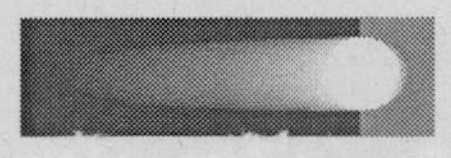

EVERYTHING TO NOTHING

EVERYTHING TO NOTHING

The Poetry of the Great War, Revolution and the Transformation of Europe

GEERT BUELENS

TRANSLATED BY
DAVID McKAY

VERSO
London • New York

The translation of this book was funded by the Flemish Literature Fund
(Vlaams Fonds voor de Letteren – flemishliterature.be)

First published in the English language by Verso 2015
Originally published as *Europa Europa! Over de dichters van de Grote Oorlog*

1 3 5 7 9 10 8 6 4 2

Verso
UK: 6 Meard Street, London W1F 0EG
US: 20 Jay Street, Suite 1010, Brooklyn, NY 11201
www.versobooks.com

Verso is the imprint of New Left Books

ISBN-13: 978-1-78478-149-1 (PB)
eISBN-13: 978-1-78478-150-7 (US)
eISBN-13: 978-1-78478-151-4 (UK)

British Library Cataloguing in Publication Data
A catalogue record for this book is available from the British Library

Library of Congress Cataloging-in-Publication Data
A catalog record for this book is available from the Library of Congress

Typeset in Fournier by MJ & N Gavan, Truro, Cornwall
Printed and bound by CPI Group (UK) Ltd, Croydon, CR0 4YY

In memoriam Alfons Buelens (1894–1975),
1st Caribiniers Regiment, soldier of the Great War

Chauvinism is the constant threat to the survival of humanity.

– Franz Pfempfert, 'Die Besessenen' (The Possessed), *Die Aktion*, 1 August 1914

Contents

1

What Was in the Air: Europe at the Start of the Twentieth Century

I have now seen four icebergs.

– Bertrand Russell, on an ocean voyage, June 1914[1]

Let us praise life and not shy from grand words. Let us be like the retired naval architect who, writing from London in June 1914, struck a tone commensurate with his ambitions, his spirit, and his age. His 'Ode Triunfal' (Triumphal Ode) is a paean to modern life, an exuberant, almost erotic celebration of the sensations excited by new vehicles, machines, factories and modes of communication in the mind of one sensitive and keenly perceptive poet. No longer will he sing of chirping crickets or the foul recesses of the human heart, but of the total autonomy of modern machinery, the hitherto inconceivable pleasures of city life, and the now of a new-fashioned world that is constantly starting afresh. 'Ah,' he sighs, 'how I'd love to be the pander of all this!'[2]

Bathed in this metropolitan glow, even political life, crime and the media acquire an unprecedented charm. Door-to-door salesmen are no longer mere peddlers, but errant knights of industry. Nor is the poet oblivious to the birth of consumerism ('O useless items everyone wants to buy'). Yet in this paradise framed in flickering neon, this 'immediate system of the Universe', he believes that something essential is coming to light. This man is a twentieth-century counterpart of Walt Whitman (1819–92). The pantheism of life on wheels is his theme, the 'New metallic and dynamic Revelation of God' – a deity not benign, but utterly amoral.

This life is decidedly not without violence and danger. But why should that trouble a poet who literally has no conscience? He hails not only new construction techniques, but also advances in the arms industry, waxing rhapsodic about 'tanks, cannons, machine-guns, submarines, flying machines'. Railway crashes, mine collapses and shipwrecks are all in the game. He compares being torn to shreds by an engine to a woman submitting to ravishment. Yes, sexuality too will be transformed: 'Masochism through machines' is his heated cry. He spurns reason and moderation, pursuing extreme experiences without bounds or scruples. Yet in contrast to his like-minded contemporaries the Italian Futurists, he does not call for the demolition of old buildings. Instead he extols the cathedrals of Europe, confessing his fervent desire to smash his head into one and be dragged off the street, bleeding like a pig, without anyone knowing who he is.

Is this modern man? Someone whose nerves are so tightly wound that he wants them to snap on his command when the time comes? From its opening lines, this ode acknowledges the dark side of the glorious new age: 'By the painful light of the factory's huge electric lamps / I write in a fever.' Writing appears to be a way for the poet to soothe himself, a surrogate for the aggression that he investigates and contemplates in his work:

> Hi-ya-ho revolutions here, there, and everywhere,
> Constitutional changes, wars, treaties, invasions,
> Outcries, injustice, violence, and perhaps very soon the end,
> The great invasion of yellow barbarians across Europe,
> And another Sun on the new Horizon!

The poet is not unenthusiastic about the coming apocalypse, but at the same time he puts these revolutionary changes into perspective. How significant are they, really, in the light of that ageless, ever-unfolding 'Moment' that underpins the experience of modernity? He no longer has an inner life; his only consciousness is of the outer world, where he is coupled to every train, hoisted on every dock, and spun in the propellers of every ship. 'Hey! I'm mechanical heat and electricity! / Hey! and the railways and engine rooms and Europe!' Swept up and pulled along in the seething roar, he is finally reduced to wordless cries. Man has become machine.

But then the pace slackens after all:

> Z-z-z-z-z-z-z-z-z-z-z-z!
> Ah if only I could be all people and all places!

He calls this a 'Triumphal Ode'? What a farce! It's nothing but a mental trip, a futuristic thought experiment that lands, with a thud, back in reality. This man was neither a machine nor the pimp of modern life. He was not Europe, not all people and all places. Nor was his vision of catastrophe – part ecstatic, part impatient – entirely unique. The author of this ode, Álvaro de Campos, was composing idiosyncratic variations on themes sounded elsewhere in the European avant-garde. And, despite his defiant extremism, his words betrayed a certain ambivalence. But how could it be otherwise? De Campos's life, work, views and visions issued from the protean imagination of Fernando Pessoa (1888–1935). These lines were written not in London but in Lisbon, at the desk of a man who rarely left the city but constructed whole worlds in his head. Pessoa took Whitman's boast, 'I contain multitudes', literally, publishing not only under his own name, but also under a series of heteronyms. He invented names, backgrounds and bibliographies for them, as well as opinions about literature that showed some affinity with his own, but which he could not (or dared not) unequivocally embrace. The spring of 1914 saw the birth of the serene, pagan master poet Alberto Caeiro and his two followers, the discipline-obsessed neoclassicist Ricardo Reis, and the occasionally manic Futurist Álvaro de Campos. That may sound like an arbitrary cacophony of voices, but their different strategies and methods were representative of almost every major current in European intellectual life.

Pessoa's poetics may appear extreme, but the deliberate ambiguity on which they were based was far from exceptional at a time when hope and despair were vying for supremacy – as were the great European powers, whose Cold War style conflicts and crises in places like Morocco (in 1905, 1907 and 1911), Bosnia-Herzegovina (in 1908, 1909 and 1912–13) and Turkey (1911) could just barely be confined to a regional scale or warded off through diplomatic manoeuvring.[3] The Russians and, above all, the colonial superpower of Great Britain feared the new German nation with its drive for economic and territorial expansion. The French shared this fear but were also out for vengeance, intent on reclaiming the Alsace-Lorraine region they had lost in the shameful defeat of 1870. The strikingly militaristic German state thus had so many enemies that it clung to its strong ties with Austria–Hungary. But the Dual Monarchy, sunk in its own arrogance, was so despised and menaced (both its own ethnic minorities and its neighbours in Italy, the Balkans and Russia were eager to see it partly or entirely dismantled) that it seemed certain to drag Germany into armed conflict. Power centres and arsenals were being expanded, alliances forged and tested. Many people sensed that this was a historic turning point.

Even though the real Pessoa lived nowhere near London, the city's normally phlegmatic literary scene was buzzing with emotionally charged rhetoric redolent of his writings in June 1914.

On the twentieth of the month, the first issue appeared of *Blast: Review of the Great English Vortex*. It was the most outspoken avant-garde voice in the English-speaking world. With a flurry of capital letters and exclamation points, its editor, Wyndham Lewis (1882–1957), made it clear from the opening pages that *Blast* was to be a forum for all the 'vivid and violent ideas' that would otherwise never reach the public.[4] The magazine's very name invoked violence and energy, an explosion and a common curse.

Lewis and his collaborators opened their magazine with a series of manifestos presenting 'vivid and violent ideas' and enumerating various categories to be blasted. Out of 'politeness', they first took on England, opening with a factor over which no one had control: the climate. What we need, Lewis and co. said, are a few good blizzards, instead of the 'flabby' English weather that weakens our spirits. Yet they seemed spirited enough, blasting their way down a long list of French shortcomings (such as sentimentality, sensationalism and Parisian parochialism) followed by an even longer series of British ones (including aestheticism and snobbery, humour as an escape from reality, and the mediocrity of the Victorian age).[5] The next 'blast' targeted about fifty organizations and individuals specified by name, ranging from socialists and welfare workers to the then-popular Continental philosophers Benedetto Croce and Henri Bergson (whose lectures Lewis had attended in Paris, and who had initially had a strong influence on his thinking). This list also included the otherworldly poet and 1913 Nobel laureate Rabindranath Tagore and the British pacifist Norman Angell, whose hugely successful *The Great Illusion* (1910) had attempted to show that a modern-day war would be financially ruinous for all parties, out of all proportion to any possible territorial gains.[6] And of course, blasts were extended to several artists branded academic – think Edward Elgar. The new art began here, with the detonation of the old.

Blast's tongue-in-cheek style, bravura and boastfulness concealed a real dissatisfaction with England's international position and the state of the British Empire.[7] Lewis might claim that there was nothing chauvinistic or patriotic about his attitudes, but the bulk of his thirty-three-page manifesto returned again and again to the theme of England's unique contribution to Western culture ('The Modern World is due almost entirely to Anglo-Saxon genius, – its appearance and its spirit'), and he felt compelled to express his 'violent' (that word again) boredom with the 'feeble Europeanism' and 'Cosmopolitan sentimentality' that he saw all around him.[8] Healthy nations should not imitate each other or strive toward some ill-defined Europudding. Rather, he protested, they should draw out and cultivate their own inherent strengths – shouldn't they?

Blast's rhetoric was more aggressive than was customary in the British Isles, but dissatisfaction and insecurity about mighty Albion's role on the world stage had been brewing for some time. These feelings were also in evidence in the essays and poems of a somewhat unlikely contributor to *Blast*, Ford Madox Hueffer (1873–1939), who was one of the leading authors of the day but had a reputation as an 'impressionist'.[9] Hueffer chose his words more cautiously than Lewis (not a hard thing to do), preferring meandering sentences and understatement to exclamation marks. But his winning eloquence could not conceal his grave concerns. He would not have been quick to admit it, but the contradictions of the early twentieth century were too plentiful even for him to gloss over. While loath to become a vulgar patriot, he was thoroughly conscious of his Englishness. He did want to keep pace with the times, but without endangering his upper-class English privileges. And although he regarded himself as a conservative, he supported women's suffrage and Home Rule for Ireland. In the first issue of his magazine *The English Review*, published in December 1908, he revealed himself as a kind of 'paternalistic socialist',[10] even advocating a public pension system and other social programmes for widows. Still, his ideas were far from revolutionary; above all, he wished to propagate a civilized way of life, if only so that he personally would be left in peace, with time for his erudite studies of the evolution of verse forms.

Yet Hueffer's own *English Review* essays on current affairs betray his profound uneasiness about European civilization. He is like a man faced with a house on fire who takes deep breaths to calm himself, in the absurd hope that he will blow out the flames in the process. Not that he was blind to the situation: 'We seem to see Great Britain drifting inevitably towards a war with Germany', he wrote in April 1909. 'There are a hundred factors that make for it; we can observe none that makes for peace.'[11] On his analysis, the panic-mongering and sensationalism of the media and parliamentarians, caught up in an arms race with Germany, only made things worse. Despite having the strongest navy in the world, Hueffer wrote, Britain behaved as if it were not ready for war, as if it were weaker, more degenerate, and less hardy than it truly was. This could, he argued, tempt Germany into mounting an attack. 'We are encouraging aggression in a manner that is fatal to the peace of Europe', he observed in dismay.[12]

England, he insisted, had to exude strength and confidence. To offer a counterweight to the Prussians, who were martial by nature, it had to establish a national army. As an 'Imperial race', England could do no less, Hueffer said: 'We stand in a different plane of civilisation from almost all our neighbours, and, since we are more peace-loving, since we are more civilised, we must be prepared, for the sake of humanity to be able, not only to maintain ourselves but to maintain the integrity of the nations most allied to us in the love for peace and civilisation.'[13] This was not to be taken as criticism of Prussia: 'That is what she stands for; that is what she is there for. And, in the infinite scale of things, who shall say that she, and not we, shall not stand for the ultimate good of humanity?'[14] Without using the term, Hueffer depicted an almost Darwinian struggle for survival between two legitimate but wholly irreconcilable ways of life – in other words, a clash of civilizations. Nonetheless, he tried to remain broad-minded. He believed that each nation, in theory, had the right to its own empire, but the British had happened to acquire one before the Germans could, and now they had no choice but to defend it. If they did not, he warned, they would share in the pitiable fate of the once-so-proud Poles and those erstwhile founders of civilization, the Greeks.[15] England would either be a world power or it would cease to be. That was its destiny as a nation born to rule.

In a less emphatic form, the same ideas pervade Hueffer's poems from this period, which include many long pieces with a smooth, virtuoso flow. In 1911 he published the collection *High Germany*, which combines a free adaptation of the work of a certain Freiherr von Süssmund with a few thoughts inspired by the title country, where Hueffer's father had been born. The thirteen-page central poem, 'To all the Dead' – part travelogue, part reverie, part elegy and part vision – includes a Gothic-tinged encounter between two lovers who rise from their German burial mounds. The locals do not seem to have shared the narrator's fearful fascination with death and decay: 'That's High Germany. / Take up your glasses. "Prosit!" to the past, / To all the Dead!'[16] A sense of utter pointlessness and a dread of decay and mortality also dominate 'Canzone a la Sonata', in which Hueffer presents his young, energetic American disciple Ezra Pound with a series of rhetorical questions that attest to a profound cultural pessimism and a fear, no longer camouflaged, of total destruction. What had the modern age actually brought forth, apart from 'nameless fear'?[17] A merrier tone prevails in 'Rhyming', in which the poet daydreams about a series of what-if scenarios. The most detailed of these fantasies, in its ostentatious innocence, perhaps reveals something of Hueffer's own ambivalence: what if we moved London to Germany and rebuilt the city there, 'like old Cokayne / Where old dead passions / Come true again'?[18] Might Britain's future lie on the Continent after all?

This almost blasphemous conclusion was also reached by the young Scottish writer Charles Hamilton Sorley (1885–1915).[19] At first he led the model British life behooving the son of a Cambridge philosophy professor: an elite education at the boarding school Marlborough College, cross-country running, and poetry. His letters show that he began reading the poems in *The English Review* at an early age.[20] It is not clear whether he also read the political pieces, but in any case his thoughts were moving in the same direction. In October 1912, the seventeen-year-old Sorley wrote a three-part poem, 'A Call to Action', which sketches in thirteen quatrains the poignant contrast between the heroic England of yore and the decadence, idle talk and apathy of his own day. It ends with the words,

> Pale, puny soldiers of the pen,
> Absorbed in this your inky strife,
> Act as of old, when men were men,
> England herself and life yet life.[21]

With his literary talents, Sorley seemed destined for the bookish future he decried, but in a letter to his parents in late January 1913, he explained that while he did wish to go to Oxford, his plan was not to study classical languages and pursue a career in India, as they had hoped, but to become a headmaster or social worker.[22] Soon after, he won an Oxford scholarship, but his studies would not begin until the autumn of 1914. His father, who had fond memories of spending summers in Berlin and Tübingen as a student, thought it would be a good idea for his son to pass the intervening months in Germany. Charles had a wonderful time in Schwerin, expounding at length on his thoughts and experiences in effusive letters to his parents and former classmates. The subject was often how very different the Germans were, and Sorley almost always meant that as a compliment. They were more spontaneous and less self-conscious, their language made the most banal reflections sound brilliant, and when they sang, especially the soldiers – 'Were they singing? They were roaring something glorious and senseless about the Fatherland (in England it would have been contemptible Jingo: it wasn't in Deutschland).' Sorley seemed not merely impressed, but actually converted: 'When I got home, I felt I was a German, and proud to be a German: when the tempest of the singing was at its loudest, I felt that perhaps I could die for Deutschland and I have never had an inkling of that feeling about England, and never shall.'[23] Surrounded by strangers in a strange land, Charles Hamilton Sorley had discovered the meaning of patriotism.

That had always been a troublesome concept for Guillaume Apollinaire (1880–1918). In the first decade of the twentieth century he had emerged as the leader and spokesman of the French avant-garde, yet he himself was not French. The son of a Russian-Polish mother and an unknown Italian officer, he was regarded as Russian by the authorities and as Polish by his friends and the press.[24] In the borderless Europe of the Belle Époque, all this had seemed unproblematic, as long as you stayed out of trouble. But in 1911 Apollinaire had to spend a week in prison and was nearly deported, having been falsely accused of stealing the *Mona Lisa* from the Louvre. When far-right journalists began attacking him with anti-Semitic slurs (for reporters of their kind, Apollinaire later remarked, any Pole was Jewish by definition[25]) the shocked poet began to wonder if he should try to become a French citizen, as he already was in his heart and mind. Despite his international orientation and cosmopolitan circle of friends, his frame of reference was thoroughly French, and he asserted his 'Frenchness' with the fanaticism peculiar to some assimilated immigrants.[26] Issues of assimilation and nationality also formed a unifying thread in Apollinaire's journalistic work. For instance, he denounced the Russification of Finland as 'a Machiavellian plan aimed at obliterating not only a culture, but also the life of an entire people'.[27] At other moments, he took an interest in the constitutional status of Bosnia-Herzegovina, took pains to keep the French public up to date on the shifting alliances between pan-Slavists, Russia and the Dual Monarchy, and quoted at length from an article about the assimilation of Jews in Poland in which all hopes were pinned on liberalism as the antidote to 'Prussian aggression and Russian barbarism'.[28]

Alongside these geopolitical structures, Apollinaire also firmly believed in a realm of European culture where kindred spirits from different backgrounds could meet to challenge and inspire each other. Artists from all over Europe came together in cities such as Paris, Berlin and Munich to experiment with new forms and values. Apollinaire's circle in Paris included the Spanish painters Pablo Picasso and Juan Gris; Max Jacob, a French poet of Jewish origin; the Swiss poet Blaise Cendrars; and the Italian poet-painter Ardengo Soffici. It was to Marc Chagall, a Jewish painter from Belarus who had likewise found a second home in Paris, that Apollinaire dedicated his poem 'À travers l'Europe' (Across Europe). Through Apollinaire, Chagall came into contact with the Berlin gallery owner and magazine publisher Herwarth Walden of *Der Sturm*. Apollinaire himself had been to Berlin in January 1913, where among others he met the poet and novelist Peter Baum (1869–1916).[29] Such contacts steadily expanded Europe's avant-garde networks. Tellingly, 'À travers l'Europe' was published in *Der Sturm* in May 1914, in French.

To Apollinaire, Europe was simultaneously a reality and a dream. It was the place he treated with irony in 'Zone', the opening poem in *Alcools* (1913), where he remarked that the conservative

Pope Pius X was the most modern of Europeans.[30] But even more importantly, it was the place he invoked in 'Vendémiaire', the final poem in the collection, in the hope that its cities would slake his unparalleled thirst.[31] Europe seemed to Apollinaire like one gigantic brewery, but his thirst was up to the challenge – 'terrible', the poet called it, inviting the question of what it was that he was so desperately thirsty for. Addressing the city of Paris, he wrote, 'You will drink all the blood of Europe in deep draughts'[32] – an image at once hedonistic and apocalyptic. Was he implying that if truly necessary the Continent would bow to the appetites of the French capital and Europe would, as a matter of course, be sacrificed?[33]

These were confusing times for Europeans. Terms like 'nation', 'race' and 'tribe' were on everybody's lips, but they were interpreted in many different ways. New nations like Germany and Italy were still trying to figure out what they really were and wanted. Other states, such as England, France and Portugal, had been been around for much longer and, according to their leading citizens, were showing signs of disrepair and decay. Then there were those peoples, much greater in number, who dreamed of a state of their own and were prepared to resort to revolution and armed conflict if necessary. And as all these groups were searching for themselves, trumpeting loudly to their neighbours whenever they thought they had found something – 'We are rational!' 'Yes, but we respect the individual!' – a new American superstate was emerging, while on the other side of the world, in the East, Europeans still felt threatened by the Mongols and Tatars, who had once (in and around the thirteenth century) penetrated deep into the continent. Was that what it meant to be European – not to be descended from Genghis Khan? Then where did Europe's eastern border lie? Somewhere around the Black Sea? Did the rebellion of the revolutionary, Francophone Young Turks in 1908 bring the Ottoman Empire into the Western camp? And what of the Russians, with their mixture of Slavic and Tatar blood that made them immune to everything German – as the Russian poet Khlebnikov, born on the steppes by the Caspian Sea, wrote in 1913?[34] Or the Jews in Galicia and the Muslims in the Balkans – did they belong? And the Hungarians – that incomprehensible amalgam of Magyars, Huns, Slavs, Jews, Sumerians, Scythians and Tatars – how European were they really?[35]

One of the many who grappled with such questions was the Hungarian poet and journalist Endre Ady (1877–1919), whose dispatches from Paris for the newspaper *Budapesti Napló* combined amusement with self-criticism. Japan had learned more from Europe in fifty years than Hungarians had in a thousand, Ady argued in May 1906, and while modern states like America and Japan were looking ahead and building for the future, Hungarians were merely cultivating the past.[36] Even Ady himself was guilty of this tendency in poems such as 'A Tisza-parton' (On the Bank of the Tisza, 1906), in which the first-person narrator wonders how, with his roots by the great Ganges, he finds himself by this great European river.[37] The backwardness of Hungary struck Ady with particular force in Paris, and with scathing irony he remarked that the Hungarian Academy's greatest contribution to scholarship was a memorandum on the use of upper- or lower-case letters in aristocratic titles.[38]

This swipe was part of an exceptionally sardonic piece from April 1905, set in the year 2085. After centuries of conflict, the European powers have finally formed the United States of Europe. This development, Ady tells us, was viewed with chagrin by the United States of South America, the United States of South Africa, India, China, Japan and Asian Russia. Ady's dividing line is revealing: Stockholm, Paris, Berlin, Geneva and St Petersburg are all, for obvious reasons, major cultural centres in the new United States of Europe. Russia is split into European and Asiatic regions.[39] Was the East–West divide the ultimate clash of civilizations?

As a Western-oriented intellectual and the later standard-bearer of the trailblazing journal *Nyugat*, whose very title ('West' or 'Occident') pointed the way for Hungary, Ady was keenly aware that diverse reactionary forces were steering his country in the opposite direction. Hungary could make it onto the right side of the border in 2085, but it would have to work hard and lay a foundation for the future. In his long, blistering article, 'In the Margins of an Unknown Codex of Corvinus' (1905), Ady used the well-established metaphor of Hungary as a 'ferry-land', plying back and forth, uncertain whether it belonged in the West or the East.[40] Nothing good could become of the country if it went on this way, he wrote. And if Hungarians were truly determined to wallow in their past, they should emulate the glorious Transylvania, a multicultural state that embraced European culture, nurtured the arts and sciences, and developed a form of religious tolerance in an age when 'the great *Kulturvolk* by the Rhine' were still burning Jews at the stake.[41] Three centuries after the Enlightenment, the dark stagnation of fundamentalism threatened to return. In another essay, Ady approvingly quoted an article by a French scholar: 'We believe that Europe belongs to the Europeans and that the path of progress is finally guaranteed. Yet when you look to the East, to Hungary, Russia, and the Balkans, you can see that in our present culture absolutely nothing is guaranteed and secure and that even today Europe threatens to gravitate toward Asia.'[42]

With the geopolitical barometer pointing toward change, the social system could not remain unaffected. Despite the elegant ring of the Belle Époque, workers and left-wing intellectuals were more than ready for something new. Social injustice and the democratic deficit had become intolerable. The Flemish schoolmaster and poet René De Clercq (1877–1932), who had earned a reputation for his poems in the tradition of Guido Gezelle about the beauties of nature and the countryside, startled both friends and enemies in 1909 with a few radical lines in his collection *Toortsen* (Torches):

> I will teach you the cry
> Of the ravening, thirsting, raging lion,
> Which sows terror and wilderness
> In the place where the wealth of the world is.[43]

In a fiery speech delivered on 1 May (International Workers' Day) 1912, Hendrik De Man, the twenty-six-year-old *Wunderkind* of Flemish socialism, decried efforts by the 'bourgeoisie' to defuse this celebration of the working class. He held up the prospect of an 'irreconcilable class struggle', made the latest in a series of pleas 'for the eight-hour day and against militarism', and warned against the 'general, catastrophic war' that the great European powers were courting with their brinkmanship. For him, 1 May was not a festival for 'Arcadian poets, with little white lambs frolicking in emerald fields'. It was a 'Norse spring in which the dark, unbending forces of winter and the nascent, warming future-power of the spring sun are still embroiled in the storm of battle'.[44]

Of course, words like 'battle', 'struggle' and 'storm' had long been part of savvy political oratory, but in this period they were more than words. A large-scale peasant rebellion in Romania in March 1907 claimed some 11,000 lives. Such explosions of violence no longer seemed to occur in the heart of Europe,[45] but the great powers could not afford to neglect the fringes of their massive continent. Political shifts or unrest in far-off places could disrupt the usually precarious balance of power.

Not that every constitutional change was necessarily accompanied by violence. In 1905 Norway dissolved its union with Sweden, and despite initial fears of war, the split went smoothly. Again, geopolitical ties were decisive; Norway inclined toward England, and Sweden toward Germany. In the summer of 1905, the great powers had their hands full with the crisis in Morocco (see below) and the Russo-Japanese War, and their main hope for the Scandinavian conflict was that it would be settled peacefully, although they probably would have intervened had negotiation failed.[46]

Further unrest could be anticipated in areas where nationalism was transforming from a romantic current emphasizing cultural identity and history to a political movement based on ethnic or linguistic particularism, which demanded autonomy or even an independent state. These developments were followed attentively, and often anxiously, throughout Europe. A randomly selected issue of *The English Review* from May 1909 addresses not only the predicament of small countries ('It [the settlement of the Balkan question] has proved that small States can expect no mercy' [357]) but also, at some length, the revolution of the Young Turks and the dismantling of the Ottoman Empire (including the massacres of Armenians), as well as the rise of a pan-Polish party and the situation in Greece. Almost the entire continent was in turmoil, and the great powers could not remain aloof. The Irish were questioning their status within Great Britain (as were the Scottish and Welsh, albeit to a lesser extent). The Russians were confronted with similar discontents among the Armenians, Georgians, Ukrainians, Poles, Latvians, Estonians, Lithuanians and Finns within their kingdom. In Germany, the Poles, Danes and French (in Alsace-Lorraine) were restive. Likewise, the Polish, Romanian, Croatian, Serbian, Slovenian, Bosnian, Czech, Slovakian, Ukrainian, Ruthenian, Italian and German minorities within the Austro-Hungarian Dual Monarchy were in pursuit of greater rights; some even sought independence or union with the mother country.

Because linguistic rights were often central to these campaigns, and the essence of a language was thought to find expression in its literature, the political struggle generally received literary reinforcement, with poets at the forefront. Their role was to find words for what lay in the hidden depths of their nation's soul, and thus to help shape that soul. Even when nationalist movements made the transition from the cultural to the political (and sometimes even the military) sphere, poets played leading roles. Besides mastering the rhyming dictionary, aspiring poets of the nation had to mount the speaker's platform and the barricade.

We see this illustrated in the turbulent careers of the revolutionary Latvian writer couple Aspazija (1865–1943) and Rainis (1865–1929).[47] The descendant of an aristocratic Latvian family, Aspazija was jolted into social consciousness by an unhappy, financially ruinous arranged marriage. Her poems and plays expressed her longing for freedom as a young woman and as a Latvian. Her official debut, in the autumn of 1887, was just six quatrains long, but from the opening couplet ('In the new year to new work / the Spirit of the Times calls us'[48]) it read as a plea for independence.

She found an ally in the young journalist Jānis Rainis, then a prominent member of the Marxist-oriented movement Jaunā Strāva (New Current). In her new lover, Aspazija saw no less than the Latvian Goethe, and she encouraged him to use his literary talents to change the world: 'I am merely the dusk of this century's close / but you are the bright dawn.'[49] Rainis responded to her urgings but was arrested in 1897 for his political activities. In prison, he continued work on a translation of *Faust* that Aspazija had begun. The almost mystical bond between them was legally formalized when they married in a small prison chapel, the bride wearing a black dress. She was permitted to accompany him into exile in Russia, but after a while, desperate financial straits sent her back to Riga, where she published a prodigious stream of poems, plays, stories and articles. A constant battle against censorship only strengthened her conviction that poetry and freedom were essentially one and the same. 'When a nation moves toward a goal in a transition period, the way of redemption is shown by the Poem, like the star in the East.'[50]

In 1903 Rainis was allowed to return from exile, and the couple soon formed the heart of a large network of nationalist authors, composers, actors, teachers and workers. Rainis developed into the spiritual leader of the Latvian Social Democratic Party, which petitioned Czar Nicholas II for national autonomy, Latvian classes in schools, women's rights and better conditions for workers. In 1905, a year of revolution throughout the Russian Empire, came an uprising against the autocratic regime of the Czar and the German aristocrats who controlled the countryside. Both retaliated forcefully, and some 9,000 revolutionaries were executed, imprisoned, deported or exiled from the Baltic provinces. Around 5,000 managed to escape, including Rainis and Aspazija. From Switzerland, they continued their literary and revolutionary work, and in particular, Rainis's play *Uguns un Nakts* (Fire and Night), frequently performed in Riga, continued to feed the revolutionary fire: 'The battle goes on and will not end.'[51]

'Battle', 'struggle', 'storm' – they make potent metaphors, but in the early twentieth century these words were often intended quite literally. The social and cultural unrest sweeping most of the Continent was often paired with a rhetoric of power and aggression. This idiom proved appealing to revolutionaries of very diverse stripes. In a climate where Friedrich Nietzsche's Zarathustra ('Therefore I must first go deeper down than I ever ascended: – Deeper down into pain than I ever ascended, even into its darkest flood!'[52]) and Henri Bergson's vitalism ('You must take things by storm: you must thrust intelligence outside itself by an act of will'[53]) had become intellectual watchwords, the urges to seek out those perilous depths, leave reason behind, and cultivate revolutionary fervour seemed to reinforce one another.

This attitude may have been most overt in the work of Filippo Tommaso Marinetti (1876–1944), the son of a wealthy Italian lawyer and a musician whose father was a literature professor. Marinetti had decided at a young age that he would use his rhetorical powers to incite a revolution against what he saw as the total apathy of Italy's art world.[54] And what better way for him to announce that the future had begun than by publishing a manifesto in a foreign country, in that quintessentially modern medium, the newspaper. With some help from an Egyptian business associate of his father's who owned shares in *Le Figaro*, Marinetti had his Futurist manifesto printed on the front page of the Paris newspaper in February 1909. In a melodramatic style, he sang the praises of speed, recklessness and revolution. Marinetti had been born in Alexandria, home to the legendary library, but he wrote of his desire to leave the past behind by demolishing libraries and museums. He also drew a startling connection between war and cleanliness: 'We will glorify war – the world's only hygiene – militarism, patriotism, the destructive gesture of freedom-bringers, beautiful ideas worth dying for, and scorn for woman.'[55] Marinetti's intent was to cause a stir, and he did. He also provoked demands for clarification. Could he possibly be serious about all this? The glorification of war, one French interviewer suggested, implied a form of barbaric regression that could hardly be called Futurist. The poet patiently explained his view: just as an individual can only rid the body of dangerous infections and excess blood through bathing and blood-letting, a nation must abandon itself to a 'glorious shower of blood' at least once per century.[56] This interview took place less than three months after 28 December 1908, when one of the greatest disasters in European history, the Messina earthquake and tsunami in the south of Italy, had claimed over 100,000 lives.[57] Although Marinetti had waited to launch his new movement until the front pages once again had room for news of the arts, the tragedy did not soften his rhetoric of death and destruction.

Meanwhile, elsewhere in Europe, the ruins, tidal waves and conflagrations of Sicily and Calabria haunted the prominent Russian poet Alexander Blok (1880–1921). At a talk in St Petersburg in January 1909, entitled 'Elemental Force and Culture', he articulated his fears in a string of apocalyptic images that reflected his Symbolist literary outlook:

> We are living between two camps – between two fires of seething vengeance. It is this that makes it so terrible. What kind of fire is it that is bursting from under the shell of lava? Is it like that which ravaged Calabria or is it a cleansing flame? Whichever it may be, we are living through a terrible crisis. We do not yet know precisely what events are lying in wait for us, but in our hearts the needle of the seismograph has already shifted.[58]

Humankind had brought this transformation upon itself, Blok said. Idle words about progress, technology and prosperity were no more than attempts to mask the spiritual emptiness of modern man. Man had conquered the sky and descended into the bowels of the earth, but as always, pride goeth before the fall. No act of culture can withstand the elemental force of nature. Blok feared the worst for the human race. The final poem in the cycle 'The Field of Kulikovo', which he completed in December 1908, opened with a decidedly ominous epigraph from Vladimir Solovyov: 'And a haze of inescapable evil / casts veils on the day ahead.' His own poem served as both a warning and as an exhortation. As a poet, he could see into the future, and the message was clear: war was inevitable. 'It is your time, now. – Pray, kneel down.'[59]

The desire for regeneration and purification often articulated in the literature of this period frequently masks a deep sense of sin. God might have been pronounced dead, but the same could not be said of the self-accusing culture of Christianity. Drought, infertility and stagnation could all be interpreted as symptoms of a sick society that had invited its own punishment. If people could truly abase themselves, mentally and physically, could they bury their excessive self-consciousness and discover a kind of passionate fervour that would bring meaning and excitement into their lives? In other words, would a little war be enough to wipe out the sins of the world?

It was still June 1914. Whole races, peoples and cultures were still in danger. On the 16th of the month, the Italian Symbolist poet Gabriele D'Annunzio (1863–1938), residing in Paris, sent a stern letter to the French ambassador in St Petersburg. Why be afraid of war? In a world where the 'Latin genius' was menaced by democracy and the 'tyranny of the plebeians', and dragged itself tastelessly through 'mud' and 'humiliation', only 'a great national war' could bring salvation. 'It is only through war that those peoples who have degenerated can stop their decline, for war unfailingly gives them either glory or death.'[60] The poet, who had just recovered from a venereal disease, was obviously eager to do great deeds.

Several key modernist works from this period link war and the sacrifices it entails to a country's regeneration and cultural survival.[61] Igor Stravinsky's *Sacre du Printemps* (1913) and T.S. Eliot's *The Waste Land* (1922) are the best-known examples. This was also a central theme in less modernist circles. We find it in D'Annunzio, for instance, as well as in the legendary poem penned by Charles Péguy (1873–1914) in 1913. Here are two stanzas from the eight thousand lines of alexandrine verse that make up Péguy's magnum opus *Eve*:

> Happy are those who died for the carnal earth,
> As long as it was in a just war.
> Happy are those who died for a patch of ground.
> Happy are those whose died a solemn death.
> […]
> Happy are those who died, for they have returned
> To the primeval clay and the primeval earth.
> Happy are those who died in a just war.
> Happy the ripened wheat, the reaped grain.[62]

Péguy believed he knew what made a war just: namely, the need to safeguard civilization. He saw it as the duty of every civilized man to defend the scattered oases of freedom and culture against barbarism. France, England, northern Italy, parts of America, and a few bits of Belgium and Switzerland – these were the world's only hope, and they were under threat. Péguy saw it as a very real possibility that these few scraps of modern civilization would go the way of the ancient European and American cultures, taking all humanity down with them.[63] He recorded these reflections in 1905, four years before Ford Madox Hueffer came to much the same conclusion (see above).

Péguy, an independent-minded Catholic and a socialist, was shocked to the core by aggressive German diplomatic manoeuvres in Morocco aimed at playing France and England off against each other.[64] This crisis, modest in the light of subsequent events, prompted no less than a conversion. Suddenly internationalism was a vacuous or even dangerous term, and patriotism was the greatest virtue. The barbaric Germans were the enemy, and the conquering hero was that modern-day Athens and Rome, cradle of the revolutionary spirit and its sole heir – yes, France. In a newly aggressive political climate, these were more than mere theoretical musings, especially given Péguy's intellectual stature.[65] Yet he was not alone in this outlook. Even though Germany had established the world's finest system of higher education and was admired around the world for its artistic and scholarly achievements, it was above all the incarnation of those aspects of modernity rejected by thinkers like Blok and Ady: the cult of technology, efficiency and progress.[66]

In stark contrast to this narrow picture of Germany was the circle – one could almost say 'cult' – that formed in the first decade of the twentieth century around the poet Stefan George (1868–1933). In his work and his actions, this pupil of Mallarmé and follower of Hölderlin almost single-handedly showed that it was still possible to embody the classic, aristocratic ideal of the poet in the modern age. For George, the Word with a capital W was at the heart of a quasi-religious celebration of beauty and higher truths, in which the life of the soul was deemed far superior to that of the mind. A poet like George had no need to read the newspapers.[67] Instead, he surveyed the world around him, and found omens of overweening pride, catastrophe and doom. These insights featured prominently in his collection *Der Stern des Bundes* (The Star of the Covenant), published in late January 1914.[68] More didactic in tone than his earlier work, it included a sketch of the Old Testament God's response to the hubris of the modern Babel-builders:

> He laughs: too late to stop, too late for medicine!
> Ten thousand must be struck by holy madness
> Ten thousand must be felled by holy sickness
> Tens of thousands by holy war.[69]

A prophecy, a fantasy, or sheer despair? The answer is often unclear in European poetry of the time. While poems can be found describing the war as a gymnastic exercise, it is striking how explosive, not to say violent, most verse from the period is: like a god, war gives and takes, especially the latter. Even in circles with very different ideas about politics and poetry than that of George and his disciples, these same ideas and images were in circulation – for instance, among Kurt Hiller (1885–1972), Jakob van Hoddis (born Hans Davidsohn, 1887–1942), and Georg Heym (1887–1912), young men generally classified as expressionist poets, whose work is permeated with an apocalyptic sensibility. At first sight, they are not as heavy-handed as George and his followers – the name of their group, the Neopathetic Cabaret for Adventurers of the Spirit, suggests some degree of self-awareness – yet their poems sketched nothing less than the end of the world. Or was that no more than neopathetic irony? Hoddis's best-known poem is simply titled 'Weltende' (End of the World). In the first verse a solid citizen loses his hat. Seven lines later, trains are tumbling into ravines. There need not be any causal connection between these incidents, and van Hoddis puts the whole thing in perspective, also mentioning that most people have runny noses. This poem, written in 1910, marked not so much the end of the world as the end of poetry – at least as practised in Germany up to that time. No deep thoughts or chains of reasoning, but pure images, presented one after the other like a film.

Nonetheless, the expressionists had much greater concerns than formal experimentation. As prophets of a new age, their primary objective was to engender an ethical revolution, to galvanize people out of their lethargy. Their targets were the *petit bourgeoisie*, who supported law and order in hope of a quiet life. Young people, on the other hand, wanted thrills and tumult. Pending the invention of guitar amps and spray paint, these young Germans poured their energy into art, literature and theatre.

For Georg Heym, the stakes were particularly high. On 6 July 1910, five weeks after attending the first Neopathetic Cabaret performance as a guest, he complained in his diary, 'Oh, it's terrible. Even in 1820, it couldn't have been any worse. Everything always stays the same. So dreary, dreary, dreary. Nothing ever happens. If only something would happen some time that wouldn't leave behind that musty aftertaste of everyday routine.' Since Heym seemed unable to find the strength to transcend mediocrity within himself, he hoped to draw it from the outside world: 'If only something would happen, just for once. If only barricades would be erected. I would be the first to mount them; even with a bullet in my heart, I would still feel drunk with enthusiasm. Or if only someone would start a war, even if there's no good reason. This peace is greasy and grimy as wax on old furniture.'[70] A month later Heym fell madly in love with a girl from Hamburg, and the pendulum of his heart swung wildly in the opposite direction. Less than a month after that, a few of his poems appeared in print for the first time, and soon afterwards he was approached by publishers. But his thoughts, and certainly his writings, remained every bit as apocalyptic. Demons and merciless gods filled his imagination; shadowy cityscapes went up in fiery blazes. Monstrous, grotesque magnifications, Kurt Hiller called them, meaning it as a great compliment.[71] Yet Heym meant it all quite seriously. In the June 1911 issue of the expressionist magazine *Die Aktion*, he expressed a deep longing for old-fashioned heroism, splendour and rapture: 'Once the world often saw the shadows of these Gods on the horizon. Now they have become puppets. War has vanished from our world, and perpetual peace has wretchedly taken its place.'[72]

Just a few weeks later, it seemed as if Heym's wish was coming true and the accursed perpetual peace was already a thing of the past. The summer of 1911 had brought a new crisis in Morocco. France had taken advantage of a minor incident in Fez to occupy the city, upon which an overzealous German foreign minister, without consulting his government or generals, had ordered the warship *Der Panther* to Agadir. England – France's ally and, more importantly, the world's mightiest naval power – was irked by this *Panthersprung* and made its position clear in a speech by Minister David Lloyd George. Mutual recriminations mounted. In September, some even suggested that Germany was preparing to invade Belgium, and rumours of mobilization sent many Germans rushing to the bank in a panic to withdraw their savings. The world appeared to be teetering on the edge of the abyss.[73]

It was in this climate, between 7 and 10 September, that Heym wrote a first draft of his poem 'Der Krieg' (War), which was never finished:

> He is risen now that was so long asleep
> Risen out of vaulted places dark and deep.
> In the growing dusk the faceless demon stands,
> And the moon he crushes in his strong black hands.[74]

A cosmic colossus has arisen, capable of reducing cities and celestial bodies to rubble in a single gesture. His power is dumbfounding.

> In the nightfall noises of great cities fall
> Frost and shadow of an unfamiliar pall.
> And the maelstrom of the markets turns to ice.
> Silence grows. They look around. And no one knows.

Unchained, he shows himself to be an agent of death, frenzied, overpowering and murderous.

> On the mountains he's begun his battle-dance,
> Calling: Warriors, up and at them, now's your chance!
> There's a rattling when he shakes his brute black head
> Round which crudely hang the skulls of countless dead.
>
> Like a tower he tramples out the dying light.
> Rivers are brim-full of blood by fall of night.

Legion are the bodies laid out in the reeds,
Covered white with the strong birds of death.

A complete regression takes place. Even the greatest creations of human hands return to the belly from which all things issue. Like a titan, he towers above the smouldering remains.

A great city quietly sank in yellow smoke,
Hurled itself down into that abysmal womb.
But gigantic over glowing ruins stands
He who thrice at angry heavens shakes his brand.

Not until the final verse does it become clear what drives this god:

Over storm-torn clouds' reflected livid glow
At cold wastelands of dead darkness down below.
That his hellfire may consume this night of horror
He pours pitch and brimstone down on their Gomorrah.

And so Heym's god proves just as wrathful as George's. The sinful world may have deserved a final chastening, but the time was not yet ripe. The Morocco crisis was averted through diplomacy and compromise, and on 15 September, Heym concluded that his was not an age for *Sturm und Drang*. 'I require intense external stimuli to be happy ... I hoped for a war at least, but even that has come to nothing.'[75] Wanting to be in the front row if something did happen after all, he tried to sign up for the army in late 1911 and early January 1912. On 16 January, something dramatic did finally happen: Heym and his friend Ernst Balcke were skating toward Wannsee on the river Havel when they fell through the ice. Labourers heard their cries for help but could not reach them. Their bodies were not recovered until days later.

Heym's parents later received word from Metz that he had been accepted for officer training.[76]

Had Heym been born in Italy, late 1911 would have offered him a very different set of opportunities. While the world was anxiously waiting to see how the Morocco crisis would be resolved, Italy struck elsewhere in North Africa, invading the Ottoman provinces of Tripoli and Cyrenaica. Why should France and Germany be the only European countries to lay claim to North African territories? It seemed obvious to the Italians that, as the former overlords of the Mediterranean, they too were a great power. On the surface, this looked like the start of just another colonial war, but the repercussions were felt throughout Europe.

Obviously, the Futurists were overjoyed. In pamphlets with titles like *War, the World's Only Hygiene* and *Tripoli Italiana*, they declared with pride and satisfaction that the masses had finally become as bloodthirsty and Futuristic as they were, and announced without further argument that the word 'Italy' should take precedence over the word 'Freedom' in every respect.[77] And their joy was beyond description when, during the war in North Africa, the Italian army used aircraft for the first time in history, first for reconnaissance and later in combat. The Futurist war appeared to have become a reality. But was this really a small, sanitizing conflict?

The sometimes consuming desire to live life to the fullest that afflicted so many young artists and writers in the early twentieth century has often been interpreted as a premonition of the coming war. It is certainly a spectacularly bitter illustration of the maxim, 'Be careful what you wish for, you just might get it', or indeed of sowing the wind and reaping the whirlwind. Yet in the opening years of the twentieth century, cooler heads were also preoccupied with the link between civilization and war. The American philosopher and socialist William James (brother of the well-known novelist Henry James) regarded himself as a staunch pacifist, but he had no intention of being naive: 'Martial virtues must be the enduring cement; intrepidity, contempt of softness, surrender of private interest ... must still remain the rock on which states are built.'[78] When he wrote this in 1910, he was making essentially the same claim as the Futurists: personal freedom was subordinate to the nation's welfare. It followed that the nation's most important school was not the university, but the military. In this sense, several countries had already established lifelong learning. In Bulgaria, for instance, all men were part of the reserve troops until they turned forty-seven. One Bulgarian general remarked in 1910 – not without pride – that his country was the most militarized in the world.[79]

This was more than mere machismo. In the geopolitical system of the time, Bulgaria, which had not gained its independence until 1908, lay on a fault line between the Ottoman Empire (Turkey) to the east and the constant ferment of the Balkans to the west. On more than one occasion, the earth shook. When the Italians drove back the Turks in North Africa, their European neighbours thought that perhaps the time had come to drive the weakened Ottomans out of the Occident once and for all.[80] In the autumn of 1912, Serbia, Montenegro, Greece and Bulgaria set aside their rivalries, agreeing to go to war together and split the territorial gains – Macedonia, Thrace and Kosovo – among themselves. And so it came to pass. Yet as one might expect, the victors did not entirely agree about who should receive which piece of the pie. Serbia had its eye on Thessaloniki, but that went to Greece. Bulgaria grabbed a stretch of the Aegean coast that the Serbians had also been hoping for. And under intense pressure from Austria, Albania was created in 1912 to contain Serbian expansion toward the Adriatic. Although this tactic did more or less bring

Serbia's expansion to a halt, Austria remained deeply concerned. Bulgaria, frustrated about giving up so much of Macedonia, then turned on its allies in late June 1913, less than a month after signing the peace treaty. This move proved disastrous; the Bulgarians were defeated by a new coalition of Serbia, Greece, Romania and, however improbable it may seem, Turkey. Alliances shifted faster than the wind, and the outcome was chronic instability.

Every time these smaller countries and peoples clashed, the interests of the European superpowers – England, France, Germany, Russia and Austria–Hungary – were also at stake. One pressing question was whether Austria–Hungary still truly belonged on this list. Hadn't it let other countries take advantage of it, time and again, and wouldn't Serbia and Russia exploit its weakness to go on dismantling the Habsburg Empire? Worse still, wasn't the Dual Monarchy laying the groundwork for its own implosion – for instance in 1908, when it recklessly annexed Bosnia-Herzegovina, thereby irritating the Germans, offending the Russians, provoking the Serbians, and alienating the rest of Europe?[81] This had left Austria, and Europe, exposed to tremendous risks. The Balkan alliance described above could easily turn against Austria, or conversely, Austria could try to forestall the alliance by starting its own Balkan conflict. If Germany rushed to support the ally that shared its language, and Russia came to the aid of its fellow Slavs, then Germany and France could find themselves obligated to declare war on each other, and England would be compelled to stand by France (under the terms of the Triple Entente between England, France and Russia) – an unimaginable continent-wide catastrophe. But surely the situation would not be permitted to reach that point, since it was obvious where such escalation would lead in a world continually developing new and ever more deadly weapons.

* * *

And still it was June 1914. A time to break down, and a time to build up, as – back in London – the contributors to *Blast* understood. The castigating tone with which they began their first issue was followed by a warm bath of praise. Their homages to England (bless her ships, her ports, her barbarous humour) and France (its vitality!, its masterly pornographers and sceptics!, the bitter stream pouring out of the wound of 1870, etc.) would not have been out of place in De Campos/Pessoa's 'Triumphal Ode'. Still more intriguing is the subsequent list of 'blessed' persons, institutions and products, with now-forgotten singers, actors, stunt pilots, boxers and cricketers rubbing shoulders with authors like James Joyce, notorious suffragettes like Lillian (Lillie) Lenton, known for her hunger strikes, armed opponents of Home Rule in Ireland, and the fundamentalist Pope Pius X.[82] Thus far, all might be described as rebels with a cause. But what was Henry Newbolt (1862–1938) doing in this company? Newbolt's distinctly premodern poems, a favourite at English boarding schools, exalted chivalry and self-sacrifice in battlefield imagery that seemed to owe more to school sporting events than to any authentic experience of war. Not long before, in 1913, he had been knighted for his patriotic, militaristic verse.[83]

What this suggests is that *The Great English Vortex* was not proposing a Nietzschean transvaluation of all values but propagating a British presence on the world stage that was assertive to say the least and, in practice, downright aggressive. Their 'blasts' had cleared the ground for the expansion of the British Empire. In this campaign, the most modern insights of the avant-garde artist ('Dehumanization is the chief diagnostic of the Modern World') mingle with his deepest, uncensorable feelings. Wyndham Lewis stressed this last point: 'Killing somebody must be the greatest pleasure in existence.' Of course, this was mere bluster. Maybe he called his abstract pictorial contributions to *Blast* 'Plan of War' and 'Slow Attack', but we should not read too much into that either. And yes, he wrote that 'Art merges in Life again everywhere', but that doesn't mean that we have to take his words literally.[84] Does it?

On 28 June 1914, no sane person in Sarajevo thought it was perfect weather for the Archduke Franz Ferdinand, heir to the Austro-Hungarian throne, and his wife Sophie to tour the city in an open carriage. Their public appearance in the annexed capital of Bosnia was a provocation in itself. Following an inspection of army manoeuvres on the Serb religious holiday of Vidovdan, it was nothing short of an insult. It may seem strange that the Serbs commemorated an utterly humiliating military defeat at the hands of the Turks in 1389, in which their ruler had been killed. Their sense of drama and pathos, as well as their masochism, was undeniable. Still, it was their national holiday, the day when they celebrated their dream of vengeance and territorial expansion by reciting one of the centuries-old poems commemorating the battle on Blackbird's Field in Kosovo.[85] The despised Ottomans had just been driven out of Kosovo at long last in 1912, and now the confounded Austrians were at the gate!

Alternatively, Franz Ferdinand may have been making a symbolic statement that it was time to shelve the dream of a Greater Serbia, which could not possibly come true under the Danube Monarchy, but that in return for their allegiance the Slavs would receive considerable autonomy within the empire. But on 28 June this alternative never had a chance. Franz Ferdinand and his wife were assassinated by a young Bosnian Serb, barely more than a boy, who was almost certainly assisted by the Serbian secret service.[86] The symbolism was readily apparent: just as one heroic Serbian had assassinated the Turkish sultan in the hour of the nation's defeat, now, on his own wedding anniversary, the hated reactionary Franz Ferdinand had met his end in the capital city of the Bosnian Serbs.

The assassin, Gavrilo Princip (1894–1918), had actually wanted to become a poet. He had read Walt Whitman and Oscar Wilde, owned books by the anarchists Bakunin and Kropotkin, and knew lines from Nietzsche's poems by heart.[87] He may have been an immature blunderer, but he was also in tune with an age when poetic and revolutionary aspirations often went hand in hand, and a man of letters could also be a man of action. When Princip had volunteered for military service after the outbreak of the Balkan War of 1912–13, he had been rejected by a Serbian officer who described him as 'too small and too weak'. Perhaps the officer should have been more diplomatic.

As news of the murder travelled around the world, misunderstandings and conspiracy theories began popping up all over. Freemasons, the German security services, the Austro-Hungarian government itself – apparently many people had their reasons to want Franz Ferdinand out of the way. According to insiders, even his uncle, the venerable Emperor Franz Jozef, mumbled that it was a 'great worry less' for him.[88]

Confusion also reigned in the circles of Miloš Crnjanski (1893–1977),[89] a Serbian–Hungarian poet who had been studying in Vienna, the imperial capital, since 1913. He had just celebrated Vidovdan in the city park with other Slovenes, Serbs and Croats living in the city, and a grand ball was to take place that evening. The Serbian envoy was planning to attend, and Crnjanski was expected to ask his wife to dance. But it was not to be. After lunch, while Crnjanski was playing billiards with his friends, a waiter informed him that the heir to the *Serbian* throne had been assassinated. Something was terribly wrong. It no longer seemed like a good day for a waltz.

The life of another young poet in the region, the Bosnian Ivo Andrić (1892–1975),[90] likewise changed forever on 28 June, when his book hit the shelves in Zagreb.[91] As a secondary student in Sarajevo, Andrić had established a secret youth organization to promote Croat–Serb unity and freedom. He translated Walt Whitman and, after reading Bakunin and Kropotkin, came to the conclusion that national liberation would lead to a social revolution and bring an end to the backwardness of his homeland. As a sympathizer with the Young Bosnia movement, Andrić seems to have believed that terror was a legitimate means of driving out the hated occupiers. The very thought of it excited him, to his own shock: 'How joyously I anticipate the days of great deeds. And the *hajduk* blood rises and burns. My life passes without the virtue and goodness of sacrifice. But I love the good. Let those live who are dying on sidewalks, unconscious from fury and gunpowder ... Let those live who, withdrawn, quiet in dark rooms, prepare uprisings and contemplate ever newer ruses.'[92] Andrić too came to Vienna as a student in 1913, but in early 1914 he moved to Kraków. When a few of his poems were published in a collection of new Croatian lyric verse in 1914, he was described in the book as a sensitive, ambitious young man 'without even the slightest Turkish atavism'.[93] In one of his poems – 'Prva proljetna pjesma' (The First Spring Song) – the poet saw the 'blossomed branch', 'flaming flowers', and 'clouds [that] sail like an army in the sky' as portents of 'great deeds': 'When will the King's army come?'[94] Perhaps sooner than he imagined or hoped. The assassination in Sarajevo made it necessary for him to leave Kraków at once. Throughout the Dual Monarchy, Yugoslavs had become objects of suspicion. In Andrić's case, that suspicion was understandable. His past as a school friend of Danilo Ilić, who would be hanged in 1915 for conspiracy in the murder of Franz Ferdinand, certainly did not plead in his favour.

The Hungarian poet Endre Ady was in the Szatmár district on 28 June, campaigning for the Radical Party. He is said to have burst into tears after crying out in a visionary moment, 'In this world war the Hungarian nation will perish whether the Entente wins or loses. Hungary will be divided ... reaction will take over.'[95]

Meanwhile, Alexander Blok had reached an impasse. As always, he spent the summer at his beloved country estate of Shakmatovo. Local farmers stopped by to pay their respects to the Symbolist master, receiving for their troubles a glass of vodka credited with healing powers. Blok's plans were no different than they had been in prior years: reading, writing, translating Flaubert, and taking endless walks through the woods and fields while musing on life and love.[96] But he ran into difficulties with the translation and was no more successful with his writing. 'Is my song really sung?' he wondered in mild distress in a diary entry dated 28 June.[97]

The Jewish German poet Alfred Lichtenstein (1889–1914) was in the middle of his year of compulsory military service when the assassination occurred. That day, in his poem 'Abschied' (Farewell), he anticipated the moment when he would leave the 'merciless mill of men'.[98] This does not exactly suggest that he had the gift of prophecy. Yet on 9 and 10 July, when the German generals had begun their summer furlough, the Serbian field marshal had gone to Austria (!) to take a cure, the British were up in arms about the possibility of civil war in Ireland, and the French were enjoying a sex scandal involving finance minister Joseph Caillaux,[99] he wrote this poem:

> Suppose war is coming. There's been peace for too long.
> Then things will get serious. Trumpet calls
> Will galvanize you. And nights will be ablaze.
> You will freeze in your tent. You'll feel hot all over. You'll go hungry.
> Drown. Be blown up. Bleed to death. Fields will rattle to death.
> Church-towers will topple. Horizons will be in flames.
> Winds will gust. Cities will come crashing down.
> The thunder of heavy guns will fill up the horizon.
> From the hills all around smoke
> Will rise and shells will explode overhead.[100]

2

A Hot Summer: July–September 1914

> To me this Prelude has a terrible beauty.
>
> – Louis Couperus, Munich, 8 August 1914[1]

On Thursday, 23 July 1914, the poet Anna Akhmatova (1889–1966), who had just turned twenty-five, arrived at Slepnyovo, her mother-in-law's dacha near Bezhetsk.[2] There she was reunited with her son Lev, just under two years old, but not with her husband, the flamboyant poet and world traveller Nikolay Gumilyov (1886–1921), who was on the outskirts of Karelia, preparing for a solitary summer on the Gulf of Finland. Although life was calm and peaceful at Slepnyovo and Akhmatova had always made good progress with her writing during her summers there, she had little love for the place. After her cosmopolitan lifestyle in St Petersburg, more than 300 miles to the north, this flat, cheerless region of the remote Tver province was an inevitable disappointment. But now that the scintillating salons of St Petersburg had shut their doors for the summer months, she was condemned to the company of two women, her mother-in-law and Gumilyov's elderly aunt, who passed the time by sewing their own funeral shrouds.[3] Life can be unbearable here, she wrote to the Symbolist poet Georgy Chulkov. The utter tranquility and tedium even prevented her from continuing work on what was meant to be her first long poem, *At the Edge of the Sea*. Scraps of news from the outside world occasionally reached her ears, but she said they struck her as 'absolutely improbable'.[4]

The Sunday after her arrival, she wrote to her husband, wondering impatiently whether he planned to join her at Slepnyovo and whether he had any news or gossip from St Petersburg. She added that she was avoiding the 'insipid' neighbours. Four days later, on Thursday, 30 July, the situation had hardly improved, and the weather was worse – 'I foresee an early autumn.'[5] She asked her husband insistently to send money. In her letter to Chulkov, she announced plans to visit Switzerland for six weeks, but in view of her chronic financial troubles, it is unclear how she intended to pay for the trip.

Before the issue could arise again, history intervened. That same day, 30 July, Czar Nicholas II announced a general mobilization. The tension between the Serbians (Slavs like the Russians) and the Austrians had mounted considerably in the last week of July.[6] After falling just short of total compliance with an Austrian ultimatum described by observers as a warmongering affront, Serbia had been compelled to mobilize on 25 July, and Austria had actually opened fire three days later.[7] Germany's goadings and provocations were making the Czar and his generals very nervous. Hesitating any longer could prove fatal, because the vast Russian Empire needed much more time to ready its forces than did Germany, its ultra-modern enemy. Kaiser Wilhelm II, Nicholas's adoring cousin, who had no clear notion of what his generals were plotting behind his back, pointedly asked the Czar to reconsider the decision to mobilize, in order to maintain 'the peace of Europe'.[8] In fact, Nicholas was already regretting this earlier decision, but he allowed his generals and ministers to convince him that they were past the point of no return. With a heavy heart, he told the Kaiser that stopping the war machine was '*technically* impossible' but that Russia was 'far from wishing war'.

The next day, there were grey skies over St Petersburg, and the weary Czar confessed in his diary that the weather matched his mood. Military preparations continued apace. Austrian troops were swiftly advancing on Serbia, leaving the border with Russia almost undefended. Obviously, this increased the pressure on the Germans, who had always counted on Austria's support in the event of a confrontation with the Slavic giant. On 1 August, the Kaiser could no longer postpone the inevitable conclusion: as Russia was continuing to mobilize and had not even responded to a German ultimatum, the German Empire accepted 'the challenge' and declared war on Russia. In truth, German military leaders had been searching for years for an excuse to blame Russia for starting the European war they craved.[9] Their plan had succeeded.

The next day, when the declaration of war reached Slepnyovo, the three women were united, for once, by shock and bewilderment. Young Lev must not have known what to think; suddenly his mother, his grandmother and his great-aunt all seemed overcome with despair. Fifty-one years later, Akhmatova still clearly recalled this moment. The women in the village broke into an impressive lament, and in that dark hour, the isolated poet shared their feelings. It was as if her whole life were falling apart. In the two-part poem 'July 1914', written that very day – 20 July, according to the Julian calendar – we hear the voice of an apocalyptic prophetess. The unusual weather ('Rain has not sprinkled the fields since Easter') and the bitter odour of burning peat, which seemed to have silenced the birds and stilled the leaves of the aspen, were all omens of an unprecedented catastrophe.

> Ghastly seasons are coming. Beware.
> Fresh made graves soon will fill every space.
> For the famines, plagues, earthquakes prepare.
> Stars will dim and the sun hide its face.

Akhmatova's visions, like Alexander Blok's, have an eschatological flavour, and they make very explicit reference to the fate of Mother Russia. The 'one-legged' messenger who recites these prophecies in the poem has faith, however, that a still greater Mother is watching over them.

> Yet our land will survive, will not fall,
> Torn in sport by our devilish foes.
> Mother Mary will spread out her shawl,
> White and healing, upon our great woes.[10]

Could a poem about the onset of war be any more ominous than this? Akhmatova first evokes the smell of a forest fire, followed by fresh graves, mass deaths, unutterable grief, war widows, and trampled fields. Her extreme, often biblical imagery, in which a prayer for rain is answered with the warm blood of soldiers, suggests that 'July 1914' was not intended as a realistic, documentary account of those dramatic days. Yet there are signs that the atmosphere of this poem did not spring entirely from her poetic imagination. Beyond the platitude that her entire oeuvre reads like an intimate diary, there does seem to have been something strange about the weather in that part of northern Europe in the summer of 1914. It is not clear whether Akhmatova and her husband Gumilyov had comparable experiences or simply kindred imaginations, but in any case, there is a remarkably similar passage in one of his poems about this pivotal moment.

> That summer, thunderstorms were unrelenting.
> And never had there been such stifling heat,
> With total darkness all at once descending,
> So suddenly the heart forgot to beat.
> The fields were strewn with spoiling unripe wheat,
> Red skies at noon as if the world were ending.[11]

Whether symbol or reality, the message is clear: at any moment, the charged atmosphere could release a great and devastating bolt. And when it did – as Akhmatova later emphasized on more than one occasion – the twentieth century began.[12]

The mood of near-hysteria in Russia at that time is suggested by a collage of contemporary newspaper clippings in Alexander Solzhenitsyn's 1971 documentary novel *August 1914*. Patriotic poetry emphasized the Slavic unity between the Orthodox Serbians and their Russian brothers. The German aggressor would be punished by God, in what seemed destined to become the last and greatest war in European history. Cast-iron sculptures were pulled off the roof of the German embassy and hurled into the Moyka river.[13] Representatives of every ethnic group and religion in the Russian Empire convened in the Duma to affirm their solidarity. Hundreds of thousands of Russians gathered by the Winter Palace and solemnly knelt down, flags and icons in their hands. God, Czar and people formed an invincible trinity.

> The Court convenes, a brilliant throng;
> Past eager crowds our staunch reservists
> Parade to cheers both loud and long.
> The Sovereign's head is bowed in prayer
> 'Midst anthems, incense, cloth of gold:
> To greet his people comes the Tsar
> Before the battle, as of old.[14]

Writers and other intellectuals, often accused of decadence and elitism, suddenly felt a fresh bond with the people and their concerns. From old-school Symbolists (such as Fyodor Sologub and Vyacheslav Ivanov) to the young, Acmeist poet Sergei Gorodetsky, they brandished both their rhyming dictionaries and their sabres, singing the praises of the honourable, holy war that would at long last revitalize the Russian spirit.[15] For them, this was a war for their culture, in which victory over the external enemy would also destroy the evil within.

The central issue looming in the background was Russia's place in Europe: could the Slavic and the Germanic characters be reconciled? To poets like Vyacheslav Ivanov (1866–1949), who like many of his Russian contemporaries had studied in Germany and been shaped by his exposure to Goethe, Novalis and Nietzsche, this was no academic question, but one that went to the heart of his own identity. To escape this dilemma, Ivanov made a sharp distinction between 'classical' Germany and the Prussian militarism and materialism of 'modern' Germany.[16] The young German state's collectivism and mania for organization clashed with his own dream of *sobornost*, a kind of organic, grassroots community based on shared spiritual values.[17] The war was an opportunity for the Russians to rediscover themselves and show Europe that their culture was far richer than was recognized by those (mainly Germans) who called it 'backward'. The role of England and France in this dichotomy was never entirely clear; they too, of course, were major Western powers that often looked down on Russia and, from the Russian perspective, did not always have the right outlook – religious, metaphysical, *Eastern*.[18] The war would make it clear who belonged with whom and why. The treaty binding Russia to France and England could potentially be transformed from a paper agreement into a spiritual pact. If Germany were not merely defeated, but annihilated, then Russia could take its place among the free European powers, without constant worries about its eastern flank.

On the very first day of the war, Valery Bryusov (1873–1924) noted in a poem he was writing that this would be a decisive European conflict: 'Across the pastures of ancient Europe / The last war is being waged'.[19] That very same day, he left his dacha and went to Moscow to look for a job as a war correspondent. History was being made, and the great poet wanted a front-row seat. Even beyond that, he hoped to be one of its chroniclers. Apparently, when history calls, even a decadent Symbolist will swallow his pride and become a reporter.[20]

The younger generation of Russian poets was also coming into action. The Futurists, especially the outspoken Vladimir Mayakovsky (1893–1930), seemed born for this type of agitation and commotion.[21] During the October Revolution of 1905, when he was barely twelve years old, Mayakovsky had told his sister Olga that they had gone on strike at school and sung the Marseillaise during the church service, upon which the school had been closed. Two years later, he was one of the first to be arrested for Bolshevik activities. He was released because of his youth, but from that time on the Czar's security services took careful note whenever young Vladimir so much as bought a loaf of bread. In January 1909, Comrade Konstantin (a name he had adopted in memory of his brother, who had died young) was arrested again and detained for several weeks. That summer, after his third arrest, he was put behind bars for six months, five of which he spent in solitary confinement at Moscow's Butyrki prison. At the age of sixteen, he had left childhood behind forever. His imprisonment left enduring scars, but as one might expect in the life story of a hero, it also marked the start of something new: in his cell, he began to read and write poetry. Although he later called the results 'inflated and weepy',[22] this was his first taste of something that could become more important to him than politics. When he was released in January 1910, he gave up his work for the Party and began teaching himself art. In August 1911 he was admitted to the Moscow art academy. There he met the Ukrainian Cubist painter and Futurist poet David Burliuk (1882–1967), an extravagant natural-born artist who helped Mayakovsky launch his career. The two men soon became the pillars of Russian Futurism.

In their manifesto *A Slap in the Face of Public Taste*, Burliuk, Mayakovsky and their poet friends Aleksei Kruchenykh and

Velimir Khlebnikov wiped the floor with Blok, Bryusov and Sologub's Symbolist generation. A new age, a new idiom and a new morality – it all began here and now, Moscow, 1912.[23] In formal terms, there can be no denying that they lived up to their ambitions; the linguistic inventiveness of Khlebnikov and Kruchenykh's poetry may still be unparalleled, and their compositional placement of letters and words on the page made literature simultaneously a form of art and music.[24] Yet when war broke out, the Futurists responded in essentially the same way as the older generation. Their mindset may have been radically different – they did not go into raptures at the thought of the Eternal Feminine or the Greek mother goddess Demeter – and their work may have been marked by greater bravura and more exclamation points, but much of their art was similarly obsessed with finding the true meaning of Russia and Slavic culture. In other words, their sense of national identity was highly developed. When Marinetti came to Russia in January 1914 to promote his brand of Futurism, the local youth stopped just short of proclaiming him the new Messiah. But the many sincere or sensation-seeking members of the public who treated Marinetti almost like a foreign head of state were rebuked by Khlebnikov and his fellow Futurist, Benedict Livshits, for 'betraying Russia's first steps on the road to freedom and honour, and placing the noble neck of Asia under the yoke of Europe'.[25] In a letter written in February 1914, addressing Marinetti as an 'untalented loudmouth', Khlebnikov confidently predicted that they would meet each other amid the roar of cannons, 'in a duel between the Italo-German coalition and the Slavs, on the Dalmatian coast'.[26] The Germanophobic Khlebnikov had good reasons for choosing this arena.[27] Something was rotten in the Balkans, and the fates had ordained that the struggle for the Slavic soul would play itself out in the Croatian part of the Austro-Hungarian Dual Monarchy.

That struggle had now begun. On 2 August, Mayakovsky entitled a new poem 'War Is Declared'. The rhetoric of the evening papers and the overheated Russians he quotes ('We shall pollute the Rhine with poison blood!') flows seamlessly into that of his own verse, in which 'crimson streams of blood' run over the square and a west wind brings 'juicy flakes' of human flesh 'like red snow'.[28] The next day, the German army attacked the Polish–Russian cities of Dęblin (Ivangorod), Kalisz and Częstochowa (Chenstokov), committing war crimes in Kalisz and Częstochowa later that month. Civilians were executed, houses were destroyed, and in Częstochowa, a pilgrimage site, the shrine of the Virgin Mary was desecrated.[29] Akhmatova's darkest visions were already becoming a reality.

The outbreak of war is attended by sweeping emotions, grand gestures and impressively loud proclamations, as well as by logistical feats unequalled in civilian life. Millions of young men are mobilized and transported across continents; automobiles, horses and carts are requisitioned in the national interest; cannons rattle down the roads; and Red Cross ambulances pop up all over.[30] Just as symptomatic of the gravity of the situation, although much less visible in the streets, are the arrests of foreigners who have suddenly become objects of suspicion. The rules change from one moment to the next: you can go to sleep a guest and wake up an enemy. Anyone who arouses suspicions is, without reservation, declared an enemy of the state.

The practical implications of all this soon became abundantly clear to the Slovakian poet Janko Jesenský (1874–1945) and his fellow authors Miloš Crnjanski and Ivo Andrić in the Balkans. Jesenský was arrested immediately for his nationalist activities, while Andrić had left for Split, on the Dalmatian coast, after the assassination of Franz Ferdinand.[31] Austria's secret police were watching him closely, along with many other young Yugoslav revolutionaries, and the Dual Monarchy's official declaration of war on Serbia on 28 July was followed by a wave of arrests. On 4 August, Andrić was on the beach, drinking coffee, when the police found him. After short periods in custody in Šibenik (now in Croatia) and Maribor (Slovenia) he was sent to prisons in Ovčarevo (Serbia) and Zenica (Bosnia). Despite the different ethnicities predominating in these regions, they were all Austrian territory at the time. Andrić had run afoul of the authorities because of the political implications of his poem 'Prva proljetna pjesma' (The First Spring Song), quoted in Chapter 1. During his long imprisonment, however, literature was also a consolation. He read the books that were sent to him and wrote poems of his own, as well the lyrical prose later collected in *Ex Ponto* (1918). Nevertheless, his imprisonment affected him deeply, as weeks passed in utter silence, 'the silence and humility with which a person becomes familiar when misfortune befalls him'.[32] Sleepless nights brought him to the brink of despair, where death seemed 'miraculous, light, and beautiful' and he wondered in anguish when the 'good word' would come and release him from the darkness. This is not an unusual reaction for someone who has suddenly been deprived of his liberty, but the political context made Andrić's feelings all the more extreme. One moment he would draw strength from the 'forgotten ties of blood' that connected him to his ancestors, and the next he would be overcome by the despairing thought that his fate was determined by his 'heritage' and 'the inescapable curse of race and blood'.[33] Like his fictional contemporary Stephen Dedalus in James Joyce's novel *Ulysses* (1914–1921), Andrić came to see history as a nightmare from which he was trying to awake. He longed for the greatest possible moral and political independence, but he was tied by blood, and often enough bound hand and foot, to the history and destiny of his own nation.

Depending on how that nation was defined, it might include

Crnjanksi, who was also a 'Yugoslav', part of a southern Slavic people, even though he had been born in the Hungarian half of the Dual Monarchy and grown up as part of the small Serb minority in the primarily Germanophone and Hungarian city of Timişoara. After the assassination of the archduke, Crnjanski had spent several days hiding in the woods in Hinterbrühl, about ten miles to the southwest of Vienna.[34] As a supporter of the political student association Zora (Red Dawn), he too was under suspicion, and after the murder of Franz Ferdinand the patriotic press had declared open season on all Serbs. In early July, the Hungarian government journal *Pester Lloyd* had declared that Serbia, to show its good faith, must 'exterminate the nest of rats' that had crossed the border from Serbia into the Dual Monarchy to sow 'death and destruction'. The Hungarian authorities were eager to display these 'pestilential rats' to the Serbian delegation.[35] Crnjanski spent most of the remainder of July in the Hungarian Serb city of Novi Sad, in the arms of a Serb woman he had met there – the wife, in fact, of a high-ranking Serbian officer. When Austria declared war on Serbia, aliens in the Novi Sad region began to be rounded up. The woman, with whom Crnjanski attempted to reach the Serbian capital of Belgrade, was detained in Szeged as a suspected spy. Since he was with her, he too ended up in prison. After long interrogation, the police found nothing to charge him with, and instead sent him straight to the army. The woman would remain behind bars until the end of the war, and the Hungarian Serb Miloš Crnjanski found himself in training to fight in the Austrian military – against the Serbians.

To call the Austrian troops multicultural would be a gross understatement.[36] The poets serving in the Austrian army included Georg Trakl, born in Salzburg; Ernst Angel, from Vienna; the German-speaking Czech Zionist from Bohemia Hugo Zuckermann; the German-speaking Jew Franz Werfel from Prague; the Czechs Rudolf Medek, Stanislav Kostka Neumann,

Miloš Jirko and František Gellner; the Slovak Janko Jesenský (after his release); the Pole Jerzy Żuławski; the Croat Miroslav Krleža, the aforementioned Hungarian Serb Miloš Crnjanski, and the Galician–Polish, primarily Yiddish-speaking Jews Samuel J. Imber, Uri Tsvi Greenberg, Jacob Mestel, David Königsberg and Melech Ravitch.[37]

Ber Horowitz (1895–1942) also ended up in the Austrian army.[38] Born in a small village in the Carpathians, he had barely completed Polish secondary school in Poland when he was conscripted. It was a new world, and he was keenly aware that as a Jew, he did not entirely fit in. In his early war poem 'Galicia 1914', he described the Poles in his regiment enthusiastically singing their national anthem, 'Jeszcze Polska nie zginęła' (Poland is Not Yet Lost), and the certainty among the Ukrainians, as the trumpets sounded, that they were marching into battle to liberate the Ukraine. The contrast with the Jewish soldiers was striking:

> When we brothers
> went to war,
> from our eyelids
> hung bitter tears ...[39]

This may have been pacifist in intent, but what seems more relevant is that these Jews had no country to liberate. Furthermore, most of their fellow Polish Jews were under Russian rule, and the young Jews sent to the Eastern front by the Dual Monarchy would therefore have no choice but to treat them as mortal enemies.[40] Horowitz makes reference to this predicament in 'Oif 'n Weg zum Exerzierplatz' (On the Way to the Drilling Field). After a typical soldiers' song in which every line ends with a firm 'Hey!', he thinks of his mother's unhappiness, and her sister in the Caucasus who is saying farewell to her son at that very moment, and a woman in Naples who is witnessing her son's departure. Then the three young men are struck by the same realization: 'You distant, dear brother / and I am to be your murderer!'[41]

To some extent, the Poles had the same problem. Spread across Russia, Prussia and the Dual Monarchy, and hence divided among different armies, they inevitably experienced the conflict as a kind of civil war. From day one, it was clear that while this could represent a turning point in Polish history, there would be a heavy price to pay.[42] Nonetheless, both in their partitioned country and elsewhere in Europe, Poles launched into a fervent diplomatic and military campaign for their nationalist cause. Right-wing Polish politicians, viewing German imperialism as the greatest threat, threw their support behind the Russian Czar in hopes of being rewarded with greater autonomy.

Józef Piłsudski, a revolutionary and the leader of paramilitary units that aimed to undermine Russian authority with acts of terror, assessed the situation very differently. He hoped to defeat Russia with the Central Powers and then to change sides, bringing Germany and the Dual Monarchy to their knees in partnership with the Allies. Even before the war he had offered his services in Vienna, and before Russia and Austria–Hungary had officially declared war on one another, he had sent reconnaissance troops across the Russian border. On 16 August, his paramilitary units were transformed into the Polish Legions. In short, this was a man of swift action and strategic ingenuity, with insight into the uses of symbolism and propaganda.

Indeed, even the name 'Polish Legions' was an overt reference to the Polish army's legendary contribution to the Napoleonic wars of the late eighteenth and early nineteenth centuries. These exploits were the subject of the poem penned by a Polish soldier in 1797, 'Jeszcze Polska nie zginęła' (Poland is Not Yet Lost), which was to become the Polish national anthem. This was one of numerous patriotic songs and poems that stirred the hearts of many Poles in the Romantic period, particularly that of Poland's foremost national poet, Adam Mickiewicz (1798–1855). In 1848, the 'year of revolutions', Mickiewicz himself had established a Polish Legion in Italy, which sought to drive the Austrians out of northern Italy with the help of their Slav brothers from the Balkans. This was meant to be the beginning of the end for the Habsburg Empire and the dawn of a new and independent Poland.[43] The plan failed, but the Polish Legion attained a legendary status. Although this glorious past was largely mythical – most of the enthusiastic Polish legionnaires had served as cannon fodder for Napoleon – Piłsudski was now trying to turn the legend into a reality. Through their dedication and self-sacrifice, the Legions were to compel the surrounding states to grant Poland its freedom and independence.

Self-sacrifice was also a central theme of what may be the best-known Polish poem of the First World War, 'Ta, co nie zginęła' (She Who Is Not Yet Lost). The title refers to Poland itself, in an allusion to the well-known phrase in the national anthem, but it also reflects the poet's firm conviction that a great deal of Polish blood would have to flow before the country could achieve a full, independent existence. Divided by cruel fate, Poles came face to face in enemy trenches. A true Pole, the poet believed, had to accept that cruel fate without complaint or any twinge of conscience, keeping in mind the ultimate goal.

> Don't think of me, my brother,
> While marching to your death:
> Stand tall in the fire of my bullets,
> Like a knight, as you draw your last breath.

Weaponry had evolved since Napoleon's day, but not the images and values of the warrior. Even though they are brothers, the poem continues, the Poles will fight each other like brave, proud knights.

And if you see me from afar,
Aim at me instead
Into a Polish heart
Fire your Russian lead.

This was no figure of speech, but a reality. This image was meant to pierce the hearts of Polish readers: Poles were killing each other with enemy bullets. But the sacrifice would not be in vain.

For I dream of her by day
And I see her in my dreams.
SHE WHO IS NOT YET LOST
Will rise where our blood streams.[44]

The author of these lines, Edward Słoński (1874–1926), had offered up no more than his words, but in the tradition of the Napoleonic Polish Legion, the young Polish poets of 1914 answered the call of duty. At least ten of them enlisted,[45] including Jerzy Żuławski (1874–1915). At first sight, Żuławski was a traditional patriotic poet, a rowdy, unreflective country boy (he was an avid mountain-climber and one of the founders of a volunteer rescue service in the Tatra Mountains) with one foot stuck in the Romantic era, only too ready to risk his life in the service of his country. In reality, he was a complex prototype of the early twentieth-century poet's many-faceted identity.[46] The son of a fighter in the failed revolution of 1863, he earned a doctoral degree in Bern, Switzerland, writing his dissertation on causality in Spinoza. He was profoundly influenced by Nietzsche and Bergson, travelled extensively in Italy, France and Germany, and is best known for his philosophical plays and the first Polish science-fiction novels, in the tradition of Jules Verne and H.G. Wells. In his trilogy *Na srebnym globie* (On the Silver Globe, 1903–10), he used allegorical tales of moon landings and moon dwellers to picture how Europe might look in the twenty-seventh century. If there was progress of any kind, then it was in transcending materialistic cravings and the tensions between nations. But in reality, Europe still had a long way to go. Before the Poles could become Europeans, they would have to achieve national independence. And in his writings on this subject – including the poems he wrote during the war – Żuławski drew on the familiar arsenal of Romantic imagery: phoenixes rising from their own ashes, and spring as the dawn of the nation. That spring began in the hot summer of 1914.

Żuławski did not hesitate to follow in the footsteps of his father and his forefathers, as he wrote in 'To My Sons'. If fate was not kind to the Poles this time, then his sacrifice would serve as an example to the next generation.

> Let's pray to God, dear sons of mine,
> That the shackles binding our legs disappear,
> And before you reach your grandfather's years
> His dream to waking truth will incline
> And the ages of blood which nourished the leas
> Will make them blossom in a Poland that's free.[47]

This is what the poet does, and what the soldier does: spill his blood on the soil for the sake of his land. In the harvest season of 1914, reaping and sowing took on an entirely new meaning.

This image acquired an enduring power. In the sun-drenched European summer of 1914, war hysteria reached unparalleled heights. Political opponents cast their differences aside, declaring that the interests of the nation outweighed all internal conflicts. On 31 July, the *Pester Lloyd* wrote that the Dual Monarchy, which had so often been an object of contempt, had now been truly united by war, and that 'unified Hungary and unified Austria' had 'found a new, higher spiritual unity'.[48] Five days later, the leading Austrian newspaper, *Neue Freie Presse*, printed the poem

'This is the Struggle' by Countess Edith Salburg. All pettiness and infighting had been foresworn in 'foaming enthusiasm', she reported in solemn jubilation. 'We go to the battlefield like priests to the altar.'[49] Much the same message was heard across the border. That same day, 5 August, the left-wing liberal newspaper *Den* reported to its great satisfaction that 'in Russia there are no longer peoples and groups of the population' and that all were doing their part for the destiny and future of the country.[50] The war was transcendent, lifting everything to a higher plane: politics, emotions and all of human life.

Nowhere was this more apparent than in Germany. After Kaiser Wilhelm announced from his Berlin balcony that there were no longer different parties or religions, but only Germans, millions of men departed for the front with a song on their lips. The Dutch writer Louis Couperus, writing from Munich on 5 August, was surprised by the 'overweening' idealism of the masses: 'and now they are making the rounds, singing songs of their Fatherland! How full of emotion it sounds. In front of the Austrian *Botschaft*, in front of the Wittelsbach Palace and Residenz, the songs and hymns are bursting from a thousand throats, full of enthusiasm.'[51] Not long after this, the Red Cross entreated the public not to give so much chocolate to the soldiers, because it was making them ill.[52]

The task that awaited these young men defies comprehension. Germany was fighting not only the Russian barbarians in the east, but also the excessively liberal, egalitarian and pragmatic heirs of the French Revolution in the west.[53] The soldiers had a well-defined mission: defeat France in a *Blitzkrieg* and then rush to the Eastern front to take on the vastly more numerous Russian forces. General von Schlieffen had planned all this in 1905: Germany would not use its western border as the main entry into France, because the French side was too heavily fortified. Instead, it would invade from the north, sweep rapidly through the country, surround Paris within six weeks, and declare victory on the Western front.[54] The plan had just one weak link: the area to the north of France was not German, but Belgian, and Belgium's neutrality was guaranteed by a host of international agreements. So Germany – one of the signatories of those agreements – asked its smaller neighbour if, for one time only, it could make use of Belgian territory.[55] According to the official ultimatum from Berlin, delivered to the Belgian government on 2 August, Germany had no other option because the French were planning precisely the same thing – that is, to invade Germany, by way of the Belgian city of Namur. The German Empire expressed its sincere hope that Belgium would remain neutral, but also that the country would open its borders. Any damage done to its material heritage by German soldiers in transit would be reimbursed without hesitation. But if Belgium refused its hospitality, then Germany would have no choice but to regard it as an enemy. This may sound like a terrible dilemma, but in truth it was no such thing. Belgium had no real choice; if it allowed Germany free passage, then it would become no more than a German vassal state. And if Germany was defeated, Belgium would have sacrificed the vital political support of France and England. The country therefore defied the German ultimatum, and King Albert personally took command of the army. On 3 August, the same day that they advanced into Russia, the Germans spread false rumours from Luxembourg (which they had already occupied) that France was planning to use the Grand Duchy as its base of operations, and officially declared war on France. The British foreign secretary Edward Grey convinced parliament, which was loath to go to war, that the nation could not stand idly by as the Germans overran the Continent.[56] Even Irish nationalist members of parliament, such as John Redmond, volunteered assistance and troops; a kingdom that had been on the brink of civil war in Ireland would march into battle more united than ever. On

4 August, when Germany declared war on Belgium, Britain was unavoidably drawn into the conflict, along with its colonies in Canada, Australia, New Zealand and large parts of Africa. From one day to the next, the European war became a world war. What the Austrians had initially seen as not much more than a stratagem for destroying Serbia – which they were already planning two weeks *before* the assassination in Sarajevo[57] – had, through a fateful mix of bravado, opportunism, ill will and misunderstanding, escalated into what quickly became known as the Great War.

From day one, everything about the conflict was worthy of that name, from the numbers of troops mobilized (ranging from half a million Serbians to more than five million Russians and Germans) to the number of poems dedicated to the conflict, which is almost inconceivable today.[58] According to the anthologist and poet Julius Bab, up to 50,000 war poems a day were written in Germany alone during the first month of the war.[59] That figure may seem implausible, but considering the huge numbers of poems written around the world for holidays such as Valentine's Day, it is not unthinkable. In some ways, Valentine's poems and war poems are quite comparable; simple rhymes are used to convey feelings of passion and connectedness. In early twentieth-century European culture, poetry was central to the educational system, and on special occasions newspapers often devoted prominent space to poetry. So the outbreak of mass versification at the start of the war was not really all that strange. From the smallest village newspapers to the most widely read dailies, the media opened their pages to lyrical contributions, and a great deal more poetry was written for private audiences. The magnitude of the event made ordinary people wax lyrical. Only a small minority of living Europeans had ever been through a war. The public was tossed on waves of emotion: suspense, excitement, anticipation, a sense of duty, and fear. Consider these famous lines from 'Soldatenabschied' (Soldiers'

Farewell), written by the poet and boilermaker Heinrich Lersch (1889–1936) at the time of the mobilization, during which he volunteered for the infantry:

> Farewell all, farewell!
> When we fall for you and for our future,
> Let these words re-echo as our last salute:
> Farewell all, farewell!
> A free German knows no cold compulsion:
> Germany must live even if we must die![60]

For some poets, strict rhyme may have been a way of keeping their panic under control. Most of them had no actual war experience, but they knew only too well what awaited them. Just before departing for the front, Alfred Lichtenstein vividly pictured his future in the poem 'Abschied' (Farewell):

> The sun is falling down on to the horizon.
> Soon they'll be throwing me into a nice mass grave.
> In the sky the good old sunset is glowing red.
> In thirteen days maybe I'll be dead.[61]

Yet for the soldier in Lichtenstein's poem, this shattering realization is no reason to bemoan his fate. No sobbing sweetheart or weeping mother could hold him back: 'I'm happy to go'. He is motivated partly by a sense of duty, but also by the feeling of participating in something larger than himself, in a collective, in history.

In those early days of August, no one expressed this feeling more poignantly than Rainer Maria Rilke (1875–1926). Born in Prague, writing in German, living in Paris by preference, and firmly convinced that he had a Russian soul, the introverted, highly sensitive Rilke was just about the last person you would expect to understand, let alone applaud, a European war. Yet he did, in a manner both unique and representative. From a very young age, he had recognized that he was not cut out for the life of a soldier. His parents, however, had seen things differently. At the age of ten, René was enrolled in the Sankt Polten military academy in Austria, and four years later in another in Mährisch-Weisskirchen (now Hranice, Czech Republic).[62] The plan was to make him an officer – an eminently respectable career choice that would open doors in the Habsburg Monarchy. This plan was not entirely successful. Although his scholastic performance was more than satisfactory, the effect of the military setting on the young Rilke can only be described as traumatic. Nevertheless, his work bears many traces of his military background and often places that world in a positive light. In fact, *Die Weise von Liebe und Tod des Cornets Christoph Rilke* (The Lay of the Love and Death of the Cornet, Christoph Rilke, written between 1899 and 1906), the prose poem that long remained his best-known work, is a remarkably virile celebration of the ecstasy in which life and death can be experienced, written from the point of view of a young ensign who goes to his death as a model of courage and heroism, his flag still burning beside him on the battlefield. The *Cornet* met with great success in 1912, when it was published as the first slim volume in the Insel-Bücherei series, and for lyrical prose of its type, it became a record-breaking bestseller. It is said to have become almost required reading in the early weeks and months of the war, finding its way into the knapsack of many a German-speaking soldier[63] – although not into that of the poet himself, who was not conscripted right away. As if by chance, Rilke was in Germany when the war broke out, having left Paris on 19 July for a quick visit to his publisher and his doctor. On 1 August, the day Germany declared war on Russia, he, like Louis Couperus, was in Munich. Their contrasting responses reflect their different personalities.

At first, Couperus (1863–1923) snobbishly dismissed the conflict as a 'gigantic, interesting thing' that nevertheless paled by comparison to the products of an imagination like his, such as a battle between all-powerful, ultra-advanced 'Martians or Jupiterians'. Still, he acknowledged that as a citizen of the neutral Netherlands, he felt '*very* small' now that this 'World Conflagration' was spreading through 'all of Europe'. The catastrophic drama of the war obviously excited him ('The red Fire, the red Blaze – oh, what a delightful image! One simply can't get enough of it!'), a reflection of his aestheticism.[64]

Of course, Rilke was just as accustomed to a sheltered existence as was Couperus, and his reflections on the declaration of war reveal as much about his personal mythos as they do about his actual political views. Nevertheless, in the long, complex series *Fünf Gesänge. August 1914* (Five Hymns: August 1914), he struck a chord that still resonates a century later. Like Couperus, he cast himself as a neutral observer, making no reference in these poems to Austria, Germany, or any of the nationalistic arguments of the day. For Rilke, the war was not a contest of nations, but an event that had suddenly and unexpectedly endowed the seemingly arbitrary and accidental acts of modern man with meaning, direction and inevitability. In a world that had declared God dead, something absolute had now arisen:

> he, who until so recently
> heard a hundred voices, not knowing which one was right –
> how relieved he is now by that single summons; for *what*
> is arbitrariness beside that joyful, beside that certain necessity?
> At last a god.[65]

This could have been a peaceful god, Rilke added, were it not that such a god no longer had the power to 'grip' us. Instead, the 'War-God' had gripped us all, and not just to take us on a family outing. He 'hurls fire', and the skies turn red, as on the earth below 'hearts are full of their homeland [*Heimat*]'. Clearly, Rilke too was fully aware of the extent of the unfolding tragedy. Yet that did not detract from the excitement, the sense of being chosen. 'Blessed am I, that I may see men gripped', reads the opening line of Part II. Imagine his good fortune to experience this. Finally, something was *really* happening. Something *real* was happening. In the midst of catastrophe, this response may seem perverse, but similar thoughts passed through many people's minds on 11 September 2001. Rilke went even further, introducing a familiar metaphor: 'the harvest begins'. Girls and women, he wrote, would be returned to their original role and status – the mothers as 'givers' and the girls as the 'legendary lovers' of ancient times. Yes, there would be yearning, weeping, moaning, but such feelings would now be given free rein, rather than suppressed or controlled. Everything would change now, even for the solitary poet. When the war god makes his entrance, the individual is consumed by the collective.

> And what of us? Glowing together into one,
> into a new creature, which he fills with fatal life.
> So too, I no longer *am*; from the collective heart
> mine beats its beat, and the collective mouth
> breaks mine open.

At this point in the third poem – written on the third day of war, the text suggests – the poet expresses his first reservations. If this god is absolute and can see what is to come, would he willingly see his own creation destroyed? Yes, he would. A terrific and terrifying regression was in progress, to a 'still unrevived primeval past' in which 'triumphantly / felt danger' made men 'holy together'. Only once does Rilke use the pivotal word, referring directly to the only thing as absolute as the god who inspires these emotions. Unsurprisingly, that word is ushered in by an adjective that transfigures it and makes it central. Each soldier, Rilke writes, undergoes a *gefürsteter Tod* – an ennobled death, a death made princely. The only thing remaining is for them to stare into the eyes of their destiny without flinching and try to outdo that horrifying God in horror. Then, out of pain and extremity – and not out of hate – they take on a new face. The confrontation with the other, 'the enemy', 'the stranger', brings new insight. The series does not end triumphantly. The soldiers may have touched the Universal, but without becoming It – they themselves remain finite. The closing lines, placed in prosaic parentheses, describe what awaits them in muted yet consoling terms: '(So that your own error / burns away in the tormented, the terrible heart.)' May their own failings and failures be counteracted, even consumed, in the heart unexpectedly touched by something absolute, the heart that is brimming with love for the *Heimat* but that will, in the end, be filled with nothing but pain and horror. It was less than a week into the month of August and the war, the air still thick with tension and expectation, but sensitive minds and hearts knew what lay in store.

Still, intimated knowledge is nothing like lived knowledge, such as we find in the writings of Ernst Stadler (1883–1914). The message of his 1913 expressionist poem 'Der Aufbruch' (Setting Out) was similar to that of Rilke's *Cornet*: life had to be lived to the fullest, even if that meant dying.

> Forward, with battle and blood in my eyes, and reins held up.
> Perhaps in the evening, victory marches would play around my head.
> Perhaps we would all lie somewhere, stretched out among the dead.
> But before the reaching out and before the sinking,
> Our eyes would see their fill of world and sun, and take it in, glowing and drinking.[66]

Yet Stadler was no ironclad militarist, but a prototypical European intellectual with Franco-German roots (having been born in Colmar a decade after the Alsace region was annexed by Germany). He studied at Oxford's renowned Magdalen College and became a professor at the Université Libre de Bruxelles in 1910.[67] In 1914, he spent his summer vacation in Strasbourg, making plans to transform the university town into a cultural centre, with leading roles for Germany, France, and prominent intellectuals from both nations, such as Georg Simmel and Henri Bergson.[68] He did not expect to be present in person for the continuation of this project, because he had accepted a teaching position in Toronto and was planning to move to Canada in early September. But then came the German mobilization, and he was ordered to report to Colmar at once as a reserve lieutenant.[69] He began to keep an understated diary, which displays nothing of the enthusiasm for war generally associated with August 1914. The people of St Moritz, where he was billeted on 2 August, were filled with dread, and his commanding officer hoped to avert bloodshed through prayer, but to no avail. At breakfast the next day, his unit was surrounded by wailing mothers, daughters, sisters and sweethearts. More than a sixth of the village's inhabitants were ordered to take up arms. The first casualties had already been reported. A Roma family with three children who crossed the German border, seemingly by chance, were taken prisoner.[70] German soldiers were killed by friendly fire: '*C'est la guerre*. Already, human lives are starting to become worthless.'[71] After opening a speech with a series of jokes, his commander abruptly changed his tone: 'In time of war, killer instincts have to be roused. It's a terrible thing, but a military necessity.'[72] The news that reached Stadler sometimes bore little relation to the truth: the Netherlands, and perhaps Sweden, were said to have allied themselves with Germany.[73] In fact, both countries remained neutral, sometimes with great difficulty. But Stadler's first-hand experiences were real enough. On 6 August, a lieutenant committed suicide; 'feverish excitement' had gotten the better of him. Meanwhile, the troops were stationed in villages where, despite place names like Bassemberg and Weiler, the locals spoke French. 'Even the mobilization order is in French', wrote Stadler, their fellow Alsatian. The atmosphere among the general population was very different, 'although people are very friendly, if only out of fear'.[74]

Like Colmar, Bassemberg and Weiler, Strasbourg too was German territory in July 1914, having changed hands in the Franco-Prussian War of 1871. Its residents were plagued by mixed feelings and revealing misunderstandings. When a messenger burst into a literary gathering to announce that Germany had declared war on France, the Alsatian poets stood up and spontaneously began singing their national anthem: 'La Marseillaise'.[75] They were not the only ones who had never entirely adjusted to being German. One man often went just across the border to the nearby city of Nancy on Sundays to watch the French forces drilling. 'I saw them', he would say afterwards with a sigh, visibly moved by his ex-compatriots, who still commanded most of his loyalty. On 1 August, this man's nephew, the young poet and artist Hans (Jean) Arp (1886–1966), took the train from Strasbourg, his birthplace, to Paris, the centre of modern art, where he had met Wassily Kandinsky a few years earlier. Near the Gare de L'Est railway station, Arp went in search of a bank where he could exchange his German currency. 'Poor boy,' the clerk said to him, 'all your money has become worthless, because war has just been declared.'[76]

Another pioneer of modern art, the poet-critic Guillaume Apollinaire, also spent the day in transit, returning in haste from Deauville with his friend André Rouveyre. He later described the drive to Paris in his poem 'La Petite Auto' (The Little Car):

> We said farewell to a whole era
> Furious giants were rising over Europe [...]
> Nations hurled together so that they might learn to know one another.

When they arrived in Paris and saw mobilization notices posted all over the city, the two friends realized

> that the little car had driven us into a New era
> And although we were both already mature men
> We had just been born.[77]

As if to celebrate their arrival in this 'New era', they had a Paris photographer make a flip book, a series of fifty photographs that look like a film when the pages are turned rapidly. The men stare into the camera, excited and sniggering: the new age starts now.[78]

This anecdote seems to suggest, yet again, that the war was greeted with excitement and enthusiasm. But it was not, or at least not as widely and unanimously as is often said or suspected.[79] On 4 August, as nearly all his male friends reported to their barracks, the poet and novelist Jules Romains (1885–1972) wrote of the 'ominous emptiness' that had descended over Paris.[80] In Germany, too, the euphoria was less than absolute. As early as 10 August, Couperus wrote of a soldier in Munich calling out to the cheering public, 'Instead of shouting hurrah, why don't you tip us; then at least we can go get drunk!!' The next day, the Dutch writer was struck by the 'weary mood' and the silence in the coffee houses. '"Give us a *hurrah!*, won't you?" cried a passing soldier, perhaps contrary to his own secret feelings.'[81] This aside suggests that all the shouting and cheering was a kind of incantation against the fear of death.

In those turbulent days, the greatest anger, despair and disbelief was to be found among the few socialists who had not caught the nationalist bug and were doing their best to make it clear that the war could never be in the interests of the working class. In the despairing poem 'Tu vas te battre' (You'll Put Up a Fight) – written on 30 June, before war was officially declared (although the poet may have antedated it later) – Marcel Martinet (1887–1944) asked workers just what they thought they stood to gain from this European conflict. It was one thing to battle against the exploiters and the bosses, 'against the rich, against the masters / against those who eat your share / against those who eat your life'. But for a foundryman from Creusot to be asked to kill a foundryman from Essen, a miner from Saxony to kill one from Lens, a dockworker from Le Havre to kill a dockworker from Bremen? It was too ridiculous for words. Look at your coarse, black workman's hands, Martinet urged them. Look at your thin, pale children, your worn-out wife, your comrades: 'And now, and now, / now go and fight'.[82]

But this was obviously a minority view. The prevailing sentiments in France were outrage and a proud determination to defend the country against the aggressors. This explains how the *union sacrée*, the truce between classes and political factions declared by President Raymond Poincaré, could unite the divided country as if by magic. In the face of such a massive threat, the old feuds – between the *communards* and those who had crushed their insurgency in 1871, between the two sides in the Dreyfus Affair, between socialists and nationalists, and between Catholics and anticlerical republicans – no longer seemed so relevant. Here too, the war seemed to lift people onto a higher plane. Not that they suddenly became superior beings, but the catastrophe led many of them to adjust their values and priorities, often quite abruptly.

In those early weeks of August, Gabriele D'Annunzio experienced just such an unanticipated change of heart. At first glance, his response to the onset of war seemed to be exactly the kind of thing one might expect from a bombastic, belligerent nationalist like him. On 13 August, *Le Figaro* proudly published D'Annunzio's eleven-part 'Ode pour la résurrection latine' (Ode to the Latin Resurrection), composed directly in French, along the bottom of its first and second pages and across the entire width. The almost masochistic way in which the opening lines link beauty to death and horror ('What terror and what death / and what new beauties / are scattered all through the night?'[83]) can be taken as characteristic of his views: this war offered the Latin race a chance to awaken from its slumber and reclaim its rightful place at the heart of world civilization. His belief that this was a divinely ordained mission forestalled almost any criticism, for who could disobey heaven's command? Accordingly, the countries that fought this battle – 'O Italy! O France!'[84] – were themselves divine. This was a poem full of exclamation marks and capital letters.

Yet in everyday life, the war forced even an aristocrat like D'Annunzio to moderate his tone considerably. It made for a painful contrast: even as his poetry voiced the pride of a chosen people, he complained in his diary of the difficulty of maintaining his impressive collection of greyhounds under such dire circumstances. On 17 August the great anti-democrat noted that war was actually tantamount to the abolition of the individual. The sight of military uniforms could still send him into raptures, but the lifeless atmosphere in the streets of Paris disturbed him. To his dismay, a bookstore's display window held nothing but titles about the art of warfare. Despite having longed for heroism, he wrote in the privacy of his diary of the overpowering 'feeling that nothing has any value any longer'.[85]

On 14 August, D'Annunzio had his poem reprinted in the Milanese newspaper *Corriere della Sera*, no mean feat considering its tone and subject matter. His editor there, Luigi Albertini, had pleaded with him on 8 August to submit a few pieces that a neutral paper could print in such difficult and delicate times,[86] when Italy was doing its utmost to stay out of the conflict. On 2 August, the Italian chief of staff had announced that there was no way his country could take part in a war, since there were not enough uniforms available.[87] The next day, Prime Minister Antonio Salandra declared in parliament that because Austria had reneged on one of its commitments, Italy would not honour its alliance with the Dual Monarchy and Germany, and would remain neutral.[88] For the most part, the Italian public was tremendously relieved; the masses had no desire for war in any case, and an alliance with the occupiers of Trieste and Trentino would have been a dreadful prospect. Germany and Austria were scandalized by Italy's decision, of course, viewing it as an act of abject cowardice. The French were relieved; no doubt the fraternal bonds between the two Latin nations were on some people's minds, but the most important reason was military. Italy's neutrality allowed France to leave its Alpine border almost undefended, so that more of its troops could be deployed against Germany.

For the Italian Futurists, these were frustrating times. A great war had finally broken out, but their country had declared neutrality. In the 1 August issue of *Lacerba*, Carlo Carrà (1881–1966) published his visual poem 'Festa patriottica-dipinto parolibero' (Patriotic Holiday – Freeword Painting), an explosion of colours, catchwords and newspaper clippings with ejaculations like 'Evvivaaa l'esercito' ('Lo-o-o-ong live the army') and 'Abbassoooo [l'Austria]' ('Do-o-own with [Austria]') that left no doubt as to his allegiances.[89] In the first collage (dated 2 August) in the series later titled *Conflagrazione* (Conflagration), Carrà's fellow Futurist Paolo Buzzi (1874–1956) proclaimed the outbreak of 'the European war' with newspaper clippings against a red background. Buzzi drew special attention to statements of Italian neutrality, adding his own question marks and exclamation points.[90] For genuinely neutral observers, this was a nerve-wracking time. From Rome, the Dutch poet P.N. van Eyck

(1887–1954) wrote to his friend Albert Verwey (1865–1937), 'For the first week I did *nothing* but await the arrival of the latest newspaper and grind away at the news with my brains like millstones.'[91]

Not everyone was paralyzed by these events. The war had scarcely begun when the Futurist in Fernando Pessoa, Álvaro de Campos, felt it calling out to him in neutral Lisbon. On 2 August, he began a 'Ode Marcial' (Martial Ode) – a variation on the 'Ode Triunfal' he had written in June, but adapted to the new situation. But what was that situation, exactly? In stark contrast to the 'Triumphal Ode', the new poem began in uncertainty: 'What is it that will change and is already changing, out there, / In the distance, in the future, in its agonies – who knows where?'[92] These questions were not purely rhetorical. Pessoa sensed that great, sweeping transformations were just around the corner, but he hardly had words for them yet. His references to approaching horsemen and earthquakes seem apocalyptic, and the figures who appear to control the action of the poem clearly come from the underworld, 'from the abyss of things ... from the place of the laws that govern everything'. Worldly leaders are like playthings in the hands of these archetypal rulers. While the poet could record the seismic waves, it was still too soon for interpretation, let alone prediction. Nations and empires would fall, but which ones?

> O you civilizations arriving at the nocturnal crossroads
> Where they have taken away the pont d'appui
> And from which crooked roads lead who knows where.[93]

This was the true state of affairs in 'confused Europe'.[94] A crucial girder had been removed, the balance had been disrupted, and the long-standing framework was collapsing. What next? Nobody knew. It made the poet uncharacteristically nostalgic. As a child he had stared at soldiers in fascination, unaware of 'the carnal and bloody reality' of their profession.[95] He was determined to find the deeper and higher meaning of these events, their mythological resonances, and the astral constellation that could explain them, but his thoughts kept straying back to

> the real war ...
> With its reality of people who actually live
> With its strategy actually applied to real armies made up of real people ...
> of real human misery, the deaths of those who truly died,
> And the sun just as real over the earth just as real
> Both real in action and the same shit between them![96]

* * *

That same day, 2 August, Charles Sorley was thrown into jail in Trier. He had spent the spring and summer in Germany, enjoying the country more and more. While he missed 'a good breakfast', British coins ('a big downright English penny'), and the satirical magazine *Punch*, he considered Germany a superior country in every other respect.[97] The growing international tensions had not escaped his notice. 'The haystack has caught fire', he had written to his parents from Jena on 26 July. Drunken *Verbindungen* (members of student associations) were parading the streets shouting 'Down with the Serbs' and snatching up the new editions of the papers that rolled off the presses every half-hour, the rumours becoming wilder with each print run. Ignoring his father's urgent request that he return home, Sorley went on to Marburg on 28 July for a week's walking tour in the Moselle valley with his friend Arthur Hopkins. When they returned to civilization on 1 August, the burgomaster of Neumagen ordered them to leave the country post-haste. The next day they found the village's children in tears and the women 'snuffling and gulping'. On the train to Trier, all they saw were silent, resigned men on the way to their barracks. Here too, there seemed to be little enthusiasm for war. The soldiers told Sorley and his friend that the entire country was in the grip of a paranoid fear of spies, and they decided it would be best to report to the next military guardpost. Unfortunately, Sorley did not have a passport with him, and the two men were thrown in prison, with 'a hissing crowd shouting "Totschiessen" [Shoot them dead]'. When they were released the next day, the same mob was waiting for them: '"Then you're not the Englishmen who poisoned the water", they said.' They were then sent off almost like departing heroes, as a rumour began to spread that England had taken Germany's side in the war.[98] That would have been the ultimate clash of civilizations: the Germanic peoples against the Slavs and the Latins.

By way of Cologne, Liège and Brussels, Sorley reached Antwerp on the evening of 3 August. The city's inhabitants made it clear just what they thought of their own forces, telling him, 'The Germans will be here in twelve hours' time, there's no doubt of it.'[99] A ship chartered by the British consul transported Sorley and a number of other stranded Britons and Americans to the other side of the North Sea.

Back at home, Sorley found an England entirely different from the one he had left seven months earlier. This was a country at war. As recently as 2 August, a massive pacifist demonstration had taken place in the streets of London, but that already seemed like the distant past. From one moment to the next, a nation of civilized cricket players had been transformed into a nation of bloodthirsty warriors.

> We mean to thrash these Prussian Pups,
> We'll bag their ships, we'll smash old Krupps,
> We loathe them all, the dirty swine.
> We'll drown the whole lot in the Rhine.[100]

There were subtler variations on this theme, but these anonymous lines encapsulate the mood in Britain. The main reason for such fury may seem incomprehensible to us today, yet both in official propaganda and from the perspective of the many thousands of young men who volunteered for military duty, the conflict centred on the fate of one country: Belgium. After foreign secretary Edward Grey's speech before parliament, the 4 August edition of *The Morning Post* reported an enormous swell of sympathy throughout the House of Commons, 'a feeling that we really meant to "play the game" as it ought to be played and stand by our friends'.[101] And so the Belgians discovered that they had friends on the far shore.

They would need all the friends they could get. The German army invaded Belgium the morning of that same day, 4 August. In his collection of war poems *Bezette stad* (Occupied City, 1921), the Flemish poet Paul van Ostaijen (1896–1928) suggests that the invasion was a cakewalk, summarizing it in four words: 'Visé marche! Liège mortars'. In reality, it took a little longer and demands a bit more discussion. The German troops entered the country at Gemmenich and were in Visé, on the Meuse river, by evening.[102] From there they launched an attack on Liège, the first key point on the Belgian lines of defence. Everyone expected the Germans to crush the Belgians, as indeed they had to if their plan of reaching Paris as quickly as possible was to succeed. Against all expectations, however, the ring of forts around Liège held out for several days. After fierce fighting and heavy losses, the Germans changed their tactics; they would prevail not by force of numbers, but with an air attack from a zeppelin and artillery fire – including from Krupp's new miracle weapon Big Bertha, which was rushed to the battlefield.[103] This strategy ultimately succeeded, but the Battle of Liège nevertheless became emblematic of Belgium's plucky resistance against the brutal German attack. All at once Emile Verhaeren (1855–1916), already revered throughout

Europe, became Belgium's unofficial poet laureate, predicting that no one would ever forget the heroes and victims of Liège.[104] Valery Bryusov mentioned both Verhaeren and Liège in his surprisingly named ode 'To the Flemish', in which he informed the vanquished that the love of country always triumphs over military might.[105] The French pacifist Henri Guilbeaux (1885–1938) showed a somewhat better grasp of geography in 'Stances à la ville de Liège' (Stanzas for the City of Liège), calling the city of fallen heroes the first 'injured metropolis' but offering as consolation the thought that it had at least been spared the sad fate of Visé and Dinant, where 'blatant rape and savage arson' had caused immeasurable suffering.[106] This assessment was not entirely accurate (sixty-seven civilians had been killed in Liège, and forty-two buildings set on fire), but it was true that Visé and Dinant had suffered much worse. In Dinant, for example, 674 men, women and children were put up against a wall and shot and about 1,100 houses were destroyed.[107] During the battle, the husband of Maria Dobler Benemann (1887–1980) was in Visé, where twenty-three civilians were executed and some 600 houses destroyed.[108] A poem she based on her husband's letters and diary, supplemented after his death later that year with stories from comrades-in-arms on leave, is shadowed by a trace of guilt.

> Behind, a heap of ashes haunts you
> an elegant house that you transformed
> when hunting for a sniper's nest.[109]

At the same time, these lines reflect the official story: German soldiers could not have acted otherwise, because they were under constant fire from cowardly Belgian snipers. The truth was generally quite different. The incidents in Visé took place almost two weeks after the occupation of the village. All the houses had been searched and all weapons confiscated long before. The German soldiers, who were drunk, may well have been sent into a panic by a shot from their own ranks. Furthermore, according to a Dutch journalist who was on the scene and spoke with Dutch Red Cross workers, the systematic devastation of the village did not begin until the next morning, when drunk soldiers once again plundered all the houses, setting them on fire and shooting at everything that moved – 'pigs, horses, cows, dogs'.[110]

Such German atrocities soon became a mainstay of Allied propaganda. The most barbaric act attributed to the Germans – chopping off children's hands – has been proved a myth after extensive research,[111] but many other horrors reported were anything but fabrications. Tales of civilian snipers that had been circulating in the German military since the Franco-Prussian war fuelled paranoia in some German soldiers, while many others were simply aggrieved that the stubborn Belgians would not allow them free passage. They used civilians as human shields, murdered, looted and raped.[112] The later destruction of the university library in Louvain and the cathedral at Reims made it difficult for the Germans to go on regarding themselves as the defenders of civilization. Allied posters, postcards and poems inscribed these events in the collective memory.[113]

> The Iron hand has struck, but in the smiting
> Its own dishonour on the wall is writing,
> And Belgium's funeral pyre the world is lighting.

So the British poet Mary Booth wrote in 'The Women of Belgium to the Women of England', which both expressed moral outrage and taught a propagandistic lesson.[114] The French poet Valentine de Saint-Point (1875–1953) is not known to have written about these atrocities in particular, but they probably did not come as a complete surprise to her. In her 'Futurist Manifesto of Lust' (1913), she explained that after a battle in which soldiers have died, it is perfectly normal for their comrades-in-arms to turn to rape 'so that life may be re-created'.[115] The physical conquest of a territory, she suggested, leads naturally to the physical conquest of its women. This connection seemed more questionable in battered Belgium. Driven by outrage and a spirit of unity rarely seen in the politically divided nation, the Belgian people resisted the invasion, and the poets played their part. Constant Eeckels (1879–1934), a usually mild-mannered Catholic poet with great sympathy for the Flemish cause, left no doubt as to the attitude required:

Our Fatherland is under attack!
Now all must join the ranks.
Proudly plant the Belgian flag.
Lions, sharpen your fangs!

The 'lions' in question are clearly the Flemish, an allusion to the Lion of Flanders. The second stanza heralds the advance of the Walloons, and in the closing lines, confident that God and Justice are on his side, the poet urges the entire country to take up arms:

Are we mere spoils of tyranny?
Will freedom, justice be denied?
Not now, not ever! Turn and flee!
The Belgians have arrived![116]

In a long letter sent from Antwerp to the Dutch critic Maria Viola, the poet Karel Van den Oever (1879–1926) described the optimism and determination of the Belgian people, who hoped, prayed and believed that their little country would become the arrogant Prussians' grave. The Germans might think of themselves as well-organized and modern, he wrote, but it took a great deal more to win a war. In Van den Oever's opinion, religious affiliation played a major role (in a subsequent letter, he told the story of a Belgian priest killed near Aarschot 'by Luther's bullet'), as did the nobility of the nation and the soul: 'The practical compartmentalization of the German soldier's knapsack does not make the German army Europe's finest, for the mathematical calculations of the German army staff can never account for the patriotic power of the people, which makes a sabre more than a strip of steel.'[117] For Van den Oever, too, the conflict was a clash of cultures, a fight to save as much of Catholic civilization as possible.

This perspective would have struck a chord with the Irish poet Tom (Thomas Michael) Kettle (1880–1916), a liberal Catholic and brilliant lawyer and economist who happened to be in Belgium, in his role as a former member of parliament, when the war broke out.[118] The arms he had come to purchase for the paramilitary Irish Volunteers were ultimately donated to the local military forces. His articles and reports show his unqualified support for the Belgian cause. 'It is impossible not to be with Belgium in the struggle', he wrote from Brussels on 5 August. 'It is impossible any longer to be passive. Germany has thrown down a well-considered challenge to all the deepest forms of our civilization.'[119] The ravages he observed across the country in the days and weeks that followed, including at the cathedral in Mechelen and the library in Louvain, reinforced his existing view that Germany – swept up in Bismarck's blood-thirst, Nietzsche's power-hungry brutality, the nationalism of historian Heinrich von Treitschke, and the militarism of General Bernhardi, pan-Germanist and author of the bestselling *Deutschland und der Nächste Krieg* (Germany and the Next War, 1911) – had embraced the 'Gospel of the Devil' and turned its back on Europe's true calling as a beacon of culture and progress. To Kettle, Europe embodied democracy and sovereignty. The German attack negated those values and therefore posed a threat to Ireland's future. This conclusion may seem surprising, since Britain, rather than Germany, formed the most immediate barrier to Irish independence, but given Kettle's European ideals, his reasoning was understandable. As early as 1905, he had averred that to become truly Irish, his country would have to be European. He saw the future not in an inward-looking nation-state, but in a carefully nurtured internationalism in which countries large and small would respect and learn from each other. Germany's actions flew in the face of that dream, and therefore had to be combated by all possible means. It was 'Europe against the Barbarians'.[120] Ireland's honour and Europe's were inextricably linked. The only way for Ireland to claim its rightful place among European nations was by fighting for justice and civilization.

Meanwhile, the Belgians were fighting for their lives. Some were valiant warriors, while others were terrified. There was widespread panic, but at the same time many heeded the call to battle. In these intense, confusing times, even cultural pessimists suddenly saw reasons for hope. The baroque poet-priest Cyriel Verschaeve (1874–1949), for instance, wrote to his friend Jozef Lootens that the war could bring about the unforeseen moral regeneration of God's people.

> It almost makes me proud, as a human being, that crowds of people are capable of such perseverance, and an endless curiosity fills me, a desire to become more intimately acquainted with the course of that terrible battle. I must confess, I was wrong about my times and thought the people of today were made of much softer stuff [...] God has handled matters well, and I believe He is using the lancets of war to cut a great deal of pettiness, indecision, and rot out of the world, and out of our nation. Let us hope that I am not mistaken, and that the dragon teeth sowed by this war, like those of ancient Greek mythology, will yield a splendid race of people, rich in love.[121]

Across the North Sea, Verschaeve's contemporary Ford Madox Hueffer was less lyrical about the situation. The war depressed him, and with the best will in the world, he could not see what good it might bring. Obviously, it had a baleful influence on society life, interfering with Hueffer's usual round of dinners, dances, parties and plays[122] – but it also had repercussions for literature. In days like these, who could find the time to read? And then there was the dreadful moral hair-splitting and all the inescapable clichés about nations that, despite their flaws, Hueffer felt were all fundamentally civilized and worthy of appreciation. Although ... 'It is extraordinary to think of the usually good and quiet Germans, the Austrians, and ourselves, all at each other's throat.'[123] He was willing to believe that it is better to die of your wounds out in the rain than 'gradually to peter out' in some stinking hospital, but he could not swallow the rhetoric in which the war was packaged. The only thing intellectuals could do in these grim times was to 'extract, for the sake of humanity and of the humaner letters, all the poetry that is to be got out of this war'.[124] For him, this categorically excluded the nationalist rantings of most of his fellow poets. Great names like Thomas Hardy, Laurence Binyon, *Blast* favourite Henry Newbolt, and Rudyard Kipling ('Stand up and take the war / The Hun is at the gate!'[125]) were offering their services to the British propaganda office.[126] That was another thing that depressed Hueffer – all those ghastly poems about 'mad dogs, and throttling fists'.[127]

Those who personally experienced the violence of war were overcome by sensations they would never have believed possible. Late at night on 20 August the expressionist poet August Stramm (1874–1915), writing from Geiswasser in Alsace to his publisher Herwarth Walden and Herwarth's wife Nell, described how the war placed everything in a new light: relationships, emotions, experiences ... nothing was as it had been. This was even true of his use of language. His sentences flowed one into the next like the experimental prose that James Joyce was just then inventing. 'War. Everything is behind me. Hope friendship and love. I love you but you are behind me far far do not be angry but another knew you another not I.'[128] The war offered him not transcendence, but regression, yet he was no less quick to embrace it. The soldiers were free to act like schoolboys, shedding their inhibitions. 'Oh power is glorious power Now we are waiting for the enemy waiting waiting he will come he must come that's what we want nothing more in the world 250 rifles my rifle will come before them.'[129] In this volley of words, a fragment like 'life has no value' could run directly into a passage that seemed to suggest the opposite ('Dear friends how are you') only to relapse into an anxious delirium ('only one fear he might not come not come go back') followed by a command ('Enemy come!') and the thought that he, Stramm, might not be able to write again, but that they should take courage, because what he could do, others could surely do better.[130] Again, we find a poet warding off the fear of death. By writing these words in a letter for others to read, Stramm may have persuaded himself to take courage as well.

No sooner had Anna Akhmatova's husband Nikolay Gumilyov heard about the mobilization than, full of chauvinistic zeal and guileless enthusiasm, he volunteered for service. 'The voice of war calls me',[131] he wrote in a poem that day, and without further ado, he left his solitary retreat in Terijoki (later annexed by Russia and renamed Zelenogorsk). On 5 August, he arrived in Slepnyovo to say farewell to his family. Akhmatova was horrified that he was going to war, but her opinion carried no weight. The next day, Gumilyov and his wife left for their home city, which, in a surge of patriotism, had recently been given the new, less German-sounding name of Petrograd. On 18 August, Gumilyov boarded the train to Novgorod, where he was to join the cavalry.

As they were parting at the station in Tsarskoye Selo, he and Akhmatova ran into their fellow poet Alexander Blok. Although both Gumilyov and Akhmatova were both Acmeists and therefore intellectual opponents of this celebrated Symbolist, Gumilyov, who was already in uniform, expressed his hope that Blok would not be sent to the front: 'It would be like roasting a nightingale.'[132] Gumilyov saw himself not as a delicate songbird, but as a mighty eagle. War offered him and his beloved Russia an opportunity for purification. The possibility of *not* joining the military never even entered his battle-hungry mind. He was intent on proving his strength and courage, on finally becoming like the conquistadors of his earliest poems.

As for Blok, he was deeply ambivalent about the war.[133] His stay in Shakhmatovo had been rudely interrupted in late July by a telegram from his father-in-law, telling him that he had to join his unit in St Petersburg right away. Once the war had begun, his loved ones had taken decisive action. His wife had gone to the front as a nurse, and his new mistress, the actress Lyubov Delmas, had followed suit. Blok, in contrast, no longer knew what his purpose was in life. He wanted to work and make a contribution, but no one seemed to have any use for his talents. He sank to alarming depths of gloom, even contemplating suicide in his diary, and his letters to his mother left her deeply distressed. Still, something drastic was obviously happening to Little Mother Russia, and that only confirmed the long-standing premonitions of Blok, the poetic visionary.

Meanwhile, the mobilization and the war were placing Russian society under considerable strain. Since the failed revolution of 1905, the regime's paranoia had known no bounds, and now that the enemy was crossing the border all systems were on red alert. The opposition and their potential sympathizers were kept under close scrutiny, and the tools of the state included censorship and terror. Social unrest went on unabated in the Russian Empire. In

1913, almost a million workers had gone on strike, and in the early summer of 1914 a half million Russians had refused to work. St Petersburg and Baku had seen mass demonstrations where red flags were openly waved.[134] A series of large, orchestrated campaigns were carried out at the start of the war to create unity and smother any revolutionary impulses with patriotic passion. These efforts were relatively effective in the cities, but in the countryside – where most of the 6.5 million soldiers mobilized in 1914 were stationed – small-scale riots erupted in almost half of Russia's 101 provinces.[135] Radical cultural or ethnic nationalist movements were monitored and severely restricted. Among the groups banned by the authorities was the Futurist cell that had just formed in the Ukraine. The three leading Ukrainian Futurists were called up for duty, and their magazine and newspaper offices were shut down.[136]

The Russians faced increasing difficulties on the Eastern front after a string of early successes on Prussian territory and suffered a humiliating defeat at Tannenberg in late August. Almost the entire Second Army, some 150,000 soldiers in all, was surrounded by the Germans. Fewer than 10,000 escaped; 92,000 were taken prisoner and the rest either killed or wounded. In disgrace, General Samsonov put a bullet through his head. For the first time since 1905, the Czarist regime was tottering.[137]

Although Serbia was where it had all begun, the shocking escalation of the war had pushed the country literally and figuratively to the margins of the military maps. Meanwhile, the Austrian army was fighting for its life and that of the great empire it represented. To its dismay, the Dual Monarchy found itself facing a war on two fronts. Instead of a quick punitive mission targeting the obstinate Serbians, in which they could have counted on victory through sheer numbers, they were forced to deploy most of their troops in Galicia, in the east. Foolishly, they decided to send a relatively small force across the Save and Drina rivers. But the Serbians (described by Kaiser Wilhelm as 'Orientals, therefore liars, tricksters, and masters of evasion'[138]) would not give up without a fight, and after an exceptionally bloody battle on Cer mountain, the occupiers had to retreat. As they did, they inflicted harsh reprisals on civilians,[139] killing children and leaving behind their mutilated bodies, raping and murdering women and dumping the corpses into a canal along with their severed breasts, and roping other victims together before executing them.[140] The Dutch medical doctor Arius van Tienhoven was part of an international commission that investigated these atrocities, and his report clearly shows that they were acts of vengeance. For example, he found the doors of ransacked and demolished houses covered with inscriptions like 'A lovely souvenir of the punitive expedition by the Austrian army – 15 August. Serbia devastated, long live the Austrian army!'[141] This was something else the troops had not yet learned in 1914: how to admit defeat.

Meanwhile, on the Western front, the situation for the Allies was going from bad to worse. It seemed as though nothing could stop the German advance into Paris, and a catastrophic French offensive in the Ardennes led to tremendous losses. Some 27,000 French soldiers died on 22 August alone. In early September, the remaining French troops and their British reinforcements retreated almost to the Seine. The humiliated soldiers had no idea what to expect, and fell prey to despair and disillusionment. The French government fled to Bordeaux in a panic.[142] In the capital, Luigi Barzini, the best-known Italian war correspondent of the day, urged his compatriot D'Annunzio to flee Paris at once.[143] But the poet refused to leave, ordering his private secretary Tom Antongini to hoard enough food to last the two of them, two female servants, and their twenty-two canaries a full year. The food shortages forced him to kill a few of his favourite dogs (not to eat them, but because there was no food to spare).

For D'Annunzio, too, the tension gradually became unbearable. On Sunday, 6 September, he wrote in his diary, 'Anxiety, dread, a choking feeling. In solitude, one's personality breaks down. It's no longer possible to be alone, to feel alone, without our universe falling apart.'[144] For Jules Romains, that Sunday was a day of horror. The universal soul so often described by Romains, the founder of Unaminism, seemed to have been completely drowned out by hate, belligerence and fear: 'Paris is becoming stifling. Panic is bringing out the worst in people.'[145]

Of course, those at the front experienced an entirely different level of tension. There was no solitude, no quiet moments when soldiers could reflect on their situation, except perhaps during Sunday mass. Charles Péguy – who when the mobilization was announced on 1 August had broken off the latest of his many polemical essays mid-sentence to fulfil his patriotic duty[146] – was attending a church service in Montmélian on 4 September. The next day, Reserve Lieutenant Péguy fought in the Battle of Villeroy (Seine-et-Marne) and was killed at the head of his troops. 'He yearned for war, and so its outbreak must have brought him joy', Paul van Ostaijen wrote some time later. 'His death was literally the apotheosis of his life.'[147] It is true that Péguy fell at an almost glorious moment. Villeroy can be regarded as the prologue to the first Battle of the Marne. From 5 to 10 September, some two million French soldiers fought for their country's survival. To some, they seemed like men reborn. Others saw grim despair and little else.[148] Nevertheless, they succeeded. Half a million fatalities later, the German advance toward Paris had been halted.[149] 'First Success for Allies', read the *New York Times* headline on 10 September.[150] Odes were composed to their heroic deeds, but the enormous losses were not forgotten.

One survivor of the battle, François Porché (1877–1944), commemorated its events in the long poem *L'arrêt sur la Marne* (The

Halt at the Marne), dedicated to the memory of his friend Péguy. Its tripartite structure reflects the way the French experienced and remembered the battle: 'L'agression' (the enemy attack), 'Paris' (the capital under threat), and 'La bataille' (the decisive engagement). The final couplet requires neither explanation nor paraphrase:

> And we live on and look back with pride
> Because of the other men who died.[151]

Those who had not been through the tragedy themselves were usually unable to remain so laconic. Anna de Noailles (1876–1933), for instance, clearly struggled to come to grips with what had happened. As a baroness of Greek–Romanian origin and the focal point of a celebrated Paris salon, she was one of France's leading republican cultural figures. The survival of her country perhaps mattered more to her than to some nameless farmer from the Vosges. But what degree of sacrifice was possible – and acceptable? In her long poem *Les morts pour la Patrie* (Those Who Died for Their Country), written in October 1914, Noailles tried to soothe her troubled conscience. In solemn alexandrines, she glorifies the victims as heroes from classical mythology. Only by placing them on an unattainably high pedestal can she make it sufficiently clear how vastly they differ from those who did not sacrifice their lives. Or, more accurately, to avoid casting herself into the very lowest depths to illustrate the magnitude of the contrast, she must elevate the fallen soldiers to the very loftiest heights. From the azure dome of the heavens, the angelic heroes can then console the mortals down on earth.[152]

In sharp contrast to this rhetoric of martyrdom were the final fragments of the 'Martial Ode' written by Fernando Pessoa/Álvaro de Campos after the Marne. He sounded a death-knell between verses ('Dong-ong-ong-ong'[153]) and opened the door to emotions that come closer to the everyday experience of war than Noailles's ceremonious melodrama:

> You still have his crib in a corner at home ...
> You still have his baby clothes saved from when he was small ...
> In a drawer you still have some broken toys ...
> Now, yes, now, go look at them and cry over them ...
> You do not know where your son's grave is ...
> He was no. such-and-such in some regiment
> And died out there somewhere near the Marne ... Died ...[154]

The bald sentimentality of these verses is kept in balance by the utter sobriety of what follows:

> Now he has turned to rot ... It took no more than a German line,
> A bit of lead the size of a nail [...]
> They will say that your son was a hero ...
> (Nobody knows, by the way, if he was a hero or not)
> His name will not go down in history ...
> '20,000 men died in the Battle of ...' He was one of them ...

Of course, soberly facing facts was easier in a neutral country far from the battlefield. The sketches and notes Paolo Buzzi made in his collage diary during the Battle of the Marne were black and white in the early days of combat, but blazed a fiery red after the headlines of 12 and 13 September. Plumes of smoke rise between crudely sketched letters spelling out 'Battaglia Marna'. The entire scene literally rests on the repeated phrase 'heaps of corpses'.[155] Buzzi's fellow Futurist Marinetti seems to have been more receptive to notions of heroism, at least at first sight. In the visual poem 'Après la Marne, Joffre visita le front en auto' (After the Marne, Joffre Toured the Front by Car), he drew the supposed route of the French general Joffre's victory tour. Yet a series of capital letters forming the word 'BELLE' (beautiful) is interrupted after the first syllable by severe rows of +, – and × signs,[156] a little graveyard amid the Futuristic furore.

Meanwhile, the Germans had retreated to a strategic position for the continuation of the war. The *New York Times* had been right. The war was not over; this was merely the first stage. The enemy had not reached Paris, but nor had he been driven back into his own country. The end would not come within the six weeks anticipated by von Schlieffen; that much was certain. After the overwhelming and exhausting events of the first forty days, it was time to draw breath, regroup and reconsider. The conflict had entered a new stage. The troops were digging in.

3

The Voice of Steel: Autumn and Winter 1914

> This great war is a European civil war, a war against the inner, invisible enemy of the European spirit.
>
> – Franz Marc, 'Das Geheime Europa' (The Secret Europe), November 1914[1]

Despite its unparalleled horrors, the war had already produced something of immense value to humanity: namely, unforgettable poetry. This, at least, was one rather amoral commonplace from the early months of war.[2] If poets had all too often been shut in their ivory towers, they were now quick to see that they could and must speak with the voice of the people. As Europe's nations rediscovered their souls, they also rediscovered poetry. 'All vagueness and hesitancy have disappeared instantly as if from the touch of a magic wand', wrote the young Russian poet Georgi Ivanov (1894–1958). 'Sadness and joy, ecstasy, and wrath – simple words and clear feelings have replaced the boring antics of poets over-satisfied with themselves. Our poetry has been cleansed by a wave of beautiful vigour, of sober and joyful enthusiasm.'[3] Ivanov was taking advantage of the war to suggest that his own Acmeist view of literature had history on its side, but this quote also reveals the bad conscience of the modern poet. As poetic diction had become more specialized, it had excluded an ever-larger group of readers. The war gave poets and the public an unexpected opportunity to renew their relationship.

Yet the price that poetry paid for this new lease of life was staggeringly high. In his poem 'Abschied' (Farewell), written in early August shortly before he left for the front, the Expressionist poet Alfred Lichtenstein had remarked laconically that in thirteen days he might be dead. That proved pessimistic; in reality, he still had some seven weeks to live. Right until the end, he went on writing poems full of level-headed, startlingly unheroic observations. In 'Gebet vor der Schlacht' (Prayer Before Battle), Lichtenstein unsentimentally exposed the thoughts that occupied the soldiers as they marched into battle, singing lustily. Honour and a spirit of sacrifice were nowhere near the first things on their minds. They just wanted to go on with their everyday lives when the war was over, milking cows, 'stuffing girls', getting drunk, and beating up some bastard now and then. They would even say seven rosaries a day for the rest of their lives, if God would just spare them and take their pal Huber or Meier's life instead. And if they had to be injured, let it be mild – 'a slight leg wound / a small arm injury' – so they could go home as heroes with bragging rights.[4] But these dreams were usually shattered by the realities of war; it was a rare soldier who suffered no more than a scratch. 'On yellow fields in red trousers, the French are ablaze, / Ashen pale from death and powder', Lichtenstein observed dryly in 'After Combat'. 'I brace myself in the greyness and take on death', he declared in 'Die Schlacht bei Saarburg' (The Battle of Saarburg), sent from the front on 16 September, just nine days before death took him.

Two days after that, Ernst Wilhelm Lotz (1890–1914) followed him in death. In the words of Lotz's friend, the Expressionist painter Ludwig Meidner, this promising young writer had left for the front full of enthusiasm, with 'Reason tucked in his coat pocket like a snuffbox, intended for only occasional use'.[5] The tone of Lotz's early wartime letters to his parents and sweetheart is vigorous and full of youthful ebullience. His fatherland – 'that invisible, floating home of the nation'[6] – had called him, and he was ready. He had always envisioned a great and meaningful future for himself ('as a factor in a new, radiant culture'[7]), but he set aside that ambition in the face of this historic moment. What had seemed like powerful metaphors in his poetry could now be experienced viscerally. In his poem, 'Aufbruch der Jugend' (Revolt of Youth), he wrote:

> A shock went through us, a cry of need, we roll on, swollen,
> Like a storm tide we have poured out into the city streets
> Washing away the wreckage of the shattered world

These piercing lines depict a new generation forcing a new age into being. Yet by 21 August, he reported that he could only speak of the war in terms of 'horror', and four days later he wrote to his girlfriend that while the vanguard had not entirely given up hope, all of their 'Hurrah enthusiasm' was gone. The next day, his company lost eighty-two men. In early September, Lotz's heart leapt with joy when he heard that the leading critic Kurt Hiller had classed him with writers such as Robert Musil, Franz Werfel, Alfred Lichtenstein and Ernst Stadler as one of the best young artists 'on the battlefield'. From mid-September onward, his company regularly engaged with French troops just a few dozen metres away. On 25 September, shrapnel from a shell flew into Lotz's trench – but the only casualty was his cigarette. 'I must have a guardian angel', he wrote to his wife in delight.[8] The next day, his angel abandoned him.

As the war continued, one promising writer after another had to be struck off Kurt Hiller's list. After Lichtenstein and Lotz, Ernst Stadler also died on the Western front, on 30 October. His war diary describing those final weeks and months is an almost clinical record of weather reports, artillery attacks, army transports, troop movements and looted houses, and of searching for food, alcohol and dry places to sleep, punctuated by scenes of mass graves and ruined cities (such as Louvain). Occasionally Stadler made note of an emotion. 'Someone whose brains were completely exposed. He is still alive. He will not be brought to a dressing station but to a house across the way, since he only has a few more moments to live in any case. The horror of war. I feel bad.'[9] On 17 October, he wrote of soldiers who had gone mad, their nerves overstrained by the war.[10] The poet understood very well what was going on, both in his own mind and on the battlefield around him. By early October, he had already more or less given up hope that the war would end soon. We could take care of the French and Russians, he told his aunt Marta, but with the English to handle too … it was a tall order. The only way he could imagine the situation changing was with the economic collapse of the warring nations, and given the dreadful losses on all sides, he did not rule out that possibility.[11] Yet he was never able to test his predictions, since he too fell in battle.

In *Die Aktion*, the Expressionist magazine for politics, literature and art, the death of Stadler, a regular contributor, was the subject of a black-bordered announcement in the 21 November issue. According to editor-in-chief Franz Pfemfert, Stadler had 'followed his friend Charles Péguy, to whose work he had introduced us'. Beneath this front-page notice were five poems sent from France by the field surgeon Wilhelm Klemm, with a stern warning from *Die Aktion* that reprinting them in 'lyrical war pamphlets or similar verse collections' was forbidden under all circumstances.[12] The magazine reported on the war, of course, but it refused to be dragged into the hate-mongering patriotism that held German culture in its grip. Accordingly, it continued to give space to French authors and reported the death of Péguy, another contributor, with sorrow and reverence. In any case, there was not much chance of Klemm's field hospital poems ending up in jingoistic magazines. The excruciating realism of 'Lazaret', which was frequently anthologized after the war, made it difficult to use as propaganda. Here is the middle stanza:

> There's a stench of blood, rubbish, shit and sweat.
> Bandages ooze beneath torn uniforms.
> Clammy, trembling limbs, wasted faces.
> Dying heads slump down, half sitting up.[13]

In the early months of the war, those dying heads included a number of other German poets, such as the widely read patriotic writer Hermann Löns (26 September), the nationalist Paul Ernst Köhler (14 October), the lyricist Justus Koch (31 October), the socialist poet Ludwig Frank (3 November), the tuberculosis-ravaged publisher and poet Alfred Walter Heymel (26 November), and the *Aktion* poet Hugo Hinz (7 December).[14] Another *Aktion* poet, the young and probably syphilitic Expressionist Hans Leybold, took his own life on 8 September after being wounded in Namur.[15] Whether it was a fantasy, a prophecy, or a dry statement of fact remains unclear, but in his poem 'Ende' (End) – published posthumously in late September in *Die Aktion* – this friend of Hugo Ball's wrote, 'In my brain an infinitely huge fist has wedged itself' and 'The waves of my gay drunkenness have subsided.'[16] By that time, Klemm felt much the same. In late August he had cried out, sure of victory and full of enthusiasm, 'Not one false note anywhere. We are living in a great age.'[17] But just a month later he wrote that the war was so terrible that you began to yearn for a bullet to free you from all the pain and panic. Meanwhile, at his field hospital, Klemm was immersed in muck, vomit and work. He had already gained so much practical experience that he could amputate limbs unassisted.[18]

War was also taking a heavy toll on the other armies, with the French making the greatest sacrifices. The 27,000 French soldiers who died on 22 August included the well-known prose author Ernest Psichari and the poets Jean Allard-Méus, Pierre Amar, Jacques Baguenier Desormeaux, André du Frenois, Jean Reutlinger and Robert de Saint-Just.[19] Three days later Pierre Boutet and the songwriter Auguste Gien were lost. On 30 August, Henri-Charles Grégoire and Antoine Yvan fell in the Ardennes, Jean-François Marichal by the Aisne, and Charles Mokel in Faux. Albert Hombek was killed in Maubeuge on 1 September. Charles Péguy died on 5 September, as mentioned above, and a day later Gustave Valmont fell at the Marne. That same battle cost the lives of the poets Jacques Balder, Henri de Boisanger and Louis Dulhom-Noguès. Even after the French claimed victory, the list of fatalities went on growing; the French poets slain in the first five months of war included Maurice Colin (12 September), Louis Granier (13 September), Paul Feuillâtre (21 September), Joseph de Joannis-Pagan (23 September), Éduard Bernard (27 September), Tony Rigaud (29 September), Robert Drouin (2 October), Charles Roguet (6 October), François de Lartigue (12 October), Louis Ménagé and Charles Perrot (13 October), Auguste Massacrier (in October), Robert Marchal (1 November), Léon Gignoux (5 November), Charles Dumas (7 November), Émile la Senne (11 November), Marcel Paoli (16 November), Pierre Corrard and Olivier Hourcade (21 November), Paul-Marie Thomas (25 November), Jean de la Ville de Mirmont (28 November), Jacques Nayral (9 December) and Louis Lemas (14 December).

The Italian Futurists did not allow this human suffering to put them off.[20] As soon as war broke out, they had but one goal: to bring Italy into the conflict. To make it clear where the movement's priorities lay, the *Lacerba* editors announced in the 15 August issue that the magazine would henceforth be devoted entirely to politics, and the price would be reduced.

Lacerba sought to present its views with complete, incendiary candour, but the censor had other plans. In the very first article, a stern essay by Giovanni Papini (1881–1956) entitled 'Italy's Duty', much of the text was blacked out.[21] It was not that the Italian authorities were opposed to all political debate, but there was too much at stake for them to take any risks. The censor proved especially averse to insulting and hostile remarks about Germany, which might yet prove an essential ally to Italy and therefore could not be treated with contempt. Prime Minister Antonio Salandra announced that his country's attitude was one of *sacro egoismo*. In other words, while the French were bound together by the *union sacrée*, a near-religious sense of solidarity, Italy planned to offer its services to the highest bidder like a flighty whore, with the ultimate goal of transforming the peninsula into a world power. Germany felt that Austria–Hungary should respond by offering up its substantial Italian-speaking territories (such as Trieste and Tyrol). But the Dual Monarchy could see that this would be the beginning of the end. If their Italian subjects were allowed to secede and unite with Italy, the Serbs were certain to make similar demands, along with the Romanians and all the other minorities.

To the Futurists, it had been perfectly clear whose side Italy should take even before the war began. A letter written by Marinetti on 12 August mentioned campaigns that his movement would organize to create a favourable climate for war against Austria. Papini, too, left no doubt about who Italy's allies should be. France was the home of revolution, the birthplace of liberty. As for the Austrians, the Futurists would use every artistic means at their disposal to tell the world just what they thought of them. Giacomo Balla (1871–1958) set the tone with his manifesto *Antineutral Clothing*, published on 11 September, presenting futuristic, nationalistic green, white and red uniforms that members of the movement actually wore at some of their many interventionist demonstrations. On 15 September, they stormed into Milan's Teatro dal Verme during the premiere of a Puccini opera. After the first act, Marinetti unfurled a large Italian flag from the highest balcony, while Umberto Boccioni (1882–1916) tore up an Austrian flag and threw the shreds of fabric into the audience. The next day, they burned eight Austrian flags during a performance on the piazza in front of the cathedral and passed out pamphlets. Clashes between students and police officers culminated in the arrest of seven Futurists, including Marinetti, Boccioni and Carrà.

On 20 September, the Milanese cell published the *Futurist Synthesis of the War*, an interventionist pamphlet signed by Marinetti, Boccioni, Carrà, Russolo and Piatti, which redrew the world map according to the national characters of different countries. The war was envisioned as a conflict between Futurist and 'Passé-ist' forces, between the future and the past. The countries that made up these camps were described in remarkably polarizing terms. The thrust of the pamphlet was that Austria (associated with stupidity, the Inquisition and espionage), Germany (country of brutality, pomposity, archaeology and scholarly pedantry), and Turkey (equated simply with a provocative '0') were arrayed against a much stronger coalition: Serbia (independent, ambitious and bold), Belgium (energetic, enterprising, industrial and excellent), France (intelligent, brave, swift and elegant), Russia (powerful, rugged and indomitable), England (practical, with a sense of duty, a spirit of fair trade, and respect for the individual), Montenegro (see Serbia), and Japan (resolute and intent on progress). The pamphlet then argued that Italy clearly belonged in the latter group, since it possessed 'all the strengths and weaknesses of genius'.[22] The Futurists saw no conflict between Genius, a quintessentially Romantic concept, and their forward-looking ideology. In fact, they derived their sense of superiority from this X factor, which they saw as giving them a moral advantage in that ultimate clash of cultures, the world war. In the *Synthesis*, the rigid, analytic and methodical characteristics of German culture stood in opposition to the flexibility, intuitive synthesis and ingenuity of the creative genius. The manifesto opened with a few surprising remarks: although the demolition of historic monuments had been part of the Futurist programme since day one, the authors sharply condemned the German attacks on centuries-old cathedrals.[23] The clumsy, medieval, plagiarist Germans, they contended, lacked the creative genius of Futurism and hence the right to destroy works of art. That right was reserved for themselves alone, by virtue of 'the Italian creative Genius, capable of creating a new and greater beauty on the ruins of the old'.[24] This turned around the argument advanced by Stefan George's disciple Friedrich Gundolf as a pretext for German depredations: 'Whoever is strong enough to create has a right to destroy.'[25]

In the neutral Netherlands, Albert Verwey, a friend of both George and Gundolf, was unimpressed by this axiom. In fact, he suggested that the endless stream of self-justifying writings and remarks by his German friends was a sign of their troubled consciences. In his insightful commentary on the war, published in his magazine *De Beweging* (The Movement) in early October, Verwey stated in no uncertain terms that Germany had wantonly violated the law of nations. Yet as he saw it, this did not reduce Germany's many justifications for war to mere rhetoric; all the warring parties were doubtless confident of their own good intentions and just cause, even though their positions were rarely consistent. For instance, Verwey acknowledged that England was playing its 'traditional role as defender of freedom and public law' in Belgium, but at the same time, by allying itself with Russia, it was posing a threat to 'Finland's freedom and public law in eastern Europe'.[26] Verwey saw it as a neutral observer's duty to do justice to all parties, an attitude that Gundolf, in a letter to George, could only describe as entirely missing the point.[27]

For Irish nationalists, assessing the competing claims of the warring nations was more than an interesting intellectual challenge. If they backed the right horse, they could win the political autonomy they had long desired, but a bad bet could be fatal to their cause. The moderate member of parliament John Redmond was quick to come to his analysis: not only had Germany infringed on the rights of small nations in invading Belgium, but by fighting side by side with the British, the Irish could assure themselves of Home Rule within the British Empire after the war. Redmond thus called on the paramilitary Irish Volunteers to enlist in the British army. His former fellow parliamentarian Tom Kettle had already taken this step. Still deeply affected by what he had seen in Belgium, Kettle launched a major recruitment campaign, making almost 200 speeches to win over his compatriots to the cause of the Entente.[28] More than 175,000 of the Irish Volunteers declared their support for Redmond, and some 80,000 of them actually enlisted during the first year of war. They formed the National Volunteers, fighting in the Irish regiments of the British army, to which Kettle devoted his poem 'A Song of the Irish Armies'.[29] In addition to Kettle himself, the poet and Volunteer Francis Ledwidge (1887–1917) also joined up. But a fanatical minority of Volunteers fiercely resisted what they saw as collaboration with the British occupiers. Claiming the name of 'Irish Volunteers' for themselves alone, they broke off from Redmond's larger group, contacted the Germans, and began making plans for an armed uprising.

After sixty days of war, amid ceaseless cultural, moral and military one-upmanship between the conflicting nation-states and cultural zones, the French poet Jules Romains very deliberately began work on a *chant de l'Europe* (Song of Europe), a seed that grew into his 1916 collection *Europe*.[30] For Romains, the driving force behind Unanimism – a system of thought that posited a single soul (*una anima*) uniting all individuals – the war was a true nightmare. The man who called Europe 'my country' on the very first page of his new poem was drafted into the auxiliary forces and discovered, from his military office in Paris, how thoroughly that country had 'fallen prey to armies'.[31] Not that Romains was advocating the abolition of the nation-state. It was through France, he wrote, that his 'body was attached to Europe'.[32] The one European soul was evidently divided into national mini-souls, and the conflict between these little souls posed an obvious and acute threat to the big one. This, Romains lyrically explained, was why he had to write an ode to Europe, declaring its birth even as its death cries echoed all around him.[33] The masses of men slaughtering each other also had the capacity to save the Continent. Romains's Europe was not an Arcadian reserve, but a place where great crowds sought each other out and were absorbed into each other: 'European crowds! European gods!'[34] The images Romains used in *Europe* to argue for the Continent's salvation are quite revealing: Europeans are said to be tied together ('Ce vieux relai noueux'[35]), and they encounter each other at a 'crossroads',[36] as well as in music halls, parks, harbours and theatres. These crowds, Romains writes, are the proof that Europe lives on; they form the antithesis of death.[37]

Meanwhile, in the prosaic realm of everyday life, the relative stability following the Battle of the Marne did nothing to make the Western front less dangerous. From mid-September to mid-November, the Allies did everything in their power to prevent the Germans from reaching the strategically vital northern French ports of Dunkirk and Calais, in what became known as the race to the sea. Oddly enough, Antwerp played a crucial part in this race, despite being closer to the Netherlands than to France. In late September, British troops were sent to Antwerp, a move that threatened to slow down the laborious German conquest of Belgium even further. That was certainly the intention; the longer

German troops were detained in the north, the easier it would be for the Allies to defend the French ports.

One of the British soldiers sent to Antwerp to aid the faltering Belgians was the promising young socialist poet Rupert Brooke (1887–1915).[38] Breathtakingly handsome, very talented, and at home in the very highest circles (he lunched with Winston Churchill shortly before leaving England), Brooke had for years felt emotionally off-kilter, sexually insecure, and morally uncertain. The war offered him a chance to give his life meaning and direction of the most radical kind. No longer would he have time to vacillate and ponder; duty and animal instinct would take control. In one of the '1914 sonnets' written in the autumn and winter of that year, he gave thanks to God,

> [...] who has matched us with his hour,
>   And caught our youth, and wakened us from sleeping,
> With hand made sure, clear eye, and sharpened power,
>   To turn, as swimmers into cleanness leaping,
> Glad from a world grown old and cold and weary,
>   Leave the sick hearts that honour could not move,
> And half-men, and their dirty songs and dreary,
>   And all the little emptiness of love![39]

Brooke, like more than a few other poets, hoped to overcome his decadent tendencies and almost unbearable guilt feelings through the purifying ritual called war. Note that when Brooke composed this ode to purity, he had already been exposed to the realities of war, the stinking corpses and bleak rows of refugees. His Royal Naval Division had arrived in Antwerp on 6 October, around the time that the Belgian army began to retreat from the city and the Belgian government fled to Ostend.

The previous day, the Germans had crossed the Nete river at Duffel, and the route to Antwerp's final ring of fortresses lay entirely open. To deprive the enemy of a crucial landmark and target, the Belgian forces tried to remove the top of the St Martin's Church tower in Duffel. The attempt failed, and the church burned almost entirely to the ground. The fire was visible as far away as the nearby town of Hove, where eighteen-year-old Paul van Ostaijen could see, as he later described in his epic volume of war poetry *Bezette stad* (Occupied City), how 'the blazing tower / went down in FLAMES'. Van Ostaijen also described the Duffel church fire in a brief newspaper article in December 1914 – the 'infernal glare of the flames, tapering into a sharp point against the blue sky'.[40] The same article describes another scene that would remain etched in his mind forever: the 'fantastically sorrowful retreat of a powerful Red Cross column', also from Duffel. This image resurfaced six years later in *Bezette stad*:[41]

> the whole country road 200 RC automobiles
> clo ven night by **200** cars
> **200 S**irens______!

As thousands of Belgian refugees – 'the fleeing the endless procession of the fleeing' (*Bezette stad*) – and soldiers hastened toward Antwerp, Brooke and his comrades-in-arms tried to hold off the enemy for a while in Mortsel Oude-God, a town just north of Hove – 'Vieux Dieu', as the British poet reported the place name in a letter to his lady friend.[42] The war seemed far away at first, but at 2 a.m. Mortsel came under fire. The British were quickly forced into retreat and found themselves amid the other refugees on the left bank of the Scheldt – 'with all their goods on barrows and carts ... white and drawn and beyond emotion'.[43] The bombardment of Antwerp began on 7 October. Those who had sought refuge there, such as the Van Ostaijen family, moved on, this time toward the Netherlands.

Goodbye menaced city
salvation to the north
fair
carousel
people and things
pram
hat box
lampshade
hours the same things
has this nation been forsaken by God[44]

The scene made an equally indelible impression on Sublieutenant Brooke. 'Make America help the Belgians', he wrote to an American friend in December. 'I saw their suffering. It is terrible. French and English suffering don't matter. But they're so helpless.'[45] In a letter to an American poet he compared the scene to 'Hell, a Dantesque Hell, terrible ... That's what Belgium is now: the country where three civilians have been killed to every one soldier ... It's queer to think one has been a witness of one of the greatest crimes of history.'[46] Everyone in England would have to make huge sacrifices, Brooke concluded. More than a few responded to his entreaty, often despite difficulties of their own. An acquaintance of Brooke's who suffered from tuberculosis and urgently needed to go to a sanatorium volunteered to assist Belgian refugees in London. Brooke put her forward as a model when asked for money for another acquaintance, who had bronchitis, so that he could go to America to recuperate. 'I feel it's not a time to be wintering in Los Angeles. I feel that if there's a ghost of a chance of – doing some good by giving his life, he should try to give it. Also, that if anyone *has* any spare money, he should be trying to assist with it some of the outcast Belgian widows and children.'[47]

The image of the Belgian refugees compelled Ford Madox Hueffer, too, to write his first war poem. In early September he had declared himself incapable of writing a poem about the war. He wished he could, but it seemed too far removed from his own life. He couldn't believe what he read about it in the papers, and without visual input he couldn't write poems. What he most sorely lacked was a clear view of the conflict, literally and figuratively: 'This present war is just a cloud – a hideous and unrelieved pall of doom.'[48] The word 'doom' became the leitmotif of Hueffer's *Antwerp*, published in book form in October, after he had been confronted, in London's Charing Cross station, with the utter dejection of the Belgian refugees. No trace of heroism there. Why hadn't the poor Belgians just let the Germans pass through? They could have 'kept their lives and their wives and their children and cattle and goods'.[49] Apparently, Hueffer concluded, there was a form of patriotism so extreme that it made people willing to tolerate even misery like this. And that made it impressive in its way – material for a poem. Hueffer had said that he could not 'make a poem out of fine words like avenging slaughtered saints or unsheathing freedom's sword'.[50] But this image, this experience, inspired him, prompting him to re-evaluate his ideas about poetry and beauty. The Belgian soldiers in their ugly uniforms could replace the proud knights and heroes of past wars. And this wretched scene, Hueffer suggested, was the source of a 'strange new beauty'. Beauty

> is the highest word you can find to say of it.
> For you cannot praise it with words
> Compounded with lyres and swords

And then, in spite of everything, this modern war poem made 'Belgium' synonymous with heroic resistance:

And that shall be an honourable name;
'Belgian' shall be an honourable word;
As honourable as the fame of the sword,
As honourable as the mention of the many-chorded lyre.[51]

Although Hueffer's elegaic ode suggested that the battle for Belgium had been lost after the fall of Antwerp on 10 October, in fact the fighting went on undiminished on the left bank of the Scheldt. The Belgian army was nearing collapse, and during their hasty retreat they also lost much of their supply system.[52] Whether in earnest or to assuage his own despair, Karel Van den Oever wrote a sonnet that same day, 10 October, about what he believed he had witnessed 'Op den oever der Schelde te Antwerpen' (On the Bank of the Scheldt in Antwerp). He described much the same horrors as Rupert Brooke had in one of his letters – 'The sky was lit by burning villages and houses ... Rivers and seas of flame leaping up hundreds of feet ... It lit up houses wrecked by shells, dead horses, demolished railway stations'[53] – but the Flemish poet heightened the mood of planetary apocalypse:

The polder skyline burns with clouds blazed dead.
Some from the crumbling, devastated bastions,
Ramparts reduced to ash, the walls rust-red,
Dripping with blood of all the world's nations
[...]
Till all is swarming, whirling, in a jumbled motion ...
And look, far off a bristling army struggles onward!
Hurrah! Belgium has thrashed a hundred thousand Prussians![54]

This final claim was extremely wishful thinking. The Belgian army did manage to bring the Germans to a halt at Ghent, but they then put all their energy into making sure they reached the coast ahead of the enemy. Starting on 12 October, the battered Belgian soldiers poured into the Westhoek, the region of West Flanders bordering on France and the North Sea, and began digging trenches. Over the next few days, the Germans captured Ghent, Bruges and Ostend. On 16 October they attacked Diksmuide. French troops retaliated. By this time, the British were present in force, and by 20 October, the British Expeditionary Force had arrived, commanded by Sir Douglas Haig. They were just in time for the Battle of Ypres.

Nor was there any pause for breath on the Eastern front, where again poets were among the fallen. On 13 September, for instance, the many-faceted Czech writer and artist František Gellner (1881–1914) was declared missing. Fierce fighting took place in the autumn, especially in Galicia. In early September, the Austrians were nearly wiped out by the Russian army,[55] losing some 350,000 men. In their hurried retreat from the Galician capital of Lemberg (Lviv), they had to leave behind some 1,000 locomotives and 50,000 railroad carriages – a logistical nightmare. Field Marshal Franz Conrad von Hötzendorf, the man whose warmongering intrigues had been so crucial to the escalation of the conflict in July, admitted to his staff after these crushing defeats that, if Crown Prince Franz Ferdinand had still been alive, he would probably have had Conrad executed.[56] But in the hell that was Galicia, it was the field marshal's Austrian subordinates who were begging for death by the second week in September. Some ninety seriously injured soldiers were left behind by their fleeing comrades in a wooden shed on Grodek's market square, without a doctor, medicine, or any other way to alleviate their indescribable pain. The impossible task of tending to their needs under these conditions fell to the twenty-seven-year-old poet and pharmacist Georg Trakl (1887–1914), an unfortunate choice. Trakl, hounded by drink, depression and premonitions of doom, could not even take proper care of himself, and the sights that confronted him now were worse even than his drug-fuelled visions of blood and destruction. The war both confirmed his cultural pessimism in its darkest forms and offered a chance for redemption. Early in the Battle of Grodek, he had been forcibly disarmed by his fellow soldiers after rushing into the firing line as if driven by a death wish. But when the ravages of war forced themselves upon him, there in the shed, he found himself defenceless. 'What can I do? How should I help? It's unbearable!' he cried, as if it were a mantra.[57] For two days and nights, dying soldiers were begging for deliverance. One of them put a bullet through his own head – his brains remained splattered on the wall. Meanwhile, Trakl's helplessness and the constant wailing were nearly driving him insane. When he ran outside in a panic, another hellish scene awaited him: suspected Ruthenian collaborators had been brought to the square, forced to put their heads through a noose, and then hung. On 22 September the poet had a nervous breakdown, crying out that he would take his own life. Again, he was disarmed just in time. Trakl's traumatic experiences formed the seeds of a poem that was to become a classic of German literature.

GRODEK

At nightfall the autumn woods cry out
With deadly weapons and the golden plains
The deep blue lakes, above which more darkly
Rolls the sun; the night embraces
Dying warriors, the wild lament
Of their broken mouths.
But quietly there in the willow dell
Red clouds in which an angry god resides,
The shed blood gathers, lunar coolness.
All the roads lead to blackest carrion.
Under golden twigs of the night and stars
The sister's shade now sways through the silent copse

To greet the ghosts of the heroes, the bleeding heads;
And softly the dark flutes of autumn sound in the reeds.
O prouder grief! You brazen altars,
Today a great pain feeds the hot flame of the spirit,
The grandsons yet unborn.[58]

The angry war god of Georg Heym's vision dwells in these red clouds. The 'shed blood' of 'dying warriors' with 'broken mouths' has saturated those clouds, as if they have absorbed not only the gold of the plains and the blue of the lakes but also all the suffering in the world. A faint glow is still visible in the heavens – the 'golden twigs of the night and stars' – but in the world below pitch darkness is descending – 'all the roads lead to blackest carrion'. This is the scene not of a clash between armies but of a primordial conflict between the elements and the species once called the crowning glory of God's creation. It is clear who is fated to lose. In its pride, determination and sensuality, the human race has destroyed its own future ('the grandsons yet unborn'). It finds itself left behind, defeated and utterly deserted.

In early October, Trakl's unit retreated to Limanow, near Kraków, behind the front line. In brief letters to friends in Vienna and Innsbruck, he spoke of his 'indescribable sorrow'.[59] On 7 October, his commanding officers committed him to a garrison hospital in Wadowice because of his erratic behavior. The next day, when he was to be transferred to Kraków, he is said to have made a desperate attempt to flee to the front line. In his barred room at the Kraków hospital, surrounded by delirious soldiers with serious mental illnesses, he was once again overcome by anxiety attacks, fearing that because of his suicide attempt he would be sentenced to death for cowardice. On 3 November he died of a cocaine overdose.

At the time, the atmosphere in Kraków was charged with tension. After the fall of Grodek on 12 September, the Russians had rapidly pressed on to the strategically crucial town of Przemyśl, the last bulwark protecting Kraków, surrounded by fortresses. On 24 September, the first siege of Przemyśl began, with a second wave of Russian attacks on 11 October and a third on 12 November. One of the soldiers ordered to defend the fortified town was the Hungarian poet Géza Gyóni (1884–1917). He was anything but a born fighter. His period of compulsory military service had been spent in Bosnia from November 1907 to April 1909, a time he did not remember fondly.[60] When he found himself on the way back to the Balkans with his regiment in 1912, he wrote the passionate pacifist poem 'Cézar, én nem megyek' (Caesar, I will not go). To outwit the censors, he placed his political message in a historical setting: 'And as for your crown / That, O Caesar, defend on your own'. Gyóni said he had no interest in going like 'an animal to the abbatoir'. When war broke out, however, he volunteered for duty and began writing fiery patriotic poems. He soon became the military house poet of Przemyśl, and his poems were smuggled out of the fortress by aircraft and distributed among the soldiers. They met with great success and went through many reprints. In one of those poems, 'Letter to the West', Gyóni sharply criticized both the cowards who stayed at home and the degenerate 'Western' ideology to which these coffee-sipping pseudointellectuals subscribed.

> Where are you now, O intellectuals,
> Sons of a sinister age, sad gentlemen,
> kneeling fanatically to the holy West,
> unbridled by the least sobriety,
> laughing at the fatherland and at ideals,
> fancying yourselves gods in Café New York,
> Promising the sacred new day tomorrow
> that we already found out yesterday is a lie.

Where are you now, tell me, O Francophiles,
Miniature giants with no god but Eros,
And are they still clattering, your little rattles,
rattling on about defeats and blunders?
Contempt for Hungary's illustrious past
Poisons the mind corrupted by the West
You wise men born before your time, sick monsters,
What do you feel in your pigeon chests?

Where are you now, O world citizens?
I don't see one of you standing in the storm.
What's keeping you? As far as the eye can see
Steel-sinewed heroes are going into battle
Against the filthy vermin of the night.
Hush, little boys, be still, for now speaks might.
'Quiet!' is your new name in this new language.
Now hear power's voice; now hear the voice of steel.[61]

In the war rhetoric of those days, the West more or less meant France and England – in other words, the enemy. To ally yourself with the culture and values of these countries was to commit treason.[62] Since the Hungarian word for 'West' is *Nyugat*, which was also the name of the leading liberal magazine, Gyóni (whether or not deliberately) was also criticizing prominent *Nyugat* poets such as Endre Ady and Mihály Babits.[63]

Yet the contributors to *Nyugat* were far from united in opposition to the war.[64] In the 1 August issue, for instance, the poet Ignotus (1869–1949), a co-founder of the magazine, made it very clear what should take priority. Even though the Dual Monarchy was anything but the liberal, Western democracy for which *Nyugat* campaigned, Ignotus wished to dispel any false notion that Hungary could remain neutral, like Luxembourg, Belgium or Switzerland. Too many Magyars lived in other parts of the Dual

Monarchy, outside strictly Hungarian territory. For Ignotus, the choice between the status quo and a shrunken Little Hungary was an easy one; he would 'passionately support the Habsburg regime'.[65]

The up-and-coming poet Béla Balázs (1884–1949) had more than just political reasons to welcome the conflict. In the 16 August issue of *Nyugat*, he announced that for him this was a 'holy' war.[66] He reaffirmed this position is his diary on 12 August, comparing the war to a moral bath and sternly commanding himself to 'pay the debt' he had incurred with his 'monomaniacal individualism'.[67] Not everyone saw the conflict in such apocalyptic terms, however. The same issue included the very personal poem 'My Brother' by the leading poet Dezső Kosztolányi (1885–1936), born in the Serbian part of the Dual Monarchy.

> My little brother's gone to the Serbian mountains to fight,
> Serving our liege on the border, marching into the fray.
> My heartbeat loyally measures the hours of the night.
> I shall light lanterns for him, and they will guide his way.[68]

The poet Árpád Tóth (1886–1928), unfit for military service because of a pulmonary condition, felt that Kosztolányi and *Nyugat* had made a poor showing. 'As the world is at war, the entirety of "modern" Hungarian literature resembles a fat, sick, tuberculotic blob trampled by a military boot.'[69] The great poet Endre Ady was never one to take a radical position, and he made no exception for politics. Instead, his perspective on the war was prophetic and mythic, and in the same 16 August issue he wrote that everything in life is predetermined and that war only breaks out when needed, 'even though it saddens me personally'.[70] The same issue also included Ady's poem 'Torony az éjszakában' (Tower of Night), in which the perfect calm of the moon in the sky is set in stark contrast to the ephemeral nature of earthly things, symbolized by a tower awaiting bloodshed 'as once more / we hear proclaimed the ancient motto / to victory or ruin'.[71] Under such circumstances, a Poet of the Nation can either flow with the current or else stand on the riverbank asking uncomfortable questions. Ady chose the latter course. In a brief essay published in *Nyugat* in mid-September, he pleaded the cause of the loners and eccentrics, 'the arrogant individualists and egotists, as that swindler Barrès sneeringly calls them'.[72] This reference to the prolific Maurice Barrès (1862–1923), a French ultra-nationalist, was clever and highly significant. Since the outbreak of war, Barrès had, if anything, become even more militant. By distancing himself from the Frenchman's rhetoric, Ady showed that he was no starry-eyed Francophile, staking a place for himself in a Hungarian social climate where, since early August, patriotism had become practically a legal obligation. In his matchlessly subtle style, with just a hint of sarcasm, Ady's short essay 'The New Militarism' expressed the belief that the war could certainly have some educational value, but would not necessarily lead to a resurgence of traditional cultural values, since militarism seemed to be taking the place of socialism among the masses. And Ady once again lived up to his reputation as a visionary, with a sibylline prophecy of major social upheaval on the horizon: 'Those who live to experience it (even two world wars will not be able to stop it) will enjoy all the pleasures generally afforded by the growth, flourishing, and decay of the bourgeoisie.'[73] His own position on this malodorous prospect remained somewhat vague. In the 1 December issue of *Nyugat*, he published the poem 'A halottak élén' (Leading the Dead), a bitter elegy in which the first-person narrator is the commander of a group of soldiers doomed to perish – a job for which Ady probably felt himself more qualified than for leading an army battalion into battle. Here is the first verse:

On the Plains we're all losing now,
And blood clouds are running unbound.
I've now found my true troops,
It's now my troops I have found:
They, the expatriates of Life.

As in Trakl's poem, the clouds have gathered up the spilled blood. But while the darkness grows ever deeper for the Austrian poet, Ady sketches a more ambiguous scene, at the strange juncture where the land of the dead meets lust for earthly life.

How beautiful this ghastly world,
How beautiful, how good to me
That in the camp of the real shadows
I can pretend to lead, you see
And that we may send a smile to Life.[74]

Within the margins established by the censors, the last issue of *Nyugat* in the first year of war was more critical of the conflict. In an essay from a series entitled *Simple Thoughts*, Menyhért Lengyel (1880–1974) called the war a gruesome anachronism, unfortunately made inevitable by the ingrained militarism of politicians and military commanders. Perhaps the most striking thing about it, he wrote, was that the soldiers, along with the rest of humanity, had regressed to an earlier stage of cultural development, effortlessly falling back on primal instincts. Progress had proved to be a complete illusion. Yes, humanity had freed itself of both the bubonic plague and slavery in the past, but it apparently could not rid itself of war. Still, Lengyel could understand why millions of people threw themselves into the war without reservation. The subjugations of modern life – the rules and laws, conventions and commandments – had been swept away by the war 'like mist by a gale'. Humankind had exchanged peace and civilization for a new form of liberation: freedom from having to provide for your own food, clothing, peace of mind and work (the army would take care of all that), and, above all, the freedom to murder and pillage with near-impunity.[75] In her long prose poem 'Záporos folytonos levél' (A Cry Through the Storm) in the same issue of *Nyugat*, Margit Kaffka (1880–1918) presented a very different perspective on the soldiers' sudden freedom. They had become like particles of dust, she said – millions of little soldiers with no idea where they were or why, marching through destroyed villages in the thick fog, expected to kill on command 'because neighbours of another tongue and place would behave thus'.[76] Obedience was expected of them, and nothing more.

In the besieged city of Przemyśl, Géza Gyóni had come to similar conclusions. In early November he wrote 'Csak egy éjszakára' (For Just One Night), often interpreted as a shrill protest against the war, although it can also be read as another condemnation of those who had stayed behind. This time, however, the poet did not direct his ire at sceptical intellectuals, but at the so-called patriots who paid mere lip service to the war from the safety of their easy chairs.

> Send them along for just one bloody night –
> The patriots of the tongue, of speech and spite,
> For just one bloody night:
> That, as the blinding star-shells leap the dark,
> And cheeks reflect the terror of their spark,
> And reeking mists are made of Magyar gore,
> They may scream out in tears: 'My God, no more!'[77]

If Gyóni had been a Russian, the tone of the poem might well have been even more strident, for despite their loud protestations of patriotism, very few leading Russian poets and intellectuals had joined the forces. One noteworthy exception was Nikolay

Gumilyov.[78] After his training in Novgorod, his cavalry regiment was sent to East Prussia, to an area captured from Russia by the Germans in early August.[79] In early October he was to see military action there himself for the first time. The experience of war was everything he had hoped it would be. In the poem 'Voina' (War), he compared the soldiers' sacrifice to farmers sowing the fields. These fighters deserved praise and honour, he concluded, because more than anyone else, they were building the future.

> And, O, verily war, this majestic
> Enterprise, is sacred and all light;
> Winged seraphim behind the warriors'
> Shoulders can be witnessed shining bright.
> And O, dear Lord grant your gracious blessing
> To the workers slowly walking there
> On the fields that blood has sprinkled, sowing
> Heroes' deeds, reaping a glory rare.[80]

Gumilyov was remarkably vague about the exact nature of the future for which the soldiers were fighting. He was not much interested in liberation from tyranny or the defence of the Slavic Soul, in either his life or his poetry. It was not the objectives of the war that justified the means, but the fight itself. A critic compared this aspect of Gumilyov's ideology with that of the Vikings.[81] Not that the poet was blind to the privations that he and his brothers in arms suffered. In the opening verse of the poem 'Nastuplenie' (The Advance), about the successful Russian offensive in East Prussia, he mentioned that they had gone without food for four days. The censors decided to leave out this verse, but the heroic mythomaniac Gumilyov had not intended it as a complaint; as far as he was concerned, the troops could subsist entirely on the word of God. Anything else they required, adrenaline and the survival instinct would provide. In the same poem, he described how his savage cries resounded like copper on copper, making him feel invincible: 'I, the bearer of a Great Idea / cannot, cannot die.'[82] He did not say what this 'Great Idea' was, but it seems as though for Gumilyov, as for some others, the war had considerable regenerative power. By renouncing everyday comforts, you could tap into the best and strongest parts of yourself. War, with its primitive, earthy qualities, was felt to connect people with primal forces that were underappreciated in the modern age. In one of his *Zapiski kavalerista* (Notes of a Cavalryman), Gumilyov wrote,

> I think that at the dawn of mankind people lived by their nerves in the same way, created much and died early. It is difficult to believe that a man who dines every day and sleeps every night can contribute anything to the treasurehouse of the culture of the spirit. Only fasting and vigil, even if they are involuntary, awaken in men special, heretofore slumbering forces.[83]

War gave Gumilyov the chance to flourish, and to develop sides of his personality that he had previously been unable to explore, except during his long African expeditions.[84]

Meanwhile, his wife Anna Akhmatova was interpreting the war in her own inimitable way. The poem below, written in September 1914, may now seem like a sarcastic jab at her sabre-happy husband, but it was taken up effortlessly by Russia's propaganda machine and included in many anthologies of patriotic poetry.

CONSOLATION

There the Archangel Michael
Has inducted him into his army.
N. Gumilyov

You'll hear no news of him from the front any more,
No more letters, not even a line.

His grave in grim Poland, scorched black by the war,
You will never be able to find.

The losses are over, be tranquil and calm.
No bad news will reach you tomorrow.
He's joined Heaven's army, can come to no harm.
For him there's no reason to sorrow.

It thus would be sinful to weep and to grieve
Safe at home. But recall every day
That he's one of God's soldiers and can intercede
In your favour each time that you pray.[85]

This poem's tremendous popularity in Russia should not come as a surprise. More even than bread, the country needed comforting in those months of horrific losses. Although Akhmatova's treatment of the theme was not original, she struck exactly the right tone: dead lovers, brothers and sons, delivered from earthly cares and woes, had been received into God's safekeeping, as personal intermediaries and advocates for those left behind. It is even more obvious why the authorities were pleased with the poem: it gave meaning to the endless series of fatalities and emphasized that the many soldiers who had disappeared without a trace or a grave were not really lost.

Around this time, Vladimir Mayakovsky was also writing what his otherwise sympathetic biographer Brown dismisses as 'jingoistic trash'.[86] For the first time, the revolutionary Futurist was composing verse on demand; in collaboration with visual artists such as Malevich, Larionov and Burliuk, he created propagandistic *lubki*, cartoon-like posters ridiculing Austrians and Germans and praising the Russian army to the heavens, in almost grotesque terms.[87] In the belief that a true poet must observe and experience every aspect of life, Mayakovsky also tried to travel to the front himself. As an only son, he was exempt from military service, but he hoped for a close-up view of the war as a correspondent. Red tape foiled this plan, however, as well as his next attempt, in which he tried to enlist as a volunteer but the Moscow police refused to give him a 'Certificate of Political Reliability'. For the time being, therefore, Mayakovsky's war efforts were limited to artistic contributions, and as befits an avant-gardist, he glossed over any distinction between his personal salvation and that of his country and its people. The poet seized the opportunity of war to proclaim the Futurists' long-awaited Great Leap Forward. In polemical, fiery and not always entirely coherent newspaper articles, he heralded the coming of a new type of human being, a new Russia, a new world, and a new form of art. He ruthlessly dismissed both Symbolists such as Bryusov and Balmont and purported modernists such as Gorodetsky (who had evidently abandoned his Acmeist faith), judging these poets to be mere patriotic rhymers, fully interchangeable. The war would not only redraw state borders, Mayakovsky believed, but also deeply mark the inner lives of humanity. New varieties of literature and art were thus needed to depict the war and the new reality. Or did the realists truly believe that they had the tools to convey how a massive tank could be demolished by a shell? That was the whole point, Mayakovsky said. Modern art does not represent; it gives form. And in the upheaval of war, new forms of art and beauty could be born: 'Now that every peace-loving family has been caught up in the cacophony of war, because of a brother, a husband, or a plundered house, over the glow of the burning libraries the prophecy of a new beauty can be kindled.'[88] In Mayakovsky's mind, there seems to have been no contradiction between charismatic persuasion and cynical calculation. As ghastly as it was, the war proved what the Futurists had always claimed – that the world would have to start over from scratch. The new, Futurist man would be fearless as never before, because he would no longer be a vulnerable individual, but part of the undying masses. This implied that the war was not fundamentally a senseless bloodbath, but 'a poem of the soul liberated and elevated to greatness'.[89] Yet this should not be taken to imply that Mayakovsky's poems were lyrical outbursts of Futurist patriotism. 'Mama i ubityi nemtsami veche' (Mama and Evening Murdered by the Germans), written in October, was a striking departure from the conventions and typical subject matter of Russian war poetry. It sketches a harsh, heart-rending scene, beginning and ending with an image likening the mourning mothers of fallen soldiers to gravestones. The patriotic press was especially outraged by the third line, in which triumphant reports of victories over the enemy were mentioned in the same breath as the tears of the bereaved mothers. The poem contained not the least suggestion of an immortal soul. It was published, along with poems by the other Futurists Boris Pasternak, Konstantin Bolshakov (who contributed 'Belgium'), David Burliuk and Nikolai Aseyev, in a Moscow newspaper of which Mayakovsky was the literary editor. He soon had to defend himself, in the same newspaper, against accusations that he had promoted unpatriotic literature, and the literary section was taken out of his hands after just one issue. Not everyone was convinced that the new age called for a new kind of war poetry.

Meanwhile, approximately 300,000 Russian soldiers were continuing their assault on the ring of fortifications around Przemyśl, although so far without much success. Support for this battle on the home front was growing steadily, both among the general public and among writers and intellectuals. Capturing Polish territory was seen as the first, crucial step toward establishing a new Poland, which would either be independent or (more likely) under Russian authority. Many Russians already regarded Galicia as 'Crimson Russia' – the true heart of the country – and hence believed that any territorial gains would contribute to the restoration of the Motherland.[90] In their minds, the borders of that longed-for country would reach as far as Constantinople, the eastern centre of the Byzantine Church. Pushkin and, above all, Dostoyevsky had fantasized out loud about recapturing this centre of Christian spiritual life from the godless Muslims. In November 1914, when the Ottoman Empire sided with the Germans against the Entente, Russia saw its opportunity: at last, the reunification of Christendom could begin. The Czar published a manifesto announcing that the historic conflicts on the shores of the Black Sea could now at last be resolved. The practical implications of this were spelled out in an accompanying poem by Sergei Gorodetsky (1884–1967): the shameless half-moon above the Hagia Sophia would be replaced with a cross. The battle would be long and hard, but what was one sacrifice more on the altars of the Orthodox Church and pan-Slavism?

In Galicia, Valery Bryusov had his coveted front-row seat for the battle as a war correspondent. Every territorial gain for Russia strengthened the conviction he had expressed early in the conflict in his poem 'Posledniaia voina' (The Ultimate War):

> To sounds of marching, bullets screaming,
> And Nieuports droning in the skies,
> The marvels of which we've been dreaming
> may soon, just possibly, arise.[91]

The war was expected to bring liberation, especially to oppressed, occupied Poland. On 2 October, Bryusov reached Jarosław, a city near Przemyśl that had just been captured by Russian forces and would be back in Austrian hands a week later, only to be retaken by the Russians on 23 October. In everyday life, it seemed to make little difference who was in control of the city. When Bryusov arrived there, Austrian policemen were directing traffic as Russian soldiers and officers paraded through town, and the ruble was an accepted currency.[92] These were signs of change, but whether for better or worse remained unclear.

Strong echoes of this tension and uncertainty are also heard in 'Those Born in the Years of Stagnation', a poem by Alexander Blok that would become a Russian classic. He wrote it on 21 September, after a string of surprising Russian victories in Grodek (Galicia, 12 September), Chernivtsi (then in Austria, now in Ukraine, 15 September), Sandomierz (Poland, 18 September), but probably partly in recollection of the calamities of recent Russian history, such as the Russo-Japanese War of 1904–05, the failed revolution of 1905, and the catastrophic defeat at Tannenberg. The past is a heavy burden for the narrator of this poem; he has seen too much, been through too much, to still interpret the bloodshed as a harbinger of better days to come.

> Dumbness remains – alarm bells clanging
> have clapped all other tongues in chains.
> In hearts familiar once with singing,
> a fateful emptiness remains.
>
> And what if dark above our death-bed,
> cawing, the ravens climb –
> Let those more worthy, God, O God,
> see your kingdom in their time.[93]

This sceptical view – although hopeful in its way – held little appeal for Russian intellectuals and poets in those often crazy months. But the Symbolist poet to whom Blok dedicated these lines, Zinaida Gippius (1869–1945), may have been receptive to his ideas. Although in August she had declared herself firmly opposed to mechanistic, militaristic, godless and (therefore) guilty Germany, her diaries and later public appearances reveal that she saw the war – however terrible the enemy might be – as an utter tragedy.[94] Gorodetsky, in contrast, had no patience for soft-heartedness of any kind, and could not understand why the Russian army showed the least consideration to German prisoners of war. His article 'Love for the Germans' baldly stated that the Russians would be better off investing 'all our Slavic love, all our softness' in the sole and ultimate goal: 'To love the German must mean to beat him.'[95]

At the same time as many Russian writers were flaunting their belligerence and chauvinism, others still saw Germany as a beacon of culture and could not repudiate the country entirely. A few lines by the young Marina Tsvetaeva (1892–1941) illustrate this suffocating ambivalence. She had learned to read and write German when only six years old, and at the age of eleven had spent time at a boarding school in Freiburg. There she had fallen under the spell of the Black Forest, the landscape of her ancestors, familiar from the German legends and sagas her mother had always read to her. In the summer of 1910 – shortly before making her debut with the collection *Vecherny Albomi* ('Evening Album') – Tsvetaeva was visiting Dresden with her sister Asha.[96] 'I have many souls, but the most important of all is the Germanic one', she once wrote.[97] When the war broke out, at first she burned with patriotic hatred of the murderous, warmongering enemy. Nevertheless, she could not betray her Germanic heart, as revealed by her poem 'Germany' written in early December.

> Your enemies would hound and flay you;
> The world is glad to have it so.
> Yet how, oh how, could I betray you?
> How could I bear to let you go?
>
> Blood begs for blood, so others reason.
> I can't see things so prudently.

It's madness maybe, maybe treason,
Yet still I love you, Germany.[98]

While Charles Hamilton Sorley's poetry was free of this melodramatic tone, he did find himself in a very similar position. He had been back on British soil since returning from his German escapades in early August, but he did not plan to stay long. On 6 August he remarked that the war was a 'beastly nuisance', mainly because it was being fought against the charming German people. Yet this, even combined with his irritation at all the patriotic prattle and his contrarian streak, did not prevent him from enlisting later that month. He even admitted (albeit in a coolly ironic tone) that he had more or less been taken in by British propaganda: 'I am almost convinced that war is right and the tales told of German barbarism are true.' His plan to study at Oxford was shelved without further ado, and he spent the next few months at training camps in Churn and Shorncliffe. He had no illusions about the military operations: 'War certain to last three years now, and to end in stalemate.' Meanwhile, his sympathy for the Germans was almost undiminished, although he now saw more and more clearly what he had noticed during his months of travel earlier that year: Germans were so confident of their own superiority that they could not conceive of other ways of thinking. That was certainly a flaw, but to Sorley the main thing was that they had principles, that they were idealists in their way, and so what they did was honourable. Writing to his former schoolmaster in Marlborough, he defended the people whom he referred to in the same letter as 'the enemy'. Expressing his hope that German was still on the curriculum, he severely criticized the ideological blindness of the British newspapers. 'If this war proves (as I think it will) that you can kill a person and yet remain his greatest friend or, less preferably, be killed and yet stay friends it'll have done a splendid thing.'[99] This was wishful thinking in a climate where ditties about fathers 'hunting the Hun' were being published in England and Ernst Lissauer's 'Hassgesang gegen England' (Hate Song Against England) was popular in Germany. The two warring countries were very far indeed from becoming friends.[100]

This fact had not escaped Rupert Brooke, who like Sorley had spent considerable time in Germany. 'It hurts me, this war', he wrote on 11 November in a letter to a friend and fellow poet in America. 'Because I was fond of Germany. There are such good things in her, and I'd always hoped she'd get away from Prussia and the oligarchy in time.'[101] While waiting for a new posting abroad, Brooke found himself back in his homeland once again. His social life was more complicated than ever, especially once he started seeing Prime Minister Asquith's daughter. As Brooke's chum Winston Churchill made plans for a new front in Turkey to circumvent the impasse on the Western front, the poet continued work on his series of war sonnets. After the Battle of Ypres, in which more than 200,000 were killed, including some 50,000 Britons, 'The Soldier', which Brooke completed around Christmas, was just what his grieving country was waiting to hear.

> If I should die, think only this of me:
>   That there's some corner of a foreign field
> That is for ever England.[102]

Yet already vastly greater swathes of foreign fields had become British – and French, German, Russian, Austrian, Hungarian and so on – than most people had imagined possible in August. For many, Brooke's soothing patriotic verses had lost their power to convince. Franz Werfel (1890–1945), a German-speaking writer from Prague who served in the east of Galicia, composed a poem in late 1914 that – unintentionally, since Brooke's sonnets would not be published until the following year – seems to invert the message of the English poem. 'Fremde sind wir auf die Erde Alle' (We Are All Strangers on Earth) left no room for imperialistic myths of conquest; even the territory claimed was no more than a patch of earth beneath a headstone. 'Under your feet those places fade away', wrote Werfel; war zones were unsuitable even as burial grounds.[103] It was self-deceptive to think that the conflict would lead to new forms of human connection. War brought nothing but utter alienation and total destruction.

> Even the beating of our heart's a lie!
> We're strangers in this world, one and all,
> And everything we grow attached to dies.

Likewise, the Viennese poet and journalist Karl Kraus (1874–1936) dissected the arguments that had convinced so many people to go to war and made mincemeat of them. In his lecture 'In dieser großen Zeit' (In These Great Times) – delivered on 19 November and printed in his magazine *Die Fackel* in December – he showed that there was no longer any clear difference between cynicism and clear-headedness. The unsparing onslaught of his reasoning seemed to mimic the realities of war. 'I know very well', Kraus wrote, 'that at times it is necessary to transform markets into battlefields so that these might turn into markets again.' This great imperalist war was to him essentially an economic matter: 'Behind flags and flames, heroes and helpers, behind all fatherlands an altar has been erected at which pious science stands rubbing its hands: God created the consumer!'[104] The disaster taking place resulted from the marriage of consumerism to the militarism of the nation-state, a marriage consummated and consumed day after day, page after page, in the newspapers, which were permanently swollen with a rhetoric ungrounded in reality. Nothing sold better than war news, and so the presses kept rolling. Kraus saw the voluntary participation of so many poets in this process – whether by producing patriotic verse or by enlisting – quite simply as the end of their poetic careers. Poets, he believed, must not perpetuate the clichés and lies of their own time. When they do, they disqualify themselves. Period.

4

The Smell of Mustard Gas in the Morning: The War in 1915

> If it were not for Mother and friends, I would pray for a speedy death. I want a genuine taste of the horrors, and then – peace. I don't want to go back to the old inane life that always seemed like a prison. I want freedom, not comfort.
>
> – Siegfried Sassoon, 3 December 1915[1]

In a typically brash display of self-confidence, the American automobile tycoon Henry Ford took a luxury liner that he christened the *Peace Ship* to Europe in December 1915 to put an end to the war single-handedly and 'get the boys out of the trenches by Christmas'.[2] But the war had a momentum of its own, and even the man who had literally set the world in motion was powerless to stop it. When Christmas came, more than a thousand British soldiers near Ypres found themselves, not celebrating the peace that Ford had predicted, but trying to recover from the latest German gas attack, launched the previous Sunday (19 December). Help came too late for 120 of them;[3] their Christmas gift that year was a wooden casket. Ford's faith in positive thinking had been painfully naive; in 1915, there were no signs whatsoever that the war was nearing its end. On the contrary, major new fronts were opened, and new powers entered the conflict. In 1915, what had from the outset been called the Great War became a true world war.[4]

At the same time, the situation on the Western front had become so deadlocked that outside interventions and diplomatic offensives seemed a more promising way out than regular military operations. After the race to the sea and the Battles of the Yser and of Ypres in the autumn of 1914, the front, in strategic terms, had stabilized. In other words, any movement had become almost impossible. From the North Sea to the Swiss Alps, the two sides had dug in at short distances from each other in ever larger, better fortified trenches, keeping the enemy under relentless fire. Their alternating attempts to force a breakthrough were unsuccessful. The losses remained as great as ever, and the territorial gains were usually negligible.

In the Belgian Westhoek, the Belgians and the French managed to halt the German advance at Nieuwpoort through creative use of sluices and canals, flooding the low-lying polder landscape so that it became a swampy, virtually impassable no-man's-land. The Flemish poet Daan Boens (1893–1977), who experienced the Battle of the Yser first-hand, described it in his collection of poems *Van Glorie en Lijden* (Of Glory and Suffering, 1917). A long series of sonnets depicted the exhausting journey to the coast, the bloody battle at the river Yser ('the sky burned red! / and then ten columns fell, and ten more after them'[5]), and the eerie calm that descended afterwards:[6]

> The sluggish water came, and slowly it spread wide
> and wider, covering the low, wide fields of green.
> The morning came and, casting gentle rays of light,
> spread peace all round that sea, unmoving and serene.[7]

'Peace' was a relative term, of course. There was never anything like a ceasefire, except at Christmas, and the threat was constant. Even around the village of Pervijze, which had a reputation as a safe haven, the Liège poet and songwriter Georges Fisse (1890–1914) died on 13 December 1914.[8] The Allied soldiers were assailed not only by Germans, but also by germs.[9] The water that kept the enemy at bay often seeped into the hiding and sleeping places of the Belgian fighters, and the corpses floating in it created stinking pools of bacteria, breeding places for rats and other vermin. Compared to French, German and British soldiers, three times as many Belgian troops died of illness. Many soldiers did not have suitable footwear, and some even went around in wooden clogs – a nightmare in itself in that muddy, boggy terrain. During inspections, many soldiers were found to keep their fork and spoon in their buttonholes, so as not to lose their few meagre possessions.

The exhausted forces used the winter and spring to recover their strength, replenish their supplies, and swell their numbers. Large-scale recruitment took place among Belgian refugees, and volunteers and conscripts from the September 1914 draft arrived from French training camps. In the spring and summer of 1915, 34,000 to 38,000 new soldiers arrived at the Yser, almost doubling the number of Belgian fighters. They included the Antwerp poets August Van Cauwelaert (1885–1945) and Fritz Francken (1893–1969), driven by a sense of duty and the desire to perform great deeds. Still, these writers did not abandon their muse. Although Francken wrote 'I'll fold the ladder to my ivory tower / Time now for acts, and not for rhymes, to flower', he deliberately couched this message in rhyming verse.[10] With encouragement from their mentor, the elder poet Cyriel Verschaeve, these young Flemish intellectuals took on three tasks: defending their country by force of arms, raising the intellectual level of the Flemish soldiers at the front (many of whom were illiterate) through their presence and good example, and inspiring courage and fighting spirit with their poetry. Yet Van Cauwelaert found little time for verse in his first months of duty. All his energy went into survival, or else into a

Flemish study circle for front-line soldiers, which he organized and led.[11]

In February, Frans Van Cauwelaert, August's brother and a leading Flemish politician, called on Flemish writers who were not at the front to acknowledge their duty and take up the pen in the service of both the Belgian and the Flemish struggle.[12] René De Clercq did not have to be asked twice. Working with other Flemish writers and intellectuals who had fled to the Netherlands, he spread the militant message in *De Vlaamsche Stem* (The Flemish Voice), published in the Dutch town of Bussum. In his eyes, the Germanic identity of the Flemish people was no reason to show any mercy to the enemy. Those who felt differently – such as the writer Stijn Streuvels, according to rumour[13] – were put firmly in their place by De Clercq's poem 'Onder den helm' (Under the Helmet): 'Whoever can stand with them hand in hand / Is a scoundrel in his heart.'[14] The enemy was, of course, much worse than a scoundrel:

> Germans, let your hordes retreat
> In silence across the Rhine.
> We could be brothers when next we meet
> If you become human again.[15]

In a poem published in the *Belgische Standaard* on 11 July 1915 (a traditional Flemish day of celebration), Theo Walter unhesitatingly applied a traditional model of Flemish heroism to the contemporary situation. And on 23 July, just after the Belgian national holiday, Henri Veuskens emphasized in *De Vlaamsche Stem* that unlike in the legendary Battle of the Spurs in 1302, this time it was not the valiant Flemish knights Breydel and De Coninck who led the troops, but 'the King of Belgium Land / honoured and praised from every side'.[16] Yet this sturdy rhetorical mask concealed a good deal of ambivalence. Both in occupied territory and in refugee circles in the Netherlands, the Flemish began to have their doubts about Belgium. The cracks in the front were slowly beginning to show. After King Albert declined to respond to a question from *De Vlaamsche Stem* about Flemish self-government within the Belgian state, the editors found themselves divided: some remained loyal to the king (Frans Van Cauwelaert was among these so-called 'passivists'), while others placed the interests of Flanders before all else, even if that meant accepting support from the still-hated occupying forces. De Clercq was deeply disappointed by the king's long-delayed and dismissive reply, summarizing Albert's message as, 'Flemings, fight and keep your mouths shut'.[17] Even so, he published the collection *De zware kroon* (The Heavy Crown) in October, with poems dedicated to Queen Elizabeth and King Albert. Likewise, his 'Belgische Volkslied' ('Song of the Belgian People' or perhaps even 'Belgian National Anthem') betrayed no sign of an impending rift:

> No internecine strife will ever shame a Nation
> That fought for hearth and home with its united power.
> Two languages rang out above the massed formation;
> Two languages pay tribute to their noble valour.
> [...]
> Stay one beside the other, joined like stalks of wheat.[18]

Nevertheless, De Clercq soon became a 'scoundrel' himself, joining the camp of the activists. The Germans skillfully encouraged this type of discontent, and through the Dutch poet Geerten Gossaert (a pen name of Frederik C. Gerretson), an advocate of political union between the Netherlands and Flanders, German funds were funnelled into *De Vlaamsche Stem* (perhaps without De Clercq's knowledge). This was all part of the German *Flamenpolitik* (Flemish Policy) of exploiting the friction between the Dutch- and French-speaking communities in occupied Belgium.

This revealed the same tensions in Belgium as occupied the minds of political leaders and intellectuals in almost all the other countries involved in the war. After it was over, where would Europe's national borders lie? Would those who redrew the map be inspired by the old Flemish saying 'The language is the whole of the people', dividing up nations along linguistic lines? How could that ever work on a continent where so many cities and towns were multicultural mixes? As the fighting continued on the many battlefields, different perspectives on nationalism and imperialism clashed in the ideological arena. Most leaders of existing nation-states supported the status quo: large rather than small countries, with whatever colonies they already had or might acquire in the future. In other words, their priority was expansion.[19] Meanwhile, linguistic and religious minorities – the Polish, Irish, Czechs, Ukrainians, Croats, Finns, Latvians and so forth – were striving toward greater autonomy, whether this meant breaking away from a larger country or, as in the case of the Italians and Romanians in the Dual Monarchy, uniting with speakers of the same language across the border. This situation gave rise to striking contrasts. While Germany was aiming for territorial and economic expansion and hence supported the activist wing of the Flemish Movement, its main ally, the Dual Monarchy, was trying to crush the hopes of its many national minorities.[20] Meanwhile, Great Britain saw no contradiction in using its troops from India, Canada, Australia and New Zealand to restore the sovereignty of ravaged Belgium. Although the great powers clearly frowned on 'Balkanization',[21] and lesser nations were discouraged from believing that they could ever form viable, self-respecting states, the British and the Germans could put up with an independent Belgium or Flanders, respectively, as long as this served their geopolitical and economic ends.

Meanwhile, the eyes of the world were still on Belgium. The pamphlets and posters of the war's early months were followed by books lionizing the country – and by humanitarian aid, which made a much greater difference to the suffering Belgians. In London, just before Christmas 1914, *The Daily Telegraph* published *King Albert's Book*, 'for the benefit of the Daily Telegraph Belgian Fund'. In it, 'representative men and women throughout the world' heaped praise on that peerless monarch and his no less courageous people. The book was explicitly intended as a tribute and a show of support for 'the martyr nation of the war',[22] according to the introduction by bestselling author Hall Caine, but it was also an attempt to bring together the Entente countries and their hoped-for allies, Italy and the United States, for a wedding at the Belgian altar: 'here, in love of justice and in hatred of oppression, speaking in many voices and many tongues but from only one soul, which enkindles the earth as with a holy fire, men and women of all civilised countries have drawn closer and clasped hands'.[23] The implication was clear; the enemy was no longer part of civilization. In contrast, the vacillating neutrals were more than welcome. Major Dutch authors Louis Couperus and Frederik van Eeden contributed, as did the American writers Edith Wharton and Jack London, the Swedish feminist author Ellen Key, the renowned Italian war correspondent Luigi Barzini, the Spanish poet and later Nobel Prize winner Juan Ramón Jiménez, the former Danish prime minister Jens Christian Christensen, and the Portuguese foreign minister Antonio Macieira. There were noteworthy contributions from the Irish nationalist politician John Redmond ('The Irish nation has many strong and tender ties with Belgium') and his countryman T.P. O'Connor, who compared the defence of Liège to the Greek stand at Thermopylae.[24] The same parallel was drawn by the well-known pacifist Romain Rolland (1866–1944), who would win the Nobel Prize for Literature in 1915.[25] These were highly significant rhetorical gestures: not only did they place the Belgians on the same lofty pedestal as the Greeks, but they also equated the German invaders with the Persians. The influential French philosopher Henri Bergson could only fully express his admiration through a comparison with classical antiquity. He had always maintained that history was nothing more than 'a school of immorality', but was forced to eat his words after the example that Belgium had set for the world. He declared King Albert to be a modern Marcus Aurelius, the most virtuous and heroic of rulers.[26] Surprisingly, the usually level-headed Dutch poet Albert Verwey came to similar conclusions in August 1915, despite generally not being all that impressed with his southern neighbours:

> The Belgium that King Albert is defending on the Yser is surely one of the most ineradicable little creations that History has ever brought forth. It does not matter if we contemporaries, attending to the facts, see nothing in Belgium but a trifling and divided band of people with little love of country and a backward educational system, who are anything but original in the cultural sphere, and who, although as brave as any, have never excelled in the martial virtues. The image of trampled, downtrodden Belgium suddenly raising its banner on the Yser, and successfully resisting the most powerful army that its mighty conqueror could muster, will be cherished forever in human memory.[27]

Even more relevant here are Verwey's remarks on the power of poetry. In literary representations of the Belgian king and queen, 'who have already assumed the status of European legends',[28] he saw evidence that poetry could still influence the real world in the modern age, and more than that – that it could be one of the forces shaping reality.[29] He pointed to the rapturous odes to King Albert and Queen Elizabeth that were inspiring the warring European nations, and predicted that political leaders would vividly recall those unforgettable images of Belgian suffering even after the country was liberated. The divided Belgians, many of whom deeply detested their own leaders, could then derive some measure of satisfaction from their terrible ordeal. Whether or not they reaped political benefits from the war, it would at least improve them morally. Verwey had a deep-rooted conviction that the future lay 'not in the isolated existence of different countries, but on the contrary, in their free and unwavering community'.[30] That community could only come about, he believed, if its constituent peoples were mature and fully developed. Verwey was impressed that Stijn Streuvels had been able to write so sympathetically about his German guests during the early months of the war, but he believed that figures like Streuvels could only emerge among the 'Belgians, who have hardly coalesced as a nation'.[31] In other words, the Belgians, with their underdeveloped sense of national identity, were not the forerunners of the 'world league' that he advocated, but rather were lagging behind the larger nations. Verwey's arguments for a global community were accompanied by a strong appeal to his own Dutch nation to cultivate 'a heightened patriotic self-awareness'. In his thinking, these two issues were intimately connected: 'countries without a strong national character' could never last in his future community. Yes, the Netherlands had a great history and the Dutch were an exceptional people, but they had to wear that identity with self-confidence.[32] The future League of Nations could avoid friction only if the participating countries felt sure that their value was fully recognized.

For Verwey, these were not mere theoretical musings on international relations. He was trying to maintain his friendships with German writers in Stefan George's circle under wartime conditions, but they were not making it easy for him. As they waged their Heroic Struggle, who was he to comment from the neutral sidelines? Verwey wrote several poems defending his position ('I am neutral, never impartial. / I do not share in your struggle, but I do uphold my Cause'[33]). Yet their points of view were fundamentally irreconcilable. While Verwey dreamed of a pan-European cultural movement run by and for poets, Stefan George was transforming (as Verwey commented in another poem) into the 'King, Ruler, Saviour, and Preacher / Confessor, and sometime Kneeler' of a German alliance. Verwey did not blame his friend for that ('How could you do anything else, when you cherished / the dream of a superpower, soul of your nation'[34]), but the Dutch poet himself had no such dreams.[35] The title of the poem, 'Van een klein aan een groot volk' (From a Small to a Large Nation), was not even necessarily ironic in tone. Verwey had great respect for Germany and his cultured friends there. But as he wrote in another poem, explicitly dedicated to the Master, while George might be the poet of the German nation, Verwey was the poet 'of my nation, which calls me so'.[36]

The longer the war went on, the more severely it tested old friendships and loyalties. As the son of a music critic born in Munich under the name of Franz Hüffer, Ford Madox Hueffer initially had difficulty seeing Germany as the great foe. Still, after six months, he admitted that even he would murmur 'Thank God' if he heard that a million Germans had been killed.[37] Alongside all his other demanding literary work – and despite his earlier reservations about other poets who had gone patriotic – he began to accept assignments from the War Propaganda Bureau in London. Yet he did not feel as if he were suddenly writing propaganda, because, as he explained in the foreword to *When Blood is Their Argument: An Analysis of Prussian Culture* (1915), his entire upbringing and career had led him to the position he was presenting in this new context. That position was simple (even though it took 350 pages to set out): Prussian militarism, materialism and mania for organization were catastrophic for humanity.[38] Of course, it was theoretically important that Hueffer made a distinction between Catholic southern Germany, where his father had spent his formative years, and Prussia, which had replaced mind-broadening 'education' with mind-narrowing 'instruction' and *Bildung* with *Kultur*.[39] But by late July 1915, when Hueffer entered the military, that distinction had become utterly immaterial. He was off to fight the Germans, that was all, and he went without hesitation. 'If one has enjoyed the privileges of the ruling classes of a country all one's life, there seems to be no alternative to fighting for that country if necessary', he wrote to his mother, who had asked him in so many words why he had volunteered for service.[40] Duty and a sense of *noblesse oblige* drove him to the front, along with a certainty that, as he had written in the final paragraph of *When Blood is Their Argument*, the war was essentially a conflict between organized, materialistic egoists and all-round sportsmanlike altruists.[41]

Guillaume Apollinaire's attitude likewise became more markedly anti-German in 1915. He could not understand, for instance, how Romain Rolland could have written even a word in favour of the Germans. 'If you let them go their way, they will consume us entirely', he wrote to a friend who had defended Rolland, author of the pacifist treatise *Au-dessus de la mêlée* (Above the Fray).[42] He felt that the Germans were heavy-handed and unfair, and he believed that their notion of patriotism had nothing to do with humanism and everything to do with a poorly concealed wish to 'Hunnify' the world.

The Germanophile Charles Sorley could not see the conflict in those terms. He told his mother how pleased he had been when, during a conversation in March 1915, a German woman had told him she was not at all proud or glad to 'give her sons to fight'. All the talk of a just war nauseated him: 'What we are doing is casting out Satan by Satan.' To be sure, Germany deserved to be punished for its selfish pursuit of *Weltmacht*, but the British Empire had failed to set a better example, and therefore deserved half the blame.[43] In late April, a month before his regiment was sent to the Continent, he enclosed the poem 'To Germany' in a letter to his mother. The two countries were both blind, the poet wrote, fixated on their own prejudices and, in the case of the Germans, focused too exclusively on their own ambitions.

> You only saw your future bigly planned,
> And we, the tapering paths of our own mind,
> And in each other's dearest ways we stand,
> And hiss and hate. And the blind fight the blind.[44]

After the war, the poem concluded, they would once again be able to see each other for who they really were, and then they could forgive. But until then, there was only 'the storm / The darkness and the thunder and the rain' – euphemisms for what the young soldier would soon experience first-hand. Sorley and his men were sent to Ploegsteert, where, other than a few minor, but generally fatal incidents, there was remarkably little going on, as he observed again and again in his letters. His main pastime, it seems, was censoring his soldiers' correspondence ('I am qualifying for the position of … post-office clerk after the war'[45]). Of course, there were also regular patrols, and the trenches were systematically fortified and defended. Sorley enjoyed his special friendships with the young men under his command, who had meant little to him a year earlier but whose lives were now intertwined with his. At the same time, he was honest enough to say flat out, in a letter to his best friend, what many soldiers kept to themselves: 'Then death and the horrible gratitude when one sees that the next man is dead. "We won't have to carry him in under fire, thank God; dragging will do".' Meanwhile, he had been promoted to captain. More and more often, his letters reported deaths. 'For the present, rain and dirt and damp cold. O for a bath!' he wrote to his family on 5 October. That same day he confessed his fears to his best friend about the next day's offensive: 'To be able to prove oneself no coward to oneself, will be great, if it comes off: but suppose one finds oneself fail in the test? I dread my own censorious self in the coming conflict – I also have great physical dread of pain.'[46] And there his letters end. Eight days later, on 13 October 1915, Sorley was shot by a sniper while leading his company near Hulluch in northern France. This poem was found in his kit-bag:

When you see millions of the mouthless dead
Across your dreams in pale battalions go,
Say not soft things as other men have said,
That you'll remember. For you need not so.
Give them not praise. For, deaf, how should they know
It is not curses heaped on each gashed head?
Nor tears. Their blind eyes see not your tears flow.
Nor honour. It is easy to be dead.
Say only this, 'They are dead.' Then add thereto,
'Yet many a better one has died before.'
Then, scanning all the o'ercrowded mass, should you
Perceive one face that you loved heretofore,
It is a spook. None wears the face you knew.
Great death has made all his for evermore.[47]

It was obvious that those millions of dead would change Europe. But how, and to whose benefit – that was still an open question. For some poets, such as Emile Verhaeren, the Continent was still divided into Good and Evil. In 'Les tombes' (The Graves), the final poem in *Les Ailes rouges de la Guerre* (The Red Wings of War, 1916), he described his vision of the future, in which the heroic Allied nations ('Belgians, English, French, Italians, and Serbs') would 'chastise' Germany to save the Greco-Roman tradition. From the soil that held and bleached the bones of the fallen, the poet wrote, an 'entirely different Europe' would emerge, 'brighter and purer'.[48] Verhaeren himself did not live to see that new Europe; on 27 November 1916 he fell under a train at the railway station in Rouen, France. His last words are said to have been 'Je meurs ... ma femme ... ma patrie' ('I'm dying ... my wife ... my homeland') – and if this is a legend, that only illustrates all the more clearly that since the summer of 1914 Verhaeren had become Belgium's unofficial poet laureate. Judging by his obituary in *The Times*, even that title did not begin to do him justice. The newspaper called him 'the greatest exponent in European poetry of universal ideals'.[49] In this context, it was perfectly obvious that 'universal ideals' corresponded precisely to those of the Entente. Most European contemporaries who sympathized with the Entente saw no contradiction there; to them, a poet like Verhaeren was both the voice of his national culture and the standard-bearer of Europe and all civilized humanity.[50]

In this choir of the prophets of civilization, the young poet Pierre-Jean Jouve (1887–1976) sounded one of the rare dissonant notes. Surprisingly, in his poem 'Les voix d'Europe' (The Voices of Europe) in the collection *Vous êtes des hommes* (You Are Men, 1915), he made no distinction between 'us' and 'them'. All the voices in Europe, he lamented, the wisest and the most truthful, the holiest and the most learned, were joined in a single cry: 'Kill! Kill!'[51] As a pacifist, a disciple of Tolstoy, and a former field nurse, Jouve tried to move beyond this troubling observation. 'Pour l'Europe' (For Europe) written in the spring of 1915, was an attempt to counter the blood-thirst with a message of hope – even if that hope was purely rhetorical, existing only in the language of the poem. 'I gather you and possess you here through the miracle of a song', he declared to the 'Peoples of France, Germany, England, or Russia'.[52] Of course, his song was in the French language – hardly a neutral medium in 1915. Jouve was aware of this problem, and his efforts to solve it made it painfully clear how hopeless his mission actually was: 'Do not worry about the language, listen to the song in all its purity', he ventured, adding in parentheses, '(It's neither a French nor a German song, but belongs to some more beautiful race'[53]). Yet Jouve was not naive. Later in the poem, he reflected at length on Germany's overweening ambition, on England's avarice, on feudal Russia, unable to decide whether or not it was part of the West, on France, hounded by its own history, and on the international rivalries that were tearing the Continent apart.[54] We will have to forswear all our lies, Jouve wrote in the final poem, 'Que faut-il faire?' (What Is to Be Done?). Civilization, national pride, the press, science, education, art, colonial conquest, prosperity, arms, industry – 'Lies, lies!' Loving your neighbour and treating other men as brothers in full awareness of your own imperfection, your own unhappiness, your own inevitable failure – *that* was how we were meant to live.[55]

In the literary review *Die Weissen Blätter* ('The White Pages'), the German poet and critic Ludwig Rubiner responded enthusiastically to the work of his French colleague Jouve, not only advancing it as evidence that poets were finally mustering the courage to take on politicians, but also welcoming its humanitarian message.[56] That review in turn struck a chord with Paul van Ostaijen, who was a loyal reader of *Die Weissen Blätter* in the municipal library of his occupied city. Rubiner's words and his quotes from Jouve's book (which, as a French publication, may well have been difficult to come by in wartime Antwerp) suggested to Van Ostaijen that his own thinking about politics and poetry was in perfect harmony with that of the European avant-garde. Accordingly, in his essay 'Nasionalisme en het nieuwe geslacht' (Nationalism and the New Generation, 1916), he rejected what he called the 'nationalism of phrases' in favour of 'the embrace of a healthy internationalism resulting from a healthy nationalism'.[57] In fact, it was far from clear that this was what Jouve and Rubiner had in mind, but Van Ostaijen took his ammunition where he believed he could find it. There was a great deal at stake for him. If he wanted to claim that his increasing support for the Flemish Movement and political activism were avant-garde activities, then he had to present examples from other countries of avant-garde writers with similar nationalist beliefs. Now he believed he had found supporting evidence on both sides of the front lines. As Van Ostaijen saw it, the point of the war was not victory for the French or German race, but the dramatic acceleration of a much deeper shift, a cultural evolution, in which nationalism would play an ever greater role in Europe. He went to some lengths to disavow the narrow brand of nationalism that sowed only hate and destruction and was responsible for the cataclysmic war. What he envisaged was a 'healthy nationalism'. It was an illusion, he claimed, to suppose that the new Europe could be built without strong, self-confident nations. The general European interest was well served not by naively trying to transcend national identity, but by immersing oneself in that identity. As he wrote in a later essay,

> Today's European movement is based on a new internationalism; the cultural community is forming across borders even as hostilities continue. Distinct national cultures will be preserved, but separately from them, and with their help, a pan-European cultural community is forming.[58]

But to take full part in that European cultural community, Flanders would have to modernize quickly and completely. 'We are lagging behind the general cultural development of Western Europe and must take pains not to lose even more ground', Van Ostaijen warned. This was an especially radical break with the provincialism in his own circle. With Europe surging forward at breakneck speed, Flanders had to jump on board, he argued, before it fell prey to a much stronger culture, whether French or German.[59]

Many writers and intellectuals of the war years were preoccupied with the 'backwardness' of their own country, people or culture. From Portugal to Poland, and from Flanders to the Baltics, Europeans were yearning for a great step forward, but they doubted whether their countries were ready. It was partly a rhetorical strategy (the further ahead of your own nation you say you are, the stronger your claim to be part of the avant-garde), but there was no denying that Lisbon, Antwerp, Warsaw and Riga had a less cosmopolitan feel than Paris, London or Berlin. Yet the solution was not simply to open the floodgates and be inundated by foreign delights and insights. Not only had the war made the borders less porous than they had been in many a year, but there was more than a little truth to Van Ostaijen's claim that nationalism and internationalism tended to go hand in hand in many parts of Europe.

Fernando Pessoa, for instance, not only developed heteronyms with a Futurist outlook, but also began announcing in the early 1910s that a new variety of national poet was on the way, a 'Supra-Camões'. This was a reference to Portugal's greatest poet, the sixteenth-century Luís de Camões. The poems Pessoa published under his own name combined elements from international modernism with local nationalist themes.[60] For instance, if Pessoa ever sincerely believed in anything, then it was in 'Sebastianism', the legend that Portugal will be saved by an incarnation of the sixteenth-century King Sebastian I.[61] In a letter on the subject that Pessoa wrote to a local expert in September 1914, he suggested that his fascination with this 'all-important Portuguese phenomenon' was linked to his patriotism and what he believed was the 'very imminent' arrival of a 'super-Camões'.[62] That same week, he told a friend about his sociological study, 'Theory of the

Aristocratic Republic', and his hypotheses 'regarding the current war and the social, national and cultural forces at work'.[63] It is unclear which writings he meant, given the immense body of work he left behind, but he may have been referring to passages from a piece later published under the title 'Ultimatum', in which he argued in favour of a 'Scientific Monarchy that will be antitraditionalist, antihereditary, and absolutely spontaneous, since the Average-King may appear at any time'[64] – an almost modernist take on Sebastianism.

As he pursued these often idiosyncratic nationalist interests, Pessoa also made a deliberate effort to elevate Portuguese culture by applying European standards. Such standards were far from being generally accepted, as we learn from an ironic letter that Pessoa wrote to his best friend, Mário de Sá-Carneiro (1890–1916), in 1913, about one of Sá-Carneiro's recent writings: 'And then, to make matters worse, you write in European! You write without seeing Portugal and its work, which I consider the work of genius; you clash with the perpetual provincialism of our mentality … O unhappy man, O unhappy man! … This is good for France, for England, for Germany…'[65] In early 1914, Pessoa and a few of his friends hatched a plan to start a magazine called *Europa*, with the objective of building bridges between 'backward' Portugal and the flourishing avant-garde movements in other parts of the Continent.[66] The magazine ultimately appeared only twice, under the name of *Orpheu*, but those two issues were enough to cause a scandal in the politically and culturally unstable country of Portugal. Another shock came in April 1916 when the *Orpheu* poet José de Almada Negreiros (1893–1970) published a pamphlet decrying a well-known academic poet and certain other gentlemen he believed had made Portugal 'the most backward country in Europe and in the entire world! The most primitive of all the Africas! Place of exile for outlaws and the indifferent! The gated Africa of the Europeans!'[67] These were words with explosive potential a month after Portugal had become officially involved in the hostilities, seizing German merchant ships and provoking a German declaration of war. For Portugal, the colonies would be the main theatre of the conflict, but if Almada Negreiros was to be believed, the mother country was even more primitive. That may seem like typical avant-garde exaggeration, but the frequency with which Portugal's government was changing hands around this time, in a dizzying sequence of coups and counter-coups, did not suggest the institutional stability and leadership of a major colonial power.

Wars are fought for territory. To protect or expand their territorial holdings, European states had forged strategic alliances. But strategy is not a static thing. Romania (an independent kingdom since 1877) and Italy (since 1860) had signed treaties allying them with Germany and the Dual Monarchy, but so far they had managed to avoid taking sides. Both the Entente and the Central Powers used every means at their disposal to win over these countries to their camp. Located on opposite flanks of the Dual Monarchy, both Italy and Romania were in a position to drive a hard bargain. Everyone understood precisely what they were after: territorial expansion into areas where Italian or Romanian was spoken.

In Italy's case, this made for a long list. Apart from its colonial ambitions in Africa and the Middle East, Italy also hoped to add Trieste, South Tyrol, Istria, Fiume (now Rijeka), and the Dalmatian coast to its territory. In the spring of 1915, an agreement seemed to be forthcoming. Although it was opposed by a large majority of the Italian people and their representatives in parliament, victory nevertheless seemed close at hand for a small group of political and cultural revolutionaries and a war-hungry triumvirate consisting of King Victor Emmanuel III, Prime Minister Salandra, and the foreign minister. Right up to the last moment, the avant-garde kept pushing harder and harder for war. For years, they had been insisting on the vital importance of a war to cleanse and modernize the country. Enough of Italy's tedious obsession with the past, symbolized by its pompous cultural centres. 'You can't live in this peace', Ardengo Soffici (1879–1964) wrote in his poem 'Firenze' (Florence). The biggest thrill in town was the tram that passed every twenty minutes. 'A poster of the Folies Bergère/ Or of Splendor / Stirs you more / Than all the resigned history' visible in the city's towers and façades. Yet this was the proverbial calm before the storm. The poem's narrator self-consciously lit a cigarette at 'La Rosa café / March 6, 1915'. He too longed to become part of the Continent's history. In a sense, he already had; Florence was no longer an international city. On all the houses where foreigners had lived, the poem tells us, there was a 'For Rent' sign, and in the streets there was 'no more yes, da, oui, ja'.[68] On 11 March, Giacomo Balla and Fortunato Depero launched the manifesto *Ricostruzione futurista dell'universo* (The Futurist Reconstruction of the Universe). While glossing over the fact that reconstruction must be preceded by destruction, the authors left no room for misunderstanding about their radical plans to change the face of the world. Both art and everyday life had to be injected with a stiff shot of 'complex, constructive, noise-producing abstraction'. Their Futurist proposals were characteristically playful and violent. For instance, they envisioned a 'noise fountain', as well as aerial concerts high above the city at which aircraft would provide the noise. The playthings that Depero planned to design were equally modern. To harden children for combat, he intended to make 'gigantic, dangerous and aggressive toys'. Of course, there would also be versions for grown-ups: 'We Futurists, Balla and Depero, will construct millions of metallic animals for the greatest war (conflagration of all the creative energies of Europe, Asia, Africa and America, which will undoubtedly follow the current marvelous little human conflagration).'[69]

It would not be much longer before Italy was drawn into that little conflagration. On 26 April, Italy signed the Treaty of London, ending its paper alliance with Germany and Austria–Hungary and offering its genuine support to the Entente countries in return for a secret promise of territorial gains after the war was won.[70] By this time the Symbolist poet D'Annunzio had returned to Italy from France, and could barely contain his excitement. On 5 May, he gave a speech in Genoa that would go down in history as his 'Sermon on the Mount':

> Blessed be those who shunned sterile loves to keep their virginity for this first and last love of their life. Blessed be those who, having opposed the event [war], will accept in silence the supreme necessity and will want to be, not the last, but the first ones [to sacrifice themselves]. Blessed be the youths who hunger and thirst for glory, for they will be sated. Blessed be the merciful ones, for they will cleanse a luminous blood and bind a shining grief. Blessed be the pure of heart, blessed be those who will return victorious, for they will see Rome's new visage, Dante's forehead crowned anew, Italy's triumphant beauty.[71]

On 23 May, Italy at last declared war on Austria–Hungary. The Futurists rejoiced. On the front page of *Lacerba*, the headline of Papini's lead article trumpeted, 'WE WON'.[72] Of course, their war had not even begun, but finally being allowed to participate may have been more important to them than the ultimate outcome. Even though the Dual Monarchy was the enemy whose territory they sought, it was Germany who the Futurists and other Italians saw as their fundamental cultural nemesis. In the same issue of *Lacerba*, Soffici railed against the imperialism and militarism of the German Kaiser and the philistine morality, gravity and rigid discipline of his people.[73] More or less the same message was conveyed by 'Wir müssen', a poem by Piero

Jahier (1884–1966) that inveighed against Germany's thirst for power and martial rhetoric, depicting German soldiers as obedient killing machines. A footnote to the title pointed out that after the massacres in Belgium, the Germans had called out to their civilian victims, 'Wir müssen' (We must). The Italians contrasted these calculating bullies, who had been plotting war for decades, with their own simple elegance, rustic conviction, and talent for improvisation.

and still we shall oppose you with our army
9 months old
never willing to oppress and torture
unlike your army with its 50 years of premeditated infamy
gemütlich with our Neapolitan tunes
allegretto con passione
onward, Italy, always freedom time never church time[74]

Not that these Italians were cheerful, irresponsible scatterbrains. In the lower right-hand corner of the final page of *Lacerba* was a notice that subscribers would be reimbursed for all remaining issues, since the editors were heading off to the front and could no longer publish their magazine. Other Futurists showed equal courage. The many volunteers among them included the poet Marinetti (the group's leader), the prominent sculptor Umberto Boccioni, the noise artist Luigi Russolo, the visionary architect Antonio Sant'Elia, and the lesser-known Mario Sironi, Achille Funi, Carlo Erba and Ogo Piatti. All these dynamic Futurists were assigned to the swiftest battalion that Italy's army had to offer: the Lombardy Volunteer Cyclists. This was perhaps not as ultramodern as they had hoped, but like Russia, that other hotbed of Futurism, Italy was not yet sufficiently industrialized to support a modern war economy. Rather than a dynamic battleground crackling with Futurist ideals of progress, the Italian–Austrian front was a place of death, drudgery and deadlock. 'To be always going forward, and soon to be about to make a great advance?' the exasperated eighteen-year-old volunteer Enzo Valentino wrote in a letter to his mother on 3 September. 'I have never heard anything of this. As to advancing, it is now a month and a half that I have been up here and *always in the same place*.'[75] Seven weeks later he was killed.

D'Annunzio was given a free hand by the Italian army commanders.[76] In a regular regiment, he might have become a loose cannon, causing chaos wherever he went, but in his ever-changing role as an aviator, infantryman, sailor and, above all, maker of outlandish plans, he was worth his weight in gold to Italian propagandists. Considering the total dedication with which D'Annunzio threw himself into all these activities, it was hard to believe that he was a decadent fifty-two-year-old poet. This was what he had been waiting for all his life, and he had no intention of holding back – not as a soldier, nor as a writer. 'I am a poet of slaughter',[77] he said, and although other European poets could make the same claim after a year of battle, no one meant it as literally as he did. He would *sing the praises* of bloody massacres, for he was the absolute poet of death, an unparalleled force of nature who never bared his soul more fully than he did in the war.

In the meantime, Italy was trying to break the impasse. Starting in late June, it launched an unrelenting series of attacks on the Isonzo front, on the border between Austria and Italy (in what is now Slovenia). In October, Marinetti and his cycling friends saw their first military action in this inhospitable region. In his diary, Marinetti complained about the cold and lack of sleep, but he was enthralled by the capabilities of modern weaponry.[78] For example, he noted that the booming cannons at the Battle of Antwerp, the previous year, had been heard even in Groningen, 270 kilometres (170 miles) away. Ever a Futurist and an artist, he filled his notebook with page after page of drawings, typographical experiments, and onomatopoeic words, trying to capture the sounds, colours and tumult of the war. This line of investigation culminated in the visual poem 'Battle at Nine Levels: Mount Altissimo', in which he covered a sketch of the mountain with impressions of combat at nine different altitudes, from 30 to 3,000 metres (100 feet to almost two miles). The poem portrays war not as a slaughterhouse but as a boy's adventure, full of *son et lumière*. Yet death also lurks in this landscape.

> **800 metres** snip snip snap fire crackling
> BOOM BOOM get down it's the Brion firing
> ssssshhhhrrrrrapnels ... PIIING... sssrr zit zit zit POW
> = gasometer exploding on the right
> Austrian candidate down   blaze subdued
> the firemen return[79]

In the four Battles of the Isonzo in the summer and autumn of 1915, the Italians lost 235,000 men, more than 60,000 of whom were killed. There were no significant territorial gains.

As for Romania, it was interested in Bukovina and the Banat, but most of all, it wanted Transylvania.[80] The three million Romanian speakers there had been eager to join their mother country for quite some time, and in 1848 had even risen up against the Hungarian authorities. The events of the summer of 1914 had aroused great expectations. The Transylvanian poet Octavian Goga (1881–1938), who had spent the previous years in a Hungarian prison because of his irredentist beliefs, had written in Paris on 30 July 1914, of 'the prelude to the victory of the dream of so many generations'.[81] Legal barriers prevented him from returning home, but he hoped to reach Romania by way of Marseille and Constantinople, so that he could be in the country to witness history in the making. Street protests and a petition signed by more than forty professors at the University of Bucharest demanded the immediate invasion and annexation of Transylvania. What the 80 per cent of Romanians who were illiterate thought about all this, we do not know. But the literary and intellectual elite knew where they stood. In the words of a 1914 tribute to Goga, 'His verses, written in 1904 – "We have a dream that should come true, the child of our griefs / Our forefathers and fathers have died grieving for it" had become a kind of watchword for all Romanians.'[82] The country did not take military action right away, however, partly because Germany had instructed the Dual Monarchy to relinquish the territories claimed by Romania in order to strengthen the alliance (as it had in the case of the Italian claim to Trieste and Tyrol). Yet no agreement was ever reached, and it looked more and more as though the Romanian prime minister, Ion I.C. Brătianu, would cast his lot with the Allies. Germany invested forty million marks in propaganda and bribes to change the Romanians' minds. In desperation, the Germans even listened to lunatics who told them that sending 200 German good-time girls to Bucharest might influence Romania's decision in their favour. But none of this helped. Still, Romania did not openly side with the Allies either, instead playing for time and pocketing the propaganda money that came pouring in from both camps.

The Treaty of London led to a new outbreak of interventionist fever in the streets and newspapers of Bucharest, and Goga made sure his voice was heard. His poem '10 May 1915', printed the following day in the irredentist scandal sheet *Epoca*,[83] was an ode to the 'Romanian hosts', which recalled the many sacrifices their forefathers had made when fighting for independence from the Turks.

As you cross frozen waters in ethereal light,
The heroes' feast-day revels stick inside my throat.
I see an army of poor skeletal recruits;
With bullet-riddled chests they seem to follow you.
They stand in each man's shadow in a single file,
And walk along beside us, dark and terrible.
Parading onward in their ruthless march, the dead
Gaze out over the mountains, arms stretched out ahead ...[84]

Goga's message was perfectly clear: 10 May 1915 should be a reaffirmation of the declaration of independence of 10 May 1877, and the start of a new war. The struggle for independence would not be over until Transylvania, the land 'over the mountains', was united with its mother country, Romania. Goga included this poem in his collection *Cântece fără țară* (Songs Without a Homeland, 1916), a decidedly traditional volume in which the sense of homelessness pervaded poems such as this one:

I am the cry steeped in the blood
Of the widows of Transylvania.
I am the messenger of love and hate
A man who dreams of victories,
And in my mouth I carry the curses
Passed down to me by my forefathers.[85]

The Hungarian poet Endre Ady could no longer understand what possessed his friend Goga. During the latter's imprisonment, Ady had sent him letters of support. He had even enraged the Hungarian establishment with his ironic suggestion of simply handing over Transylvania, including his own birthplace of Erdmindszent, to the Romanians – even though he also speculated that they might choke on it.[86] But now that there was a real chance the region might be lost – Goga was even negotiating for it with the Hungarian government – Ady could no longer stand it. 'I cannot bear this nauseous game either as a player or as an onlooker', he wrote in an open letter to Goga in late January 1915, adding with a heavy heart that he could hardly shake his friend's hand any more.[87] Ady had never taken offence at Goga's nationalist poems, but he now argued that in the turbulent modern age, a 'Hungarian man of culture' simply could not act as if it were still the nineteenth century, as if he were a Romanian Déroulède (the French super-patriot) or Garibaldi (the icon of Italian unification).[88] In this passage, Ady first referred to Goga as Romanian and then as Hungarian, thus indicating the boundaries of what he considered possible. Ady's ideal Hungarian state was still a distant dream, but if Transylvania were to pass into Romanian hands, then not only would his friend Goga cease to be a Hungarian, but Ady himself would be forced to abandon his multicultural dream for his native land. 'The nation that can permit itself the luxury of internationalism *today* has won its case', Ady argued.[89] It was unthinkable to him that anyone would be willing to trade one form of state nationalism for another. In the meantime, the Romanian government was stalling. The situation on the Eastern front changed so dramatically in May and June that siding with Russia began to look like a very bad idea.

In the early spring of 1915, prospects had looked much brighter for the Czar's troops. On 22 March, after a siege of several months, they had finally captured Przemyśl, taking more than 100,000 prisoners of war. For Valery Bryusov, who arrived on the scene as a war reporter just a few days after the city fell, it was a crowning moment in Russian military history. Przemyśl would become the jewel in the crown of the new Russian province of Galicia. He was unconcerned about demographics – 44 per cent of the population was Polish and 36 per cent Jewish – nor did it worry him that the Russian positions he had visited were strikingly primitive. But his confidence proved to be severely misplaced. As the prisoners of war, one of whom was the Hungarian poet Géza Gyóni, began their nine-month march to Siberia, the Central Powers prepared for a massive counteroffensive.

Now that the Western front was stable, Germany could spare men and materiel for the Eastern campaign. This was how August Stramm ended up near Gorlice. He scoffed at the Austrians he met there in late April, calling them flabby weaklings unworthy of the name of *Bundesbrüder*, but the determination of his own boys made him glow with an almost fatherly pride.[90] Life there was no bed of roses – despite the sweltering heat, Stramm and his men had to avoid drinking from wells and rivers because of the risks of typhus and cholera – but he felt as strong as an ox. Their full-scale attack began late at night on 1 May, and brought humiliating defeat for the Russians, who resisted with all their strength but had a shortage of guns and ammunition. Russian soldiers often had to wait for one of their brothers-in-arms to die before they could lay claim to a weapon. The Russian army lost more than 400,000 men in Galicia in May.[91] Whatever they could not take with them as they retreated, they set on fire.

On 13 May, Stramm had the first opportunity to catch his breath and write a letter to his wife, full of the same short sentences and exclamations found in his poems. Despite his adrenalin rush and self-confidence, he was often on the verge of tears. Homesickness drove him half-crazy. The fighting went on day and night, leaving Stramm so numbed that he scarcely knew who had been killed and who had not. 'It sometimes surprises you, when you recover consciousness, that you are still alive.'[92] He went through an unforgettable, incomparable sequence of emotions: blind rage, gallows humour, utter panic, and an overpowering instinct to survive. A group of Russians broke through the German lines, and Stramm's major, a close friend, was one of the first casualties. His fury returned: 'shoot, hack, stab, strike'. A half-hour later, every last Russian was dead. He and his brothers-in-arms had taught them the price of taking on Prussian soldiers.[93]

This was just one in a string of successful German military manoeuvres. Gorlice was taken on 2 May. Przemyśl was recaptured on 3 June, and Lemberg on 22 June. On 23 May, Whit Sunday (Pentecost), Anna Akhmatova responded to this tragedy for Russia with the poem 'A Prayer', in which she promised her life and soul if only her beloved country would survive and rise again:

> Give me bitter years of sickness,
> Suffocation, insomnia, fever,
> Take my child and my lover,
> And my mysterious gift of song –
> This I pray at your liturgy
> After so many tormented days,
> So that the stormcloud over darkened Russia
> Might become a cloud of glorious rays.[94]

Nikolay Gumilyov was furious when he read this poem.[95] How could his wife offer up her health, her talents, her child (*their* child), and her lover (Gumilyov himself) for Russia's sake? In their ever-fragile marriage, the poem could have been her revenge for his decision to join the army the year before, which had horrified her. She may have felt that he had already sacrificed their domestic happiness for a higher purpose. But Akhmatova was also sincerely patriotic, willing to offer up a great deal, perhaps everything, for the good of Mother Russia. Her personal bond with her country was so powerful that she was prepared to do penance on its behalf.

By late June, combat had left Stramm utterly drained and more lonely and homesick than ever. Feigning illness so that he would be sent home on leave was beneath his dignity as a German soldier – and as a German poet, he emphasized in a letter to his friends Herwarth and Nell Walden.[96] For months his nerves had been strained to the limit, and there had been no time at all to come to grips with his experiences, he wrote. Nevertheless, he became an increasingly frequent contributor of war poems to the Waldens' Expressionist magazine *Der Sturm*. The July 1915 issue included 'Triebkrieg' (War Instinct), which condensed the most extreme of experiences into the most compact verse to issue from the war.

Eyes flash
Your look cracks
Hot
Streams the bleeding over me
And
Drenches
Runnels of sea.
You flash and flare.
Life forces
Flame
Mildew deludes
And
Knits
And
Knits.[97]

In August, however, Stramm was allowed to spend a few weeks at home. When he returned, he discovered that his company had been almost obliterated near Brest-Litovsk. Only twenty-five soldiers remained; the rest had been either killed or injured. 'Oh, my dear', he wrote to his wife on 18 August, 'it is appalling and yet magnificent'. He told her not to fret about him: 'I am strong and shall return! For certain! How fine it was to spend a little time at home!'[98] These were his last words to his wife. August Stramm died in battle on 1 September.

The collapse of the Russian positions in Galicia was not by any means the only setback for the Allies in 1915. In the Baltics, the German forces took Vilnius on 18 September. On the Western front, the Allies were unable to reap the benefits of Germany's concentration of troops in the east and the north. Despite crippling losses and a massive inflow of materiel, the British and French were unable to break the stalemate. In both the second and third Battles of Artois, the Allies lost two to four times as many soldiers as the Germans, without significantly weakening the enemy positions.[99] The Battle of Loos was especially traumatic; on 25 September, the British were the accidental victims of their own gas attack, blown back onto their trenches by a strong wind. The next day, Britain's Volunteer Army went out to meet the enemy in ten columns of one thousand men each, as if on a parade ground. The Germans could hardly believe their eyes; never before had they been presented with such easy targets. The British were felled by the hundreds. Not until they reached the second, impregnable German line of defence did the survivors begin to turn and flee. Overcome with pity, the Germans stopped shooting. More than 8,000 of the 15,000 infantrymen in the 21st and 24th Divisions were killed or wounded.[100]

Two days later, on 28 September, the Swiss avant-garde poet Blaise Cendrars (1887–1961) lost his right arm in combat at Navarin (in the Champagne region). This earned him a medal ('Although gravely injured … and exhausted from loss of blood, he went on leading his squad in battle, remaining with them until the end of the attack') and, eventually, the French nationality he had coveted for so long.[101] He learned to write with his left hand, and what he wrote included the following passage, which – probably not coincidentally – focuses on the *manual* work of war.

> I've faced the torpedoes, the cannons, the mines, the fire, the poison gas, the machine guns, the whole anonymous, demonic, systematic, blind machine. Now I face a man. An ape like me. Eye for eye, tooth for tooth. It's up to the two of us now. Fists swinging, knives slashing. No mercy. I leap at my opponent, landing a terrific blow. His head's half off his body. I've killed the Kraut. I was sharper and faster than he was. More alert. I struck first. I'm more in tune with reality – I, a poet. I acted. I killed. Like someone who wants to live.[102]

In other parts of the Continent, it was the Germans who were sharper and faster. In October, German and Austro-Hungarian troops and their new Bulgarian allies – led by German General August von Mackensen, who had engineered the victory in Galicia – succeeded where the Austrians had failed so miserably in the summer of 1914, managing to drive back the Serbians. It was a traumatic experience for the dauntless Slavic warriors. In no time, they were beaten back as far as Kosovo. Engaging in combat on that holy ground struck the Serbian commander as a very bad idea,[103] but surrender was not a real option either. The result was a different kind of race to the sea: through neighbouring Montenegro and the inhospitable mountains of Albania, in brutal winter weather, the Serbian army tried to reach the Adriatic coast. Many of the soldiers made this journey with their families and possessions loaded onto wobbling carts. Some 25,000 Austrian prisoners of war were also forced to join the exodus. The Serbians had begun the campaign with 420,000 soldiers; approximately 100,000 were killed or injured, and 174,000 taken prisoner or went missing in action. No other army sustained such heavy losses, relative to its size. The survivors and more than 10,000 horses were evacuated from the coast near Corfu in Allied boats. On 11 April 1916, the first ships began transporting the Serbian soldiers to Thessaloniki, which had been claimed by the British and French as an Allied bridgehead in spite of Greece's neutrality. Their strategic value in that location was very limited, and they paid a heavy price for being there. Ten times as many Allied soldiers in Thessaloniki lost their lives to malaria and other diseases as died in action.[104] For about a year at least, the former child prodigy Milutin Bojić (1892–1917) was one of the survivors.[105] In Corfu, he managed to publish a play he had carried with him throughout the campaign. His poem 'Plava Grobnica' (The Blue Tomb) honoured the memory of his companions whose corpses had been tossed into the sea and torn to shreds by the transport ships. For Bojić, this image symbolized the humiliations that were once again being visited on his nation. But like other war poets, he saw in these sacrifices the seeds of a great future:

> But this graveyard, where the great and terrible
> Secret of our age lies buried in the night
> Soon will be the fount of presaged miracles
> Where the soul will come to seek its guiding light.[106]

The Serbian host had been defeated and uprooted, but its spirit and its backbone remained unbroken. Without fear or protest, it would move on to new graveyards, until it could finally reap its rewards. This is the mournful yet majestic signification of *Pesme bola i ponosa* (Poems of Pain and Pride), the volume of war poetry that Bojić published in Thessaloniki in 1917. Serbian fighters learned his verses by heart, but the success came too late for the poet himself, who died of tuberculosis on 8 November 1917, not long after his twenty-fifth birthday.

The worst disaster to befall the Entente in 1915 occurred not on the Western or the Eastern front, but in Turkey.[107] The Ottoman Empire, enfeebled by earlier Balkan wars, decided that the best defence was a good offence, while their opponents were not averse to opening a new front in the region. The Russians, as noted above, had their eye on Constantinople, and for the Entente it was vital to ensure access to the Black Sea through the Dardanelles Strait. Furthermore, if all went well, the campaign might even draw German troops away from the Western front. The Central Powers hoped that with Romania, Bulgaria and Turkey on their side they could form a powerful bloc in south-eastern Europe, while the British believed that the swift conquest of Constantinople would win those same countries over to the Entente. Turkish naval attacks on Russian ports such as Odessa and Sebastopol, along with the closure of the Dardanelles, very soon made the situation precarious for the Allies, who decided it was time to teach Turkey a lesson. But naval attacks by French and British warships did not achieve the desired results, and landings in April and August proved no more effective. Approximately half a million soldiers died, in roughly equal numbers, on the Turkish and Allied sides. The enormous losses incurred, especially by troops from Australia and New Zealand, fed the flame of national identity in those colonies, putting the British Empire under strain. The best-known literary fatality of this campaign was Rupert Brooke, who came down with dysentery on the way to Gallipoli and died of sepsis. In *The Times*, Winston Churchill predicted that Brooke's war sonnets would inspire thousands of young men. His collection *1914 and Other Poems* was published in June, and over the next ten years more than 300,000 copies were sold.[108]

As the war dragged on and continued to escalate, there was a growing need for more troops. Some aspiring soldiers who had been sent away after their first inspection were welcomed into the army just a few months later – one such case was Guillaume Apollinaire.[109] Born in Rome as Gugliemo Alberto Wladimiro Alessandro Apollinaire de Kostrowitzky, the poet was undeniably unique, and noble blood undoubtedly flowed in his veins, but all that did not make him French. His mother was a Pole from Russia, and not one official document gave the name of his Italian father. As long as millions of 'normal' Frenchmen were volunteering in Paris, the French army had little interest in this foreign mongrel, no matter how celebrated he was in Parisian literary and society life. But in late November 1914, Apollinaire managed to enlist, signing not only a contract with the army but also a fresh application for citizenship. The great champion of Cubism was now a second-class gunner. Of course, his patriotism was not of the traditional variety, but as an eternal outsider he delighted in the army uniform that allowed him to blend into the masses. As a black alter ego put it in his poem 'Les soupirs du servant de Dakar' (The Sighs of the Gunner from Dakar), 'I'm a soldier of France and so they turned me white'.[110] The war and the army had turned Apollinaire into a Frenchman.[111] Meanwhile, his poetry became more playful and self-confident. The propaganda he made was not only for the war, but also for himself and his radical view of literature.[112]

H
A
I L
W O
R LD
WHOSE
ELOQUE
NT TON
GUE I A
M THAT ITS
M O U T H
OH PARIS
STICKS OUT AND
ALWAYS WILL
AT THE
GER MANS

The Eiffel Tower had become a poem, the poem had become a picture, and the combination formed an icon of the proud, modern French nation. And it was not just at the enemy that Apollinaire stuck out his tongue – he treated the entire conflict with the same irreverence. He knew very well that he might not survive, but that was all part of the extraordinary adventure. In 'La nuit d'avril 1915' (April Night, 1915), he said simply, 'We love you oh life and we get on your nerves'.[113] That was how he lived and how he looked at death. But the unhappy conclusion of his love affair with Lou (Louise de Coligny-Châtillon) also played a role. It was partly in haste to turn over a new leaf that Apollinaire volunteered for the front.

That same spring of 1915, Ypres was once again the focal point of heavy fighting on the Western front – a battle that later went down in history as the first to involve the use of poison gas.[114] The German gas attacks provoked outrage, and Berlin launched a propaganda offensive, as it had after the atrocities during the invasion of Belgium and France.[115] Karl Kraus's lucid analysis of earlier war crimes ('If one side claims the other is killing women and children, they will both believe it and do it'[116]) turned out to have considerable predictive power. Despite the profound dismay and rage among the Allies, the British also began using gas barely two weeks later. But on that historic first occasion, at 6 p.m. on 22 April, German soldiers had opened almost 6,000 cylinders of chlorine gas – a line stretching from Steenstrate to Poelkapelle – releasing a green and yellow cloud that spread slowly toward the enemy. The French and Algerian troops had no idea what had hit them. This was genuine asphyxiating gas. Hundreds of panicking soldiers fled the front line in search of oxygen, but oxygen could not heal their corroded lungs. Toward the end, the victims often went into terrible spasms as their faces turned greenish-black and yellow fluid poured out of their mouths. According to the most conservative estimates, 800 to 1,200 men were killed and 2,000 to 3,000 were injured. The Allies and neutral observers were horrified, and the use of gas was added to the list of German war crimes in capital letters. Just a few weeks after this gruesome milestone, poison gas found its way into a poem.[117] In 'Wir müssen', quoted above, Piero Jahier derisively emphasized the cowardliness of this new weapon.

> Fill new cans with brave fragrances
> Boldly pack explosive mixtures
> Compress
> 'IMPERIAL CYLINDERS OF MILITARY ASPHYXIATION'[118]

It would not be the last military innovation to change the face of the war in 1915. Between April and November, in the margins of the Ottoman campaign, Turkish troops systematically murdered more than 600,000 Armenians. Their victims included the leading poets and intellectuals Siamant'o (1878–1915) and Daniel Veroužan (1884–1915). Another half a million Armenians were then deported to Mesopotamia. On the way, many of them died of exhaustion, were shot, or were burned or buried alive. Fewer than half of the 1.8 million Armenians in the Ottoman Empire survived this genocide.[119] Yet the dream of an independent Armenia lived on.

5

A Europe of Words, a Europe of Action: Nationalism and Revolution, 1915–1916

Zoo ver staan we.

– Roughly: 'This is how far we've come.' Flemish soldiers' expression indicating total bewilderment about the progress of the war[1]

Nations may be driven to war by fury or cool-headed calculation, and often by a combination of the two. A state of 'cool-headed fury' may sound somewhat contradictory, but to politicians it comes naturally. They understand that the enemy will do whatever it takes to sabotage their long-term plans, and this knowledge keeps the flames of their hostility burning. The enemy stands in the way of the future – that is what makes him the enemy. Many people in Germany and the Dual Monarchy believed that the future's name was *Mitteleuropa*: a customs union from the North Sea to the mouth of the Danube and from Scandinavia to the Dardanelles that would exert tremendous cultural influence while meeting Germany's burning need for expansion. France and England had amassed their wealth overseas, but Germany intended to build its empire in its own back and front yards.[2] Self-determination for national minorities in the Dual Monarchy had no place in this plan, which was based on the frankly imperialist idea that a large economic area under centralized authority was the *ancien régime*'s best hope for survival in the twentieth century and would serve as a barricade against liberal democracy in the West and pan-Slavism in the East and the Balkans.

Of course, those were precisely the regions that put up the strongest resistance to this proposal. Exiles, irredentists and refugees from the areas threatened by pan-Germanism began a major lobbying campaign to dissuade the Entente from agreeing to peace terms that would allow the Central Powers to carry out any part of the *Mitteleuropa* plan. Their cause was supported by many leading intellectuals, scholars and scientists in England and France. One of this group's chief mouthpieces was the London weekly *The New Europe*, which made its debut in October 1916. Contributors included Tomáš Masaryk, a Czech nationalist who had fled the Dual Monarchy in 1914; Jules Destrée, a socialist in the Belgian parliament; Paul Sabatier, a Nobel Prize–winning French chemist; Peter Struve, a Russian ex-Marxist who had become a liberal politician and journalist; and Ramsey Muir, the British liberal thinker and historian. Their leader was another historian, R.W. Seton-Watson, a leading advocate of national self-determination. Like-minded individuals from Serbia, Italy, Romania and Japan later joined them. In the opening issue, the editors explained that the new Europe for which they strove would be based on 'nationality, the rights of minorities, and the hard facts of geography and economics'.[3] These intellectuals saw it as their duty to lay the groundwork for the postwar peace conferences where Europe's future would be decided. 'After our armies have won the war, our statesmen will have to win the peace.' Nationalist poets such as the Romanian Octavian Goga and the Belgian Émile Cammaerts, who was working in London, also participated in this European think-tank, which was much more than a Sunday debating society. As horrifying as the war was, it provided a historic opportunity to resolve all sorts of political issues at once. If handled properly, the dismantling of the Habsburg Empire could bring freedom to its many national minorities. At the same time, a string of new and old countries – Greece, Bulgaria, Romania, Hungary, Bohemia, Poland and what Seton-Watson was already calling Yugoslavia – could form an ideal buffer between Germany and Russia. There was no talk of independent Baltic states in *The New Europe* – that region still officially belonged to Russia, an Allied power.[4] It would not do to interpret the right of national self-determination too rigidly.

In France, Guillaume Apollinaire responded to the *Mitteleuropa* plans with a mixture of scorn and alarm.[5] They could never truly succeed, he contended, and that was what made them potentially dangerous; if Germany could not have its way, it might try to Balkanize the entire continent, dividing it into so many mini-states that stability would become unattainable. In Austria, anti-German sentiment was growing, along with a desire for peace. Obviously, this tendency did not please Berlin. Instead of loyally declaring his support for the *Mitteleuropa* project, the new Austrian emperor, Charles I, incurred the wrath of his German guardian when he opened his own independent negotiations with the Czechs and the Slavic peoples in the Balkans, protecting his own sphere of influence to Germany's detriment. Meanwhile, Apollinaire concluded that Germany was trying to undermine the Allied vision for Europe by arousing nationalist sentiments among a range of minorities in prison camps and occupied territories, with the goal of weakening Russian sovereignty.[6] It did not seem to Apollinaire that Europe was in need of a new state system.

There were also critics of the *Mitteleuropa* plan within the Dual Monarchy. Although Endre Ady had fallen out with the Romanian poet Octavian Goga, and understood only too well that the right of national self-determination would mean the end of his Transylvanian dream, a future under any form of German authority struck him as much worse still.[7] Nor were the national minorities within the Dual Monarchy necessarily supporters of *Mitteleuropa*. One opponent was the Croatian poet Miroslav

Krleža (1893–1981), born in Zagreb, who knew whereof he spoke.[8] During his studies at an elite military academy in Budapest, the First Balkan War had hit him with the force of a revelation. If little Serbia could fight for its survival, why not Croatia? In a sense, the Second Balkan War answered that question, when the former allies Serbia and Bulgaria betrayed their Pan-Slavic ideals out of cynicism and avarice, squabbling over the spoils of the previous war. In late 1915, Krleža himself was called up for duty in the Austro-Hungarian army, but because of his poor health he only had to serve for two months, behind the front in Galicia. During his journey home, he began to question his own identity:

> In Pest, I thought that I was a European, that things were clear to me, while in fact I'm just as confused as anybody else. Who am I today? Not one of us will raise his voice in the great forums of the slaughterhouse where the true Croatian question is being resolved, and no one will make it clear to the world what is fundamentally at stake. After being so severely tested, we now labour under an even greater burden: uncertainty about our own existence.[9]

Arguments with a Hungarian friend, the *Nyugat* poet Dezső Kosztolányi, made it painfully clear to Krleža what it really meant to belong to a national minority. Kosztolányi liked to rant about the utter bankruptcy of Hungarian culture; no one read any more, and no one had a solid grasp of anything. 'Hungarian Jews alone will ensure the survival of Hungarian literature. Who created the Ady cult? Who reads Babits? Two or three prostitutes – that's what the Hungarian reading public amounts to.'[10] As Krleža discovered, this was the cultural pessimism of the snob whose culture is in no way endangered or oppressed. When he confronted Kosztolányi with the way their fellow citizens, the Ruthenians, were being hung on gallows as traitors at the front, his friend turned out to be a patriot after all: 'If someone has to win this war, I'd prefer it to be my own fatherland!' When Krleža retorted that Kosztolányi was not the only one with a native country – 'we all have one too, we second-class Hungarian citizens, but I would never be able to fight for my country if its cause were unjust' – Kosztolányi had no idea what he was talking about.[11] In the Dual Monarchy, some were more equal than others. Krleža was not eager to see this situation exacerbated by absorption into a kind of Greater Germany. 'We are waging battle like Teutonic hordes, but in fact we are prisoners of war, not even protected by the Geneva Convention – instead we wage war and commit high treason against our own people. If that is not perverse, I do not know what is', he noted in his diary on 15 March 1916.[12] He would have liked to embrace Nietzsche's legacy, but he could not understand how anyone could seriously believe the German propaganda depicting *Mitteleuropa* as the triumph of a unique race. 'What on paper was merely poetic mysticism is now a political tool of the *Junker*, while the rest of Europe, instead of dismissing their ridiculous serial novels as absurd speculations, blithely accepts these (pan-German) absurdities.'[13]

This was indicative of the atmosphere in the Dual Monarchy. Tensions were rising, not only between the national minorities and the Austro-Hungarian majority, but also between leading representatives of that majority. In late 1915, for example, Endre Ady became embroiled in a very revealing conflict with Jenő Rákosi (1842–1928), a well-known critic and the editor-in-chief of *Budapesti Hírlap*, who was one of the most outspoken advocates of the Magyarization of Hungary's minorities.[14] This was essentially a war-fuelled continuation of a debate that had been in progress for almost ten years between, on the one hand, the Jews and radical bourgeois affiliated with the periodical *Nyugat*, who had an urban, cosmopolitan outlook, and, on the other, the traditionalistic nationalists at their conservative counterpart *Új Idők*

(New Times). This time, the confrontation was triggered by a Budapest reprint of Géza Gyóni's patriotic war poems, originally published in Przemyśl in the autumn of 1914. Gyóni had dedicated the book to Rákosi, who wrote a glowing foreword to the new edition, praising not only the patriotism of the soldier-poet but also his fierce attack on effete, pro-Western internationalists. Rákosi's message was obvious: Gyóni not Ady was the true poet of the Hungarian nation. The next step in the conservative campaign was to arrange for Ady to undermine his own credibility. Rákosi had a schoolboy write a letter to Ady asking his opinion of Gyóni. Ady fell into the trap, responding that not even a world war could make a poet out of Gyóni, who was little more than a journalist trying to make easy money from 'this horrible war, which has cost so many lives'.[15] That was all Rákosi needed to caricature his enemy as an otherworldly decadent with the audacity to use a child to disparage a great patriotic poet. The conflict escalated when Rákosi went on to attack Mihály Babits (1883–1941), demanding that he be fired from his job as a teacher. In this case, his ammunition was a poem published in *Nyugat* in August 1915, entitled 'I Played with Her Hand', in which Babits had written that he would take more delight in spilling his blood for the pinky of his beloved than in doing so for a hundred kings and flags. Practically the entire Hungarian cultural world was suddenly expected to take sides. Margit Kaffka and Ignotus were among those who supported Ady and Babits; their opponents were mainly from clerical and nationalist circles. The smear campaign had a real impact: Babits lost his job, although he was allowed to return in late 1916. But he would not be intimidated, and on 26 March 1916 he took advantage of an afternoon benefit for blind soldiers organized by *Nyugat* to read his poem 'Before Easter', which includes the following lines.

I scorn the victor's glorious fame,
the blind hero, the folk-machine,
the one, who spells death wherever he goes,
whose gaze can maim, paralyse the word,
whose touch betokens slavery,
but I'll sing, anyone who may come,

the one, the first, who comes to pronounce the word,
the one, who first will dare to say it aloud,
thunder it, oh fearless, fearless,
that wondrous word, so waited for
by hundreds of thousands, holy,
mankind-redeeming, breath-restoring,
nation-salvaging, gate-opening,
liberating, precious word:
it's enough! it's enough! enough now!

come peace! come peace!
peace, oh peace again!
Let us breathe again![16]

Although this passionate outcry was not in the patriotic spirit that had become *de rigueur*, the Hungarian censors chose not to intervene. Meanwhile, Ady saw the often anonymous attacks on the *Nyugat* poets as proof that the life of the mind was another casualty of the war in Europe. Nearly all his poems from this period urge vigilance, but their dense metaphorical style tends to leave it unclear whether the looming menace is the war, or those whom Ady regarded as enemies of beauty and culture.

O watchmen, keep not the city in vain,
life lives, desires to live
and does not offer up its beauty

to fall before the charge
of bloody and insensate beasts.
How sorrowful is man,
how horrible the animal cries,
but the star-bolting nights
will not let us forget
the fate of man is splendour spun.
You who still stand upon the lonely posts,
O watchmen, keep not the city in vain.[17]

However humanistic the intent of Babits and Ady's appeals to their countrymen, some of their contemporaries interpreted them as defences of the cultural, political and social status quo. More than a few politicians, intellectuals and poets of all stripes saw the war as a way of finally redressing long-standing grievances. Sometimes nationalism and internationalism seemed almost to merge harmoniously in the rhetoric of war. To the formerly anti-militaristic socialist Gustave Hervé, for instance, the French foreign regiments were portents of a bright new future. He considered the French *union sacrée* a pilot project for a *Union Européenne*. In his newspaper *La guerre sociale*, he welcomed the foreign warriors with visionary fire.

Italians, Trente and Trieste are going to come back to their noble Italian fatherland!
Roumanians, your brothers of Transylvania will be given back to you!
Servians, your brothers of Bosnia and Herzegovina and of Croatia are going to be brought to you!
Hungarians, the great dream of Kossuth is going to be realized; Hungary is going to recover its independence with the establishment of a republic!
Czechs of Bohemia, Moravia and Silesia, tomorrow your

> Czechs' republic will be
> established, free from the German yoke you have submitted to for five centuries!
> Poles, Poland has half left its tomb already, and is going to be resuscitated among its dead!
> Jews, I do not know whether Zion will be revived some day; but you have heard the good news. Your brothers are going to receive civil and political equality even in Russia!
> May you prosper, army of the nations! Forward, United States of Europe![18]

This idea of a United States of Europe had been under discussion for some time in the socialist movement,[19] but the war gave it new urgency. Hervé tried to present France's national army as a liberation force for oppressed peoples. After this phase of liberation, Europe would naturally coalesce into a new union.

The radical socialist Dutch poet Herman Gorter (1864–1927) thought this was shockingly naive. In his study *Het imperialisme, de wereldoorlog en de sociaal-democratie* (Imperialism, the World War and Social Democracy, 1915), he suggested that the nation-state was complicit in the ceaseless bloodshed of the war. This was the very essence of imperialism, Gorter emphasized: using the nation as an instrument of economic expansion for the greater glory and, above all, prosperity of its ruling class. Whether the Germans won or the French and British, victory would not automatically bring an end to this imperialist project. The financial interests of the victors would only grow, and that might well expose them to greater risk. At the same time, all the new nation-states would try to accumulate as much capital as possible, plunging the world into new and ever greater wars. The only way to avoid this scenario, Gorter concluded, was the internationalization of capital. A United States of Europe, while preferable to the present situation, was certainly not the path to peace.

> It is said that Leagues of States should be formed. A League of European States. But the interests of Germany, Russia and England are opposed to it. States may join together into leagues: Germany with Central Europe, Germany with Russia (a very real future threat, perhaps immediately after this war), Germany with France, or Germany with England, but it will be to pool their strength, the better to wage War and exploit the weak.[20]

Gorter rejected every argument for world peace, disarmament, pacifism or interstate organizations. Only thoroughgoing internationalism and a world proletarian revolution could call a halt to the fateful march of imperialism. He was not alone in taking this radical position. In mid-March 1915, the Russian socialist Lenin wrote from exile in Switzerland to a Dutch comrade of Gorter's that with the help of a Dutch–German dictionary he had been able to understand 30 to 40 per cent of the *Imperialism* brochure, and he wished to congratulate the author.[21] But Gorter was more than a politician. He poured the same passion – and ideas – into his poetry. In an astonishing adaptation of some of the main themes of the legendary volume *Mei* (May 1889), which had established his name as a (or the) leading Dutch poet, his new, greatly expanded version of the epic poem *Pan* (1916) depicted the fate of fettered humanity:

> The earth was full in the glorious light of May,
> And the surface of the glittering sea was full
> Of their drifting corpses, millions, millions,
> Such as the world had never seen.[22]

Pan went on to describe a world revolution that put an end to the slaughter, but meanwhile, in the world outside the poem, the war raged on. Some socialists were trying to forge new coalitions in an attempt to alter the situation. In the summer of 1914, socialism –

an internationalist ideology at least in theory – had taken a heavy blow as Europe was swept up in the nationalistic frenzy of war and figures like Gustave Hervé instantly metamorphosed into jingoists. Now one strand of the socialist movement was trying to stem the tide of this quasi-socialist chauvinism. In early September 1915, delegations from some ten European countries held a top-secret conference in Zimmerwald, Switzerland. Gorter was not there, but another Dutch poet, Henriëtte Roland Holst (1869–1952), was,[23] along with the radical Swedish poet Ture Nerman (1886–1969). The meeting was not a great success. As the leader of a radical revolutionary group of eight that also included Nerman, Lenin argued for 'transforming the imperialist war into a civil war for socialism'.[24] The others were unwilling to go that far. The closing manifesto rallied the 'Proletarians of Europe' with fiery rhetoric ('Europe is like a gigantic human slaughterhouse'), placing most of the blame for the conflict on imperialism, which it described as 'military dictatorship'. Yet the manifesto did not declare a revolution. It did, of course, call for renewed dedication to the class struggle, but without questioning the legitimacy of the nation-state. The guiding principle it identified was the 'right of self-determination of nations'.[25] This must have warmed the hearts of the Latvians and Poles in Zimmerwald, but it was not nearly enough to appease the radicals. In early 1916, Lenin frankly acknowledged that self-determination, however important it was, was not his top priority, emphasizing 'the necessity of subordinating the struggle for this demand, as well as for all the fundamental demands of political democracy, to the immediate revolutionary mass struggle for the overthrow of the bourgeois governments and for the achievement of socialism'.[26]

The Swedish socialist poet Ture Nerman also hoped that his next collection of poems would bring the world closer to revolution. When a plan to visit the warring countries proved impracticable, he decided to take an imaginary tour of Europe instead and to report on his travels in verse.[27] His itinerary included the Netherlands, where he visited the Peace Palace in The Hague, which – as the title of one poem suggests – had become a 'Ghost Castle'. The poem laments the hypocrisy of all the crowned heads of state and bemedalled diplomats who came to The Hague and orated about peace at richly laden tables, only to go on to orchestrate the greatest catastrophe in history. Yet all was not lost. The Peace Palace was a ghost castle not solely because the peace conferences had ended; for Nerman, it was also a place where the skeletons might soon come out of the closets to torment consciences and incite revolution.

> Corpses are not good stones
> for your glorious towers.
> It is possible that below
> one stone in that heap will soon come loose,
> one corpse out of many,
> but it is a dangerous beginning.
>
> It is possible that late at night
> one corpse will go out to some haunt
> in an alley in Hamburg or Petrograd
> or London to see his friends.
>
> He may ignite the flames of hatred,
> the dangerous dull hatred
> Berlin saw in '48
> and Paris in '11.
>
> You may awaken
> one day, crowned heads,
> in a nation that takes your words
> about a 'war for freedom' seriously.[28]

The rhetoric that had helped to set armies on the march was about to turn against the ruling class, Nerman believed, and a reprise of the French Revolution or those of 1848 would shake the Continent's foundations as never before. But in neutral Sweden, freedom had not yet dawned;[29] the authorities decided not to run any risks with their radical socialists, and in March 1916, Zeth Höglund (1884–1956), who had accompanied Nerman to Zimmerwald, was arrested and sentenced to three years in prison for high treason.[30] In his cell, he wrote *Bläck och blod* (Ink and Blood), another volume that used poetry to foment revolution: 'I am starting to believe that only blood, lead, / and iron, and not words, can build a new age.'[31] Although these poets were anti-militaristic and vehemently opposed to the war, it would be a definite mistake to call them pacifists. Even though they would never lay down their lives for imperialism, it was clear that their revolution would not be a peaceful affair.

In Switzerland, another neutral state, the French poet Pierre-Jean Jouve – who was rapidly radicalizing – speculated in his four-part poem 'Á la Belgique' (To Belgium), written in January 1916, that the revolution might begin in the downtrodden country of Belgium. Since the start of the war, propaganda poets had praised Belgium as a model state, but Jouve had a different perspective. As he saw it, there was little love lost between the devout firebrands of Flanders and their jovial neighbours in Wallonia. The rich exploited the poor; the authorities exploited the masses. Nonetheless, Belgium had been a peaceful place where life was good, a genuine home for its people. Now that its throat had been slit, Jouve wrote, now that the vulgar bitch of war was prostituting humanity for her own amusement, and now that those who claimed to be prosecuting the war in God's name had covered themselves with shame and guilt, perhaps the butchered country could become the cradle of revolution.[32]

Other socialists were less optimistic. Adama van Scheltema

(1877–1924), perhaps the most popular socialist poet in the Netherlands, was thrown into a profound crisis by the war and found it difficult to see any silver lining: 'My own world is passing away – / Is what I have gained so much more beautiful?'[33] A deep longing for peace and quiet came over him, probably brought on by concerns about his personal financial well-being in the unpredictable war years.[34] Suddenly, revolution seemed more like a nightmare than a fantasy.

Albert Verwey did not think in those terms; analyzing the situation as rationally as possible, he concluded in August 1915 that the war would inevitably lead to revolution. Europeans were still inspired by the 'dream of a free human community' kindled by the French 'national structure', and there would be no stopping them. Characteristically, Verwey then moved directly to the subject of poetry: 'Precisely in a time of misery and dire need, the dreams of the poets may have the power to draw people out and inspire them to action.' He pointed to the example of the Italian revolutionary Cola Di Rienzo, under whose regime poetry (Verwey was probably thinking of Petrarch) was, for a time, transformed into action.[35]

There was no direct connection, of course, but the first European revolution to take place during the war was in a country where writers and poets played a uniquely central role in politics. Yet it was not the kind of social revolution Verwey had in mind, but one that showed once again how attached Europeans were to their 'national structure'. In late April 1916, Dublin became the scene of the Easter Rising, a revolt against the British crown with the aim of independence for Ireland.[36] The name 'Easter Rising' suggests a mass insurrection of devout Irish Catholics who, with a fitting sense of drama and symbolism, chose Easter as the time to end the British occupation and put a stop to the senseless slaughter of Irish boys on the battlefields of France and Belgium. But in reality, the uprising began on Easter Monday, 24 April, when the average Dubliner took advantage of the public holiday to go to the horse races. The group of Irish Volunteers who marched to the General Post Office on O'Connell Street consisted of barely more than a hundred men, and in the preceding months the British army had easily recruited three times as many Irishmen as did the Irish nationalists. The rebels were defeated in less than a week. Fourteen days later, fifteen leaders and purported leaders of the Rising had been put to death for high treason, and more than 1,500 prisoners had been sent to jails on the far side of the Irish Sea. Yet despite its apparent failure, this 'poets' rebellion' sent political ripples far and wide.[37] Although the Easter Rising had won little sympathy and even less active participation, the leaders so mercilessly killed by the British were revered as martyrs by their countrymen. Tom Kettle believed that the Easter rebels had spoiled the dream of Irish independence, but he also sensed a fundamental shift in Ireland's political climate and prophesied that they would go down in history as heroes and martyrs, while he himself would 'go down – if I go down at all – as a bloody British officer'.[38]

At least five of the executed men had some reputation as a poet. This group also included three of the seven signatories of the 'Proclamation of the Irish Republic' – Patrick Pearse (1879–1916), Thomas MacDonagh (1878–1916) and Joseph Plunkett (1887–1916). As good romantic nationalists, schooled in Celtic literature and mythology by the Gaelic League, they sincerely believed in the power of their words to bridge the past and future. To quote a poem by MacDonagh printed in the *New York Times* on 7 May in the major article 'Poets Marched in the Van of Irish Revolt':

> But his songs new souls shall thrill
>   The loud harps dumb
> And his deeds the echoes fill
>   When the dawn is come.[39]

The information in the article was provided by Padraic Colum (1881–1972), an Irish poet who sympathized with the republican cause, and rather than 'On a Poet Patriot', he told the newspaper that this poem was called 'Of a Poet Captain' – an interesting mistake, which suggests just how intertangled nationalism, poetry and militarism had become in the minds of these writers. The true avant-garde reasoned that even if they only represented a tiny fraction of the population, they were leading the Irish into the future. Their words would transform into action and change history.

A few months before the Easter Rising, Eoin MacNeill, a professor of medieval history and the true leader of the Volunteers, had written an article emphasizing that Ireland was not the 'poetical abstraction' of the country's popular patriotic literature and that there was no chance of a revolution succeeding unless it resulted from widespread popular discontent. That condition had not yet been met, he wrote, and so any speculation about a revolt was utterly baseless. But the Irish Republican Brotherhood, a splinter group within the Volunteers, saw things differently. It was not that they believed the masses were behind them. On the way to the Post Office, the socialist leader James Connolly said in so many words that they had no chance of success and would undoubtedly be massacred. Their decision to continue all the same had everything to do with their firm belief that their sacrifice would turn a literary myth into a reality. Although Connolly was not a practising Catholic, he had argued in an editorial in the *Worker's Republic* that February that 'without the shedding of Blood there is no Redemption'.[40]

This opinion was gaining currency elsewhere in Europe, too. Its most obvious manifestation was the war itself, but bloody self-sacrifice was also wholeheartedly espoused by the anti-war revolutionaries who opposed their countries' policies. When this attitude combined with nationalist ambitions, sparks flew.

Ireland would soon be 'West Britain' no longer, but a Gaelic nation reborn, Padraic Colum wrote in his foreword to *Poems of the Irish Revolutionary Brotherhood* (1916), an anthology combining the work of the executed poet-rebels with 'The Song of Red Hanrahan', an older poem by William Butler Yeats (1865–1939).[41] This volume also included two poems by Sir Roger Casement (1864–1916), a world-famous diplomat and Irish nationalist. Three days before the Rising began, Sir Roger had been put ashore by a German submarine in Tralee Bay, in the west of Ireland. The day before that, a ship with 20,000 German guns and ammunition had arrived in the same place, but before it could be unloaded, it was intercepted by the Royal Navy, and the captain saw no alternative to scuttling the ship and its cargo. If the Irish revolutionaries had ever truly hoped to succeed, this setback would surely have convinced them to put their plans on hold. Casement certainly thought that would be prudent, but before he could make contact with the revolutionary leaders, he was arrested. After his trial, a high-profile media event, he was hanged on 3 August for high treason. In the light of his prolonged, detailed negotiations with Germany in the middle of a world war, this sentence was not disproportionate. But considering the outcry over the earlier executions and the many requests for a pardon from prominent figures around the world, the British took a grave political risk by carrying out the sentence. Although Casement was not directly involved in the Easter Rising, he became its sixteenth martyr. In his poem 'Sixteen Dead Men', Yeats would insightfully comment that the dead men remained 'loitering there / To stir the boiling pot'.[42] While Yeats was often absorbed in esotericism, the historical significance of the Rising was not lost on him. In his great elegy 'Easter, 1916', he foresaw that nothing would ever be the same again.

I write it out in a verse –
MacDonagh and MacBride
And Connolly and Pearse
Now and in time to be,
Wherever green is worn,
Are changed, changed utterly:
A terrible beauty is born.[43]

Despite its cruelty and horror, violence could give birth to beauty. This message struck a chord with many on the Continent – though certainly not with everyone. On 26 April, a London correspondent for the Dutch daily newspaper *NRC* submitted an article insisting that the revolutionaries were 'people with wild ideals ... opinions utterly divorced from reality, the progeny of a wicked past, out of place in this century'.[44] Opinions on that last point diverged radically, however. All over Europe, small groups were becoming convinced that ideals were not enough – action was what made a difference, especially violent action.

In Flanders, the young activist poet Gaston Burssens (1896–1965) also appears to have reached that conclusion. In any case, he had given up on obedience to authority. The Belgian government-in-exile in Le Havre had declared it illegal to study at the University of Ghent, which had been transformed into a Dutch-language institution by the occupying power, but that did not stop Burssens. What was truly illegitimate – a student's desire to be taught in his mother tongue or the government that denied its citizens that right? But Burssens's political engagement went beyond that. In his poem 'Sir Roger Casement' (1916), he made a direct connection between idealism and the very real sacrifices it sometimes inspired: 'The steel of every sacred resolution / reflects the blind, incisive leer of death.'[45] Death 'leers' – idealism may or may not cost you your life, but death is always lurking in the shadows. Its 'blind, incisive' expression says something about the cruelty and injustice of life; death (justice?) makes no distinction between opportunists and idealists. But death may not be the only blind one here. In the second part of the poem, Casement himself speaks. He is blameless, he says, because he did all he could and was true to what he believed. 'I sail in the full sunlight now / toward death.'[46] This 'full sunlight' casts a special glow on his life and ambitions, but the full light of the sun can also make it impossible to see exactly what you are doing. This is another of the sacrifices every idealist makes: when ideals are brought into the real world, something real must inevitably be sacrificed, namely the people and institutions that disagree with the ideal.[47] They must be put out of commission – eliminated, physically or otherwise. By this stage of the war, activists were prepared to take that step. Burssens's contemporary Van Ostaijen seemed to be thinking along the same lines in 1916, in a poem that envisioned a reprise of the sacrifice with which the Flemish had won the legendary Battle of the Golden Spurs in 1302:

> But nineteen hundred and sixteen
> still (onward we go)
> will (row upon row)
> see the active army grow
> in will and action, marching on,
> backs bent and fists clenched, striking their foe
> and the night; the day breaks through the dawn.
> Nineteen hundred and sixteen, year that became word,
> word that became flesh,
> army of our land,
> guardian deed to guardian word and hand.
> Resolute, we stand
> in our struggle. We stand.[48]

Even if intended purely metaphorically, the bellicose imagery is revealing. Political adversaries are now the 'foe', activists form an 'active army', and that army will march, 'row upon row', to its 'struggle'. The mythology and ultimate objective of the poem are more or less the same as those of the Irish Republican Brotherhood; the word becomes flesh and that flesh forms an army of independence, ready to make 'our land' an independent state.

The main difference between the Irish and Flemish nationalists was that the latter did not yet have their own martyrs. Flemish boys were constantly dying at the front, of course, and under the most horrifying conditions, but the same could be said of the Irish soldiers in the British army, and their sacrifice had not pushed their island to the brink of revolution. The best-known candidate for Flemish martyrdom was the poet René De Clercq, who had been fired from his job as a secondary school teacher by royal decree after ignoring a request from Prosper Poullet, the Belgian Minister of Science and Fine Arts, to resign from the editorial board of the activist newspaper *De Vlaamsche Stem*. The Flemish nationalists were outraged that the Belgian authorities would deprive De Clercq of his livelihood, regarding it as further evidence that the Belgian authorities saw the Flemish as second-class citizens. De Clercq himself responded with a series of battle songs – collected in *De noodhoorn* (The Alarm, 1916) – that combine a sense of moral outrage with an unambiguously threatening tone. If the king allowed this sort of thing to continue, De Clercq warned, then the Flemish would rise up and demand self-rule.

> Can the King, *our* King, not know
> His captive people's suffering?
> If Flanders cannot be our own,
> Then from its shield the Lion will spring!
> For without rights, I have no land,

And without bread, I fear no brand,
Flanders, Flanders, with heart and hand,
I stand before you,
Fighting for you![49]

De Clercq became a model for younger poets. In a poetic homage that appeared in the activist magazine *Ons Land* (Our Country) in June 1916, Burssens described him 'as a man of words and action / standing firm / girded for battle'.[50] At least one thing was clear: for the new generation of Flemish idealists, words were not enough. At the front, they had learned the meaning of self-sacrifice. There too, the Flemish were becoming more radical. They no longer took it for granted that fighting and dying selflessly for King and Country was the right thing to do. Respect for Flemish language and culture seemed the least their country could offer them in return.

For the most part, however, they were not granted that respect, which led to growing resentment, especially among the soldiers who belonged to the Flemish elite. Other armies dealt with comparable issues in very different ways. The British army had separate regiments for different regions, so that English, Scottish, Welsh and Irish troops all fought in their own homogeneous units. In the Dual Monarchy, commanders were expected to speak the language of the troops – or languages, if the regiment was multilingual. The Austro-Hungarian army also had ethnically defined units: Krleža, for instance, served with other Croatians. Within the Russian army there were Czechoslovak legions composed of ethnic Czechs and Slovaks who lived on Russian soil, along with a growing number of Czech and Slovak deserters from the Austro-Hungarian forces. By fighting alongside the Russians, these defectors hoped to win the favour of the Entente so that they would be permitted to secede from the Habsburg Empire after the war. Among those who went over to the Russian side were the Slovak poet Janko Jesenský and the Czech poet Rudolf Medek (1890–1940), the first after deserting and the second after being taken prisoner by the Russians. In '1914', Medek looked back on the day he had seen Austrian troops arrive in his Czech village as the low point of his existence. What an insult the Austrian marching music had been, and how humiliated the Czechs had felt when they were expected to sing along with the imperial anthem. In every 'farewell' uttered by a Czech man leaving for the front, the poet heard a despairing 'why?'[51] The Czech units would avenge this disgrace while fighting for the freedom of their nation.

The Russians also allowed some of their national minorities, such as the Latvians, to form units of their own. Russian army commanders had understandable misgivings about this idea, but the Latvians' exceptional fighting spirit and pronounced hatred of all things German finally won them over.[52] When the Germans menaced the Baltic region in the spring of 1915, occupying some areas, the Latvian poet Rainis sounded the alarm from his exile in Switzerland:

> We are in the greatest danger, and all of our people should defend themselves and help the Russian army; for all of us are aware that we shall persist against the unsystematic attempts of Russification but not against the systematic Germanization, as it is practised in Belgium. Against the burning out of the whole land, against the slaughter and expulsion of the whole population, we, as a small nation, shall not persist.[53]

While the Germans were clever enough to speak Latvian with the locals, the inflexible Russians responded in precisely the opposite way, coming down just as hard on those who spoke Latvian as on those who spoke German. They had no idea how much good will they were throwing away. The Latvians wanted their own Baltic regiments and, if at all possible, autonomy within the Russian

Empire. The Czar had no intention of granting the latter request, but in the summer of 1915, he gave them their regiments, commanded by Latvian officers speaking Latvian. Rainis understood that this was a historic achievement: 'If this time is slept away we shall sleep not hundreds but thousands of years.'[54] And the Latvians answered the call. In no time, 130,000 soldiers had volunteered, and they managed to stop the Germans from entering Riga. Meanwhile, in his poem 'Latvyu bataljonem' (The Latvian Batallions), the revolutionary poet-soldier Kārlis Skalbe (1879–1945) made it absolutely clear that these warriors were not simply fighting for the Russians:

> We stand, like mighty oaks, to guide
> Our people ever on.
> Latvia's battalions, full of pride,
> Will one day claim their crown.[55]

And that may have been one important reason why the Belgian army kept its multilingual battalions. Depending on the battlefield situation, Flemish regiments could otherwise have joined forces with the enemy and fought for their independence. That scenario was not entirely hypothetical. In the summer of 1916, after yet another military triumph that had cost the lives of thousands of Poles, Commander Józef Piłsudski had demanded that the Central Powers guarantee Poland's independence, and to add weight to his request, he had tendered his resignation. Germany conceded, allowing the establishment of the Regency Kingdom of Poland, although it remained to be seen whether this was a truly autonomous country or merely a puppet regime. This turn of events only reinforced the hopes and determination of Flemish activists and front-line soldiers. Apparently, change really was possible.

This was how far Europe had come. While the carnage continued to escalate on the war's several fronts, poets, diplomats and politicians dreamed of new state structures. The most important step toward preventing future wars was thought by some to be the integration of as many countries as possible into a pan-Germanic or liberal economic union. Radical socialists, in contrast, saw anti-imperialism as the strongest basis for a League of Nations, because it seemed to them that the formation of large economic blocs only led to still larger wars. Many other observers believed that division was a precondition for union. They argued that new countries should be founded for all the peoples who felt oppressed in Europe's various empires. Nationalist sentiments like these were prevalent far beyond the Austro-Hungarian Empire. The Baltic peoples, Finns and Ukrainians in Russia, the Irish in Great Britain, and the Flemish in Belgium were counting on the war to expand their rights or even bring self-rule. Their discourse of liberty was buttressed by great humanistic or liberal ideals, but when push came to shove, their loyalty had to be bought with political guarantees.

6

Writing Poetry After Verdun and the Somme: The Battles of 1916

Just eaten my last orange. I am looking at a sunlit picture of hell.
– Siegfried Sassoon, diary entry, 1 July 1916[1]

'According to popular belief, cannon shot attracts clouds', Virginie Loveling (1836–1923) wrote in her war diary on Saturday, 9 January 1915. War brings rain – so it was in the Great War, and so it had been in the nineteenth century. The memory of this grande dame of Flemish literature went back a long way: 'Walking along the canals, struggling against the wind, I remember that in 1870, during the Battles of Gravelotte and Sedan, it rained as hard as this, and those who recalled the Battle of Waterloo told us that during the fighting, from the sixteenth to the eighteenth of June 1815, there had been a veritable deluge.'[2] Among historians there was a growing consensus that weather conditions had played a decisive role in war – not just at Waterloo, but in many land and sea battles.[3] Be that as it may, from 1914 to 1918, the weather and the war gods seemed virtually inseparable. No other factor shaped the experience of the Western front as profoundly or exhaustively as the pounding rain, which made a swampy mess of the landscape and had a similar effect on morale. Rain and sludge form the central theme of the war books *Le Feu* (*Under Fire*, 1917) by Henri Barbusse and *Undertones of War* (1928) by Edmund

Blunden, and are ever present in poems by soldiers who fought in France and Flanders.[4] 'All winter there was rain', begins a 1916 poem by Marc de Larreguy de Civrieux (1895–1916).

> My God, the sky was gloomy
> All winter there was rain
> again and again, again and again.[5]

In the French, the similarity of the words *plus* ('more, again') and *plu* ('rained') heightens the drenched feeling.

If the rain had meant a quicker end to the war, the soldiers might have gladly put up with it. But it bogged down all the belligerent nations equally, only compounding the general misery and never decisively affecting the odds of victory. After a year and a half of conflict, the rainfall had created a uniquely powerful metaphor for the situation at the front: the war had become a quagmire. Yet stagnation never leads to victory. The attacks had to go on, even though they rarely if ever yielded significant territorial gains. Meanwhile the fatalities mounted – in 1915, 349,000 French fighters died, including almost a quarter million in the Battles of Artois and Champagne[6] – but the lines were not significantly weakened. So in 1916 the armies changed tactics. The objective was no longer to capture territory but to kill as many enemy soldiers as possible. As the German chief of staff Erich von Falkenhayn wrote around Christmas 1915, 'Within our reach behind the French sector of the Western front there are objectives for the retention of which the French General Staff would be compelled to throw in every man they have. If they do so the forces of France will *bleed to death*.'[7] The war of position thus became a war of attrition.

The place chosen by von Falkenhayn was Verdun, and his offensive, codenamed *Gericht* ('judgement' or 'place of execution'), began at 7 a.m. on 21 February with a bombardment that did not end until nine hours later. After two days the French divisions defending Verdun had already lost more than 10,000 of their 26,523 soldiers.[8] Yet the troops were not exhausted by the offensive, because General Pétain introduced the 'noria' system, in which divisions were rotated constantly like the beads of a rosary. The advantage was that French soldiers were only briefly exposed to the worst of the fighting. The disadvantage was that almost all of them were exposed to it. By the end of June 1916, sixty-five of the ninety-five French divisions available had already been through Verdun – invariably coming out much smaller than they went in.

Compared to the number of vehicles required to bring a division to the battlefield, only half as many were generally needed to carry it away. In other words, every rotation in Verdun halved the number of soldiers in a division. 'That's not an army any more, it's a bunch of cadavers', said a passer-by who saw one division being withdrawn.[9] Around Verdun, the kind of fighting one generally associates with war took place only rarely. For the most part, the soldiers were cannon fodder. The French and Germans fired 140,000 shells at one another – each day. Every fourteen seconds a new truck carried munitions down the main French supply road, which Maurice Barrès dubbed the Voie Sacrée in one of his countless odes to the war.

Among the gunners was the Breton lawyer Albert-Paul Granier (1888–1917). For the first four days of the battle, from 21 to 24 February, he worked on a poem between bombardments. 'L'attaque' (The Attack) is both a dispassionate account of the minor inconveniences resulting from enemy fire (a soldier is forced to eat snow or, more precisely, to go in search of white, uncontaminated snow after his canteen is shot to pieces and the gas drives him half-mad with thirst) and a hopeless attempt to counterbalance the violence with imagination and wit. One gunner points out in a conversation with his captain that the continual gunfire shows no sense of rhythm. The timpanist should tune his instruments and focus on the 'la' sound of the thunder. But again and again, reality intervenes. Harmony and orchestration of any kind are impossible, because not one messenger has returned and no one has the slightest idea what is going on.[10] That sense of utter disorientation was fundamental to life in the Verdun front lines. The channels of communication were constantly being broken, and soldiers often felt they had been abandoned to their fate. They subsisted on bread and cheap wine. Although there seemed to be more than enough water – during this battle, again, the rain never stopped – all the water reservoirs (that is, bomb craters) had corpses floating in them, the entire battlefield reeked of rot and decay and there were rats and bugs everywhere. The living and the dead were stuck in the sludge together, for reasons no one could understand. Verdun put the 'mud' into 'muddling through'.

On the other side of No Man's Land, Anton Schnack (1892–1973) developed a wholly original poetic form to convey his experiences: protracted, epic sonnets full of pathos, their meandering, complex sentences laden with apocalyptic detail, both hyperrealistic and mythical, like a moralizing nightmare. The soldiers in Verdun were experiencing a daily assault on their persons and their senses for which no human being could possibly be prepared. Schnack tried especially hard to find words for the almost constant din of battle: the explosions, the violent screams, the bowels of the earth rumbling, 'as though a great mouth were calling out in its sleep'. But there were also unexpected moments of silence, unsettling portents of new calamities. 'Then a grenade fell into the trench; it hit sleeping men.'[11] Schnack never evades the central issue. 'There was much death', he remarks laconically in 'Ein Tag' (A Day at Verdun), 'but who cares about death any more', when it had become as common as day-old bread? 'Everything passes; only death remains.'[12] Always death is lurking, poised to strike, standing straight ahead and taunting you, or deviously stabbing you in the back. Its nearness turns the soldiers pale. They lose their souls, their faith, and time and again, their lives. To escalate the violence, to sow still more death and horror, not only to bleed the adversary to death but also to burn him alive, the army in Verdun used flamethrowers on a large scale for the first time. Afterwards, Schnack looked back in astonishment at the almost sensuous way he had literally sown death and destruction with his hand grenades:

> … that I threw death, laughing, malicious, into the tumult,
> booming under smoke and soot, bellowing after the gas,
> which was already far away, already to the north; that I threw
> it in an arc, skilfully, ten times, still more often, faster
> toward their blue weariness … oh why wasn't that time more
> sacred, more divine, brighter, more aglow with love, brotherly
> kiss, humility, dream depths, how could I forget myself so
> horribly in darkness and death?
> Oh, that I threw death like a happy game, like a stone at
> yellow birds, at their storm, lost, magnificent, wild,
> with a light touch, curious, delighted when I hit the mark,
> when I saw them tossed into the air like fish and falling on their
> backs
> with suddenly outstretched hands, groaning, soundless,
> heavy, collapsing in the red smoke of their young blood, to go on
> playing with life[13]

His shame was undoubtedly sincere, but so was his excitement. The war was an orgy – of violence, but also of spectacular lights and sounds, which in those days before Hollywood held a certain magic for receptive observers. And no poet was more receptive to that magic than the co-founder of modern French poetry, Guillaume Apollinaire. 'How lovely all these flares are', he wrote in 'Merveille de la Guerre' (Wonder of War), yet he was not blinded by their beauty.

> [. . .] it would be finer still if there were still more of them
> And yet I see them as a beauty who offers herself and immediately swoons away
> I seem to be at a great feast lighted *a giorno*
> A banquet that earth offers herself
> Hungrily she opens her long pale mouths
> Earth is hungry and here is the feast of this cannibal Balthazar[14]

While the spectacle could offer its human observers temporary transcendence or numbing amazement, in this show they would never be anything more than expendable extras. Higher forces were at work, exploiting both the pageant and the participants to feed their own insatiable appetites. In wartime, there could be no art for art's sake. Chance beauty was a by-product of war, like lice.

Combat could drive men mad with fear but could also induce ecstasy. Thousands of young men discovered the practical meaning of the will to power described by Nietzsche. Power over life and death was in their hands. They had the right – no, the obligation – to transgress the moral boundaries of bourgeois society. Or, as August Stramm had put it in a letter written early in the war, 'Killing is duty is heaven is God'.[15]

Peter Baum, the German poet who had met Apollinaire in Berlin as recently as 1913, had a very different wartime duty. While he too saw and described the fireworks over the battlefield, he was a stretcher-bearer, more often focused on the ground at his feet. 'Many an arm is missing its body', he remarked tersely in one of his *Schützengrabenverse* (Trench Poems).[16] In the late afternoon of 5 June 1916, he was digging graves for the soldiers killed that day when a piece of shrapnel hit him. He just barely lasted the night, dying early the next morning.[17]

Meanwhile, Paul Samuleit reported that Western culture was thriving, with a flood of poems to match the supply of munitions, and morale was unbroken. Samuleit, headmaster at a secondary school in Berlin, noted to his satisfaction in March 1916 that the fourth war-bond drive had been a great success and that the Prussian minister of culture had been shown that the war was by no means leading to neglect of young people or to delinquency. In fact, even the smallest children seemed aware not only of the war's importance, but also of its value. For decades, the German people had made a priority of their own *Bildung* (self-cultivation), ruthlessly pulling weeds and making the most of valuable seeds.[18] In this campaign to uplift the nation, literature had always played a central role, but even so, vigilance was called for. Weeds can take root anywhere. The published version of Samuleit's report to the Zentralstelle zur Bekämpfung der Schundliteratur (Central Office for Combating Trash Literature) includes long lists of banned books: adventure and mystery novels, questionable books for children and young adults, pornographic writing (including works of a 'medical nature'), and even 'dubious patriotic publications' (such as *Mit den Türken zum Suezkanal*; 'With the Turks to the Suez Canal').[19] These lists, signed by generals and police officers, do not include poetry, but that does not mean it went uncensored.[20] Any piece of writing that had anything to do with war or the army – and, most emphatically, anything that might disturb the *Burgfriede*, Germany's version of the *union sacrée* – had to be vetted prior to publication. In Berlin alone, more than 250 civil servants were working full-time in the censorship office to enforce such rules. Anyone flouting them received a reprimand and a black mark on their record. Repeat offenders could even be stripped of their right to publish. In September 1915, for instance, Wilhelm Herzog was forced to stop producing his magazine *Das Forum*. His advocacy of 'rootless aestheticism or Europeanness' had been interpreted abroad as a sign of German disunity and hence of weakness. According to the censor, it therefore bordered on high treason, and Herzog should be grateful merely to be barred from publishing. The poem 'An Deutschland' (To Germany) by the radical left-wing expressionist Johannes R. Becher (1891–1958) was banned by the censor in 1915. In all probability, no more than a glance at the opening couplet ('Germany, land of drudges mashed to a pulp / Rich in barbarians, stinking blood-shit-empire'[21]) was needed to decide that these lines would not be conducive to national unity and fighting spirit. But overly vivid or moralistic descriptions of what took place at the front were also prohibited. The censors did not lift the ban on Schnack's poem 'Verdun' until 1919. It may have scored poorly in all the above respects.

> Uncanny, never seen before, full of cruelty; in its skies strings of
> fire, streamers of smoke, white arrow lines, a greenish glow;
> Its name: agony, bleeding-to-death, a thousand forms of death, a
> running sore, place of murder, grave, butchery, evil labyrinth;
> Sent up from way behind their targets, on winter nights,
> monstrous, crazy, infamous, rumbling, full of ice and wind
> And with no moon, suddenly fired upon by the candles sticking
> up out of the woods, big, ponderous, brutal;
> Drowned by big guns, old-fashioned, powerful, never-ending;
> smothered with a pall of fire, sulphur, gas, and chlorine,
> By the stench of the dead, by portents and thunderbolts, gold and
> night, by fragments of clouds, great fountains of explosions[22]

And then the summer came, but the rain continued. On 8 and 9 July, the young English officer Siegfried Sassoon (1886–1967) described in his diary how everyone had spent the night in the wet, muddy trenches, soaked to the skin.[23] There was a major offensive on the Somme planned for 29 June, but three days of pouring rain from 26 to 28 June necessitated a 48-hour delay.[24] From 24

June to the start of the attack on 1 July, the British artillery fired more than one and a half million shells at German positions. The explosions could be heard on the far side of the English Channel. This unprecedented barrage indicated how much was at stake in the coming battle. Nevertheless, some brigadier generals tried to convince their troops that it would be a cakewalk for the infantry: 'You will be able to go over the top with a walking stick, you will not need rifles. When you get to Thiepval you will find the Germans all dead, not even a rat will have survived.'[25] Not everyone felt reassured by this pep talk. A few days before the attack, the Scottish poet Ewart Alan Mackintosh (1893–1917) pictured how the bagpipes would stop playing among the 'broken regiments': 'Between the battered trenches their silent dead will lie.'[26] Sassoon tried to show a brave face, bragging in his poem 'Before the Battle' on 25 June that he had no need to pray to dispel his fears, but the italicized closing line shows that he knew better: '*O river of stars and shadows, lead me through the night.*'[27] William Noel Hodgson also asked for help in saying

> good-bye to all of this; –
> By all delights that I shall miss,
> Help me to die, O Lord.[28]

Hodgson was one of the 19,240 fatalities on the British side that first day of July – the largest massacre in their history. Including the wounded, the British suffered 57,470 casualties on the Somme that day. The dead included the poets Henry Field, Alfred Victor Ratcliffe, Alexander Robertson, John William Streets, Gilbert Waterhouse and Bernard White.[29] The German defensive line proved to have stood up to the bombardment much better than expected, and the British attackers went like lambs to the slaughter.

On 18 July, Second Lieutenant Ford Madox Hueffer arrived on the Somme with his regiment. Certain that his final hour was near, he wrote a farewell letter to his two daughters: 'I am just going up to the firing line – so that seems a proper moment to write to you both – though I do not seem to have much to say – Or rather, I have so much that it wd. be no use beginning.'[30] But because of his age, Hueffer was positioned just behind the front line; on 28 July he reported that the incessant noise of the bombardments had become a kind of ongoing background drone, 'so continuous that one gets used to it, as one gets used to the noise in a train and the ear picks out the singing of the innumerable larks'.[31] Less than twenty-four hours later he was knocked to the ground by an exploding shell. His teeth and his brains were thoroughly rattled, and for a while he suffered memory loss. For the first thirty-six hours after the incident, he could not even remember his own name. For the rest of his life, he searched for a literary form to capture the panic that seized him when he awoke from the dead.[32]

In September, following his recovery, Hueffer was stationed near Ypres. Alongside his military duties, he tried to take on more assignments for the official British information service. The result of this attempt, 'A Day of Battle', went unpublished. 'I have asked myself continuously', he complained in this essay, 'why I can write nothing – why I cannot even think anything that to myself seems worth thinking – about the psychology of that Active Service of which I have seen my share. Any why cannot I even evoke pictures of the Somme or the flat lands round Ploegsteert.'[33] In fact, he was capable of visualizing those scenes, 'but, as for putting them into words! No: the mind stops dead.' The prolific Hueffer, who had once found it easy to produce up to twenty pages a week, no longer had words for what occupied his mind. He thoroughly appreciated the historic importance of the events he had been through – 'a million men, moving one against the other and impelled by an invisible moral force into a Hell of fear that surely cannot have had a parallel in this world' – but that was as far as words would take him. 'There we were, those million men, forlorn, upon a raft in space.'[34] Two years earlier, in 1914, he had not yet been able to write a war poem, because he could not picture the war itself. But now he had seen too much, more than he could combine into a meaningful whole. This was his greatest challenge as a writer after experiencing the First World War directly: to give meaning to the indescribable events that had played out before his eyes. The few poems Hueffer wrote in the summer and autumn of 1916 were, in that regard, not terribly ambitious. In 'Nostalgia' he interwove the violence of war with memories of romantic outings in the British countryside, while 'A Solis Ortus Cardine' was intended as a fitting farewell to dead comrades.[35] For the time being, there was no way he could give meaning to it all.

Those who had not experienced the bloodbath for themselves and had to rely on the newspapers for information were not usually anywhere near as troubled by such issues. For many of them, the war was still a clash of good and evil. Who had the time for shades of grey? 'Despite fierce resistance from the Germans, the battle is proceeding satisfactorily', both the conservative newspaper *Le Figaro* and the leftist *Le Petit Parisien* declared on 2 July, relying on British sources.[36] In another front-page article, they noted the capture of 3,500 German soldiers; as ever, they made no mention of Allied losses. In the weeks that followed, these newspapers reported a string of triumphs, while cautioning that a decisive victory was not yet in sight. The tone and purpose of war journalism had not changed in any fundamental way since August 1914. Maintaining the unity of France was imperative. There was no place for weeping and mourning, unless you could keep your eyes firmly on the future.

On 1 November (All Souls' Day) newspapers traditionally devoted considerable space to the dead. But even in this context, the number of fatalities remained undisclosed. Nevertheless, readers could draw their own conclusions from *Le Figaro*'s front-page appeal to readers to take in war orphans. An article in *Le Petit Parisien* called 'The Voice of the Dead' provoked Anna de Noailles to comment that every day was the day of the dead for her.[37] And there was some truth to that. The once frivolous, scintillating star of the Paris salons now composed lament after lament, often dwelling on the deaths of the young soldiers, just a few years older than her son Anne-Jules. 'Look carefully at that man dying there, and see / What this horrific war is constantly consuming', she wrote in 'Celui qui meurt' (The Dying Man).[38] She herself was one of the survivors, a position in which every day she was newly confronted with the injustice of the war. She tried to lighten her heavy burden of shame by voicing it openly, and by making herself useful as a *marraine de guerre* ('wartime godmother'), sending not only her own husband at the front but also a collection of friends and strangers – both soldiers and prisoners of war in Germany – a steady stream of bread, chocolate, letters, reading material and woollen clothing (much of which she knitted herself). She was so well known that even letters from total strangers addressed simply to the 'Comtesse de Noailles' in 'Paris' were delivered to her door. A Corporal Lacoste wrote to tell her how moved he had been to discover one of her volumes, as if by chance, in a library, and asked if she would be willing to correspond with him, so deeply did he long for a woman's words. The baroness evidently agreed to this request, since ten days later Lacoste sent his profuse thanks: in the midst of the violent, painful, dirty, selfish, vile life of a soldier, her poems embodied the beauty and culture he sorely missed.[39]

Thanks to her contacts in the political and military elite, Noailles knew very well what was going on at the front. She did her best to keep her chin up and to embody what she, a Romanian–Greek aristocrat, saw as the values of the French Republic, but the immense suffering sometimes threatened to drag her down.

'How are we to live today? All beings are left in solitude / The dead have killed the living', she reflected,[40] although her intention was not to indulge in self-pity. As a flamboyant member of high society, she had grown accustomed to being the centre of attention, and for her the war was a sustained lesson in humility. 'We understand', she wrote to her husband in late January 1916, 'it is thanks to you that we are drunk with pride, and that we imagine we ourselves are serving our Homeland and Victory.'[41] For the next few months, the Marquis de Noailles served in Verdun, a place consecrated by battle and soldierly sacrifice, where his wife received a personal tour at the end of the summer from General Charles Mangin. 'Silence cloaks this world-famous name', she wrote after her visit, in the poem 'Verdun'.

> Blood pours in such plenty that no human voice
> May mingle its vain and febrile complaint
> With the endless vapors of this earthly incense
> In the carved and scarred plain here you see
> The sainted, unsounded power of the land
> Whose finest hearts lie at rest beneath.[42]

Around this time, Noailles's friend and kindred spirit Edmond Rostand (1868–1918) wrote the poetic introduction to a book that took an inventory of the literary output over the past two years of world war. In alexandrine verse, the author of *Cyrano de Bergerac* (1897) used allegory to explain what purpose he believed the war still had after more than 700 days. France, keeper of the clear light of Reason, had been viciously attacked by demonic forces that used perverse rhetoric to present their barbarism as a philosophical exercise. Very slyly, Rostand made this point by reference to Goethe's tragedy *Faust* (1808). By making it explicit that he was quoting Germany's great national poet – a passage from the Walpurgis Night scene in which a witch tries to lure

Faust into buying implements of death and violence – he implied that German *Kultur* ('koultour', as Rostand mockingly wrote the word) had given rise to terror.[43] The catalogue of German crimes had grown even beyond what Goethe's witch had described; Rostand mentioned rape, amputation of fingers, and other horrors from the list of war crimes committed by the German army when it invaded Belgium and France. 'The thought [also a word for 'philosophy' in French] is the mother of the *schlague* [flogging, a kind of corporal punishment used in the German army]', Rostand concluded, in a stanza that also denounced Hegelian thinking. He contrasted this German witch with another saleswoman, one for whom 'goods' were synonymous with 'good'. Compassion, grace, order, dreams – she had it all in stock. This personification of French values came from a region 'where Might has never yet made Right'.[44] She was the bright fixed star that Victor Hugo had called 'Stella'; not at all the same star, Rostand pointed out, as the dancing one that Nietzsche had evoked in *Zarathustra*. The reader was not to suppose that the two cultures at war had much in common.

But for the men in the trenches, it was increasingly difficult to believe that they were fighting for their culture. Poison gas, massive bombardments, the deliberate mass killing of enemy soldiers – by 1916, the two sides were using essentially the same tactics. The Verdun offensive was mirrored by that of the Somme, and both had led to similar results. The major attacks intended to break the stalemate had taken an unparalleled human toll on both sides. The combatants were well matched, even in their rate of attrition.

On 18 November, after a long series of pointless attempts to gain ground, and more than a million casualties all told, the British high command brought the Battle of the Somme to an end.[45] The Irish poet Tom Kettle was one of the many who did not survive. An uncanny silence ensued. 'Thiepval Wood's ghostly gallows-trees made no sound nor movement', wrote the British war poet Edmund Blunden (1896–1974), who had taken part in the final stage of the battle. 'Thus, then, beyond doubt, the gigantic clangor of the Somme offensive had ceased.'[46] Meanwhile, the *Guardian* saw no reason to temper its rhetoric. Its 22 November issue hailed the battle as the finest of all time. 'It was heroic in every turn and phase. And the heroism was nowhere vain. Everywhere it won its end – yea, and more than its end. Nor was its cost beyond measure as figures go.'[47]

A month later, on 18 December, the Battle of Verdun ended too. There had been some 500,000 casualties for territorial gains of less than fifteen kilometres.[48] On 18 November, Marc de Larreguy de Civrieux died at Froideterre, near Verdun, and four days before the battle ended, Norbert von Hellingrath (1888–1916), poet and editor of the collected works of Friedrich Hölderlin, died at Douaumont.

On 20 December, Jules Romains's volume of poetry *Europe* was published in Paris, in a deluxe limited edition of 150. He decided to print so few copies not out of elitism or decadence, but in a deliberate attempt to evade the censors, who might otherwise have banned it for its revolutionary and pacifist ideas. This was no unnecessary precaution; even in a review in England, the bulk of a quotation from the book was blacked out.[49] When Romains read from the volume in a Paris bookshop in March 1917, the scene reminded him of a meeting of the early church in the catacombs. It was not clear whether this time what remained of the congregation would be thrown to the lions.

7

Café Dada: Anti-Semitism, Pacifism and the Avant-garde

Why are there not a few, three, five, ten, who stand together and cry in the public squares: Enough! and who will be shot down and will at least have given their lives that it should be enough.

– Rainer Maria Rilke when called up for duty, October 1915[1]

It starts out as a very ordinary poem – ordinary, at least, in the universe of George Bacovia (1881–1957). Like most of the poems in his debut volume *Plumb* (Lead, 1916), it wallows in a decadent, autumnal atmosphere of rain, decay and death. Then, all of a sudden, it turns weirdly specific:

But look, that's a Jewish corpse ...
The weather's soggy, mud and rain –
To the strange semitic murmuring
I add myself, and fall in line.[2]

Is the poet very deliberately moving beyond his usual repertoire of images, or would this visual detail – a Jewish corpse in the street – be considered typical local colour in Romania? Within the confines of Bacovia's relentlessly morbid atmosphere, the poet seems to be expressing his solidarity with the Jewish figure. He too is an outcast, although – despite his fearful fantasies ('One thought masters me, / Hounds me and goads: / – Vanish faster!') – he is still alive. The image is potent, but there is also something coy about it. The poet may fancy himself an outsider, but Jews were quite literally outcasts in Romania, the only country besides Russia where they had not yet been emancipated. Romanian Jews had no civil rights and could not buy real estate.[3] For many authors and intellectuals, Romanian nationalism and anti-Semitism went hand in hand. In both the cities and the countryside, Jews were viewed with suspicion, because they were overrepresented among professionals, journalists and stockbrokers. On 27 August 1916, when Romania – after two years of waiting, hesitating and negotiating – finally declared war on the Dual Monarchy, pogroms erupted in various parts of the country. Jews had to flee for their lives, and many sought a safe haven in Budapest, in the territory of the official enemy, seemingly confirming the unsavoury rumours that they were German spies, or some other kind of fifth column.[4]

Samuel Rosenstock (1896–1963) was out of the country at the time. He had flown the nest in the autumn of 1915, feeling suffocated in the home of his well-to-do parents in Bucharest, and gone to Zurich on the heels of his school friend and fellow Jew Marcel Janco (1895–1984).[5] Around the same time, Rosenstock had a poem published in the Romanian magazine *Chemarea*, the first to appear under his new pseudonym, Tristan Tzara. These lines were more savage in tone than the average war poem being written in the belligerent countries, and were also experimental in a new way. The poem seemed to leap without warning from scene to scene and emotion to emotion:

Light burst from shells
And lightning cracked in our hands
Just as God's hand split into five fingers
We come up on the troops from behind and cut them down

We trample corpses left in the snow
We open a window to the drowned darkness
Through valleys that sucked the enemy dry
They have killed them to the distant blue.
Frost: bones splinter, flesh crumbles
We let our hearts weep.[6]

'The Storm and the Deserter's Song' was not autobiographical – after all, Romania was not yet at war – and Tzara's decision to go to Zurich could of course be seen as a deliberate attempt to avoid the turmoil of the conflict. Although the country where he ended up, Switzerland, maintained a firm policy of neutrality, the turbulence of war was felt even in that mountain confederation.[7] As the Swiss themselves liked to say, using an image that was ubiquitous at the time, there seemed suddenly to be a trench (*Graben*) running between the German- and French-speaking areas, and tensions were rising. On both sides, some advocated fighting alongside those who shared their language, and both groups accused each other of violating Switzerland's neutrality and consorting with the enemy. Yet the very use of terms like 'enemy' showed that the accusers themselves were far from neutral.

Still, not all the accusations of partisan bias were groundless. Some newspapers clearly took sides. The Swiss army went even further than sympathizing with the Germans – since the outbreak of war, its intelligence service had virtually become an arm of the German military. When this became public knowledge it provoked an outcry, as well as court proceedings that further poisoned the atmosphere. Meanwhile, the Swiss army was doing its best to defend the country's borders, a mammoth effort involving a quarter of a million soldiers, many still untrained, who often had to go without adequate food or pay. Yet the army was also a potential vehicle for restoring national unity, at least in the eyes of the Swiss Folklore Institute, which published multilingual brochures containing traditional proverbs, military slang, poems and song lyrics that were said to illustrate Switzerland's true national character.[8] Swiss soldiers from the different cantons got to know each other in the army, and would bring the songs and sayings of their fellow fighters back home with them after the war, creating a more unified national corpus of Swiss songs and, by extension, a Swiss culture.

Yet not everyone agreed on how to define that culture. The Francophone poet Jules Carràra believed the best way for Switzerland to be true to itself was by declaring its solidarity with trampled-upon Belgium. In the title poem of his collection *Solidarité* (1914), published to raise money for a Belgian relief fund, 'conscience' and 'the poet' enter into dialogue with the descendants of war heroes from Swiss history, statesmen, and sites of historical significance (such as Winkelried, Grandson, Marignan and Berthelier). All of them seemed to agree that the only way for the Swiss to live up to their history was by rushing to the defence of small, courageous countries. The poet's closing lines combined pride with ferocity: 'O Switzerland, the nations can expect much more from you / A great task lies ahead, if you can see what you must do.'[9]

The leading Swiss author of the day, the German-speaking poet, novelist and essayist Carl Spitteler (1845–1924), also saw a great task awaiting his country, but a very different one. In 'Unser Schweitzer Standpunkt' (Our Swiss Point of View) – a much-debated speech delivered on 14 December 1914 to the Neue Helvetische Gesellschaft, an association founded before the war to strengthen the bonds between German- and French-speaking Swiss citizens – he stressed that strict neutrality was the only viable approach.[10] Because he believed that each language group was responsible for the level of its own public debate, his speech – which is still quoted today – dealt primarily with wrongs, prejudices and misconceptions among the German-speaking Swiss, who made up some 69 per cent of the population at the time. Spitteler knew only too well how normal it was for people to feel the most sympathy for those who spoke their own language, yet he warned that succumbing to that urge would threaten the integrity of the state. The Swiss are not joined by language or blood and have no royal house to create unity, nor even a generally accepted capital city. Their only national symbols are the flag and the principle of neutrality. That principle, Spitteler argued, took priority over linguistic and cultural ties; after all, war and politics were not matters of philology. He added that it would be extremely short-sighted of the Swiss to reserve all their sympathy for the Germans, when Switzerland owed at least as much to France. Ideals such as freedom, democracy and tolerance – once guiding lights for all of Europe – were of unquestionable importance to the Swiss. Similarly, Switzerland had close ties with England and Russia, and Spitteler pointed out that the Swiss should be able to identify only too well with the woes of small countries like Serbia and Belgium. In other words, the so-called enemies of the German-speaking Swiss were not enemies at all, but valued neighbours and friends. Spitteler was also disturbed by the sense of superiority exuded by more than a few of his countrymen. The scorn, sarcasm and *Schadenfreude* that he observed in the streets and in the press were, in his opinion, entirely inappropriate. Before all else, the Swiss had to become better acquainted with the other people with whom they shared their country. Spitteler suggested that newspapers carry translations of articles from other communities, to counter prejudice and strengthen national unity. Besides, the Swiss had no justification for flaunting their superiority: 'It goes without saying that we, being impartial, see many things more clearly and judge many things in a more accurate way than those who are caught in the passion of fighting. This is an advantage of position, not a spiritual advantage.'[11] The poet concluded that as long as the war lasted, the Swiss – like chance onlookers at a funeral procession or theatre-goers watching a tragedy – should maintain a humble, solemn and respectful silence.

Most of the artists, pacifists and revolutionaries from warring countries who had ended up in Switzerland had no interest in Spitteler's arguments. They had come not to keep silent, but to exercise the rights of free expression stifled by censorship in their home countries. The first issue of the pacifist magazine *Demain* (Tomorrow) was published in Geneva in January 1916, under the editorial leadership of the French poet Henri Guilbeaux (1885–1938). Driven by outrage and shame at living in a world where scientists used their skills to build better weapons, thus placing the ideals of the Enlightenment and the French Revolution in the service of death, Guilbeaux hoped to bring together voices from all over Europe to devise a radical internationalist alternative. As the magazine's name suggested, the intention was to move beyond the horrors of the present day and contribute to a new world – not a reconstruction of the past, but an entirely new edifice, in which new structures and new materials would generate new forms of hope and life and create new opportunities for love, truth and science.[12] Above all, in the chauvinistic climate that prevailed throughout Europe, *Demain* sought to give internationalism another chance. To that end, the magazine recruited writers from across the Continent; its contributors included the Belgians Frans Masereel and Jacques Mesnil, the French authors Romain Rolland, Pierre-Jean Jouve and Marcel Martinet, the Dutch poet Henriëtte Roland Holst, the Swedish writer Ellen Key, and the British novelist Ethel Sidgwick.

Shortly after arriving in Zurich, Tzara likewise found himself in a milieu of radical experimentation with new forms and structures, but these experiments were very different from Guilbeaux's. The movement Tzara co-founded, Dada, may have shared Guilbeaux's opposition to war, but it proposed a very different remedy. According to the Dada artists, 'truth' and 'intelligence' were part of the rhetoric that had brought about the war and continued to fuel it. In the process, they had lost every shred of meaning. While the socialist pacifists of *Demain* denounced the militaristic propaganda that led countries and individuals to fight to the bitter end, the Dadaists gnawed at that same propaganda with relish, as if it were a juicy bone. They were determined to keep gnawing until all the meat was gone and Western culture was nothing more than a bare skeleton, picked clean. In other words, Dada was not a pacifist movement (wasn't pacifism just another strain of traditional Western thinking?) but distinctly violent.[13] Beneath their playful anarchism, the Dadaists were children of their time, who had understood perfectly well that aggression was the secret of success in the twentieth century.

At the hub of the Dada movement was the German poet and playwright Hugo Ball (1886–1927), who had followed a very unusual path to Zurich. On 29 July 1914, he had sent his sister an enthusiastic letter from Munich, letting her know how much he was looking forward to collaborating with artists like Wassily Kandinsky and Paul Claudel, and how proud he was to be exhibiting the most radical styles of painting ('mainly French and Russian') in the lobby of his theatre. But less than ten days later, he volunteered to join the army and fight his French and Russian contemporaries, telling the same sister that events had made art utterly ridiculous.[14] The army rejected him three times because of a heart condition, but that did little to dampen his enthusiasm for war. In the poem 'Glanz um die Fahne' (Splendor of the Flag), he declared that the world could be liberated from its agony by abandoning itself to the primitive energy released by the conflict. That was before he saw the fighting up close, as a war tourist. As early as November, he wrote from the Belgian front that the world had fallen prey to diabolical madness.[15] The tone of his poems then changed radically, showing the strong influence of

Georg Heym's apocalyptic verse. Ball became more and more politically engaged, openly pinning all his hopes on Russia. If the war led to a revolution there, then the slaughter would finally have some meaning, he wrote on 13 March 1915. Europe would be shaken to its foundations, and an entirely new world would become possible.[16] A few months later, he moved to Zurich, where in the January 1916 issue of the radical leftist magazine *Der Revoluzzer* he published the poem 'Totentanz 1916' (Dance of Death, 1916):

> And so we die, and so we die,
> we're dying every day now,
> for it's such a comfort to welcome death.
> In the morning still asleep,
> by afternoon we're down.
> In the evening well and truly underground.
>
> Battle is our bawdy house,
> Our sun is dark and bloody,
> Death our only watchword, our only sign.
> Wife and child we leave behind –
> still, what do we care?
> No one minds as long as we are there.[17]

In this sarcastic parody of a well-known eighteenth-century German marching song and the cabaret hit 'So leben wir' (That's How We Live), Ball dealt a crushing blow to Prussian morality.[18] His next artistic move was also inspired by the rich tradition of German cabaret. On 5 February, he opened the Cabaret Voltaire at Spiegelgasse 1. Yet these were performances such as had never been witnessed in Berlin – or, in all probability, anywhere else. Admittedly, the opening night was not all that radical. Tristan Tzara recited a few of his Romanian poems, Emmy Hennings

(Ball's future wife, who had performed in the Neopathetic Cabaret in Berlin) read original work and sang a few songs, and a balalaika orchestra played Russian folk music.[19] Soon enough, however, there were recitations of adapted 'Negro poems', simultaneous poems (performed by Tzara, Janco and Richard Huelsenbeck, a friend of Ball's summoned from Berlin), and sound poems, for the performance of which Ball dressed up as a cross between a shaman and an explosive shell. That was also how he sounded. Instead of using existing words, he invented new concatenations of sounds, like 'gadji beri bimba glandridi laula lonni cadori gadjama gramma berida bimbala glandri galassassa laulitalomini'. Keeping in mind the context of the war, this technique comes across as simultaneously desperate, absurd and appropriate in 'Totenklage' (Dirge):

ombula
take
bitdli
solunkola
tabla tokta tokta takabla
takatak[20]

Ball explained that he had founded the Cabaret Voltaire to show that 'there are still a few independent-minded people who stand for ideals other than "war" and "homeland"',[21] although he neglected to specify what those ideals might be. In any case, the acts on the programme confirmed that 'homeland' was not sacred to the Dadaists. Russian music, Italian Futurism, German popular songs, French lyrics – what the war had divided into enemy camps, the Cabaret Voltaire reunited. For the first few months, the Dada texts made surprisingly little mention of the war, and when they did, it was with artful ambiguity: 'We want to change the world with nothing, we want to change poetry and painting with nothing, and we want to bring the war to a stop with nothing.'[22] If they did want to end the war, then their strategy certainly was the celebration of 'nothing', a gleefully destructive nihilism that would only make room for reason ('Voltaire') when it consented to play the fool.

Tzara, too, threw himself into this new way of thinking and being. The final sentence of his Romanian poem quoted above ('It's so dark only the words are light') could be seen as defining the essence of his literary output from then on, which was written in French. The words of his writings seem both weightless and like beacons of a new kind of understanding, shrapnel bombs of meaning that send readers in all directions at once, hinting at a deeper significance without ever making it clear. A case in point is the *Manifeste de Monsieur Antipryene* (Monsieur Antipyrine's Manifesto), which he read aloud on 14 July 1916, at the first Dada soirée – the Cabaret Voltaire having been forced to close. It contains such enervating pearls of wisdom as: 'And while we put on a show of being facile, we are actually searching for the central essence of things, and are pleased if we can hide it.'[23] Two weeks into the offensive on the Somme, this verbal display of mislaid knowledge included a few allusions to the war. 'Dada is our intensity', the manifesto began, 'it sets up inconsequential bayonets the sumatran head of the german baby'. Ordinary syntax has been tossed overboard, but the mentions of babies and bayonets would immediately have been understood by contemporaries as a reference to one of the war crimes of which the Germans were accused after the invasion of Belgium in 1914: impaling infants on bayonets.[24] Tzara's talk of German babies can be interpreted as a typical Dada reversal, and the invocation of the 'sumatran head' lends those *Kultur*-babies the aura of primitivism that the Dadaists adored. All of these poets seem to have felt certain that so-called Western civilization was on its way out. 'Dada remains within the European frame of weaknesses', Tzara said, 'it's shit after all but from now on we mean to shit in assorted colours and bedeck the artistic zoo with the flags of every consulate … HoHiHoHo Bang'.[25]

In September 1916, the volume *Phantastische Gebete* (Fantastic Prayers) by Richard Huelsenbeck (1892–1974) was published in the Collection Dada series, with seven woodcuts by Hans Arp. This little book thoroughly lives up to its title: litany meets parody in intense, complex texts that evoke incomprehensible adventures. Cubic sound poems entitled 'Chorus sanctus' alternate with off-colour intermezzos and pseudo-mystical reflections like 'I am the beginning of the world because I am the end'. Again, amid this maelstrom of words and images, the war surfaces in several places. 'Flüsse' (Rivers) seems to describe both the execution of a modern painting ('From the spotted tubes the rivers pour') and primitive, erotically charged rituals.

> a misfortune has befallen the world
> the breasts of the giant lady went up in flames and a snakeman
> gave birth to a rattail
> Omba umba the Negroes are somersaulting out of the chicken
>   coops and the spray of your breath is grazing their toes
> a great battle passed over you and over the sleep of your lips
> a great slaughter filled you out[26]

The poem is nothing if not ambiguous. It may suggest a connection between the bloodshed that was well under way in Europe and ritual outbreaks of violence in primitive cultures, but it could just as plausibly refer to the export of the war to Africa by Europe's colonial powers, which had forced local populations there to participate in the butchery. The final sentence quoted above (in the original German, 'ein großes Morden füllete euch aus') suggests that slaughter gave a unique sense of fulfilment. In 'Der Redende Mensch' (The Speaking Man), the puns and proverbs are interlarded with phrases like 'dulce et decorum est pro patria mori or always be loyal and honest or well I never'.[27] This is wisdom according to Dada: the solemn pronouncements with which young men are sent to their deaths are no better than sanctimonious clichés or barroom exclamations. Dada comes into its own in the deliberate annihilation of ordinary language use and prevailing aesthetic standards. Its target was not so much the war as the belligerent rhetoric and lying propaganda on which the war machine depended.

The Russian Futurists too were now summoned by that machine. Even Mayakovsky, rejected in 1914 because of his earlier revolutionary activities, was conscripted on 21 October 1915. By posing as a technical draftsman, he contrived to be assigned to the Automobile School in Petrograd.[28] One of his associates there, the composer Vladimir Shcherbachov, provided the musical notation that served as a soundtrack for what would become Mayakovsky's greatest, most experimental war poem – the cynical and lyrical, despairing and prophetic, aggressive and anti-militaristic, humble and egomaniacal *Voina i Mir* (War and the World, 1915–16).[29] Like the Dadaists, Mayakovsky unmasked the propaganda of the war and, at least on the surface, seemed thoroughly uninterested in basic human values. Yet a closer look suggests that his caustic tone may have been the only way for him to salvage those values, so that they would have another chance after the slaughter ended. Again, there was a time to break down and a time to build up. In any case, Mayakovsky had no pity for those who had come to regret their eagerness for war in the summer and autumn of 1914.

> It's too late already!
> No second chances!
> No time for this softness of yours!

Our thousand-armed medics
Have all been issued lancets
Straight from the arsenal's stores.[30]

The poet then presents the warring countries, one by one, as grotesque characters with their own self-serving (and disillusioning) reasons to wage war with such ferocity. Italy, he writes, is fighting for 'king or barber',[31] Germany to defend its 'thinkers, museums, poets', and the French because 'raping, burning, choking' to 'machine-gun music' makes a welcome change from their usual amorous entanglements. Nor does Mayakovsky spare his own country, playing the anarchist, pacifist disciples of Tolstoy off against the rapacious, adrenaline-fuelled Russians with their (barbarous?) Asian roots. In the following section, the poet imagines the war as the ultimate spectacle, a performance to make Nero proud ('all the world's now one huge Colosseum'), but adapted to the sentimental, commercial conventions of the new art of film ('More widows in this shot! Nowhere near enough widows on screen!'). Not that the poet-cameraman is blind to the unfolding tragedy – he describes how a sky 'like a chandelier' holds 'all the fire of blazing Europe'. After the battle ('once all who fell upon each other / had fallen'), death wanders the battlefield, beginning its *danse macabre*. Even the survivors are hardly worthy of the name.[32]

Five days, so far,
Trains have roared around curves
And through bullet-holes drilled in my brain.
In this festering car
Forty men must be served
By the four legs that remain.

Part IV, which follows, begins as a discourse on poetry in time of war. Mayakovsky anticipates the criticism that he has had no personal combat experience and tends to get carried away much too easily by his own verbal artistry. As self-confident as ever, he turns this complaint on its head. No 'poesy' for him, no 'lyre' – it's not his lyricism that's inappropriate, but that of conventional patriotic poets. Like a Futurist Christ, he then takes all the sins of the world upon himself, paving the way for spiritual cleansing and, in the final part of the poem, for resurrection. The Day of Judgement has arrived: the Rhine flows into the Danube, severed limbs go in search of their former owners, and thousands of rainbows arch over 'the unscathed', those who have survived the catastrophe. In this new age, countries and continents offer up their greatest talents as gifts to humanity. This reversal, this turnabout, is almost too good to be true. And of course, it wasn't true. Mayakovsky, like millions of others, longed for a different world, a different Russia ('And then, believe me, / at last, / long awaited, / he'll come, / the free Man / of whom I roar!'), but as this utopia blossomed in his mind, it was 1916, and the war was only escalating.[33]

Meanwhile, Aleksei Kruchenykh (1886–1968) was going to greater and greater lengths to find a suitable new mode of expression. In 1913, he and Khlebnikov invented a radically new form of poetry, *zaum* (a compound word literally meaning 'beyond reason'), in which the words of a poem were chosen not for their dictionary meanings, but because they formed an intriguing pattern of sounds, structures and etymologies, offering a glimpse of the fundamental laws of existence. In the volumes *War* (1915) and *Universal War* (1916), Kruchenykh and his collaborator, the visual artist Olga Rozanova, went still further, eliminating the distinction between poetry and abstract art and presenting the two forms jointly as *zaum*.[34] According to the poet, the universal war of the title would be fought in 1985 (by Europe and Asia, as the poets Drieu la Rochelle and Pessoa also predicted around that time). This inspired poems such as 'battle between india and europe':

> drove
> toughguy
> fluff
> so
> the kid
> mind
> rat
> unshoeing the armchair[35]

Germany is mentioned in the following titles, but that does not make the poems any easier to grasp. When approached with the reasoning mind and the dictionary, these poems remain uncommunicative. Yet their subtle sound patterns, in dialogue with Rozanova's polychromatic collages, engendered not merely new meanings but, more significantly, a new experience of reality.

Kruchenykh evaded conscription by moving to the Georgian capital of Tbilisi,[36] but his Futurist comrade Velimir Khlebnikov did not escape. On 21 April 1916, he was called up for duty. Although in 1914 he had come out vocally as a bloodthirsty, almost xenophobic pan-Slavist, Khlebnikov was bewildered to find himself in the army. In the opening lines of his next poem, he protested that he was unsuitable for military service because his poetic personality was irreconcilable with the brutal violence of the war.

> Who, me? Me too? This triumph of torpidity?
> This anti-Onegin?
> Me, offended that people are the way they are?
> Me, who watched the *R* depart from Russia,

Me, reared up by all that is best in Russia, brightest and best,
Me, tangled in the brightest of bird-song?
I've got witnesses!
You thrushes, swans, and cranes!
Me, who dreamed my life away?

Me too? You mean I'll have to grab a gun
(a dumb thing, heavier
than handwriting)
and go marching down some highway,
beating out 365 × 317 regular heartbeats a day?
Knock my head to fragments.[37]

The number of steps he expected to march each day was anything but arbitrary. All his life, Khlebnikov had been trying to crack the universal code, and the figures 365 and 317 were central to his numerology. Like some miraculous mixture of Saint Francis (who talked to the birds), Nostradamus (who tried to look into the future), Einstein (who was in search of a unified theory), Zamenhof (the inventor of Esperanto) and Rimbaud (the alchemist of the word), this mathematically trained ornithologist and etymologist – who was at least as much a futurologist as a Futurist – tried to cram as much empirical information as possible into his framework in order to lay bare the all-powerful law of the universe.[38] As a poet, he was of course interested in everything related to language, but numbers also played a crucial role in his investigations. He had spent the first few months of the war frenetically analyzing all sorts of data and deduced that the sea battles of the world war would parallel the key dates in the struggle between Islam and the West since 1095. His brochure on this topic, *A New Theory of War: Battles, 1915–1917* (published in 1914), described the future course of the conflict. On 28 December 1914, when the great sea battle that he had predicted failed to take place, the news merely encouraged him: 'Now that I have understood my mistakes, I'm free.'[39] He returned to his calculations and, on 31 January, swore to his publisher that if his next prediction came true, his complete timetable of future naval battles would have to be published immediately. 'That is how I will go down in history –' he wrote to his family in August, 'as the discoverer of the Laws of Time.' But the Russian army was uninterested in his research and summoned him to serve in the 93rd infantry regiment. It would be the death of the child in him, he feared, and his few surviving letters show how severely his sensitive, inquisitive, absent-minded nature jarred with the totalitarian discipline and faceless collectivism of the army. As it happens, the aversion was entirely mutual. Khlebnikov was referred to not as 'him' but as 'it'. He had become a thing, ill-suited to serve his country but nonetheless required to do his duty. He could not even pledge allegiance to the army, because he was already a loyal servant of poetry. But would the poet within him survive this ordeal? 'Marching, orders, it's ruining my sense of rhythm, and makes me crazy by the end of the evening detail, and I can never remember which is my right foot and which my left', the raw recruit complained. 'Thanks to the continual monotonous cursing and swearing, my feeling for language is dying within me', he wrote to Nikolai Kulbin, a patron of the Futurists and a physician to the general staff of the army. Khlebnikov hoped that some influential friend would be able to free him from this mind-numbing situation: 'I am a dervish, a Yogi, a Martian, anything you want, but I am *not* a private in a reserve infantry regiment.'[40] His friends did their best, and the poet often spent several weeks in hospitals or on leave near Astrakhan, his region of origin. This did nothing to change his fundamental attitude:

> I am a captive of malicious graybeards
> Though I am merely a scared, shy rabbit

And not the king of the realm of time,
As people call me.[41]

* * *

But things could always be worse. In late October 1915, Khlebnikov talked to a female friend, possibly Jewish, with whom he was secretly in love, about the pogroms taking place in Russia.[42] During its Great Retreat in 1915, the Russian army had made systematic use of the scorched earth method, looting and burning down Jewish shtetls, houses and temples. Jews from Galicia, Lithuania, Courland and Latvia were deported in droves by the Russians because they were seen as traitors whose sympathies lay with the Germans. Families were split up, including many with fathers serving in the Russian army. There was hardly any means of transportation and next to no housing. Perhaps as many as a million Jews became refugees in their own country, cast almost completely outside the law.[43] Life had always been hard for Jews in Russia, but as the German army pressed ever deeper into Russian territory, even the assimilated, intellectual Jews of Petrograd began to fear a recurrence of what had happened in Spain in 1492 – mass expulsion.[44] This prospect seemed quite likely to the brother of Sophie Parnok, a Russian Jewish poetess who was then romantically involved with Marina Tsvetaeva. Tsvetaeva herself also took the situation very seriously. Her elegy 'To the Jews', written in 1916, began with the words, 'Who has not trampled you, burned you alive?'[45] But Alexander Blok, whose poetry she admired, sided with the tramplers. 'Hang them all, the yids', he said in an unguarded moment,[46] and when a group of Symbolists including Konstantin Balmont, Fyodor Sologub and Zinaida Gippius compiled a book against anti-Semitism in 1915, Blok was the only major figure in the movement who never responded to their request for a contribution.[47]

In England and the United States, committees were established to aid the Jews. Their propaganda brochures pointed out that the

Belgians were receiving more assistance than the Jews (in proportional terms), even though they had not been as hard hit, and despite the more than half a million Jews fighting in the Allied armies.[48] The many hundreds of thousands of Jews who had fled Galicia after earlier pogroms and settled in the United States were following events closely, and they were actively involved in charity work and in raising public awareness of the situation. The poet Zishe Landau (1889–1937), who had emigrated in 1906, had no doubt what was going on. This was the end of traditional Jewish life in Galicia and the Baltic region.

> Now, for our shattered Jewish life
> I kneel, and pray to you for grace;
> I weep for our old mother Vilna,
> For Brod; for every holy place;
>
> I weep for Warsaw, Kovno, Lemberg,
> For every large and little town
> Whereon the foe of old has fallen,
> And which the foe will fall upon.[49]

In 'A Nakht' (A Night, 1916), a disturbing medley of grotesque and realistic images, the poet Moyshe-Leyb Halpern (1886–1932), another emigrant from Galicia, described what was happening to those he had left behind.

> A Jew runs down the street,
> Blood dripping from his head,
> I see how he leaps with pain
> And he weaves himself into the circle,
> Jews come one after another,
> Bleeding from heads and arms.
> People emerge dancing

From the *shul* and the *kloyz*.
Women, too, come running,
Feathers flying from their bellies.
An old Jew on fire comes whirling,
Cradling a Torah in his arms.
Weaving a round dance are
Jews, not fully slaughtered yet,
With a murdered child in her arms,
And her hair loose in the wind,
And eyes large and green,
A crazy woman comes flying.[50]

In this long poem, Halpern presented the destruction of Jewish life and the Jewish people as a harbinger of the Apocalypse – the work of the Messiah himself, heralding the end of the world.[51] This time it was not the poet who had the wildest imagination.

8

Total War: Peace Plans, Revolution and Mutiny in 1917

> I see the horror and absurdity giving rise to a collective fatigue among the men. It is true that war devours a person's innards. You could almost call the war galvanized flesh, a corpse, a slab of meat in combat.
>
> – Zinaida Gippius, diary entry, 8 March 1917[1]

'People have more desire *to experience things* than *to live in peace*', Albert Verwey wrote in the summer of 1914, trying to work out for himself how such a devastating war could be taking place in modern Europe.[2] Three years later, even the most decadent sensation-seekers had presumably had their fill of experiences, but the war showed no sign of ending. The great cultural transformation so many intellectuals and poets had dreamed of had now come about, but not quite as they had imagined it. No longer the sleepy continent that had swerved between indecision and grand plans, Europe was now permeated with an almost totalitarian *culture de guerre*, a culture in which the thoughts, utterances and actions of soldiers and civilians alike were moulded entirely by the war, by the need to survive it and the desire for unconditional victory.[3] Idleness had no place in this new culture – and in truth, neither did freedom. Even the Futurists had conceived of the war – 'the world's only hygiene' – as a temporary condition. Spending all day in the bathtub is no way to build muscles.

By this stage, the situation on the ground no longer had any real connection with the ambitions and ideals that had led the nations of Europe into war. Yet the exigencies of war made it impossible to pause for reflection or put things into perspective. And without any exit option, it was vital to give the war some kind of meaning. As long as parts of Belgium and France remained occupied, the war was billed as a fight for the Liberation of Nations. Yet for the British and German soldiers putting their lives at risk on foreign soil, liberation seemed a rather abstract notion. Their own countries were in little if any peril. From early 1915 onwards, German zeppelin raids did do damage to British targets but did not form a serious threat to the sovereignty of the British Isles. Official propaganda had always described the war as a battle between good and evil, between civilization and barbarism. This image was used to recruit millions of soldiers in the early months of the war and later, when investigators reported on atrocities committed during enemy advances.[4] Yet in the trenches, terms like 'civilization' and 'barbarism' quickly lost all meaning. The soldiers kept fighting because they were forced to, or in solidarity with the rest of their unit, or to show they were as brave as the next man.[5]

The sacrifices made by civilians and politicians were in no way comparable. That made it both easier and harder to give them meaning. As long as your own life is not at stake, it is easier to go on believing in the absolute justice of your cause and your ideals. But at the same time, your physical distance from the reality of war can undercut your sense of urgency. The culture of war took steps to prevent that. The propaganda continued incessantly, and the many government measures to deal with shortages made the public more keenly aware of the situation. There was famine in large areas of Europe, and hundreds of thousands of civilians starved to death.[6] In Germany, the army came first when the country's ever scarcer resources were allocated. Seventy per cent of the food supply was automatically reserved for the troops. Inflation reached record highs, and many people could no longer afford meat or vegetables. Potatoes often had to be replaced with turnips, a traditional form of cattle feed that was now also used in bread dough. In August 1916, and again in January and February 1917 food riots broke out in Hamburg and other major cities. At the very bottom of the food distribution list were the occupied territories. In Belgium, Virginie Loveling reported in her war diary in 1917, hunger was so widespread that well-dressed middle-class men were coming to her door to beg for bread.[7] There was hunger in Austria because Galicia, the country's breadbasket, was occupied by the Russians, and because the Hungarians, who were increasingly separatist in outlook, no longer wished to share their food with their brothers in empire.

This was Europe at war: millions of deaths on the battlefield, hardship on the home front, faltering economies, and as a result, increasing political and social friction. But what could individuals do to relieve this unprecedented suffering? For soldiers, the choices were few. Deserters paid with their lives, and other forms of insubordination were severely punished. For civilians, the options were just as limited. They could not exercise any real political influence, through referendums or even through elections. They could take to the streets in protest, but the occupied territories had degenerated into police states, and the food riots in Germany itself were put down forcefully by the police force and the army (which were beginning to take the possibility of civil war quite seriously). Politicians, too, felt they had very little room for manoeuvre. The governments of the warring nations had worked themselves into positions from which peace talks were virtually unthinkable.

In this sense, they had become the victims of their own propaganda machines. If you claim to be fighting for the survival of civilization and humanity, there is little room for negotiation. You can't half-save civilization, and how do you compromise with people you've described as monsters? Furthermore, politicians had stressed that civilians would have to make unheard-of sacrifices, and most families had actually done so by this time. This made it almost impossible to win public support for concessions of any kind. Nor was there much scope for diplomacy.[8] To expand their alliances, the major powers had made all sorts of promises to lesser states, and there was no way they could all be kept. The Entente, for instance, was fighting for Serbian sovereignty, while the Central Powers had promised the Macedonian part of the Serbian Empire to Bulgaria, to reverse its territorial losses in the Second Balkan War. The Polish and Belgian questions also promised to make negotiations exceedingly complex. Germany wanted to turn both countries into vassal states, with foreign policies dictated by Berlin. Belgium would then serve as a buffer between Germany and England, while Poland would keep the Russians at a safe distance. This scenario was unacceptable to the Entente. The British Empire had gone to war to liberate Belgium, and Russia had declared its intention to make Poland a nearly autonomous province and certainly could not permit the German Empire to expand, through a vassal state, right up to Russia's western border. For Germany, some form of territorial expansion was a non-negotiable demand; there could be no return to the situation before August 1914. Yet that was precisely what most of the Entente countries required, at a minimum, and some of them could not conceal their hopes of reparations for damage done. Belgium dreamed of Luxembourg and parts of the Netherlands, and France wanted to return to the pre-1790 borders, which embraced not only Alsace and Lorraine but also the resource-rich Saar region.

Yet the many peace plans developed by neutral organizations and other advocates of peace recognized no role for annexation.[9] Nations could not be shoved back and forth at will, like pawns on a geopolitical chessboard; they had the right to decide for themselves who would govern them. The case for self-determination was often accompanied with arguments for minority rights, democratic control of foreign policy (since secret agreements had played a central role in the escalation of the war in 1914), and various forms of international arbitration and consultation. Despite the general emphasis on self-determination, there was no clear definition of 'people' or 'nation'. Italy believed that it had a claim to Tripolitania because the region had once been a province of the Roman Empire. And Greek nationalists demanded Macedonia because Alexander the Great was said to have been born there, while the Bulgarians asserted their right to the same area of land because it had been the heart of the Bulgarian Empire in the tenth century.[10] For major powers on both sides of the struggle, strict application of the self-determination principle would have led to total upheaval; both Russia and the Dual Monarchy were essentially multi-ethnic states. On 12 December 1916, the German chancellor Theobald von Bethmann Hollweg floated a peace proposal in which he emphasized that his country had always seen the conflict as a war of self-defence. Yet just a few weeks earlier, he had proclaimed the formation of the Kingdom of Poland in parliament, essentially redrawing the map of Europe and making a peace treaty with the Russians next to impossible. France and Great Britain raised a different objection to Bethmann's proposal: Germany's annexationist politics in Belgium had nothing to do with self-defence and only proved that the Allies had justice on their side. Accordingly, they rejected a plan put forward by the American president Woodrow Wilson for 'peace without victory'. Germany was in the wrong, they reasoned, and therefore had to be punished. Or in the words of one of the many poems about the German peace proposal, 'In this Dance of Death / the man who called the piper's tune must pay.'[11] The Hungarian prime minister István Tisza commented that the right of self-determination propagated by Wilson was a fine principle, but exceptionally difficult to apply in multi-ethnic areas. Who would assume control there? Wouldn't the majority impose its will and 'national identity' on the minorities? The Germans intimated that they were open to negotiation, pointedly remarking how dearly they would like to see Ireland and India avail themselves of the right of national self-determination. In the same memorandum, however, they also announced a policy of unrestricted submarine warfare, in protest at Britain's strangulating maritime blockade of German ports. The goal was to disrupt British supply lines, but the effect was to provoke the United States to break off diplomatic relations and, ultimately, to declare war on Germany. This illustrates how peace proposals (sincere or otherwise) further escalated the conflict.[12] As much as everybody loathed the war, peace seemed almost as unattainable as victory.

The year 1917 began in deadlock – military, political and diplomatic. Then a first dramatic crack began to show. In Russia, the new spring dawned in the depths of winter.[13] The average February temperature in Petrograd was 12.1 degrees below zero (Celsius).[14] Civilians, mostly women, had to queue for bread outdoors for up to forty hours a week in these conditions, often only to discover that there was none to be had, owing to shortages of ingredients or of fuel for baking. On 8 March, International Women's Day (23 February according to the Russian calendar),[15] the women of the city had had enough, and took to the streets by the thousands. It was the start of the February Revolution. Soldiers and labourers joined the uprising, which was boosted by a sudden relatively warm spell.[16] It seemed as if spring were truly ushering in a new world. Three weeks later, Czar Nicholas abdicated and was replaced by a Provisional Government.

The revolution unleashed an avalanche of emotions. Mayakovsky, for one, could hardly contain himself. On 12 March a friend ran into him early in the morning. After lifting him off the ground and kissing him with wild enthusiasm, Mayakovsky seemed eager to hurry on to the station. 'Where are you going?' his friend asked. 'Why, they're shooting over there!' 'But you're not armed!' Mayakovsky did not see the problem: 'I've been running all night to where the shooting is.' 'What for?' 'I don't know why! Let's run!'[17] The Futurist leader may have been more impetuous than the average civilian, but Anna Akhmatova also spent the first day of the revolution wandering the streets as if hypnotized, seemingly oblivious to the danger.[18] The Symbolist poet Zinaida Gippius likewise noticed that the revolution had released extraordinary energies. It both fascinated her and filled her with fear. She did not doubt for a moment that the revolutionaries would succeed: 'Everything about the war cries out, "Retreat!" And everything about the revolutionary movement shouts, "Advance!"'[19] That made all the difference in the world.

In other countries, the revolution engendered great expectations. The young Flemish socialist Richard Minne (1891–1965) was hopeful that the future would come from the East, because Russia was where 'the marvellous schism lies / between old faith and new'. Now the challenge was for enough people to choose the right side, so that 'new values' and 'a new order' could emerge spontaneously.[20] Géza Gyóni, still a prisoner of war in Siberia, also took heart from the revolution. He hoped that it would spread to Hungary[21] and 'dance along the world smelling of blood',[22] as he wrote in the poem 'Utólso tánc' (Last Dance) on 22 March. Gyóni would never witness the outcome. He died on 25 June, his thirty-third birthday, just a few weeks after his beloved younger brother Mihály had perished in the same camp. In May, Romain Rolland, Frans Masereel, Pierre-Jean Jouve, Marcel Martinet and Henri Guilbeaux published *Le Salut à la Révolution Russe* in

Switzerland.[23] In his poem 'Mars 1917' (March 1917), Guilbeaux interpreted the revolution as an inspiring struggle for liberation from the tyranny of capitalism and war and paid homage to all the deportees, prisoners and 'martyrs' who had made all this possible through their courage and spirit of sacrifice.

> Peoples, to your feet,
> proletarians, form a chain around the world, unbreakable and unending,
> liberate humanity from its torments, from its agonies,
> create life, create peace, for the Revolution.[24]

What was striking in Russia, however, was that the revolutionaries seemed unconcerned about peace. Not only was their uprising extremely bloody,[25] but they did not even really call for a ceasefire. Although the war had thrown the Russian economy into such disarray that a revolution had ensued, democratization and social reform were felt to be more urgent than ending the bloodbath that had already been so catastrophic for the country. By the fourth day of the revolution, Zinaida Gippius observed that the slogan 'Down with the war' was remarkably unpopular. It seemed as if, in all the commotion, the people had forgotten the war entirely. 'Understandable, only too understandable', the poet reflected, 'after all those government campaigns and the dictum … "Everything for the war!"'[26] But of course, the war would not let itself be forgotten. Day after day, she wrote two weeks later, military regiments passed her window with banners like 'War until victory', 'Comrades, make shells', and 'Guard our new-won freedom'. According to her friend Alexander Blok, mobilized in July 1916 and now in Petrograd for a short time, there was not much evidence of any revolutionary spirit at the front.[27] Gippius believed that the Provisional Government, in which her friend Alexander Kerensky played a leading role, was making a grave error by keeping its war plans firmly under its hat.

For the time being, none of this could put a dampener on the festivities. On 5 April, the day after he visited Gippius, Blok wrote to his mother,

> I walked the streets watching this spectacle, which is like nothing ever experienced before in the world or in history, and saw happy, friendlier-looking people assembling on the unswept streets, without bodyguards. The extraordinary feeling that nothing is forbidden, that almost anything can happen. Not one of us could ever have expected to witness these simple miracles that are now daily occurrences. You might think that it would all be very frightening, but it isn't at all – this majestic freedom, these army vehicles with red flags, soldiers' greatcoats with red armbands, the red flag on the roof of the Winter Palace.[28]

Yet in the fluid environment of a revolution, conflicting interpretations of the new situation can quickly emerge. The end of the monarchy was regarded as a great emancipation in the non-Russian areas of the empire. People spontaneously began to sing the Marseillaise and raise the national flag: the Finnish flag in Helsinki, the Ukrainian flag in Kiev, and the Georgian flag in Tbilisi. It seemed inevitable that the fall of the Czar would bring a new European state system. On Sunday, 25 March, some 100,000 demonstrators took to the streets of Petrograd with the lemon-yellow and blue flags of the Ukraine and slogans like 'Federal Republic' and 'Autonomy'.[29] The next day, about 40,000 Estonians marched through the city, including 12,000 armed soldiers. They too demanded independence.[30] But the Provisional Government's initial policy documents said as little about the rights of national minorities as they did about the war.[31] In practice, most of the Petrograd revolutionaries turned out to be fervent Russian patriots. Some of them were open to the idea of a federal solution to the problem of other nationalities – Switzerland was cited as a model – but there could be no question of dividing Mother Russia.[32] One exception was permissible to the new leaders. On 29 March, they decided that Poland – then occupied by Germans and Austrians – could have its independence. But beyond that, national unity was their watchword. The un-Russian monarchy had been deposed, a great patriotic revolution had taken place, and the revolutionaries had finally established the *sobornost* (spiritual community) of all Russians that they had longed for. They were not about to let peripheral upwellings of nationalism spoil their achievement.

This uncompromising attitude only encouraged the nationalists to fight back. In this respect, public sentiment in the Ukraine and Finland followed much the same course as that in Ireland or, to a lesser extent, Flanders. Those who had once been moderate supporters of autonomy (or Home Rule) now demanded unconditional liberty. On 6 July the Finnish Sejm (parliament) declared the country's independence, whereupon the Provisional Government sent troops to Finland to crush the independence movement and dissolve the Sejm. The crisis did not reach this stage in the Ukraine, where the Provisional Government tried to appease the nationalists with promises of autonomy. This went too far for the Russian nationalists in the government, who resigned in outrage, bringing the new regime to the verge of collapse.

And indeed, lack of clarity on the two leading political issues – the war and non-Russian nationalities – soon led to the downfall of the civilian regime. General Brusilov, the celebrated leader of a successful Galician campaign in 1916,[33] had been placed at the head of the armed forces by the Provisional Government, but even he could not prevent war minister Kerensky's summer offensive from ending in catastrophe.[34] The objective was to recapture Lemberg, but after two days of steady progress, the war machine stalled, and increasing numbers of soldiers simply gave up the fight. Approximately 400,000 Russian soldiers were killed or injured, and many more deserted. While Maxim Gorky had regarded the offensive as a last-ditch attempt to bring some order to the chaos of Russia, and Blok had also patriotically supported the action, the reality was a far cry from their expectations. The nationalist insurgency in the capital meant little to the soldiers. The revolution had undermined their respect for the officers' orders, and the army descended into anarchy. Soldiers eagerly accepted German offers of drink or brothels, or suspended hostilities on their own initiative. The retreat turned into an utter fiasco, with pervasive drunkenness, rape and pogroms forming a painful contrast to the exalted rhetoric of the home front:

> And if, swirling with pain, I fall in the name of Mother Russia,
> And find myself in some deserted field,
> Shot through the chest on the ground,
> Then at the Gates of Heaven,
> In my dying and joyous dreams,
> I will remember – Russia, Liberty,
> Kerensky on a white horse.[35]

Many Russian poets had been quick to embrace the revolution. However patriotic they were, they had never cared for the Czar, and the new civilian authorities were closer to the world of their own experience. As mentioned above, the socialist Kerensky was a friend of Gippius's, and one of Blok's former publishers was now the minister of finance.[36] Meanwhile, the other Symbolists were squabbling over who would write the lyrics for the new national anthem. Some of them, guided by their Russian national pride, emphasized the importance of the Orthodox Church. Bryusov, on the other hand, believed that it should be an anthem for all the people of Russia and for all religious groups. Shunning the chauvinism and militarism of some of his fellow poets, he stressed Russia's devotion to the struggle for peace and freedom. In poems like 'Freedom and War' and the pamphlet *How the War Should Be Ended*, he argued that the war should be continued until the Poles, Belgians, Serbians and Armenians were also liberated.[37] Gippius, Sologub and Balmont wrote poems expressing similar views. Remarkably, the rhetoric had not changed in any fundamental way since 1914. Soldiers still had to fight bravely for their country and transform the world into a healthy, devout, strong community. In these elite circles, far from being a cry for peace, the Revolution fuelled the old militaristic dream. Those selected to fight for that dream at the front were beginning to see matters quite differently.

It would be an exaggeration to suggest that the climate among Belgian soldiers was also ripe for revolution, but there were more deserters each year, and a swelling mood of general discontent.[38] Anything else would have been surprising. The winter of 1917 was the longest and fiercest that anyone could recall. Until April, temperatures were sometimes so far below freezing that the sentries had to be relieved once an hour.[39] The Belgian front was not the most dangerous, but unlike their British, German and most French counterparts, the Belgian soldiers could never visit home, and after three years the separation from their families in the occupied country began to take its toll. Behind the front, in De Panne, writer and patron Marie ('Mamieke', or 'little mother') Belpaire (1853–1948) became a mother figure for Flemish authors and intellectuals. One of the regular visitors to her villa was her distant relative Georges (later Joris) Van Severen (1894–1940), writer of occasional poetry. In his reading and his own writings, he was highly susceptible to D'Annunzio's exaltation, but his own perspective on the conflict differed drastically from his idol's. 'Idiotic, foolish war. My hatred of the ruling powers burns and consumes me through and through, my hatred of people like Mamieke, drowsing in the sappy-sweetness of their calm, warm, peaceful lives. Rebellion flares bitterly in me.'[40] Around the time of this diary entry (8 January 1917), intellectuals who supported the Flemish cause found themselves united in their protest against the current situation. The Flemish study groups organized in 1915 for the cultural and moral edification of the troops were banned by the army leadership on 11 February, a step that only encouraged covert Flemish radicalism. The poet-priest Cyriel Verschaeve supported this Front Movement morally and logistically. The poets Filip De Pillecyn (1891–1962), Jozef Simons (1888–1948), Armand Suls (1893–1948) and Van Severen were among its day-to-day leaders, and Van Severen saw himself more and more as a revolutionary.[41] Yet this rebellious spirit does not surface in their surviving poetry from this period, except perhaps in these lines written by De Pillecyn in April 1917 about horses that had to be freed from their harness.

> Give rein and let the horses rear up free.
> Revolt is blowing in from distant skies.
> Don't mount the saddle, for the weight of sleep
> May blind you to their fitful, fiery eyes.[42]

The poet may have adopted this highly figurative style in response to the new rigour with which senior army officers and military intelligence (whose sympathies lay with the French-speaking community) were cracking down on the leaders of the Flemish movement. Everything the Flemish leaders did was suspect, and every expression of Flemish pride was equated with seditious activism and punished with imprisonment or demotion.[43] As the Allies were making a case for the liberty of Poles and Czechs in magazines like *The New Europe*, these Flemish authors and soldiers felt oppressed in their own country and army. In response to these developments, poets with a much less radical image also grew more defiant. August Van Cauwelaert, 'the full and flawless youth with the pure heart and the pure mind of a poet', was severely injured in early April 1916. While recuperating in France, he sent passionate letters to friends at the front,[44] encouraging them to keep him thoroughly informed so that he could influence the king through his brother Frans, a prominent politician. Although the king was personally responsible for appointing anti-Flemish ministers and army commanders, he was still deeply respected by most of the soldiers. The government, however, could no longer count on much sympathy. In a long and uncharacteristically militant poem, Van Cauwelaert made it clear that he too had lost his patience with the wartime cabinet in Le Havre.

> How long will you placate with pledges and smirks,
> As if tossing a few scraps of bread to a cur,
> and say with a shrug, 'Stop your shouting for rights,
> just bow down and take it, just shut up and fight.'[45]

Van Cauwelaert's sympathizers undoubtedly recognized the allusion to an earlier war poem by René De Clercq, the poet whom both the occupied nation and the generation on the front had come to know as the Voice of Flanders. 'For without rights, I have no land, / And without bread, I fear no brand', De Clercq had written in 'Aan die van Havere toen zij vergaten dat ook Vlaanderen in België lag' (To Those in Havre When They Forgot that Flanders Is Also Part of Belgium, quoted in Chapter 5).[46] As the title indicated, De Clercq's ideal was not necessarily Flemish independence, but respect and acknowledgement of the Flemish role in the war. Van Cauwelaert took the same position; in lines like 'Our people has shared in the pain of our country', 'our country' always referred to Belgium. Van Cauwelaert did not leave any room for doubt that Germany was the greatest enemy ('the villains from the Rhineland'). But he described the Belgian government in terms that were almost as scathing, presenting them as an elite alienated from the people, who after the war would shamelessly take the credit for the price the Flemish had paid in blood.[47] The Flemish soldiers had obvious reasons for their anger, but similar complaints were heard surprisingly often among the Walloons. Louis Boumal (1890–1918), a poet from a working-class family in Liège – and, incidentally, another visitor to Marie Belpaire's villa and an acquaintance of Van Severen's – also complained in his diary about a lack of respect for ordinary soldiers among the general staff and the arrogance of some officers 'who in hanging around in the barracks and the pubs have developed a second nature, drunken and coarse. To them, soldiers are no more than registration numbers, convenient, conscripted things.'[48] There was undoubtedly a 'Flemish question' on the Yser, but as in all the other armies, there was also a social question.

In that respect, the Battle of the Chemin des Dames (or Second Battle of the Aisne), from 16 to 20 April, was a landmark event in the war as remembered by the French. Whereas Verdun had symbolized heroic fortitude, 'Chemin des Dames' became synonymous with 'tragic debacle'.[49] The scenario was all too familiar by this stage in the war. Poor coordination of artillery and infantry was compounded by misevaluation of the German defence lines, and the result was yet another massacre. The *rupture* anticipated by General Nivelle never took place.

In the rain, fog, snow, freezing cold and hail, 29,000 French soldiers died and another 100,000 were injured or went missing in action. It was the last straw. Soldiers from fifty-four divisions, almost half the French army, refused to go on fighting. Although the word 'mutiny' is used in many accounts of the event, they did not desert or flee the trenches. They simply made it clear that they would not leave the trenches for another senseless attack. They were prepared to defend their country, but to lay down their lives because some general thought it would bring him eternal glory? Never again. The best-known literary expression of this uprising is the anonymous, orally transmitted 'Chanson de Craonne', whose title recalls a village on the front line that was wiped off the map by no fewer than five million shells, and rebuilt in a nearby location afterwards.

> Those who have the dough, they'll be coming back,
> 'Cause it's for them that we're dying.
> But it's all over now, 'cause all of the grunts
> Are going to go on strike.
> It'll be your turn, all you rich and powerful gentlemen,
> To go up onto the plateau.
> And if you want to make war,
> Then pay for it with your own skins![50]

This was a symptom of a still deeper crisis. Across the country, workers were going on strike, not to demand peace and surrender, but to protest against the war profiteers: arms manufacturers and other industrialists who were growing rich on the backs of self-sacrificing soldiers and of men and women who were working themselves to the bone. It was clear to the French government that the implicit contract between the government and its citizens was at risk of being terminated. Petain was appointed to replace General Nivelle, and a battery of measures, mainly social in nature, along with a limited number of executions (49), restored order to the French ranks. For the time being, no more major offensives were undertaken.

On 27 February 1917, Chancellor Bethmann made an all-out effort in the Reichstag to emphasize the battle-readiness and unity of the German people, citing both Goethe and Karl Bröger (1886–1944), a working-class poet who was both a Catholic and a socialist. Were they not all living in 'a nation about which one of our poets at the front said the moving words, "Its poorest son is also its most loyal son?"'[51] The applause came from every bench after this reference to 'Bekenntnis' (Confession), a popular poem during the war. There could be no mistaking the chancellor's point: social friction did not exist in Germany. The country might be under siege on all fronts, and its enemies might have gravely misunderstood its people's fundamental desire for peace, but at least the Germans would be united in resolute struggle to the finish.

In theory, at least. In practice, the number of deserters from the German army in 1917 was (as in other armies) double or triple the figure for 1916. And proportionally, no fewer soldiers were court-martialled than in the French or British armies.[52] On the home front, too, unity was a relative term. Survival was becoming increasingly difficult, and therefore took priority over shows of support for official war propaganda. At the same time, the sacrifices demanded were becoming more and more extreme. The Hindenburg Programme required all men between the ages of seventeen and sixty not eligible for military service to work in the war industry (factories, agriculture or administration). After food, clothes and shoes were also rationed. Germans who planned to buy a new piece of clothing had to turn in an old one to the authorities in order not to exceed their quota. Women were not allowed to own more than two pairs of shoes or boots.[53] Production for the war effort was all there was now. This was total war. There was no escaping it any longer.

Everyday life could hardly have been less like the world Bethmann described in his speech. 'The great war has renewed our people', he claimed. 'This is not about rewarding the people for what they have done … but all about finding the appropriate political and constitutional expression of what this nation is.' Meanwhile, the people were expressing themselves through mass demonstrations and food riots. And when they protested, their leaders' political and constitutional response was simply violent repression.

The front had also seen the emergence of a new breed of man. Again, this new life bore little resemblance to the chancellor's high-flown description. Lieutenant Carl Zuckmayer (1896–1977) was so ashamed of the poem '1917', in which he took stock of his life as a soldier, that he did not publish it until fifty years later:

> I haven't eaten for seven days
> And shot a man right in the face.
> When I scratch, the bright blood runs.
> I'll soon be turning twenty-one.
> When I'm drunk, I'll plant my fist
> In those pasty faces. Rage is my hymn.
> Lice and fleas eat from my shins.
> My stubble sprouts like garden cress.
> And so I take my seed in my hand –
> Europe's future, black-specked spawn;
> A god drowns in a sludge-filled pond! –
> And shit my legacy on the wall.[54]

By this time, Pierre-Jean Jouve had also abandoned the tone of his early war poems, benevolent, hopeful, and full of unshakable love for humanity. Anger and despair had come in its stead. This pacifist poet could no longer build a new world, and only the thorough destruction of the existing one seemed of any use at all to him. In *Danse des morts* (1917) he presented an illusion-free analysis of the war, given voice by the figure of Death. All the phrases used to sell the conflict (holy war, for our homeland, for democracy, peace, the victory of justice) were shown to be no more than cynical masks disguising pure imperialism. Everyone wanted a piece of the pie, and so they shamelessly exploited other people's suffering. One had his eye on Belgium, the Balkans or Poland – and above all, their mining basins – while another was more tempted by Trieste, Trento and Dalmatia. Europe had left its great ideals far behind and was teetering on the brink of moral and intellectual bankruptcy.

> Hey! Hey! Hey!
> Europe's gone the barbarian way!
> She's wallowing in it and having a ball,
> Enjoying herself and ending it all.[55]

But those who were able to go on believing in the primacy of the nation-state and in France's national culture tended to see matters rather differently. From his sick bed, where he found himself in March 1916 after sustaining a serious head injury at the front, Guillaume Apollinaire, finally granted French citizenship, decided that there was no higher calling than writing odes to the heroes and achievements of his adoptive country. Future generations and politicians, he told Pierre Albert-Birot of the avant-garde magazine *SIC*, could find inspiration in his work and discover that freedom and art can exist only in a society with a strong will.[56] He was one of those French heroes himself; along with the rest of his regiment, he had received the Croix de Guerre in May. His injury completed the picture. Not that he bragged about it, but his friends let it be known that a very risky trepanation had been required to save his life.[57] It was felt that it would be too dangerous for Apollinaire to return to the front, and the military went in search of a desk job for him. The press office had no desire to work with the notorious king of the Cubists, but the censors had a place for him. When Henri Guilbeaux heard of the transfer in the summer of 1917, he had harsh words in *Demain* for the standard-bearer of modern art and literature. 'Like journalism, Cubism can apparently open any door.'[58] Even though he considered Apollinaire a charlatan, taken seriously only on the banks of the Seine and the Spree (apparently, there were gullible snobs in both capitals), the shamelessness with which he had segued into censoring the writings of his peers disgusted Guilbeaux. Apollinaire himself found the new job more hilarious than anything else, one of the war goddess Bellona's more amusing whims. With mock solemnity he vetted the poems of his young friend Albert-Birot and the other *SIC* writers.[59] Yet wartime conditions did change his perspective on the avant-garde. For instance, he distanced himself from his reflexive pre-war cosmopolitanism. When Tristan Tzara asked him to contribute to Dada publications, Apollinaire replied that he could not possibly become involved in an international art movement with German participants.[60]

After the tragedy on the Somme, the atmosphere in the British army was worse than ever, yet there were hardly any acts of rebellion beyond jocular, *sotto voce* griping. For example, on 15 January 1917, Siegfried Sassoon commented on the other officers he met in England: 'What earthly use are all these people? They don't instruct anyone; they simply eat and drink. I think nearly half the officers in our army are conscripted humbugs who are paid to propagate inefficiency. They aren't even willing to be killed; I can at least say *that* for myself, for I've tried often.'[61] Yet soldiers rarely questioned the fundamental nature of their mission. After sustaining a serious injury, Somme veteran Robert Ernest Vernède was promised a safe office job, but he would have none of it. In his 1917 poem 'A Listening Post', he sketched the contrast between the higher goal of making sure that the world would not 'lie in chains for years / and England be a bygone tale / And right be wrong / And laughter tears' and the way the soldiers were expected to achieve that goal: the cold-blooded 'murder of our fellow man'.[62] But he left it up to God to resolve this discord, went back to work, and died on 9 April of fresh wounds incurred in Havrincourt (Cambrai).

Sassoon felt convinced that his work at the front would lead only to 'madness' and that the soldier had degenerated from a noble figure into 'a writhing insect among this ghastly folly of destruction'.[63] He wrote these words on 15 February 1917, on his way back to the front after being sent home with trench fever in late July. On Good Friday, 6 April, after a few weeks in France, he told a very different story: 'If I had the choice between England tomorrow and the battle, I would choose the battle without hesitation.' When the spring offensive began three days later, his tone changed slightly, although even after six days of combat during which he never slept longer than an hour at a time, he still described himself as 'fit and cheery'.[64] He realized that the Germans he had shot to pieces would remain burned into his memory until his dying day, but that did not seem like such a terribly long time, since he was convinced he would die the following Monday. Fate decided otherwise. He was hit by a sniper, but the bullet merely went through his shoulder. At first the dauntless Sassoon carried on in spite of his injury, but at the end of the day he decided to stop by an aid station, after which (much to his disappointment) he was sent back to England again.

The diary entries that follow are mildly amused pieces about dinners, parties and outsiders' naive comments about the war. On 15 June, he sent a statement to a few politicians, pacifists, writers and government officials, and the head of British war propaganda, Arnold Bennett. One of the members of parliament read it aloud in the House of Commons on 30 July. A day later, the statement was printed in *The Times* and the author became world-famous:

> I am making this statement as an act of willful defiance of military authority, because I believe that the War is being deliberately

> prolonged by those who have the power to end it. I am a soldier, convinced that I am acting on behalf of soldiers. I believe that this War, upon which I entered as a war of defence and liberation, has now become a war of aggression and conquest. I believe that the purposes for which I and my fellow-soldiers entered upon this war should have been so clearly stated as to have made it impossible for them to be changed without our knowledge, and that, had this been done, the objects which actuated us would now be attainable by negotiation.
>
> I have seen and endured the sufferings of the troops, and I can no longer be a party to prolonging those sufferings for ends which I believe to be evil and unjust.
>
> I am not protesting against the conduct of the War, but against the political errors and insincerities for which the fighting men are being sacrificed.
>
> On behalf of those who are suffering now, I make this protest against the deception which is being practised on them. Also I believe it may help to destroy the callous complacence with which the majority of those at home regard the continuance of agonies which they do not share, and which they have not enough imagination to realise.[65]

There is every reason to believe that it was not the war itself, but the rhetoric of war, that had suddenly become too much for Sassoon. The governing class, the propaganda services, and fanatical nationalists droned on and on about the Beastly Hun, all the while annihilating their own country's young generation. In the trenches, Sassoon's irritation had been outweighed by his dedication and fighting spirit. But when immersed in the complacency of the British upper classes, he could no longer keep himself in check. In the privacy of his diary, he came to conclusions that were remarkably similar to those of the Russian revolutionaries. 'The rulers of England have always relied on the ignorance and patient credulity of the crowd. If the crowd could see into those cynical hearts it would lynch its dictators.'[66] Sassoon demanded that the British Empire openly declare its terms for peace, so that negotiations could have some chance of success. As long as it would not, it invited the suspicion that it harboured secret and deceitful plans. His public statement received the vocal support of pacifists such as Bertrand Russell and Lady Ottoline Morrell, but most of his friends and acquaintances were appalled. Just as the United States had finally decided to join the Entente and 'safeguard the future of liberty and democracy', just as the demoralized Russian army had realized that it would have to go on fighting for the sake of its freedom, Sassoon was undermining Britain's moral ground, and hence endangering its liberty.[67] Bennett suggested that Sassoon simply lacked the wider view required to judge the situation, adding that the army would have no choice but to declare Sassoon 'daft', even though he had been completely lucid when he made his statement.[68] And he was right; that was the only option short of a court martial, and after the bad publicity Sassoon had already brought them, the authorities wished to avoid any further embarrassment. The rebellious young officer was examined by the Medical Board, declared mentally unsound, and sent to Craiglockhart War Hospital to be treated for shell shock. It was there that he met the volunteer soldier Wilfred Owen (1893–1918), who really was suffering from shell shock.

Italy's post-unification army had never been noteworthy for its unity or undying devotion.[69] Its poor and largely illiterate soldiers were expected to take orders from the landowners who exploited them in everyday life, now dressed in officers' uniforms. The inequality was also geographical: farmers from the impoverished south of the country were commanded by privileged northerners in a war that served the interests of the northern elite. The grunts expressed their dissatisfaction in many ways, including a flood of anonymous letters to the Italian king. If he wanted to stay on the throne, they warned, then he would have to make peace, and quickly. In their eyes, the real enemy was not the Austrian emperor, but that 'buffoon and murderer D'Annunzio Gabriele who persuaded the ignorant masses to chant "Long live the war"'.[70] This was no lie. While maintaining a tireless commitment to speechmaking, D'Annunzio had flown high-profile propaganda missions over enemy territory, propagating death-defying heroism and nationalism as the ultimate Italian virtues.[71] Admittedly, he was not entirely numb to the suffering caused by the war. When one of his fellow pilots crashed, D'Annunzio watched over the body until it literally decomposed before his eyes and the stench became unbearable. In January 1916 he was temporarily blinded after a flying accident, and the 10,000 one- or two-line reflections that he jotted on notecards in the following months provided an inside view of the visions that tormented him on his sickbed. They occasionally offer a glimpse of the hell into which he had so eagerly plunged.

> I lie all night on the barbed wire that defends the hill. I count the corpses. They are caught in the steel thicket, they wrap themselves around the curls of the cut wire, hang in between the stakes, like robbers badly nailed to crosses, they twist like animals caught in the snares. They have no eyelashes, no lips. I see their staring and naked eyes. I see their fixed and naked teeth. I see blood dripping from the wood and the steel, curdling, blackening, viscous like the thick substance that covers the stakes. In the world there is no more dew, there is no more dawn.[72]

This was a sobering thought, but the poet did not let it lower his spirits for long. Once he recovered his vision, he was once again the heroic fighter who had discovered through personal experience that bloodshed and self-sacrifice are the road to an authentic life. Others reached a different conclusion. In May, there were violent street protests in Milan and elsewhere, and in April and August the number of deserters doubled.[73] In July 1917, members of the Catanzaro brigade refused to go back to what they called the slaughterhouse of the Kras plateau. They killed three officers and four military policemen and laid siege to the house where they believed the heroic poet was staying, shouting 'Death to D'Annunzio'.[74] In conformity with ancient Roman practice, the regiment was then decimated. In other words, thirty-eight soldiers were put to death, all of them boys from the south. D'Annunzio came to witness the executions. The sight sickened him, and a friend saw him trying to control his trembling lower lip. But you would never guess any of this from his aestheticized written account of the event, in which he delivered a judgement on the young men that they would never be able to appeal. 'You are peasants. I recognize you as such from your hands, from the way you hold your feet on the ground. I do not care whether you are innocent or guilty.' Referring to a Roman king who had seen fit to kill all his soldiers too short to reach the hilt of their sword, he sentenced them again: 'You, men of the plough, men of the sickle, are of mediocre height.'[75] Meanwhile, he played the role of the great, stoic man, but that was not always how he truly felt. A few weeks after the executions, the stress and excitement almost overwhelmed him, and he seriously considered taking the poison pill that he always brought with him on dangerous missions. 'I want to tear my heart out and to burn out my brain.'[76] Once again driven by an unquenchable desire for death, he completed his next mission safely.

Most other soldiers were not protected by such a death wish. They wanted to survive, but one in ten Italian infantrymen was killed. These regiments lived in an atmosphere of tension, fear and resignation. Piero Jahier, one of the other cultural leaders who had argued in favour of intervention, devoted his 'Primia marcia alpina' (First Alpine March') to a sense of solidarity that was not only largely fictional but also somewhat easier to maintain in the relative safety of the training camp where he was writing:[77]

> If you ask for kidneys torn up by a mine
> if you ask for wrists worked to the bone
> if you ask for knees that climbing has bent
> if you ask for love that no suffering will end,
> then we say: here we are, Alpine soldiers all,
> and we come running when you call.[78]

In reality, mines tore up more than kidneys. High in the mountains, in terrain completely unsuited to ordinary military tactics, the two sides were constantly trying to place mines beneath each other's positions. Excessively ambitious tunnelling projects sometimes led to spectacular explosions and often to fatal injuries. By this point, successive waves of attacks had caused 570,000 fatalities among the Italian forces in this border region. There were some 600,000 infantrymen at the front at this time. In other words, there were almost as many dead soldiers as there were active ones at the front.[79] Against this backdrop, it is nothing short of miraculous that the troops along the Isonzo river were willing to attack for the eleventh time, on 19 August 1917. The resulting carnage – the worst in the Italian campaign thus far, with another 100,000 Italian soldiers lost in less than a month – made no immediately visible dent in the confidence of the elite. Ardengo Soffici, another firm advocate of Italian intervention, was injured in this attack on 23 August and reported on his state of mind in a poem from, and about, his hospital bed.

> The white walls of the room
> are like brackets;
> the spirit rests here

between the burning fury of yesterday's battle
and the flowery enigma that will commence again tomorrow.

Bright shining pause, simmering of multiple senses,
here all converges into an inexpressible unity,
mysteriously I feel flowing a time of gold
where everything is equal:
the fields, the highs of victory, the howlings, the sun, the blood
of the dead[80]

The sickroom makes reality seem parenthetical, as every image, thought and feeling is absorbed into the white glow of the moment. But again, even after all those months of death and destruction and the near-destruction of the poet himself, we hear yet another expression of the same old outlook on the war, the outlook that had led so many in the elite to welcome it with open arms. Destruction, he concluded, leads to new life, a 'flowery enigma'. The nature of the process was mysterious to Soffici, but this conviction gave him enough reason to hope that the war would continue.

It became clear how unpopular this point of view had become in late October, when the Central Powers launched a counter-attack. The Italians were massacred. In the space of just a few weeks, they were chased out of the mountains for which they had spilled so much blood by their very aggressive opponents – Bosnians, among others – and driven back to the Piave river. Italy lost 700,000 men in that brief period, only 40,000 of whom were killed or injured. Some 350,000 soldiers surrendered, often without any semblance of a fight. According to the Italian chief of staff Luigi Cadorna, the Caporetto disaster showed what a sorry bunch of bunglers he had under his command, but the government suspected the reverse and replaced Cadorna. The army was not so easy to replace, of course, and instead every possible step was taken to boost its morale. Living conditions for the troops were improved, and the propagandists set out to convince both the public and the soldiers that this was a social struggle that would lead to better lives for wage labourers and raise every Italian's standard of living to up to level of 'any other European'.[81] In other words: no need for a revolution, the war is the revolution.

The indefatigable D'Annunzio also did his bit to fan the flames of heroism yet again, alternating severe and soothing words. It was fortunate for him that the troops were now along the Piave, as it offered an ideal source of metaphors: this sacred watercourse was the artery that carried the lifeblood of Italy; this was the water of regeneration, the new baptismal fount. But of course, the troops had to prove themselves worthy of that water. Then D'Annunzio cracked the whip. Yellow-bellied runaways would hear their own mothers deny them: 'I have not borne you!' And as if rejection by *la mamma* were not bad enough, he compared their muddy faces, 'as of some excrement', with the faces of the enemy, devoid of all manliness. Their debased attitude could no longer be tolerated. Not one more 'nail's breadth' of Italian ground would be given up, he pontificated, and the soldiers certainly should not count on forgiveness or indulgence from the enemy. 'This war is without pity; this world war is without mercy.' After Caporetto, peace was no longer an option. The enemy had to be crushed completely, because he was savage and cruel and, in his malevolent bestiality, formed a threat to the nobility of Roman-Italian culture. D'Annunzio's message was straightforward and concrete: 'The Italian who kills most today shall be the best beloved son of Italy in arms.'[82]

There was no shortage of single-minded passion in 1917, but that was something of which Fernando Pessoa was still not capable. On 24 October his heteronym Alberto Caeiro interpreted the carnage according to his own impregnable logic:

War afflicting the world with its squadrons,
It's the perfect type of error of philosophy.

War, like everything human, wants to alter.
But war, more than everything, wants to alter and alter a lot
And alter quickly.

But war inflicts death.
And death is the Universe's disdain for us.[83]

It was a fallacy to think that people could bring about fundamental change by force. Things are what they are. But Pessoa's other heteronym Álvaro de Campos could not live with that detached conclusion. In November, he published a manifesto in *Portugal Futurista* with the telling title 'Ultimatum'. Like the Dadaists, de Campos met violence with violence. No one need hope for sympathy or compassion. His dream was to build a tremendous fleet on which he could assemble all the things he disliked about Europe and expel them from the continent. It was a long list, ranging from bloodthirsty prophets and nationalists (D'Annunzio, Kipling, Maurice Barrès, Charles Maurras) to pacifists like G.B. Shaw, and including almost all the continent's political leaders, from Kaiser Wilhelm to Venizelos in Greece and Boselli in Italy, and from the British and French prime ministers Lloyd George and Briand to their on-and-off Spanish counterpart Eduardo Dato Iradier. He wielded his rhetorical sledgehammer without mercy, for they had authored their own destruction with their hypocritical rhetoric. 'Proclaim loud and clear that nobody's fighting for Freedom or Justice! They're fighting in fear of everyone else!' de Campos urged.[84] All those who lacked the strength and authenticity to make a real difference to their continent were sent packing. 'Europe wants Masters! The World wants Europe! Europe is sick of not existing!'[85] And that process of continental self-realization was certainly not helped along by the interminable war, which had become a squalid, uninspiring farce, abhorrent to anyone who longed for a great future.

> Who believes in Them?
> Who believes in their counterparts?
> Make those *poilus* shave!
> Take away the herd's helmets!
> Send everyone home to peel symbolic potatoes!
> Give this mindless pandemonium a bath!
> Couple this war to a locomotive!
> Tie it to a leash and go show it in Australia!
> Men, nations, objectives: all a huge zero!
> All are to blame for the failure of everything!
> The failure of everything is to blame for all them!
> Completely, utterly, and unequivocally:
> **SHIT!**[86]

9

Last Man Standing: Endgame, 1918

> I hate the twentieth century, just as I hate this rotten European continent and the whole world over which this wretched Europe has spread like a grease stain.
>
> – Georges Duhamel, 1918[1]

So that was the First World War: two hundred and fifty fresh corpses every sixty minutes, a Twin Tower every afternoon. On an average day, 900 French soldiers died, 1,300 Germans and 1,459 Russians.[2] For the survivors, life on the front was typically tedious, anxiety-riddled and dirty. But the soldiers were more than mere cave-dwellers. If they managed to keep their footing in this inferno, it was because in spite of all the letdowns, losses and rude awakenings, they still cherished the belief that the war was not absurd. Yes, it was ghastly, inhuman and revolting, but not futile, not without meaning. Events in international politics reinforced that belief. The Fourteen Points proposed by the United States president, Woodrow Wilson, on 8 January 1918 gave hopes of freedom and autonomy to the Polish and other national minorities in Austria–Hungary, along with the occupied Belgians, French, Romanians, Montenegrins and Serbs. For many artists and writers, the meaning of the war was as clear as day. Without making light of the violence and the horror, they felt a deep conviction that this cataclysm would bring a new kind of art, one that would help to conceive and nurture a new and better world order.

In theory, this could be a fully cosmopolitan order, but not many people considered that likely. The nation-state seemed poised to come out of the war stronger than ever. In fact, applying the right of self-determination would mean recognizing many new nation-states. And it went without saying that they could not all be model nations, especially in their attitudes toward modern art. From the opening words of his lecture 'L'Esprit nouveau et les poètes' (The New Spirit and the Poets), delivered on 26 November 1917, Guillaume Apollinaire stressed that the new spirit would spread around the world, and that it was nowhere so clearly in evidence as in France. He also believed that the characteristics of this new spirit were fundamentally French. The *parole in libertà* (words in freedom) of the Italian and Russian Futurists, in which the words zigzagged across the page with no apparent system, were too free for his taste. French art was not fond of chaos. But Wagner's romantic German pathos was just as alien to the spirit Apollinaire had in mind. Artists and movements influenced each other, of course, but it was wrong to think that different national views on art would tend to converge over time. The revolution (Apollinaire spoke of 'social events') would never lead to the end of national literatures. Increasingly, he argued, art would have 'a homeland', and he did not mean that metaphorically. Apollinaire's position was that even though every artist, poet and philosopher belongs to the same human race, they all express their individual races and milieus in different ways.

> Art will only cease being national the day that the whole universe, living in the same climate, in houses built in the same style, speaks the same language with the same accent – that is to say never … From ethnic and national differences are born the variety of

> literary expressions, and it is that very variety which must be preserved.[3]

A cosmopolitan form of poetry would be as devoid of character as the cliché-ridden rhetoric of international diplomacy and politics, Apollinaire believed. Not everyone agreed. Around this time, Wilson's Fourteen Points were inspiring Europeans in a way that poets seldom could. And the Russian Revolution ... well, even Wilson himself was enthusiastic about that.

The president's words of admiration were not expressions of pure idealism. They appeared in a passage intended to nudge the peace negotiations in Brest-Litovsk toward an outcome favourable to the Russians (and thus to the Allies). That was the leading news in early 1918; a separate peace treaty for the Eastern front was close to being signed. In the summer of 1917, the collapsing Russian army had taken the Kerensky government down with it. British and Belgian troops were trying to fill the gaps left in the front line by Russian deserters, but it was a hopeless task.[4] The fall of Riga (Latvia) to the Central Powers on 2 September noisily heralded the beginning of the end.[5] Bolsheviks took to the streets with signs reading 'Peace Now!' In Finland and the Ukraine, nationalists declared independence. Everyone was turning against everyone else; the extreme right-wing Black Hundreds against Jews and Bolshevik workers, the Bolsheviks against the Cossacks, the farmers against the landed aristocracy, and the rich against the revolutionaries. The Provisional Government pondered reorganizations and reforms, but as Zinaida Gippius sternly remarked in her diary, all of her friends' good intentions came too late. 'Again, it's like it always is here, "It's too soon! Too soon!" until suddenly it's "too late!"'.[6] And it *was* too late.

Led by Lenin, whom the Germans had only too happily permitted to return from Swiss exile to his tumultuous homeland in a sealed train, the Bolsheviks seized power in early November. Gippius kept close track of developments, chronicling them as they took place. On 28 November, she already knew what to expect: 'How will they govern? Whoever survives will see. I suspect there will be few survivors among those who think.'[7]

While most poets – Symbolists, Acmeists and Futurists alike – had enthusiastically supported the war in 1914, the October Revolution created deep divisions, especially among the Symbolists.[8] Most Futurists saw the uprising as the start of the long-anticipated transformation and modernization of society. 'Accept or not accept? There was no such question for me, or for the other Moscow Futurists. My revolution', Mayakovsky later wrote.[9] Finally events were keeping pace with his own energy and ambition. Khlebnikov, too, was delirious with joy. 'The cannons were silent. We ran through the streets of the city like kids after the first snowfall.'[10] The revolution also gave both men the opportunity to bid farewell to military life – another fine reason to celebrate.

The Acmeists took a less rosy view of the situation. Like almost all other leading intellectuals, they had welcomed the resignation of the authoritarian Czar. But now that the Bolsheviks were coming into power, they feared the prospect of an even more repressive regime. In late November, Osip Mandelstam (1891–1938) publicly reflected on the fall of the Provisional Government. In a socialist revolutionary (but non-Bolshevik) newspaper, he defended Kerensky, associated the new leaders with a 'yoke of violence and hate', and predicted that Russia would 'descend to deepest hell'.[11] Meanwhile, Nikolay Gumilyov was in Paris, having returned from Transjordan, where he had apparently fought alongside the British. At the Russian military headquarters in the French capital, he met the anarchist Victor Serge, for whom Gumilyov sketched his own self-portrait: 'I am a traditionalist, monarchist, imperialist, and pan-Slavist. Mine is the true Russian nature, just as it was formed by Orthodox Christianity. You also have the true Russian nature, but at its opposite extreme, that of spontaneous anarchy, primitive violence and unruly beliefs. I love all of Russia, even what I want to fight in it, even what you represent …'[12] Although Gumilyov was no revolutionary, he did his best to find a way of returning home.

Anna Akhmatova, who would officially divorce Gumilyov later in 1918, was equally concerned. Life would change profoundly, she thought, and the situation could easily degenerate into violence, as it had during the French Revolution. Her popular war poem 'Prayer' was reprinted in December, in an opposition newspaper. In this context, the lines 'So that the stormcloud over darkened Russia / Might become a cloud of glorious rays' sounded like a condemnation of the godless Bolsheviks.[13] Marina Tsvetaeva had fled Moscow and experienced the revolution in Feodosiya, in the Crimea. What made the strongest impression on her were the drunk, disorderly soldiers.[14] *Innere Emigration* seemed her only escape:

> Hear the city romp and moan,
> Moonlight through a cloud of wine.
> There is not a living soul
> Can touch this poor, proud life of mine.[15]

The Symbolists Fyodor Sologub, Vyacheslav Ivanov and Konstantin Balmont believed that the Bolsheviks had betrayed the war and, by extension, their country. Gippius was even more damning: the Bolsheviks were born imbeciles, half-witted fanatics, riffraff, and German agents.[16] She could not begin to understand why her friend Blok supported their cause and regarded it as no less than heresy – a term the deeply religious Gippius did not use lightly.[17]

Blok was generally ill informed about the details of Russian politics, but his intuition suggested to him that it was time for a fresh start and that this would inevitably mean violence. He had long since given up his faith in the transformative potential of the war, which he now saw purely as a symbol of the repugnance and deceitfulness of the prewar regime. European culture urgently needed to be rescued.[18] But how? On 19 August 1917, before the catastrophic fall of Riga, Blok had reverted to his former role as a seer. In 1909, after the Messina earthquake, he had foreseen a consuming fire, but had been uncertain whether its effect would be to purify or merely to destroy. Now he realized that it was up to Russia's cultural leaders to determine which it would be. The air in Petrograd was once again filled with the odour of burning peat, as it had been during the ominous summer of 1914. For Blok, this was a sign that the blaze of revolution would quickly spread across the country. The crucial thing would be to destroy only what had to be destroyed. The conflagration could clear away the old, if it were guided in the right direction; he hoped 'to place on destruction such limits as will not weaken the fire's pressure, but organize this pressure; to organize the violent freedom'.[19] To him, the Bolsheviks seemed perfect for the job. Immediately after the takeover, he publicly expressed his support for the regime, explaining that what mattered most to him was 'the soul of the revolution'. The great upheaval he had prophesied some ten years earlier was now taking place before his eyes. He was not at all surprised that eruptions of violence were part of it. In the light of October's greatness, the disturbances were no more than October grimaces, he believed.[20] All the same, those grimaces were a central theme of Blok's first major poem about the revolution, 'The Twelve', written in January 1918. Lines such as 'Grip your gun like a man, brother! / Let's have a crack at Holy Russia!' and 'To smoke the nobs out of their holes / We'll light a fire through all the world' indicate the tone of this twelve-part poem,[21] which shows yet again that even after four years of war, violence was still regarded as a legitimate way, perhaps the only way, to bring about fundamental change. And this time the sacrifice would truly be rewarded; at the end of the poem, the twelve revolutionaries in the title transform into apostles, led by Christ himself. Utopia becomes reality.

> So they march with sovereign tread …
> Behind them limps the hungry dog,
> and wrapped in wild snow at their head
> carrying a blood-red flag –
> soft-footed where the blizzard swirls,
> invulnerable where bullets crossed –
> crowned with a crown of snowflake pearls
> a flowery diadem of frost,
> ahead of them goes Jesus Christ.

That was poetic exaggeration, of course, although the Bolsheviks did keep the most important of the promises with which they had gained political supremacy. They had committed themselves to land reform, but above all to peace without delay, and they immediately announced a ceasefire. The peace negotiations in Brest-Litovsk, however, were not going smoothly.[22] Although a swift end to the war appeared to be in the interests of both parties – the Central Powers could redeploy their troops on other fronts, and the Bolsheviks needed all their resources to consolidate the revolution in Russia and to propagate world revolution – their territorial demands were incompatible. While Poland and the Baltic region were yearning for independence, they were the subject of endless to-ing and fro-ing between the Russians and Germans in Brest-Litovsk. The Ukraine was also in the balance at these negotiations. The Ukrainian leaders who had declared independence chose the lesser of the two evils; they would be better off as a German protectorate than under the iron rule of the

Bolsheviks. This too strengthened Germany's bargaining position. Meanwhile, the Russians deliberately drew out the talks to give revolutionary forces in the West (particularly in Germany and Austria) time to gather strength, in the hope that an international revolution might bring a general peace.

In late January – in this climate of 'neither war nor peace', to use Trotsky's phrase – Blok wrote another long, programmatic poem, 'The Scythians', as he saw almost all his Symbolist friends and fellow poets turn against the revolution, reluctantly siding with the bourgeois enemy. A desperate cry for peace and, at the same time, a near-hysterical provocation aimed at Europe, it was the most peculiar poem in Blok's rich oeuvre. Blok felt that in refusing to make peace, Germany was failing to recognize, or else flatly denying, Russia's role in history just as the revolution had ushered in the most critical period thus far. The title 'The Scythians' referred to a nomadic people from Iran who had ruled the Russian steppes in the centuries before Christ and were regarded by many Russian intellectuals as their true ancestors. The 'yellow threat' that struck growing fear into the hearts of Europeans was embraced by these Russian authors as the untamed, passionate, Asian part of their Russian identity.[23] Blok tried to play on this European fear. The motto of 'The Scythians' set the tone: 'Panmongolism! Uncouth name, / yet music to my ear'. Russia would no longer content itself with a place on the margins, but would step forward as a self-confident nation, asserting the strength of its numbers and of its distinctively intense, un-European temperament.

You have your millions. We are numberless,
numberless, numberless. Try doing
battle with us! Yes, we are Scythians! Yes,
Asiatics, with greedy eyes slanting!

For you, the centuries; for us, one hour.
We, like obedient lackeys, have held up
a shield dividing two embattled powers –
the Mongol hordes and Europe![24]

But they would be lackeys no more. Russia was taking its fate into its own hands. The Europeans who had been so awed by the destruction of Messina in 1908 would not know what had hit them, Blok boasted, when Russia transformed from an exploited buffer state into an open door for the barbarian hordes. Russia was a superior country, Blok went on, because it combined the best of all worlds. It could feel love and hatred simultaneously (a clear message to Western powers that the giant's mood could change at any time) and understood both French wit and German metaphysics. While decadent Europe grumbled its way forward, weak of limb and weary of life, Russia stood for boundless, unbridled passion. And it was not yet too late. Europe could still answer the call for peace and ride the irreversible revolutionary current of history.

Come to us – from your battlefield nightmares
into our peaceful arms! While there's
still time, hammer your swords into ploughshares,
friends, comrades! We shall be brothers![25]

This was a plea, an order, and a threat in one, or as Blok had written in his diary a few days earlier: 'If you do not wash away the stain of your warlike patriotism with a democratic peace, if you destroy our revolution, then you are no longer an Aryan. Then we will open the wide gates of the Orient.'[26] In 'The Scythians', he did not hesitate to repeat that message in rhyming quatrains:

We shall ourselves no longer be your shield,
no longer launch our battle cries;
but study the convulsive battlefield
from far off through our narrow eyes!

We shall not stir when the murderous Huns
pillage the dead, town turns to ash,
in country churches stable their squadrons,
and foul the air with roasting flesh.

Now, for the last time, see the light, old world!
To peace and brotherhood and labour –
our bright feast – for the last time you are called
by the strings of a Scythian lyre![27]

But history took a different course. The Germans had a plan of their own for bringing reluctant negotiators in line: Operation Faustschlag ('Punch'). When they had grown tired of Russia's delaying tactics, the German army swept almost unhindered across Russian territory until it neared Petrograd. On 3 March, the Russians saw no alternative to accepting the German peace terms. It was an exceptionally bitter pill. Russia ceded all its occupied and annexed territories, losing a quarter of its surface area, a third of its inhabitants (62 million), and more than half its industrial capacity.[28] But as Lenin emphasized, 'It is a question of signing the peace terms now or signing the death sentence of the Soviet Government three weeks later.'[29] That was also how Gippius felt, and precisely for that reason, she could not forgive the Germans for agreeing to the treaty. If they had persevered a little longer, Bolshevism might have been no more than a bloody historical sideshow. 'Germany consented to this horse trading. Germany left the Bolsheviks in place. Germany has fallen prey to mental exhaustion. One consolation (however meagre at present): Someday Germany will pay.'[30]

* * *

For the time being, it was others who were paying. German and Austrian troops took the Ukraine without batting an eyelid, and it soon became clear what this meant, especially in the countryside: not only was the country virtually annexed, but agricultural produce was requisitioned for German use. This led to peasant revolts and guerrilla warfare.[31] Full-scale civil war broke out in Finland in the spring of 1918 when it appeared that the Germans would try to assert their authority there too. 'The moon knows ... that blood will be shed here tonight', wrote the Swedish-speaking Finnish poet Edith Södergran (1892–1923),[32] and this ominous prediction came to pass. Just short of 40,000 casualties later, the Finnish White Guards, supported by the Germans, defeated their Red opponents.[33] Otto Ville Kuusinen (1881–1964), leader of the short-lived Finnish Socialist Republic and author of the revolutionary ode 'Torpeedo' (Torpedo), fled to Russia.

Not everyone in Europe lay awake at night wondering how the map of the Continent would be redrawn. Most soldiers simply wanted to survive, and their national pride did not extend much further than the regional limits of their regiments. On the Western front, the focus of the action shifted north in the course of 1917, along with Lieutenant Edmund Blunden, whose battalion was redeployed from the Somme to take part in the Third Battle of Ypres. At first, Blunden had no objection to West Flanders. There were notices at the post office in Poperinghe regarding wind movements,[34] useful information in a war zone where gas was being used. Of course, the Ypres Salient, the area around the town projecting into enemy territory, was no summer camp. British soldiers had altered the place name Hallebast to 'Hellblast',[35] even before the fighting began in earnest, at a time when – in retrospect – some circles of hell had yet to be reached. Not that the latest battle, which began on 31 July 1917, was all that different from the earlier rounds of organized carnage.[36] And yet, by this stage the battles of the Great War had come to resemble Olympic events – ever higher, further, faster, greater. If a million shells had been fired across the front lines during the prelude to the Somme, this time there would be four million. The purpose of these bombardments was to soften up the enemy, but again, they proved tougher or more numerous than expected – in any case, strong enough to give the advancing British infantrymen the shock of their lives. Again, the artillery and the infantry were poorly coordinated, and some unfortunate soldiers were killed by 'friendly' fire. Again, thousands on both sides died anonymous deaths, without aid or comforting words or family beside them. At battalion headquarters, Blunden saw a soldier with a fatal back injury. 'This poor wretch again and again moaned, "I'm cold, cold", but seemed to have no other awareness of life. The doctor looked at him, and shook his head at me. A medical orderly looked at him, and answered me he could do no good.'[37] Between 31 July and 3 August, around 35,000 men were killed or injured or went missing in action in the British and French armies. The German losses were comparable. After the Somme, this seemed like progress.

Among those who died on the first day were the Welsh poet Hedd Wyn (Ellis Humphrey Evans) and the Irish poet Francis Ledwidge (1887–1917),[38] who had written in one of his last letters to a friend, 'If you visit the front, don't forget to come up the line at night to watch the German rockets. They have white crests which throw a pale flame across no-man's-land and white bursting into green and green changing into blue and blue bursting and dropping down in purple torrents. It is like the end of a beautiful world.'[39]

In early August the battle came to a temporary halt. It was raining so hard that men, horses, carts and artillery were in danger of sinking into the mud. As the region had been under fire almost continuously since 1914, not only was all vegetation destroyed, but almost anything that might be called 'terrain'. This did not escape the attention of the anonymous poet for the immensely popular trench newspaper *The B.E.F. Times* (previously *The Wipers Times*). In the 15 August 1917 issue, he opened with a brief sketch of the situation ('Belgium, rain, and a sea of mud, / The first seven years are, they say, the worst') and offered a final impression in the closing verse:

> Maybe one day we'll forget the rain,
> The mud and the filth of a Belgian scene;
> But always in mem'ry I'll see again
> Those roads with the stumps where the trees had been.[40]

Around that same week, Ivor Gurney (1890–1937) and his company arrived in Ypres from France. Gurney was a talented composer of art songs who was also becoming a poet of some note. During the many dreary hours behind the front line, he was constantly occupied with the compilation, planning, editing and production of his debut volume *Severn and Somme*. He too had found Flanders a decent enough place at first. More than that – it seemed as if the beautiful houses, good-natured people and rosy-cheeked children reminded him why he had come to that stinking, swampy battleground in the first place: 'The men that would have destroyed and mastered this country have a great guilt, for such peasants are the salt of the earth; the only true test of good foundation.'[41] Gurney did not care for the war – as a highly sensitive, possibly manic-depressive artist, he had not been born for tribulations of this kind. But that did not mean peace was his highest ideal. When an overwhelming majority of British trade unions voted against participating in the socialist Stockholm Peace Conference, he called this 'very good and encouraging'.[42] Soon after – possibly the very next day, 10 September– he fell victim to a gas attack. In a letter written on 21 September, he tried to muster his courage while lying in the field hospital, but it was not easy: 'By conquering fear-of-Life one may learn at once to love Life and to scorn death together; but neither has come yet in reality.'[43] Gurney would never return to the front, nor to his old self.

Many thousands of others would never leave the Ypres Salient. More than 50,000 British soldiers were swallowed by the mud, their bodies never recovered.[44] Heavy fighting continued in the area until 10 November, and Langemark and Passchendaele became emblematic of pointless suffering. On 26 October, when Canadian troops began their final advance toward Passchendaele, the British poet Herbert Read (1893–1968) wrote in a letter to his family, 'We have had a terrible time – the worst I have ever experienced (and I'm getting quite an old soldier now). Life has never seemed quite so cheap nor nature so mutilated. I won't paint the horrors to you.'[45] Seventy thousand British soldiers lost their lives there, and more than 200,000 were injured or listed as missing. The Germans lost some 200,000 men.[46]

At Craiglockhart War Hospital, Siegfried Sassoon was by this time thoroughly fed up. Just as he had once been plagued by visions of the corpses he had left behind, now his conscience was sorely burdened by the spirits of the 'silent dead', his blood brothers whom he had abandoned.[47] He could not fathom how his good friend the poet Robert Graves could go on using terms such as 'good form'. If Graves agreed with Sassoon that soldiers were being sacrificed by callous bastards 'in all countries (except some of Russia)', then how could he stand idly by like a coward?[48] Sassoon's new friend Wilfred Owen needed no such convincing. With Sassoon's encouragement, he wrote and rewrote his critical war poems. In mid-October 1917, he completed 'Dulce et Decorum est', a head-on challenge to 'the old Lie' that it is glorious to die for one's country. The scene he painted in the first two quatrains certainly lacked the glow of heroism:

Bent double, like old beggars under sacks,
Knock-kneed, coughing like hags, we cursed through sludge,
Till on the haunting flares we turned our backs
And towards our distant rest began to trudge.
Men marched asleep. Many had lost their boots
But limped on, blood-shod. All went lame; all blind;
Drunk with fatigue; deaf even to the hoots
Of tired, outstripped Five-Nines that dropped behind.[49]

In late October, Owen was discharged from Craiglockhart. In March 1918 – as Sassoon was fighting in Gaza, Palestine – he was sent back to France, but not until June was he declared healthy enough to return to the front.

1914, 1915, 1916, 1917, 1918 … On the Belgian front, Corporal Daan Boens was heading into his fifth calendar year of war. The titles of the poems he wrote on the Yser reveal how drastically his mood had changed in that time. While *Van glorie en lijden* (Glory and Suffering, 1917) had included poems like 'Albert I', 'Helden' (Heroes), and 'Pro Patria Mortuus', his following collection *Menschen in de grachten* (People in the Trenches, 1918) contained such grim titles as 'De Dood' (Death), 'Onder maaiende kogels' (Under Mowing Bullets), and 'Het afgerukte hoofd' (The Torn-off Head). Hardly any European verse darker than 'Doods-wensch' (Death Wish) came out of the Great War.

Vanish, you moon! – I long for night and darkness,
so that the world around me chars to coal forever
and the life within me dies – no hope, and no distress,
I want the mighty, windless void, sheer nothingness.

No, no more rubble – I myself am rubble,
No, no more dreams – I was myself a dream,
no song, no sun – the Void, where all is black,
and I'll not see what once was fine and sweet.[50]

Yet Boens had not become a cynic. Words like 'glory' had not lost all their meaning for him. But it stands to reason that the Belgian soldiers had shed many illusions along the way. In the lecture 'Moed in lijden' (Courage in Suffering), delivered to Belgian refugees in London in December 1917 and behind the front line in 1918, Boens described how the soldiers' initial romantic 'zeal' had been eroded by exposure to 'naked suffering'. What weighed heaviest on them was the knowledge that none of their actions had brought peace any closer and that they would have to live and fight as 'scruffy wretches'. But his story also had an optimistic side. Boens considered it a hopeful sign that soldiers on the front did their duty in spite of everything. To him, this suggested not that they were slavish followers of the culture of war, but that they realized a new world was taking shape. Postwar society would be different: better, broader, deeper, less focused on the individual. At the front, they had learned and experienced what it meant to pursue a higher goal.

> We are fighting for the principle of Justice and Equality. We want peace, as a gift for those who will issue from us, and whom we will never know, but in whom we will someday live on – in other words, to later generations – a broader, fairer way of life, in which the smaller peoples no longer have to fear the larger nations.[51]

Boens believed that the war would benefit those smaller peoples, as well as the little people of this world. Rich and poor were fighting side by side, looking the same death in the eye together. After that, there could be no return to the old ways. What Boens had in mind was not a social and political revolution, but a change in mentality that would occur naturally and inevitably. 'Love' would flourish between these very different groups of people, and that would make all the difference in the world. Now they were fighting each other, but soon they would all be brothers:

> Self-sacrifice, a sense of duty, benevolence and brotherly love have become the essential components of our conduct. The tragic dimension of our lives today allows us to live at the poles of our personal identity, so to speak. We live larger, more intensely and purely true to ourselves. Love has found such powerful expression in our least thoughts and actions that we cannot but achieve a greater, deeper consciousness of our feelings – an understanding that it is perfectly natural to act out of love, in other words to act with pure humanity.

This new sense of fraternity, this solidarity, so natural under the circumstances, would radically alter relationships between people and between states. No, all the suffering was far from pointless. It taught the human race a lesson that apparently could not be learned any other way, and Flanders and Belgium would be among the greatest beneficiaries. Boens, who often wrote in French in his diary in the early days of the war, noted contentedly that 'Flemish consciousness' had taken 'giant steps forward'. His message was clear: 'The Flemish on the Yser want a free Flanders in a free Belgium. They want this right not as alms from bloody hands, they want it neither as a favour nor as a reward. It is simply what is due to a centuries-old culture; rightly understood, it is a question of fairness and justice.' Therefore the Flemish would not request compensation for their war efforts, but simply wanted what they had a right to expect as a mature, assertive culture (more assertive than in the past, perhaps, because of the war).

Earlier sections of Boens's argument – possibly relating to specific military operations and losses incurred – were struck out by the Belgian censor, but these passages about a Flemish variant of Irish Home Rule were left untouched. Of course, they hardly formed a threat to the state, but the same could be said of most expressions of Flemish identity at the front, and yet they usually met with a severe response. What Boens demanded for Flanders was what he had fought for and defended for Belgium: 'As we now do battle for the independence of small peoples, for the rights of those small peoples, we wish Belgium to remain free and untarnished as a nation, and in this independent Belgium, we wish the necessary struggle to take place for the rebirth of a people, that can and must be itself so that it can become European.' This was an explicit endorsement of the Flemish intellectual leader August Vermeylen's famous words from 1900: 'We want to be Flemish so that we can become Europeans.'[52] Boens expressed the emotions and ambitions of many small nations who wished to follow an autonomous course of development so as to claim their rightful place in Europe.

Although Boens himself disapproved of activism,[53] he had much the same faith in fraternity and the new place of Flanders as did the activists in the occupied country, such as Paul van Ostaijen. In the winter and spring of 1918, as Van Ostaijen became increasingly engaged in the political and even law-enforcement activities of an activist Flanders that imagined itself independent, he was writing poems in Antwerp in which love, fraternity and the inevitable dawning of a new age were the central themes.[54] There is no way of telling to what extent this optimism was motivated by the spectacularly successful German spring offensives on the Western front.[55] Nor is it clear how the increasingly radical socialist Van Ostaijen imagined an independent Flanders might look after a German victory. But a number of his poems testify to his belief that history was taking a decisive turn. 'This song that will stand in the reality of things', he wrote in 'Het stille lied' (The Silent Song), 'like the emergence of a wider Spring, after the hopeless turnings of long years'.[56] After a long and evidently infertile period, it was finally blossom time. The new world had arrived. 'Februarie' (February) addresses this theme even more explicitly. The poem describes the pivotal moment just before the onset of spring, which is pictured as a time of both upheaval and liberation. 'The wind that has found a joyful independence this year, for the first time ever. / Of being only wind, unbridled, wanton, and unfettered.' These are nature poems about spring, but at the same time, they describe a new world order and the avant-garde art that is its herald. 'Age of the good news, / independent age that creates a life of its own: / its own birth, its own life, harvest, and death.'[57] Worn-out traditions and coercive bonds would be left behind; the principle of self-determination was as relevant to art as it was to statecraft. The independence of which Van Ostaijen wrote did not in any way imply that different realms would act in isolation from one another. Time strove toward synthesis, and developments on all these different fronts were part of the general intellectual climate in Europe. In parallel with these poems, Van Ostaijen wrote long theoretical essays about developments in art, and the fact that similar trends were visible across Europe only fuelled his hope and expectation that a new spirit was in the air across the continent: 'While the rapid domination of all Europe by a localist tendency could be explained away as sudden snobbery, this synchronicity points to a revitalizing, pan-European vital urge.'[58] For Van Ostaijen, nationalism and internationalism were ever more intimately linked, and this theoretical belief informed his perspective on the two neighbouring countries locked in a life-and-death struggle not far away. In the spring of 1918, he wrote what became the title poem of the collection *Het Sienjaal* (The Signal), published later that year:

> Sing that glorious anthem, the Internationale, yet not in denial of
> each individual's ethos, but in understanding of them all; this
> is what it means to love.
> Judge the Germans according to their ethos and the French
> according to theirs; in each poet there is a ball of love or the
> materials for it; this ball you must find or form.

> Understand the love of the French Catholics and their antique, heroic soul; understand the old race of the French spirit, still growing in the ever-renewed shadow of the cathedrals of Chartres, of Reims, and of Rouen;
> Understand the youthful lust for life of Germany, seeking its place in the sun; above all: understand France's place on the highest peak and Germany's ascent to the highest peak.[59]

It could hardly have escaped Van Ostaijen that Germany, while seeking its place in the sun, had destroyed the cathedral of Reims. This raises the suspicion that in his idealism he was abstracting away from certain realities.[60] He was after something more exalted, the love and generosity that do not begrudge anyone a place in the sun, and the way 'that glorious anthem, the Internationale' announced the right of self-determination for all peoples. It followed that those peoples were not enemies, but brothers in a world that was liberating itself. Or as Van Ostaijen wrote in 'Februarie', directly referring to the song of the socialist revolution:

> Fraternal greetings to the people from across the borders!
> The wind of our port that refreshes all peoples.
> The music of the wind: the double basses underscore it with an Internationale![61]

There was hope in the air, perhaps inspired in part by the degree of autonomy the Flemish believed they had been granted by the Germans, but much more importantly by the Russian Revolution and Wilson's Fourteen Point Plan. In his speech announcing the plan, the American president had praised the unyielding moral will and resilience of spirit shown by the Russian people. This section moved Joris Van Severen so deeply that he recorded it word for word, in French, in his diary. He was delighted that the great president shared his opinion: 'my admiration for the

Russians grows day by day'.[62] A mighty nation seemed to be actively taking its fate into its own hands.

For the military and political leaders of the Entente, the end of the war in the east was mainly a source of headaches. The additional troops that Germany could now deploy on the Western front might prove to be the decisive factor. On the other hand, the incoming American troops could equally well tip the scales. After endless months of stagnation, it seemed that in 1918 the war would become a race against the clock.[63] The Germans would have to strike decisively before the Americans reached Europe in large numbers. On 21 March, they began their offensive. There was fog that day – a deadly fog, with admixtures of phosgene, chloric and mustard gas. Toward the end of the day, it looked as though the British army was experiencing its first true defeat in Europe, even though more German than British soldiers had been killed. Over the following days and weeks, there seemed to be no stopping the German advance – until the engine began to stall. The supply network could not keep pace with the fast-moving troops. German soldiers were trapped in the barren landscape of the Somme. They drowned their sorrows with the food and, above all, drink they found left behind in the British lines, and were caught unprepared when the British launched a counterattack on 4 April. The French, German and British armies lost half a million men, all told, in this battle. The British poet Isaac Rosenberg (1890–1918) died in combat on 1 April. As the son of a working-class Jewish family, he had joined the military purely for the money, and he loathed the militarism and nationalism he found there. The main characters in his poems are threadbare soldiers, lice and rats.

> Droll rat, they would shoot you if they knew
> Your cosmopolitan sympathies

(And God only knows what antipathies).
Now you have touched this English hand
You will do the same to a German –
Soon, no doubt, if it be your pleasure
To cross the sleeping green between.
It seems you inwardly grin as you pass:
Strong eyes, fine limbs, haughty athletes,
Less chanced than you for life;
Bonds to the whims of murder,
Sprawled in the bowels of the earth,
The torn fields of France.[64]

And now he lay sprawled there himself. Just a few weeks earlier he had written in a letter: 'No drug could be more stupefying than our work (to me anyway), and this goes on like that old torture of water trickling, drop by drop unendingly, on one's helplessness.'[65] Yet some drops took the form of shrapnel and ended the torture after all.

On 9 April, the Germans tried again, now in West Flanders. The British, supported by the Belgians, held their ground. The Kemmelberg fell into German hands, but the objective – the French Channel ports – was never attained. The attackers lost more than 100,000 men. After a preliminary barrage with two million shells, the Germans gave it a third try on 27 May. These words from the final passage in Van Ostaijen's volume of Great War poetry, *Bezette stad* (Occupied City), sum up the situation as it appeared to him:

and then
aushalten
brave *Pommern*
victory goes to the ones who can suffer the most misery

In reality, however, victory went to those who could muster the greatest manpower. Even with the new troops from the east, the German army had reached its limit. It had almost literally used up all its soldiers. Not only could the Entente count on the Americans, but a year after the Chemin des Dames, the French army had recovered much of its strength. When the Germans tried to break through to Paris on 15 July, they were almost obliterated by French and American forces. The Germans had crossed the Marne – only four years later than planned, but they could not savour their victory for long. For the first time there were complaints and refusals to work from German troops. Some surrendered in large groups. When the Allies counterattacked in August, they needed only a few weeks to recover the territory lost in the spring. On 28 September, British, French, Belgian and American forces attacked once again. The endgame had begun in earnest. A day later, Bulgaria requested an armistice in Thessaloniki.

For the first time, a negotiated peace was under serious discussion in German circles. Leaders in Berlin and Vienna tried to stop the dam from bursting by democratizing their institutions, but it was too late. On 24 October, the Italian army won a decisive victory in the Battle of Vittorio Veneto. It had given its utmost, realizing that with peace talks on the horizon, every morsel of occupied territory would count. A week later, revolution broke out in Vienna and Budapest – an ideal opportunity for the Italians to strike again. D'Annunzio addressed the troops on 1 November, giving a whole new meaning to this day of the dead with his own surprising version of the Lord's Prayer:.

> O dead who are in earth, as in heaven,
> Hallowed be your names,
> Your spiritual kingdom come,
> Your will be done on earth.
> Give our faith its daily bread;

Keep alive in sacred hatred, as we shall never deny your love.
Deliver us from every ignoble temptation;
Free us from every cowardly doubt,
And if necessary
We shall fight, not until the last drop of our blood,
But with you, until the last particle of our dust.
If necessary
We shall fight until Just God
Comes to judge the living and the dead.
Amen.[66]

That same day, the Serbians entered their capital city of Belgrade and the Entente troops reached the Danube. Two days later, Austria–Hungary asked for an armistice. By this time, there were strikes and mutinies throughout Germany. When sailors mutinied at a naval base in Kiel, not primarily for military or professional reasons but for democratic reform and peace, the death-knell seemed to be sounding for the German Empire. On 9 November, the Kaiser abdicated, going into exile in the Netherlands. Germany had played for high imperial and military stakes and now seemed to have lost everything. The fledgling German republic's delegation to the negotiating table was made up of civilians.

In this final stage of the war, the casualties remained staggering. Daan Boens survived a gas attack, but Gerrit Engelke (1890–1918) was not so fortunate. He had made it through Verdun, the Somme, Champagne and Langemark, only to be fatally wounded in the British attack of 11 October. In 'An den Tod' (To Death) he had begged death not to take him until his life had been lived out. Apparently, that time came on 13 October. He died in a British field hospital.[67] In July, he had completed his poem 'To the Soldiers of the Great War (In memoriam August Deppe)'. The union of war and lyricism had always struck him as highly problematic;

the war was too complex and soulless to capture in a poem, unless it was presented as a 'time-dictated great and insanely bloody event'. In contrast, true culture was a by-product of peace, existing to serve and preserve that peace. Engelke simply could not comprehend how war could strengthen civilization, as the propagandists went on claiming. Pan-Germanist sentiment could not be expected from him. The only causes he wished to promote were peace and fraternity,[68] and it was these ideals that animated his last major poem, a passionate appeal to soldiers of all countries, ranks and classes to come out of the trenches and throw aside their guns. Didn't they all have mothers; didn't they all love their wives? Hadn't they been together in Diksmuide; hadn't they reduced Ypres to rubble together? Didn't they all have their scars, cruel marks of a hopeless struggle? Hadn't they all lost friends, brothers, fathers?

> Frenchman from Brest, Bordeaux, Garonne;
>
> Ukrainian, Cossack from the Orals, from Dnjestr and Don;
> Austrians, Bulgarians, Turks and Serbs;
> All of you in the raging whirlpool of action and dying –
> Britisher, from London, York, Manchester,
> Soldier, comrade-in-arms, truly fellow human being and best of men[69]

It was the birth of a new world that Engelke proclaimed. He called his poem a psalm of peace, reconciliation and revolt. His contribution to civilization.

When the Entente struck on 28 September, Wilfred Owen was in the vanguard of the Fourth British Army in France.[70] The advance was difficult and took a heavy toll, among both enlisted men and officers. On 2 October, Owen lost three stretcher-bearers in a row.

He ordered his men to be especially cautious, although he himself could hardly be restrained. 'I came here to help these boys', he wrote to his mother two days later, 'directly by leading them as well as an officer can; indirectly, by watching their sufferings that I may speak of them as well as a pleader can'.[71] Yet another major attack took place on 4 November. Again, the British encountered fierce resistance from the Germans, who managed to hold off the advance for the time being. The next morning, however, the British accomplished all their objectives – but without Wilfred Owen. He had been fatally injured on 4 November. The 5 November newspaper reported that he had been retroactively promoted to lieutenant. On 8 November the regimental journal reported that he had been awarded the Military Cross. Three days later, on the eleventh, the news of his death reached his mother by telegram.

Guillaume Apollinaire spent 1918 writing and working like a man possessed, but it seemed unlikely he would ever return to his old self. His lecture 'L'Esprit nouveau et les poètes' was delivered by an actor because of the poet's poor health. On 2 May he married Ruby (Jacqueline-Amélia Kolb), whose praises he sang in 'La Jolie Rousse' (The Pretty Redhead). It read like a combination of a love poem, a meditation on tradition and renewal, and a memoir of the war years. But most of all, he seemed to be saying farewell.

> But laugh at me
> Men from everywhere especially men from here
> For there are so many things I dare not tell you
> So many things you would never let me say
> Have pity on me.[72]

On 9 November, his strength utterly sapped by his injuries, Apollinaire succumbed to the Spanish flu.

10

11/11 and After: Europe, 1918–1925

So still we face the question: what to do with Europe?

– Paul van Ostaijen, 1920[1]

And only when it was finally over did it truly begin. Although the world seemed to turn a page on 11 November 1918, when the Armistice was signed in a train carriage in the French town of Compiègne, Europe was still far from closing the book. Politicians and diplomats from almost every country met in Paris to hammer out a series of treaties – the best known being the Treaty of Versailles, which specified how Germany would pay for its role in the war. Indescribable, incurable suffering had to be expressed in hectares of territory and in francs, pounds, dollars and, above all, gold marks. The result was more frustration and despair, because no financial compensation could ever be enough, and no serious plans were made to reintegrate either the losers or the victors into European society. In Germany, this created a breeding ground for radicalism on the extreme left and the fascist right and would eventually topple the unstable Weimar Republic. Meanwhile, the Allied countries were eager to get on with business as usual, but inflation, the postwar political situation, and new forms of social unrest made that impossible. Understandably, a good deal of the poetry published in the war's wake gave voice to conflicting feelings. In neutral Norway, Arnulf Øverland (1889–1968) gave an apparently optimistic twist to the metaphors of harvesting and reaping that for years had been exploited by warmongers: 'It seems the time has come now after all / To set to work with seed and with the plough.'[2] But it soon became clear that the sole means of expression left to him were despair and sarcasm: 'Justice has prevailed / We find a people starved and massacred.' The contradictions with which the war had saddled the world were too painful to be smoothed over with rhetoric. Those who rubbed the soot of war from their eyes and welcomed peace ('what the world needs now is rest and healing!') were dismissed by Øverland as complacent. There was no 'Thousand-Year Reich' of peace ahead:

> because we vaguely sense that the holy
> star of Bethlehem
> will show the bloodthirsty choir of our children
> the way to the next barracks!

In fact, millions of soldiers were still in the last barracks. Not only were most armies not demobilized until late in 1919, but even after the Armistice and Versailles many parts of Europe remained at war – in the name of two inspiring political principles. These principles were ideological echoes of the slogan with which the Great War had begun in 1914: 'the war to end all wars'. Both revolution and self-determination aimed to eliminate the causes of war, the first by bringing down imperialism, the second by liberating oppressed peoples from foreign domination. Again, the expectations were high. Again, levels of energy and violence were attained that would hardly have been conceivable before 1914.

After the Armistice, Europe became, in the words of the Czech philosopher and politician Tomáš Masaryk, 'a laboratory over a gigantic cemetery'.[3] In his London lecture *The Problem of Small Nations in the European Crisis* (1915), he had said that the war could have no meaning unless it led to 'the liberation of the small nations'.[4] Three years later, another contributor to *The New Europe* implicitly questioned this claim when he wrote that simply dividing Austria, for instance, could not be an end in itself. In his essay 'From Nationalism to Federation', John Mavrogordato, a pacifist with a socialist outlook, argued that a country like Austria should be strengthened, not by amputating it, but by transforming the empire into a federation. If Austria were carved into pieces, then the Allies would accomplish exactly what the Germans had tried to accomplish in Belgium with the help of the activists in the Flemish Movement: Austria would be left so feeble that it would be easy prey for its annexation-hungry German neighbour. Mavrogordato proposed a similar solution to the Irish problem: the British Empire, too, could become a federation. It would then become clear that the Great War had been the death throes of the old Europe of nationalist states, a necessary transitional stage between the fall of the Roman Empire and the rise of 'the organization for the United States of Europe'.[5] Likewise, he interpreted socialism as the synthesis of the feudal system and the anarchy that had followed it. It seemed obvious to him that national autonomy was the foundation for internationalism. From that perspective, the two principles of revolution and self-determination were two sides of the same coin.

Herman Gorter saw things a bit differently. An absolute insistence on the right of self-determination would lead to the creation of a surplus of new countries and would inevitably strengthen imperialism, thus laying the groundwork for future wars. In a letter to Lenin in 1918 the Dutch poet explained his position:

> As you know, my view on the self-determination of peoples also differs slightly from yours, although I understand and admire how you have turned this question into the lever of revolution

> in Eastern Europe. If I were an Eastern European, I would have acted, and would act, in the same way as you. But in Western Europe I must take a different course of action. Here it would not be right to make the questions of Alsace-Lorraine, Ireland, Flanders, Denmark, and so forth the centrepiece of our campaign, because that would lead people to act precisely in the spirit of imperialism.[6]

The revolution took priority over the right of national self-determination. It would be international by definition – and, in late 1918, it looked close to becoming a reality. On 2 November, Gorter reported from Switzerland that 'everything is churning and coming into motion'.[7] The Swiss government had the same feeling, and both the local strikers and the Soviets who were in the country were promptly imprisoned or expelled. In solidarity with his Russian friends, Gorter spent ten days in prison in the German border town of Konstanz. There they sang battle songs and discussed revolution night and day.

Still, the flames of revolution were unlikely to find much fuel in the Netherlands. The communist, working-class poet Sebastiaan Bonn could just picture the miraculous event ('Blessed are we who in this hour / can feel the glow of the worldwide fire / burning and purifying our hearts'[8]), but on 12 November, when the socialist leader Pieter Jelles Troelstra decided that the 'historic moment' had come and called for revolution, remarkably little happened.[9] At a demonstration in Amsterdam, three people were killed and six injured when soldiers, whom the socialists were trying to recruit for the revolution, suddenly began shooting into the crowd. There could hardly have been a clearer illustration of the country's lack of revolutionary sentiment. Of course, this was not so surprising. While the people of neutral states like Switzerland and the Netherlands had gone through hard times during the war, they had never experienced the galvanizing depths of suffering.

So all eyes were on Germany. If the revolution took hold there, it could spread throughout Western Europe, utterly transforming the continent. After the revolutionary spirit and general war-weariness had led to the implosion of the empire in early November, soldiers', workers' and farmers' councils took power in some areas. From Munich, Rainer Maria Rilke reported to his wife Clara on the morning of Friday, 8 November, that Kurt Eisner, a Jew from Berlin, had declared himself president of the Bavarian Soviet Republic. The transition had been smooth and uneventful – a welcome, if unexpected and almost unbelievable, farewell to the culture of war that had held the country in its grip for so long.[10] Rilke acknowledged that the revolution could always take a fatal wrong turn, but for the time being its prospects looked bright, and the poet was very excited to think that he might have a front-row seat.[11]

Rilke's mother was in Prague at the time, but as a German-speaker she still felt safe and secure in the new state emerging there after the collapse of the Dual Monarchy.[12] Among Czechs and Slovaks, the war had accelerated the development of a national identity. Under the leadership of Masaryk, whom Rilke greatly admired, the still-unfounded Czechoslovak state had acquired French, British and American support. By energetically seizing the reins of the 50,000-man strong Czech legions in Russia, Masaryk – still officially an Austrian citizen – had positioned himself as an Allied leader. He had pledged to send his troops to the Western front, where they were sorely needed, by way of Vladivostok, but during their 10,000-kilometre trek across Siberia, the Legionnaires clashed with Hungarian ex-prisoners of war who were on their way to support the Bolshevik revolution.[13] A few months later, when the war ended in the west, the Legions were most useful to the Allies in Russia, where they could reopen the front against the Red Army. This made them a significant force in the swiftly escalating Russian civil war.

It was in the defeated armies that soldiers were most likely to become voices of revolution – quite literally in the case of the Czech teenager Miloš Jirko (1900–1961). His 'Victorious Retreat', written in September 1918, cast the military defeat of the Austrian army as the start of the long-awaited liberation of the many peoples and workers in the Danube Monarchy:

> I, student and poet, born in the year nineteen hundred,
> And also a soldier, – of the heavy, heavy guns, –
> The Bosnian who treats us to raki,
> The workman from Vienna slums,
> The Pole, with whom I talk in the goodly language,
> Bringing to my lips the savour of sweet fruits,
> The Ruthene student from Kolomea,
> The Magyar who boasts of his pig-breeding,
> The pale youth from Prague
> And the farmer from Hana,
> We,
> We all,
> We are not retreating,
> We are advancing.[14]

In 'To All!', the radical left-wing German poet Oskar Kanehl (1888–1929) called on both his fellow soldiers and the war widows and orphans to rise up and transform their suffering into revolution.

> Soldiers! All!
> Bare your scars on the market squares.
> Tear open your wounds.
> Lift your crutches, war cripples, in the busiest streets.
> If the war blinded you, show your empty sockets.
> If the war made you sick, openly show your sores.
> Show your starved bodies, fighters of the home front.

Kanehl presented desertion as a sign of love for one's fellow man and the rejection of any national identity as a sign of civilization.

> We have no homeland.
> National pride is unknown to us.
> We make no distinction between the violence of different homelands.
> To us, border posts are prison bars,
> Politics is human trafficking.[15]

But most soldiers and poets did not go so far. After Czech politicians confidently seized power on 28 October, Jan Rokyta (a pseudonym of Adolf Černý, 1864–1952) wrote the jubilant poem 'We Are Free!'[16] The revolutionary poet Stanislav Kostka Neumann (1875–1947) responded to the same historic event in 'October 28th, 1918', in the voice of Czechoslovakia itself. While the German and Austrian emperors fled to safety, he wrote, the new country was proudly coming forward as a free state and swearing a solemn oath: never would it slacken in the defence of liberty. 'All must be alike in freedom now.'[17]

In practice, the situation was not so straightforward. Czech troops under Allied command took Bratislava, a largely German–Hungarian city (Pressburg/Pozsony) that was then on Hungarian territory. The planned structure of the new state also raised many questions. For instance, if every people was supposed to govern itself, why did the Czechs and Slovaks have to share a country? Yes, they were both Slavic peoples and spoke closely related languages, but the Slovaks had long been accustomed to a Hungarian cultural framework, while the Austrians had controlled the Czech lands. Nevertheless, the Allies had a preference for larger states. Just as they tried to avoid Balkanization in southern Europe by merging Croats, Serbs, Slovenes, Montenegrins and Bosnians (including Muslims) into the new kingdom of Yugoslavia, they also opted for a union of Czechs and Slovaks. And when a revolution in Hungary brought the Bolshevik Béla Kun into power, it seemed all the more worthwhile to establish a sturdy Czechoslovakian buffer between Poland and Hungary. Masaryk, who was half-Slovak, had no objection whatsoever. Cooperation between Slavic peoples was his fondest dream, and in Versailles he even negotiated for a corridor that would link his new state to Yugoslavia – a first step toward a Slavic Federation. Nothing came of that proposal, but his territorial gains were nevertheless impressive. His delegation made skilful use of the terminological obscurity of Wilson's Fourteen Points to gain control of all Slovakia, emphasizing the right of self-determination. Czech territory, in contrast, was defined on the basis of so-called natural borders, a method that instantaneously turned three million ethnic Germans (the 'Sudeten Germans') into Czechs. Not by chance, this placed an economically crucial region on the 'right' side of the border. Czechoslovakia guaranteed that the Germans could use their own language, practise their religion, and enjoy all other minority rights. Rilke, at least, seemed satisfied with that. After a brief spell as a stateless person, he eventually became a Czech national.[18] This was little more than a symbolic decision; until his death in 1926, the poet spent most of his time in hotels and castles in Switzerland and Italy. While the Germans now living in Czechoslovakia were not by any means oppressed, they did not feel welcome or at home there either. This was a clear case in which the right of self-determination had been trampled underfoot.

The Austrians had a similar experience. As 'Germans', they would have liked to unite with Germany, but the resulting increase in size and population was unacceptable, especially to France. This left an Austrian rump state, which came close to being fragmented still further at the talks in Versailles, when the German-speaking Vorarlberg region sought to join Switzerland because it was tired of provisioning the once-indolent and now-drained capital. It was clear to all, including the Allied leaders, that the climate in Vienna was ripe for revolution. The Allies sent huge shipments of food aid, and when the communists tried to seize power in Vienna in June 1919, they failed.[19] All the same, the peace terms were a heavy blow. Three days of national mourning and bitter commentaries in the press (even on the political left) were intended to show the world that not only Austria's pride had been hurt but also its sense of justice as a great European cultural power. After another round of negotiations, the Allied leaders made a few concessions, at least one of which was in direct conflict with Wilson's articles of faith. After fighting broke out in Klagenfurt, on the border of Austria and the new Yugoslavia, the locals were allowed to decide in a referendum (the Carinthian Plebiscite) which country they wished to join. Although most of them were Slovenes (and therefore 'Yugoslavian'), almost two-thirds voted for annexation by Austria.

Hungary, another defeated power, was even harder hit. In late 1918, when it became apparent that the Dual Monarchy had lost the war, the deathly ill Endre Ady delivered his last address as the great poet of his nation. In 'Üdvözlet a győzőnek' (Greetings to the Victor) he asked the victorious powers to be gentle with his country, which had itself been the victim of a foreign and reactionary regime.

> Don't you step too hard on it
> Don't trample too hard on it
> On the beauty that's our torn heart
> Which someday may yet wish to soar.
>
> A sad, an ill-fated tribe we are
> We lived in revolt and to tame us
> Scoundrels cursed even in their graves
> Brought upon us the plagues of war.

Empty and mute stand our caserns
Silent witnesses of the carnage
Nothing but mourning, nothing but crypts
Nothing is left but catafalques.

We were the prize dupes of the world
We poor, foolish Magyars
Let the victors go now ahead
Greetings to the victor![20]

Serbia and Romania were unimpressed by this respectful plea and occupied large parts of the country. On 11 January, Romania annexed Transylvania, and after a communist regime headed by Béla Kun was installed in Hungary on 21 March, the Allies allowed neighbouring countries to nibble away even more territory in the interest of fighting the Bolsheviks. Masaryk's coveted corridor to Yugoslavia thus ended up as part of Austria. Defeated states fared better if they picked the right side after the Armistice.

The fall of Kun in August cleared the way for a new Hungarian regime that was more to the taste of the Allies. They ultimately negotiated the Treaty of Trianon, which required Hungary to give up 71 per cent of its prewar territory and 60 per cent of its population. Again, self-determination had its limits. The agreement placed three and half million Magyars outside their country's borders, including in Ady's beloved Transylvania, which went to Romania. The poet's death spared him the news of this humiliation. Ady died on 27 January 1919. Not long before, he had been elected president of the Hungarian writers' academy, but his poor health had not permitted him personally to deliver his acceptance speech on the European future he saw for his country. In Transylvania in the years that followed, Hungarian literature flourished as never before. Talented poets and dilettantes alike saw it as their sacred duty to save the Hungarian minority and defend Ady's ideal of a multi-ethnic Transylvania. Between 1919 and 1926, no fewer than 330 Hungarian-language periodicals were published there. The poet Sándor Reményik (1890–1941) became the lyric conscience of the Hungarian minority in Romania, and his immensely popular poems also appeared in newspapers and magazines in Budapest.[21]

The aftermath of the war and the territorial shifts were a source of enduring trauma for many Hungarians. Árpád Tóth (1886–1928) had seen it coming. In his poem 'Holy Cripple, Take Alarm', written in November 1918, he had called on his countrymen not to stand by like pathetic dunces while the 'happy peoples' of the world were noisily celebrating their victory.[22] Mihály Babits had equal difficulty accepting the amputation of his country. The rancorous nationalist poems he wrote about the subject were later omitted from his collected poems, so as not to offend the national sensibilities of neighbouring peoples.[23] The usually apolitical Dezső Kosztolányi, in his poem 'The Cry of Hungarian Poets to the Poets of Europe', responded to the changes with shock. His birth village of Szabadka had become Yugoslavian territory. Was anything sacred, when even your cradle could suddenly be whisked away onto foreign soil?

By mid-December 1918, little of Rilke's initial enthusiasm for the revolution remained. It had offered the liberating prospect of starting with a clean slate, but in the hands of mediocre, uninspired leaders it had quickly become diluted or derailed. This did not really surprise Rilke. The end of the war should have been more than a refreshing moment of relief, he wrote, but the revolution had shattered the peace into a thousand fragments, and no one could offer a level-headed analysis of the situation any longer.[24] After Eisner's assassination in February 1919 the chaos escalated into a true civil war, and by early May it was open season on revolutionaries. Some of these 'Spartacists' were murdered, while others – like the poet, Great War veteran and Red Army commander Ernst Toller (1893–1939) – were thrown in prison.

The situation in Berlin was no less dramatic. Poems and pamphlets called on the people to assassinate the revolutionary leaders Rosa Luxemburg and Karl Liebknecht. Early January 1919 saw a new attempt at revolution, with strikes and violent demonstrations. The bourgeois counter-revolutionary forces that had tried to crush the November revolt once again took charge, with the aid of reactionary, paramilitary *Freikorps*, and on 15 January Luxemburg and Liebknecht were arrested, interrogated, beaten and killed. In this respect, the autumn of 1918 and spring of 1919 were reminiscent of the summer and autumn of 1914: people dreamed of a new beginning yet soon found themselves bogged down in blood. But as long as the transformation lasted, the revolutionaries felt possessed by a sense of direction, determination and destiny they had experienced only once before, during that unforgettable August.

In Russia, the Futurists tried to hold on to that feeling for as long as they could. They regarded themselves as the only truly revolutionary artists and wanted to be acknowledged as such by the new regime. It seemed such a natural step; hadn't the Futurists always been revolutionaries? They managed to gain control of the magazine *Iskusstvo Kommuny* (Art of the Commune), published by the Literature and Art Department of the new Soviet Union's Commissariat of Education.[25] In his poem 'Prikaz po armii iskusstv' (Marching Orders for the Army of the Arts), published in the newspaper's first issue on 7 December 1918, Mayakovsky left no doubt about the role and responsibility of the new artists in the new world: 'The true communist / burns his bridges behind him.'[26] And that implied not only that Russian poets had to write about new subjects in a new way, but also that they could no longer inhabit the boudoirs and ivory towers that seemed to have become their natural habitat. Futurist art would be communist and therefore proletarian in its objectives, subjects and means:

> Streets are our brushes,
> the squares our palette.
> The book of time has loads of room
> for songs of revolution, see!
> Hey! Futurists, take to the streets,
> Percussionists of poetry![27]

There was nothing casual about this announcement. Artistic freedom was now out of the question, their publisher Osip Brik emphasized. In the new Russia, all labour was proletarianized, and art was no exception. The poet and theoretician Viktor Shklovski protested that the Futurists' greatest achievement was the triumph of form and the autonomy of the word. In the 15 December issue of *Iskusstvo Kommuny*, Mayakovsky went a step further. In 'It's Too Early to Rejoice', he slammed the artists, buildings and ideas that were stuck in the past or incarnated traditionalism.

> It's time to make
> museum walls
> a target.
> Let the mouths of big guns shoot the old rags!
> Sow destruction in the enemy camp.
> Watch where you're going, capitalist soul![28]

The Russian Futurists were no more pacifists than were their Italian counterparts, or the German and Romanian Dadaists. They believed in clobbering White Guards and chucking traditional art, architecture and literature (Raphael, Rastrelli and Pushkin) out of the window.[29] The publication of this poem caused an immediate and huge commotion. The bureaucrats were confused; it was gratifying to see those talented Futurists throw their weight behind the Revolution, but how dare they suggest that Pushkin and other icons should be destroyed? The official Soviet line was that all state property, and especially the artistic and historical heritage, should be protected. Alexander Blok was also very concerned. He had enthusiastically signed up for the revolutionary project, but the attitude of these avant-garde artists was abhorrent to him. In an unsent letter to Mayakovsky, the Symbolist suggested that the younger poet was the one stuck in the past, a past in which pain outweighed joy and revolting against tradition had become a tradition in itself. 'As long as we keep destroying, we will remain slaves of the old world.'[30] Mayakovsky may actually have agreed with Blok about that. The final couplet of 'It's Too Early to Rejoice' declared that the true communist comrade did not change only his outward appearance: 'Turn your own self inside out!'[31] But this was too much to ask. Workers, peasants and officials may have been ready for radical political and economic upheaval, but modern art was too much for them. Just as Arthur Rimbaud's new style had been out of tune with the taste and aspirations of the Communards in 1871,[32] now the Futurists could not find a place for their most extreme experiments in proletarian art and culture. Mayakovsky responded by changing his working method. He spent all of 1919 churning out drawings and poems for agitprop posters for the propaganda agency Rosta. At the same time, he was working on a long epic poem, '150,000,000'. With the encouragement of the new head of the literature department, the Symbolist poet Bryusov, Mayakovsky published this poem anonymously, explaining in an accompanying note that any reader could improve on it or add to it. This was true communist, collective art. Even Mayakovsky, with his outsize ego, was trying to make himself useful and encourage his comrades to become artists themselves. His propagandistic message also hit the right tone. He ridiculed the capitalist leaders of the Entente and held them responsible for the hardships of the Russian people: 'we did not sign a treaty in Versailles / so now we are starving like animals'.[33] But the 150 million Russians would prove unstoppable – his anonymous collaborators had no need to question that.

Yet question it they did, in a paranoid reign of terror that suffocated the promise of revolution in blood. 'A different time is drawing near / The wind of death already chills the heart', Akhmatova wrote in 'Petrograd, 1919'.[34] Her ex-husband, the highly decorated veteran Nikolay Gumilyov, was the first famous writer to be eliminated. In August 1921 he was arrested by the secret service Cheka on suspicion of involvement in a monarchist conspiracy. No evidence for this charge was ever found. Nor was his body.

Zinaida Gippius had seen it all coming. Day in and day out, she criticized the Bolsheviks in her diary, and in her anger and desperation she also increasingly lashed out at the European leaders who had allowed all this to happen. On 22 November 1919, she wrote, 'If, in the twentieth century, there can exist in Europe a country where generalized *slavery* prevails, in a phenomenal, historically unprecedented form, and Europe either does not comprehend the situation or else accepts it, then Europe deserves to be swallowed up by the darkness that surrounds it.' She had no doubt her attitude would be decried as counter-revolutionary, but she was only trying to save the true revolution. '*There is no* revolution', she insisted. '*There is no* dictatorship of the proletariat. *There is no* socialism. Even the much-vaunted soviets *do not exist*.'[35] By late 1919 she could no longer stand it and went into exile with her husband. From Polish-occupied Minsk, and later from Warsaw, she tried to organize the military opposition to the Bolshevik regime. When that effort failed, she moved on to Paris.

In Western Europe, the Armistice eventually led to peace, but revanchist sentiments among the victors made it difficult for the defeated nations to rebuild their futures. The worst punishment was, of course, reserved for Germany.[36] To begin with, it was stripped of all its overseas colonies. Alsace-Lorraine was returned to France, Belgium received a few cantons, the strategically important Rhineland was demilitarized, and the industrial Saar region was placed under the purview of the new League of Nations for fifteen years, after which the locals could return to German rule if they so chose (which they did in 1935). Denmark regained a part of Schleswig that it had lost in a war in 1864. East Prussia was separated from the rest of Germany to give Poland a small corridor to the sea – an inelegant solution and a lasting source of irritation for all involved. On top of these territorial losses, Germany also had to pay phenomenal reparations and was expected to take moral responsibility for the war. In the neutral Netherlands, Albert Verwey commented as early as the spring of 1919 that the Entente had chosen a very risky course. Verwey's beloved Germany was being humbled, even though the new leaders in Berlin did not bear any personal responsibility for the war, and so the revolutionaries, those propelled by 'the momentum of a future world', were being forced by the chauvinism of the 'Parisian League of Nations-builders' into a powerless position that the great German nation could not possibly tolerate for long. The world was in the midst of a profound transformation, but the West seemed more interested in settling old scores than in the needs and possibilities of the present and future.

> All countries, including Belgium, including the Netherlands, are now succumbing to the folly of organizing to defend the old, instead of working toward what lies ahead. Punishing activists is not as important as doing justice to the Flemish. Raising militias is not as sound a policy as reforming labour and business so that they become the indivisible body of the community.[37]

In Belgium, the king and government did not see it that way. The idea of self-determination for the Flemish was dismissed out of hand. National unity and the protection of the bourgeois regime were what mattered most. Without consulting parliament, King Albert staked all the credit he had earned during the war on a calculated round of political roulette. Commitments made by the regime as early as 11 November 1918 showed where its priorities lay. The country's leaders sought to neutralize any threat of revolution by introducing general suffrage (for men) and forming governments of national unity – in other words, including socialists. But this solution left many people dissatisfied. The alliance between the activists (some of whom had narrowly escaped prison) and the radicalized pro-Flemish soldiers of the Yser front gave birth to a political movement whose rallying cries were Flemish self-administration and 'War: Never Again', but which never managed seriously to influence the regime. Major and minor poets supported this Front Party: Paul van Ostaijen wrote pieces for the party newspaper *Ons Vaderland* (Our Homeland), and the veterans Filip De Pillecyn and Ward Hermans (1897–1992) also contributed. Strikingly, the Flemish sympathies in Hermans's poetry increasingly took the form of explicit antipathy toward Belgium. Hermans had been disciplined for his political activities at the front and sent to the 'lumberjack platoon' on the Orne in France, where he had to spend months felling trees in the company of conscientious objectors, Jews and nine other soldiers who had not shown sufficient patriotism. They were not permitted to stop until July 1919. This disciplinary measure had pernicious consequences. Whatever patriotism Hermans had once felt, the Belgian authorities' heartless actions had extinguished it forever.[38] The government persecution of the activists did not do much for the cause of Belgian patriotism either. Poets like Gaston Burssens and Wies Moens, who had chosen to study at the University of Ghent after its conversion to a Dutch-language institution under the German occupation, found themselves behind bars.

Paul van Ostaijen, in exile in Berlin, was going through a long, deep crisis. While his activist friends in Belgium were in prison, his life was – well, 'easy' was not the word, in a country struggling with inflation and poverty, but still, it ate at him that he could no longer have any serious influence on events, whether artistic or political, and whether in Flanders or in Germany. He tried to argue the Flemish case in the local press, but was scarcely able to convince the German revolutionaries that his Flemish nationalism was consistent with their postwar internationalism. In the summer of 1920 he began work on a major poem analyzing his own political engagement and ideals against the backdrop of his life in occupied Antwerp. There is not much room for illusions in *Bezette stad* (Occupied City). While three years earlier, in 'Zaaitijd' (Sowing Time), he had written that 'the seed fell on good ground' in the trenches on the Yser,[39] now he was forced to admit that no fruit had grown and no harvest could take place. The poet, like so many others in the avant-garde across the continent, had assumed that the breakdown of the old order would lead to a new world, but he came to the embittered conclusion that the flowering of revolution had been nipped in the bud and that instead the bourgeois Restoration had come to fruition in Western Europe.

all the hope
all the idiocies
the red flood will not swell
the red armies will not rise
and nothing will break

and nothing will   break

Belgian state nationalism reigned triumphant ('patriotic films / patriotic beer / patriotic veal') and the trinity he hated and mocked with equal passion, 'Religion & King & State', were firmly enthroned again. The 'communist European Federation' he described in his essays was not a short-term possibility.[40] In *Bezette stad*, Europe appears in two guises: as a polyglot quilt in which the sounds of Dutch, English, French, German and Latin all mingle, and in an ironic passage about a map:

EUROPE according to its EROTIC BEDDINGS
we have known Europe *so* long *so* long-
drawn-out outstretched flat and in relief
geologically
hydrologically
politically
religiously
commercially
and so on and so forth

but
this   EROTIC MAP   is a necessity
soon teaching assistants will
give lessons
on this invention for the good of humanity
here's what the women are like on Corfu

legs thighs breasts Berlin **Germany** **BRUSSELS** **Amsterdam** Bucharest **London** PARIS
hair **parfum** fleurs Houbigant Lonchamp Maisons-Laffitte ***mec maquereau***
niche rigoler gigole gousses **ehrliche Frau**

and for 5 minutes you saw
the necropolis
of the Acropolis

Whereas in the title poem of *Het Sienjaal* (The Signal), Van Ostaijen had emphasized how unique the 'ethos' of each European country was,[41] he now drew attention to how diverse European women were. It is not clear how much cynicism should be read into this, but the closing lines of this passage provide a clue. The knowledge that had seemed so essential to the ever-analyzing and categorizing academics, tourists and anthropologists of Europe was in fact a symptom of the continent's deep cultural crisis. If sexuality and the experience of lust were investigated and exploited academically and commercially, then it really would mean the end of Europe's great culture: 'the necropolis / of the Acropolis'. The 'highest peak' of culture that Van Ostaijen had praised in *Het Sienjaal* now seemed a grotesque farce.

Learning to live with disappointment – it was a task that awaited many soldiers, intellectuals and writers after the war. The glorious words of August 1914 had been unmasked as dangerous bombast, and the promise of November 1918 seemed to have brought still further disillusion. Siegfried Sassoon was not about to be deceived again. On 11 November 1918, he could already see that events were taking an unpromising turn. The triumphalism and vengefulness of his countrymen disturbed him ('One feels that England is going to increase in power enormously. They mean to skin Germany alive. "A peace to end peace!"'), and the omnipresence of what he called 'mob patriotism' made him sick. 'It is a loathsome ending to the loathsome tragedy of the last four years.'[42]

For others, however, the end of war was also a step forward. Ford Madox Hueffer had gone to the front out a sense of duty liberally laced with guilt – hadn't he taken life too easily? hadn't he done more than his share of damage in his amorous misadventures? – and he saw his serious injury as repayment of a debt. The fact that he had survived that abysmal experience placed him on firmer footing after the Armistice, and when he officially changed his name in June 1919, it put the seal on his rebirth. Ford Madox Hueffer became Ford Madox Ford – an irreversible farewell to his German roots and a new *nom de plume*. In the postwar novels that are the cornerstones of Ford's enduring reputation, the main character consistently comes face to face with death through war or attempted suicide, but ultimately survives.[43] From this perspective, the First World War seems to have saved Ford's life.

Yet many other lives had been ruined. British soldiers who had believed in their cause to the last and been welcomed home as heroes had terrible difficulty returning to civilian life.[44] Many ended up as jobless vagabonds. It was especially hard for them to readjust in a society where, aside from a passing interest in the most spectacular battlefield tales, most people were not able or willing to understand the Tommies' traumatic experiences. After all, they had survived, and now they were national heroes – what could be so traumatic about that? While arguments broke out around village pumps about the design of the memorial for those who had made the supreme sacrifice, many battle-scarred veterans withdrew from civilian life. In his war memoirs *Goodbye to All That* (1929), the British poet Robert Graves described how dreadfully difficult it was to put the war behind him. His dreams were haunted by visions of deadly explosions, unknown passers-by on the street took on the features of his fallen comrades, and on country walks his best-loved British landscapes spontaneously transformed into battlefields.[45]

What had turned into a nightmare for Graves had become an addiction for Gabriele D'Annunzio, who was caught unawares by the Armistice and regarded it as a grave injustice. He had only just performed his most heroic act – in August 1918, he dropped propaganda leaflets in the colours of the Italian flag over the enemy city of Vienna – when all of a sudden his life of self-sacrifice and derring-do was over. Just as he was about to sink into a mire of lethargy, a new cause appeared to which the poet could devote his boundless energies: the fate of the port city of Fiume (Rijeka) on the Dalmatian coast.[46] The city was not mentioned in the secret Treaty of London that had brought Italy into the Allied camp in 1915, but nevertheless, the Italians believed they had a right to it. The situation would have been problematic enough even without this complication; President Wilson wanted to tear up all the old secret agreements and use his own Points as the only guide. But that is just what the Italians claimed to be doing when they laid claim to all the regions promised to them plus Fiume, a multi-ethnic city with an Italian middle class surrounded by Croatian labourers and peasants. The Italians were clearly testing the limits of self-determination. In Fiume's city centre, the Italians did form a bare majority, but the area as a whole, including the surrounding towns, was incontestably Croatian. Wilson was not inclined to accept Italy's reasoning. He had already gone against his principles in granting them the German-speaking region of Tyrol, but they could forget the Dalmatian coast, and especially Fiume. In nationalist circles in Italy, the tension mounted rapidly. In Mussolini's newspaper *Il Popolo d'Italia*, D'Annunzio wrote derisively of the 'crippled peace' that was being fobbed off on the country. How scandalous it would be for Italy to consent to the Allied peace proposals in all their mediocrity. 'What peace will in the end be imposed on us, poor little ones of Christ? A Gallic peace, a British peace, a star-spangled peace? Then no! Enough. Victorious Italy – the most victorious of all the nations – victorious over herself and over the enemy – will have on the Alps and over her sea the Pax Romana, the sole peace that is fitting.'[47]

At the Versailles talks, Fiume became a sticking point. The Italian delegation suggested that a civil war was in the air. When Wilson placed a personal appeal to the Italian people in the local newspapers, asking them to give up their territorial ambitions, D'Annunzio jeered at him, calling him a 'croatianized Quaker' with thirty-two false teeth.[48] Nor did Wilson receive the support of parliament, the Italian in the street or the newspapers. On 19 June, nine days before the Treaty of Versailles was to be signed, the Italian government fell. Just prior to that, the Italian prime minister Vittorio Emanuele Orlando had mentioned to his British counterpart that he feared his successor would be D'Annunzio. That particular spectre did not materialize, but on 11 September a group of 200 veterans, fascists and anarchists set out for Fiume under the leadership of the poet-pilot. Instead of waiting any longer for a political solution, they took the city without a fight the next day. The Italian soldiers who were supposed to stop D'Annunzio joined him instead, and the poet became *Il Duce* of Fiume. The oratorical orgasm that followed was his most impressive yet. Heroism had triumphed over politics, courage over prattling cowardice. And once again, a form of energy was released that had no outlet in ordinary civilian life. Fiume soon needed a special hospital for venereal diseases.

The international authorities were, as one might imagine, not amused by D'Annunzio's exploits, and their irritation grew when he began touting the Belgian poet Léon Kochnitzky's plan to establish an alternative League of Nations.[49] Fiume's League would be a League for Oppressed Nations, emphatically opposed to the growing power of the United States and supported (according to D'Annunzio's plan) by Egypt, India and Ireland, and the Flemish, Maltese, Catalans and Montenegrins.

The Futurists were noted participants in the Fiume campaign.[50] Although they had branded D'Annunzio the archenemy of Futurism in a 1911 manifesto,[51] the rivals were now united by their love of showy patriotism and muscular action. By this time, Marinetti had founded a Futurist political party and was convinced that his movement was ready to lead the country into the future at long last. Twelve Futurists had died in the war, and almost all the others had been injured at least once; surely these sacrifices had shown that their fate was intertwined with that of their country. During the war, the Futurists had become friendly with the elite Arditi troops, who idolized D'Annunzio. Together, they expected to change Italy, and Fiume seemed like the perfect test case. The city became one big countercultural experiment, bursting with free love, dance, Bolshevik soviet democracy and Futurist poetry. It seemed as though anything was possible, and everything permitted. In Fiume, the interplay of art and life that was the Futurist ideal became a reality. At least in this one spot, the war seemed to have brought an end to bourgeois decadence.

As the party went on in Fiume, the outside world was looking on in growing chagrin, wondering what on earth to do next. In the Italian elections in the autumn of 1919, the military and political supporters of the Fiume escapade paid a high price. Meanwhile, the north of Italy had become almost ungovernable, with constant street fighting between fascists and communists. The word from America was still that Fiume could not, under any circumstances, come under Italian rule. Every time this message was repeated, D'Annunzio would seize the occasion to make an impassioned speech urging his followers not to give up.

He stressed that while it might seem like a territorial conflict, in fact they were fighting for their very souls, and he described the maimed veterans in his military force as trees 'pruned to yield larger fruits'.[52] But the reality was less heroic. When Rome came up with a compromise and presented it directly to the people of Fiume, D'Annunzio's soldiers intimidated the supporters and rigged the election. The poet's love for his people suddenly seemed to have cooled. 'The voice of Fiume has changed', he cried out to them. 'I no longer recognize it ... What sudden disease have we fallen sick with?'[53] Italy and Yugoslavia ultimately reached an agreement: Fiume would become a free state. D'Annunzio was furious, and on 1 December 1920, he declared war on his own country. By Christmas Eve, the Italians had lost their patience and opened fire. Fifty-six people died, and 100 were injured. D'Annunzio himself narrowly escaped death and surrendered. It looked like an inglorious defeat, but Mussolini had been observing the experiment from a distance, and sometimes from close by. D'Annunzio's combustible mix of rhetoric, nationalism and violence was a major source of inspiration for his March on Rome in 1922.

While waving the banner of grand ideals, the government leaders in Versailles were trying to solve the daunting geopolitical problems of their day through coddling, compromise and endless consultation. Fiume was not the only place where the outcome was called into question. Many Serbs, for instance, found it hard to see why they were being asked to share a single country with the Slovenes, Croats and Bosnians, who had served loyally in the Austro-Hungarian army until the very end of the war, shelling the Serb capital of Belgrade and spreading terror among its residents.[54] But the ethnic composition of the region was highly complex. The poet Ljubomir Micić (1895–1971), for example, belonged to the Serb minority in Croatia and had also ended up fighting for the Dual Monarchy. He escaped the Galician front by having himself declared insane, and in 1918 was elected as a representative to a council of the southern Slavic peoples that ultimately formed Yugoslavia. The postwar doings of the great European powers made him very suspicious. As a declared pacifist and the founder of the Serb avant-garde movement Zenit (Zenith), he took the epithet 'barbarian', often applied to his people by outsiders, and wore it as a badge of pride: 'From the Balkans we cry: anti-culture!

... Anti-Europe!'[55] To him, Europe stood for the culture that had produced the war and the lies that followed it. As a rebel poet and a modern incarnation of the traditional Balkan *hajduk* (rogue fighter), he would battle for liberation from this cultural tyranny. He championed an anti-cultural revolution, and like other avant-gardists of his time, he did not rule out the use of force: 'Lady Europe! We spit in your unwashed face and before your boil- and syphilis-ridden footsoles. We hurl the bombs of our poems into your mutilated European skies. We fire the cannons of our new ideas at the peak of the silk-veiled bourgeoisie. At the peak, that's right, and not at that imaginary divine navel, the only symbol of all European geniuses.'[56] His style, more strongly influenced by the European avant-garde than by traditional Serb ballads, did not stand in the way of his outraged message. For Micić, resistance to militarism and imperialism and resistance to Europe were one and the same. Only Balkanization could save the Continent.

In this aggressive pacifist manifesto, written in 1925, Zenitism seemed related to the course that Dada was pursuing. After Zurich, the Dadaists had settled and flourished in Berlin. In early 1918, even before and during the German spring offensive, radical artists stormed the cabarets and theatres with their sound poems and their absurd, offensive declarations. They soon found kindred spirits in the empire's rising revolutionary movements. They rejected the mentality that had brought the country to ruin. The social democrats' use of reactionary stormtroopers to crush the revolution had damaged their credibility beyond repair. The Dadaists could not understand why the patriots who had caused their country so much misery were not being held accountable for their actions. They regarded German culture and its exponents as responsible in large part for the catastrophic war. 'What is known as the German mentality has become notorious ... there is hardly any official person who has not been compromised. Pastors and poets, statesmen and scholars have vied to spread the most sordid possible image of the nation', Hugo Ball wrote in 1918 in 'Kritik der Deutschen Intelligenz' (Critique of the German Intelligentsia).[57]

Dada itself went on surprising, provoking and confusing. When D'Annunzio conquered Fiume, he received a telegram of congratulations through the *Corriere della Sera*. Maurice Barrès, in contrast, was prosecuted in a show trial held by the Paris Dadaists for his 'attack on the security of the spirit' because he had succumbed to nationalism. Inconsistent? Not necessarily. Although D'Annunzio's rhetoric was typically just as pompous and hollow as that of Barrès, the Dadaists were being true to their artistic views when they cheered on his aggressive intervention as a 'great Dadaist achievement'.[58] Who else had ever ridiculed the bourgeois powers-that-be with such flair? Nor were the Dadaists put off by the Italian Futurists' continued attachment to violence and nationalism; the programmes of Dada performances included poems by Marinetti, Buzzi and Altomare. Of course, in April 1918, reading from the work of enemy soldiers was a provocation in itself.

Dada attacks on nationalism were just as revealing. When the well-known novelist Rachilde accused Dada of being a German movement, Francis Picabia (1879–1953) congratulated her on her exclusionary French patriotism, claiming that he himself was of mixed Cuban, Spanish, French, Italian and American descent, and took pains to point out that Kaiser Wilhelm II thought, just as she did, that he was the sole representative of his nation.[59] In the same style, the Berlin 'Dadasopher' Raoul Hausmann (1886–1971) opened an essay with the words, 'Art is a matter for the nation. Nationality is the difference between polenta, bouillabaisse, powidl, roast beef, pierogi, and dumpling soup.'[60] This seems to imply that the Dadaists did acknowledge cultural differences between nations, but mainly when they showed up on the dinner table.

It was only on the Western front that the Armistice led directly to a laying down of arms. In the Balkans, the Baltics, Finland, Poland, the Ukraine and above all Russia, the fight for power and dominance dragged on for years in the name of justice and equality. In Western Europe, there was the occasional death in a street protest – when the young activist Herman van den Reeck was killed by a policeman's bullet during a banned pro-Flemish march in Antwerp, almost all the Flemish avant-garde poets wrote poems in his memory[61] – but the numbing violence of 1914–18 seemed to have ended.

The exception was Ireland, where the violence had begun well before the war on the Continent ended.[62] There, conflicting views on self-determination came into bloody collision. One key moment was the announcement of election results on 14 December 1918. Redmond's Nationalist Party, which had almost won the country Home Rule in 1914, suffered a crushing defeat, and the winner was the extremist Sinn Féin. Two years after the Easter Rising and the execution of its leaders, which many in Ireland had seen as disproportionate, the election results showed a clear, general shift toward radicalism. In fact, most of the elected Sinn Féin leaders were in prison. In a sense, the Irish electorate had rejected the British laws holding them there. Home Rule would no longer be enough; the ties with the British Empire would have to be severed completely.

In January 1919, the members of parliament who were not behind bars assembled in Dublin and declared the independence of the Irish Republic, in an attempt to lend official force to the proclamation made during the Easter Rising in 1916. This new state no longer wanted anything to do with the British Empire and its royal house. But President Wilson objected to Irish nationalism and refused to support them, saying that the Irish already lived in a democratic country and could therefore sort out their problems through more appropriate democratic channels.[63] And of course,

Ireland's rush to independence was equally unwelcome to the leaders of that democratic state – the British Empire, that is. After fighting a war of independence against the British (1919–1921) in which some 2,000 were killed, and a civil war (1922–1923) estimated to have cost twice as many lives, the Republic was transformed into the Irish Free State, and the island became part of the British Commonwealth. To most Protestants, religion was at least as important as ethnicity, and the Protestant majority in the north chose not to become part of the Free State. They had no objection to being both Irish and British, with the kind of layered identity taken for granted by most people in Scotland and Wales.

The fact that the Irish nationalists had carried out their uprising with German support – and in 1916, that year of horrors – had pushed the Protestants/Unionists toward a more extreme position. The south had seen a similar shift toward radicalism since the Easter Rising, and people there were quite willing to sacrifice the unity of Ireland in order to found a Catholic, Gaelic state. Yet even this solution left the country with dissatisfied minorities. The Catholics in Northern Ireland felt disadvantaged and politically powerless and tried to improve their status, often by violent means. The Protestants in the Free State saw with heavy hearts their country, even after independence, becoming less and less tolerant of diversity. Papal pronouncements seemed to have become more influential than those of Irish politicians.

The Free State also had fundamentalist tendencies in the cultural sphere. Soon after independence, a plan began circulating to use only Gaelic on street signs, even though most Irish citizens spoke only English. Thomas Kettle's Irish internationalism seemed a world away. This worried some, such as William Butler Yeats, now a senator – who happened to be a member of the Protestant minority. In 1925, when a bill was introduced to prohibit divorce, he summoned all his rhetorical gifts to convince his fellow lawmakers that the convictions of Ireland's crucial

Protestant population should not be ignored. 'We are one of the great stocks of Europe', he intoned. 'We have created most of the modern literature of this country. We have created the best of its political intelligence.'[64] Two years earlier, Yeats had become the first Irishman in history to win the Nobel Prize for Literature. When he talked about modern Irish literature he was, of course, partly talking about himself. But above all, he was reminding all concerned that, as he had stressed in his acceptance speech to the Swedish Academy, it was perfectly possible to be an Irish patriot, a Protestant, and a writer in the English language.

Three years before that, on 11 November 1920, the Swedish Academy had made a similar point when it announced that the 1919 Nobel Prize for Literature would be awarded to the Swiss poet Carl Spitteler for his epic poem *Olympischer Frühling* (Olympian Spring, 1906, 1909). The date and the winner were not without symbolic significance. The first prize awarded after the war went to a representative of a neutral country, the author of a work that, as the jury remarked, could not be fully appreciated until after the war. Spitteler's visionary tales of the wartime use of wondrous machines and poison gas 'testify to the decay that threatens mankind when it pushes too far a self-confidence based on material power'.[65] The Academy, which was supposed to be politically neutral, could hardly have taken a clearer stance. Deep in a subordinate clause in a long list, it also implicitly gave its opinion on the burning European issue of nationalism and self-determination. The poet's language was not only masterly, powerful and splendid, but also 'unmistakably Swiss'. In other words, the Academy believed it was possible to forge a national culture in a multi-ethnic area.

In the new states that rose out of the debris of the world war, building a national culture was a central task. When the Latvian writing couple Aspazija and Rainis returned to their native soil in April 1920, after years of exile in Switzerland, they were welcomed as national heroes. During the bloody struggle for Latvian independence, Rainis had written the dramatic ballad *Daugava* in a fit of passion. He believed it would give the soldiers all the moral sustenance they longed for. Rainis designed a national flag, offered historical grounds for the Latvians' right to their own nation, described the heroic deeds of Latvians in days of old, and celebrated the heroes of the fight for independence.

> Barefooted battalions
> Men with the endurance of oaks:
> They will recapture the Latvian land
> From the enemies' despotism.[66]

Daugava was a huge success; in just two weeks, all 4,000 copies sold out. According to the nationalist legend, the poem had an enormous impact on the troops. Soldiers carried it in their boots and shouted out passages to each other, until at last victory was theirs. Ironically, this belligerent bellowing was just the opposite of the ideal that Rainis cherished for his country. All European nations were founded on brute force and militarism, the poet observed. Why not try to build a country and culture based on a poetic, human ideal? And in that case, why shouldn't he become both the National Poet and the Founding Father? His writing received all the recognition he had hoped for, but he had to settle for a place in parliament – his secret ambition, the presidency, was just not on the cards.

As long as you were part of a country's ethnic or religious majority, self-determination was a wonderful principle. Otherwise, it carried the risk of discrimination, persecution or death. The young states wanted to carve out their place in the world, often at the expense of whatever and whoever did not fit into the official picture – whether Jews, Roma or other minorities. When the Transylvanian poet Octavian Goga was appointed minister in the Romanian government, he became one of the greatest advocates of a strong, unified Romania. Under his nationalist regime, the long-standing problem of anti-Semitism took on even more troubling proportions. Goga argued that the newly annexed territories had to be made exclusively Romanian, and he had scathing words for the 'fortune-seekers' and 'parasites' who were descending upon Romania and corrupting the pure souls of its peasants.[67] In Ukraine and the new Poland, violence against minorities was severe and widespread. No sooner had these regions been 'liberated' from Russian and German occupation than the pogroms began. In late November, the Yiddish poet Uri Tsvi Greenberg (1896–1981) saw Polish soldiers savagely demolish the street where his family lived in the Galician capital of Lemberg. 'Within two or three days the Lemberg Ghetto was turned into heaps of smoking debris', wrote a shocked *New York Times* correspondent.[68] The press reported more than a thousand deaths, a figure that was never confirmed by any official source, but which explains why Lemberg became synonymous with Jewish suffering. A preliminary investigation led to the conclusion that it had been a punitive action, because the Jews had remained too neutral when Lemberg was attacked by the Ukrainians in early November. A total of 7,000 residents of the city were physically assaulted and lost their homes and possessions, and according to the report, at least 150 were killed.[69] Greenberg went to Warsaw, where he became associated with the Jewish Expressionist magazine *Di Khaliastre* (The Gang). In 1923, he published his long poem 'In Malchut fon Tzelem' (In the Kingdom of the Cross) in Berlin's Yiddish avant-garde magazine *Albatros*. In the kingdom called Europe that he described, Jews were compelled as a matter of course to bear the cross time and time again. A year later Greenberg emigrated to Palestine.

The forest's black and dense; it grows out of the flatlands.
Such depths of grief, such terror out of Europe.
Dark and wild, dark and wild, the trees have heads of sorrow;
From their branches hang the bloody dead – still wounded.
All the faces of the heavenly dead are silver,
And the oil that moons pour out on mines is golden;
And if a voice shouts, 'Pain!' the sound's a stone in water
And the sound of bodies praying – tears falling in a chasm.
I am the owl of that sad wood, the accusing-bird of Europe.
In the valleys of grief and fear, in blind midnights under crosses,
I want to raise a brother's plea to the Arab folk of Asia:
Poor though we may be, come lead us to the desert.
But my sheep are fearful, for the half moon is descending
Like a scythe against our throats.
So I, heart-of-the-world, complain at random. Oh, terror, and oh, Europe!

In the land of grief, its throats outstretched, the lamb lies,
And I, wound-of-the-world, in Europe, spit blood upon the crosses –[70]

Most Poles were probably either genuinely or wilfully ignorant of the atrocities. After their humiliating subjugation at the hands of the Russians, Prussians and Austro-Hungarians, they could finally see independence on the horizon in those turbulent November days of 1918. For 120 years their country had existed only in imagination and memory. The national anthem 'Mazurek Dąbrowskiego' (Poland Is Not Yet Lost) had given them courage all those years, but its words had also been an inevitable reminder that they *had* lost their country. Finally, that period seemed to be over. On 10 November 1918, Marshal Józef Piłsudski was released from imprisonment in Magdeburg. He had been held captive after refusing to swear an oath of loyalty to the Austrian emperor in the summer of 1917, but now his greatest moment was drawing near. When he took over power from the Germans in Warsaw, the rejoicing defied description.[71] But the truth of the situation would soon put a dampener on things. Poland had been plundered and lay in ruins. What was left of the rail infrastructure was hardly usable, because there were no fewer than sixty-six different systems. And although there were millions of Poles, no one was quite sure where Polish territory began and where it ended. By 1921, Piłsudski would fight six wars with almost all the neighbouring states to establish the borders of his new country.

On Friday, 29 November 1918, a few young Polish poets associated with *Skamander* magazine performed at the opening of the Picador Café, a cabaret in Warsaw. The evening could best be described as Dada on rations.[72] Since there was hardly anything to eat or drink, the penniless poets put their own poems on the menu, including prices for dedications. They could even be hired to make marriage proposals. The assimilated Jew Julian Tuwim (1894–1953) read a translation of Rimbaud's 'Le bateau ivre', along with classics from the Polish Romantic period by Cyprian Norwid and Adam Mickiewicz. Antoni Słonimski (1895–1976) recited a satirical poem he had just finished, 'Alles alles über Deutschland', which not only celebrated the implosion of the German Empire and poked fun at countries that had left it in the lurch, like Italy and Bulgaria, but also pointed out the painful contrast between the fashionable discourse of self-determination and the harsh reality.

> Here and there, the goal's the same;
> On either side, there's lies and crime.
> In their bloody altercations,
> If anyone should be ridiculed
> Then surely it must be the fool
> Who takes on twenty-two nations![73]

Of course, the future was also discussed that night. Tuwim's speech – which in the best avant-garde tradition was entitled 'Inwektywa' (Invective) – tore into the bourgeois figures who would no longer play a role in the new Poland. 'With laughter and disdain the future smacks your face, you sick weeds of the Great War, big city licks, blasé dissemblers ... lazy servants of fashion and luxury, bloodless and mediocre dandies of an old Europe. You must bleed and die in a great pool of blood!!! The Time of the Workers is at hand.'[74] It was less clear whether the time of young, democratic art was also at hand. Picador was successful at first – more than a thousand copies were sold of a volume self-published by the poets[75] – but its popularity soon waned. To give their movement a fresh start, they agreed to collaborate with the local Futurists Anatol Stern (1899–1968) and Aleksander Wat (1900–1967), who had moved into the basement of the very chic Hotel Europejski. It was a debacle. The elegant location clashed with their poetic ambitions and was out of the financial reach of their intended audience. And inevitably, there were artistic disagreements between the Picador poets, whose work was highly traditional in form, and the revolutionary Futurists.[76] To make the disaster complete, Stern was arrested in December 1919 on charges of profanity after a reading in Vilnius. Słonimski immediately started a petition, but despite his efforts, Stern was sentenced to a year's imprisonment and spent months in jail.[77] Politically, Poland was slowly moving toward autonomy, but the young men who tried to open its eyes to the latest European artistic movements found they were less free than they had thought in the heady days of 1918.

The 1920s were later referred to as 'roaring' or 'gay', but that reputation is based mainly on a handful of overblown anecdotes taken as representative (such as Josephine Baker's banana skirt, or the enthusiasm surrounding Charles Lindbergh's flight across the Atlantic) and on the short-lived economic boom between the hyperinflation that followed the war and the Wall Street crash of 1929. But what dancing there was took place in the crater of a volcano, in an often desperate attempt to forget the suffering, suppress the sight of the mutilated veterans, and pretend the world was headed for better days. In 1920, Ivo Andrić wrote, 'Over the years I hear the clamour of victory, but there is less and less bread on earth, less and less strength in people.'[78] Andrić himself had not been released from prison until 1917, and since that time he had been trying his luck at Zagreb's national theatre. But even his first artistic successes did not blind him to reality. It was humanity as a whole that had lost the war. No words could right that wrong, and certainly not the nationalist rhetoric that had already done so much damage since the summer of 1914. 'What else are today's victories but tomorrow's defeats?'

And those defeats were legion. Democracy was teetering, hunger was gnawing, and after the avant-garde's exhausting journey from prewar Cubism, Futurism and Expressionism to Dadaism and Surrealism, the dream of a new art also seemed to have ended. In 1925, the Polish poet Anatol Stern took stock. His oracular collage *Europa* was designed to be a 'seismograph of the subconscious',[79] but never moved beyond the level of an (admittedly impressive) apocalyptic rant. The words 'abecedary of slaughter / of dirt lice fires' opened his excruciating dissection of the ideological and idealistic blindness that had driven the continent into a frenzy of destruction and threatened to do the same thing again. As Stern saw it, the moral panic of the postwar world had sent the Europeans, like lemmings, plunging into the deep chasm of 'the massage of propaganda / the gospel of terror', a gap

into which we jump
since we cannot jump
into heaven.

Deprived of grand words in which to believe, Europeans apparently preferred to hurl themselves off cliffs. But it goes without saying that they went in style. Like Mayakovsky in *Voina i Mir* (War and the World) and Van Ostaijen in *Bezette stad* (Occupied City), Stern staged the action of war in *Europa* as if it were a film. But instead of grotesque Cecil B. DeMille–style pageantry, he offered a sobering demonstration of incongruity.

film of world war
directors
cameramen
blinded
all captions erased
impossible to understand
the howling gesticulation
of a milliard arms
the ham acting
of the players' eyes
film of folly
stuffed with the vermin of
numbers
which explain nothing

That may have been the world leaders' greatest mistake after the Armistice: the belief that self-determination for national minorities could bring some consolation to Europe's millions of battered, dazed, uprooted, horribly maimed survivors. Even in Poland, described by outside observers as proud and nationalistic, ordinary people had very different concerns. Pain would always be pain, an amputated limb would always be an amputated limb, and even if you could ask for it in your own language, black bread would never be more than black bread. And as for their moral agony … how could they even begin to face it?

but who
but who
fights
for that – dearer than all the silesias of the world
dearer than all the independences –
the liberated
heart of
man ?![80]

Afterword

In 1919, almost anyone could have drawn the same conclusion, but when the leading French poet and essayist Paul Valéry (1871–1945) drew it, it took on the authority of a verdict: 'The illusion of a European culture has been lost.' His essay 'The Crisis of the Mind' opened with the words, 'We later civilizations … we too know that we are mortal.'[1] It was no longer inconceivable that the great lost cultures of the past – Babylon, Elam, Persepolis – would soon count Europe among their number. The First World War was a European creation that demolished almost everything Europe stood for – culture, science, enlightenment, morality – in a destructive fury unlike anything seen before. During the war, Europeans did their best to find a response to the conflict, frantically writing, pondering, studying and praying, but in the end they failed. Europe's spiritual crisis had spread to its marrow. In the panic with which Europeans ransacked their intellectual and scientific traditions for a remedy, Valéry saw a lack of direction and coherence. What had traditionally been Europe's great strengths – openness combined with an enormous capacity to assimilate and transform its many different influences and impulses – now seemed to have become part of the problem. Europe in 1914 had been not so much a beacon of progress as an intellectual way station. While there was something undeniably *modern* about that, what was clearest to Valéry, five years later, were the dangers. Or had Europe chosen this path deliberately – the path from Leonardo da Vinci's dream of human flight to the invention of aerial bombing, from Kant to Hegel to Marx to ... (an ellipsis that Valéry did not fill in, but which must have represented Lenin and Bolshevism), and from Pythagorean geometry to Krupp's weapons of mass destruction?

European supremacy had always been based on *quality*. In quantitative terms (population, area, natural resources), the continent was nothing special. The traits that, according to Valéry, had always made the European mind superior ('a driving thirst, an ardent and disinterested curiosity, a happy mixture of imagination and rigorous logic, a certain unpessimistic scepticism, an unresigned mysticism') had now evolved into a menace. Knowledge was no longer primarily the expression of a philosophical or poetic approach to the world; instead, it had become a commodity and an instrument of power. As a commodity, it could come into anyone's possession, anywhere in the world. Thus, according to the poet, Europe had forfeited its only trump card. In the future, power and force would be expressible solely in *quantitative* terms – mass, figures, tables, statistics. In fact, this change had already taken place during the war. The sheer quantities of men and munitions available had played a decisive role in the conflict. For a long time, Europe had seemed to be an exceptional region of the universe, but it would soon be rudely awakened to its new status as a mere stepping stone to Asia. The great European Mind would be diffused among more and more people in Europe and throughout all the other continents and cultures of the world. The result could be a thin, flavourless brew, but it was also possible that water would miraculously transform into wine, dramatically increasing the quality of life around the world. To Valéry, however, this seemed like no more than a theoretical possibility. And so he called on his readers to resist, telling them – implicitly, because a poet does not raise his voice – that civilized Europeans do not have to resign themselves to democracy, the spread of technology, and the general exploitation of the globe. If they wanted to defend themselves against this 'threatening conspiracy', then they could start here and now, by making quality central to their lives again. It was not the group that deserved attention, but the struggling, creative individual. That was the only way to avert the crisis of the European mind. Valéry's radical aristocratic individualism was not the only option. Europe could also choose the path of quantity, staking everything on transformation and massification. The exceptional interest that European writers and intellectuals showed in the Soviet experiment was one expression of that tendency.[2] In various parts of Europe, left-wing, pacifist Clarté circles were organized on the initiative of novelist and veteran Henri Barbusse. Like Valéry, they invoked the heritage of the Enlightenment, but they interpreted this very differently. In the years following the war many people, especially on the far left, were inclined to give equality and fraternity priority over liberty. Despite the size of some of the egos involved, in their artistic and political activities the individual was subordinate to the collective. Paul van Ostaijen, for example, pursued a form of poetry in which the poet's personality played the smallest possible role. Under the leadership of Valéry's disciple André Breton and of Philippe Soupault, the French Surrealists developed all sorts of techniques for collective artistic creation. These young middle-class men had embraced the dictatorship of the proletariat as a political dogma, and while they strongly opposed aggressive nationalism, they did not rule out the use of force.

Avant-garde artists seemed especially toughened by the war; before the summer of 1914, they had assaulted the tradition of Western art with fierce tirades and grand dreams, but afterwards many of them retreated into pitch-black, destructive cynicism. With lascivious pleasure, they unmasked the reconstruction mentality of the petit bourgeois – *allons travailler* ('let's get to work!') – as escapism. Their project was not a search for a remedy, but a deliberate subversion. Or to be more precise, while they were always ready for revolution, campaigns for the eight-hour working day or women's suffrage seemed less inspiring. It was the subconscious they wanted to explore, not the diplomatic options of the League of Nations. They revelled in their parodies of inflated bourgeois language, but their own vocabulary showed the same dramatic, overblown tendencies. They too were often fascinated with the absolute, although they sought it not in the All but in Nothingness – a shift that in a sense had taken place between 1914 and 1918, on the battlefields of Europe.

In the words of the philosopher Peter Sloterdijk, author of *Theorie der Nachkriegszeiten* (Theory of the Post-War Periods), only after another world war would Europe be ready to decide against an existence in tragic and epic style.[3] The continent learned in the school of hard knocks that a healthy indifference can be safer, more peaceful, and in fact more productive than the deadly embrace in which many countries, particularly the archenemies France and Germany, had held each other since Napoleon's time. In the interest of keeping the peace, Sloterdijk concludes, newspapers should send their most soporific correspondents to neighbouring countries. Above all, passions should never be aroused and nations never encouraged to imitate, let alone outdo, each other.

The splendid little wars that Europe waged, not once but twice, in hopes of regeneration, led to ever greater catastrophes. After Auschwitz, Stalingrad and Dresden, the cynical stability of the Cold War gave the old Europe a chance to reinvent itself and adjust its priorities. Postwar Europe became a beacon of peace, prosperity and stability. There were occasional deaths during demonstrations, and the media and public fretted about separatist movements and left-wing terrorism, but Europeans seemed to have decided that the large-scale use of force was no longer legitimate.[4] Considering the complex politics involved, the democratization of Greece, Portugal and Spain and the implosion of the communist East Bloc proceeded remarkably smoothly. Earlier, the end of Western colonialism had signalled that Europe no longer considered its imperial ambitions affordable, either financially or morally. In this climate of opinion, the explosion in the Balkans in the 1990s and the geopolitical responses to the attacks of 11 September 2001 came as a shock to many Europeans. Perhaps they did not live in the best of all possible worlds after all. The rhetoric of the clash of civilizations made a vigorous comeback, as did the discourse of nationalism, which in its extreme form led to ethnic cleansing, while more banal forms postulated a homogeneity of language and national culture that very rarely corresponded to European history and reality. The Euroscepticism that now confronts the European Union is prompted not only by the flaws in European institutions – their democratic deficit and lack of transparency – but also by a sometimes acute fear that nations will lose their identities. A true European Federation or United States of Europe seems further away than ever. The more the world becomes a 'global village' under the influence of economic and cultural globalization, the more its inhabitants want their world to provide the same sense of familiarity and security as a real, old-fashioned village. The virulent chauvinism of the early twentieth century survives today only in the soccer stadium, but milder forms of nationalism are gaining ground in almost every part of Europe, most definitely including Eastern Europe and the former Soviet Union, where most of today's countries were formed only recently.

In this climate, the continued study and analysis of our shared history is anything but a luxury – not because it provides us with a melodramatic *Warning: Danger Ahead* (history never repeats itself so superficially), but because it heightens our sensitivity to the rhetoric that peoples and ethnic groups use to describe, stigmatize and provoke each other. In that respect, the poetry of the First World War remains fascinating. This also explains why a phrase like 'poets of the Great War' does not have the same ring as 'watercolourists of the Holocaust'. Most of these war poets never intended their verse to alleviate Europe's indescribable suffering. Their work accuses, analyzes and describes, although sometimes it also goads or whitewashes. Above all, it is the work of *participants* – poets who stood not above events, or on the sidelines, but right in the middle of the action. From the start of the conflict, poets played a central role in mobilizing large groups of people. The war culture that characterized the First World War was, to a large extent, a literary culture, and more specifically a poetic one.

Given that fact, it is surprising that literary historians have so rarely embarked on a comparative study of these writings. Over the past century, bookcases have been filled with publications on the poetry of the First World War, but with a few rare exceptions, these studies have restricted themselves to a national paradigm.[5] What makes this even more surprising is that the intensely studied avant-garde of the period was profoundly influenced by the war, and some of its leading representatives either fought in the war or wrote about it. This book is a first attempt to tell their story, and that of the Symbolists and traditionalists who fought and wrote alongside them, in the context of nationalism – a political movement that since its origin has been interwoven with literature.[6] In this light, poetry is not an ornament fabricated by and for aesthetes, but a source of knowledge about the past and a demonstration of how that past was shaped by words.

Acknowledgements

Without America, this book about Europe would never have been written. The idea came to me in the spring of 2005, when I held the Peter Paul Rubens Chair at the University of California (Berkeley). Most of the research and writing took place during a Kluge Fellowship at the Library of Congress, from 1 February to 31 July 2008. I extend my thanks to Tom Lanoye, who shares my passion for the First World War and invited me, at an early stage, to do the research for *Overkant. Moderne verzen uit de Groote Oorlog* (*Other Side: Modern Verse from the Great War*), which taught me that no book like this one yet existed and inspired me to write one. To the Flemish community, which sent me to Berkeley for a semester to share my knowledge of the Low Countries and European literature with students there; to the University of Antwerp, which allowed me to go; to the Cal students who took my seminar and formulated extremely insightful readings of the texts that we discussed; to the Dean of Humanities, department chair Tony Kaes, Inez Hollander and the rest of the staff of the German Department and Dutch Studies in Berkeley, who spared no effort to make my stay there pleasant and productive; to Robert Holub, who largely remained stoic as I shamelessly converted his tidy office in Berkeley into a paper reconstruction of a First World War battlefield; to Kitty Zijlmans, who was my next-door neighbour that semester and remained an exceptionally inspiring colleague afterwards; to Johan Snapper and Riet Samuels for their remarkable hospitality; to my Belgian, British, German, Italian and Dutch colleagues who attended the fascinating ACUME conference *Writing and Visualising War* in Giessen in the summer of 2005, especially Max Saunders for the valuable information about Ford Madox Ford, Dan Todmann for pointing me toward the revisionist school, and Astrid Erll for her comparatist tips from the German school; to my colleagues at the Dutch Department, the Research Institute for History and Culture (OGC), and the Faculty of Humanities of Utrecht University, which made it possible for me to stay in Washington; to all the staff members and guests of the Kluge Center at the Library of Congress; to the phenomenally helpful staff of the Main Reading Room, especially Thomas Mann; to my Kluge colleagues Karen Carter, Owen Stanwood, Kate Nichols, Subarno Chattarji, Joel Seltzer and Chitralekha Zutshi for our many inspiring conversations and enjoyable lunch breaks, and above all to Blayne Haggart, who was kind enough to copy large stacks of materials for me; to David Van Reybrouck, who introduced me to *Drummer Hodge*, pointed out the importance of subtitles, and offered constant encouragement; to Harold Polis and Johan de Koning for their support at the start of this project; to my indefatigable student assistant at Utrecht University, Willem Bongers, who lugged many pounds of research materials and calmly suffered through the reprimands of library employees when he tried to borrow more books than the rules allowed; to Janneke van der Veer for her assistance with the bibliography; to Piet Joostens, who helped me with the interpretation of passages in Italian texts; to Miriam Van hee, Willem Weststeijn, Martina Louckova and Agnieszka Marczyk, who did the same for Slavic sources; to Peter Vermeersch for his inexhaustible fund of expertise about Central and Eastern Europe; to Michaël Stoker, who sent me a survey of relevant Pessoa materials; to Claes Ahlund, Bjarne Søndergaard Bendtsen and Lisette Keustermans for information about Scandinavian matters; to Györgyi Dandoy for her advice and her spontaneous translation of a complex Ady passage; to my parents for their moral and logistical support, and especially to my mother for transcribing a few handwritten documents; to Haye Koningsveld, Laurens Ubbink and Fieke Janse of the Ambo publishing house, who gave the term 'call of duty' new meaning; and to Sascha van der Aa of Poetry International for assistance with the anthology of First World War poetry *Het lijf in slijk geplant*. For advice and support of all kinds, my thanks go to Anne Becking, Christian Berg, Hubert van den Berg, Dorian Van der Brempt, Bert Bultinck, Evelien Edelbroek, Laurens Ham, Kristina Van Hecke, Kris Humbeeck, Jos Joosten, Martin Krol, Joep Leerssen, Vivian Liska, Ton Naaijkens, Hendrik Neel, Peter Nijssen, Luc Rasson, Matthijs de Ridder, Ann Rigney, Hubert Roland, Sophie De Schaepdrijver, Roel Smeets, Jan Stuyck, Thomas Vaessens and Luc De Vos. And to Annette, who was there, in Europe and in America.

The translator would like to thank Lydia Razran Stone for generously translating several excerpts from Russian poems into English specifically for this book, as well as the complete poem 'Consolation' by Anna Akhmatova. An earlier English translation of Chapter 7 by Liz Waters was a welcome source of inspiration. David Colmer kindly granted permission to reproduce his complete translation of Carl Zuckmayer's '1917', and Beverley Jackson offered useful comments on the opening section. Finally, thanks to Fleur Veraart for her constant support and her valuable input on translation issues.

Notes

On the Translation

Where non-English-language sources are quoted in English, the translation is by David McKay from the Dutch edition of this book unless otherwise noted. Translations by David McKay from other languages are indicated by a phrase such as 'DM from the French'. Quotes from English-language sources are authentic except in a few cases where the original source was unavailable to the translator. In such cases, the phrase 'DM from the Dutch' is used in the note.

1 What Was in the Air

1 Quoted in Marjorie Perloff, *Wittgenstein's Ladder: Poetic Language and the Strangeness of the Ordinary*, Chicago: University of Chicago Press, 1996, p. 33.

2 Translation by Richard Zenith available at jorgecolombo.com. The penultimate line ('Z-z-z-z-z-z-z-z-z-z-z!') has been altered to reflect the interpretation in the Dutch edition and in other English translations.

3 This passage is based on A.J.P. Taylor, *The Struggle for Mastery in Europe, 1848–1918*, Oxford: Oxford University Press, 1971, passim; Martin Gilbert, *Atlas of World War I: The Complete History*, Oxford: Oxford University Press, 1994, pp. 1–12; Gary Sheffield, *Forgotten Victory: The First World War: Myths and Realities*, London: Review,

2002, pp. 25–49; and Hew Strachan, *The First World War. Volume I: To Arms*, Oxford: Oxford University Press, 2001, pp. 1–102.

4 The quotes from *Blast* are taken from the online versions in the collection of the Modernist Journals Project at Brown University, available at library.brown.edu. This first quotation is from Issue no. 1, 20 June 1914, p. 7.

5 Ibid., pp. 10–12, 13–14, 15–20.

6 On Angell, see e.g. James J. Sheehan, *Where Have All the Soldiers Gone? The Transformation of Modern Europe*, Boston: Houghton Mifflin Company, 2008, pp. 31–4.

7 On this subject, see Paul Peppis, *Literature, Politics, and the English Avant-Garde: Nation and Empire, 1901–1918*, Cambridge: Cambridge University Press, 2000, pp. 83–95.

8 *Blast*, no. 1, 20 June 1914, pp. 34, 39.

9 The following sketch is based on my own research and on Max Saunders, *Ford Madox Ford: A Dual Life*, Oxford: Oxford University Press, 1996 (2 vols.), and Peppis, *Literature, Politics, and the English Avant-Garde*.

10 The phrase is used by his biographer, Saunders, *Ford Madox Ford*, vol. 1, p. 251.

11 The quotes from *The English Review* are taken from the online versions in the collection of the Modernist Journals Project at Brown University, available at lib.brown.edu. This first quotation is from the April 1909 issue, p. 136.

12 *The English Review*, May 1909, p. 359.

13 *The English Review*, April 1909, p. 144.

14 Ibid., p. 137.

15 *The English Review*, May 1909, p. 357.

16 Ford Madox Hueffer, *Collected Poems*, London: M. Secker, 1916, p. 51.

17 *The English Review*, April 1909, p. 59.

18 Ibid., pp. 52–3.

19 Sketch based on Thomas Burnett Swann, *The Ungirt Runner: Charles Hamilton Sorley, Poet of World War I*, Hamden CT: Archon Books, 1965, and annotations and introductions in Charles Hamilton Sorley, *The Poems and Selected Letters of Charles Hamilton Sorley*, edited and introduced by Hilda D. Spear, Dundee: Blackness Press, 1978, and *The Collected Letters of Charles Hamilton Sorley*, ed. Jean Moorcroft Wilson, London: Woolf, 1990.

20 Sorley, *Collected Letters*, pp. 47, 52.

21 Sorley, *Poems and Selected Letters*, p. 33.

22 It was not unusual for Cambridge and Oxford graduates to become social workers. On this subject, see a 1910 article by Guillaume Apollinaire in *Œuvres en prose complètes. Vol. 3*, Paris: Gallimard, 1993, pp. 441–2.

23 Sorley, *Collected Letters*, p. 81.

24 See Thomas Compère-Morel (ed.), *Apollinaire au feu*, Paris: Historial de la Grande Guerre, Péronne (Somme) / Réunion des Musées Nationaux, 2005, p. 27, which includes a quote from an official document describing him as a *sujet russe*.

25 Guillaume Apollinaire, *Lettres à Madeleine. Tendre comme le souvenir*, Paris: Gallimard, 2005, p. 108. See also Jacqueline Stallano, 'Une relation encombrante: Géry Pieret', in Michel Décaudin (ed.), *Amis européens d'Apollinaire*, Paris: Presses de la Sorbonne Nouvelles, 1995, p. 22.

26 See also Walter L. Adamson, 'Apollinaire's Politics: Modernism, Nationalism, and the Public Sphere in Avant-garde Paris', *Modernism/ Modernity* 6 (1999), p. 39.

27 Apollinaire, *Œuvres Poétiques*. Paris: Gallimard, 1971, p. 451.

28 Ibid. 449, 456–8, 454.

29 See Gerhard Dörr, 'Apollinaire et *Der Sturm*, Berlin, janvier 1913', in Décaudin, *Amis européens d'Apollinaire*, pp. 157–8.

30 Guillaume Apollinaire, 'Zone', trans. Samuel Beckett, in Tim Cross (ed.), *The Lost Voices of World War I: An International Anthology of Writers, Poets and Playwrights*, Iowa City: University of Iowa Press, 1989, p. 208

31 Guillaume Apollinaire, *Alcools. Poèmes 1998–1913*, Paris: Gallimard, 1920 (1913), p. 162.

32 Ibid., p. 167. DM from the French.

33 Cf. Veronika Krenzel-Zingerle, *Apollinaire-Lektüren. Sprachrausch in den Alcools*, Tübingen: Narr, 2003, Chapter 5.

34 Velimir Khlebnikov, *Collected Works, Volume I: Letters and Theoretical Writings*, trans. Paul Schmidt, ed. Charlotte Douglas, Cambridge MA: Harvard University Press, 1987, p. 245.

35 For detailed accounts of the history of the Hungarian people, see e.g. András Róna-Tas, *Hungarians and Europe in the Early Middle Ages: An Introduction to Early Hungarian History*. Budapest/New York: Central

European University Press, and Miklos Molnár, *A Concise History of Hungary*, Cambridge: Cambridge University Press, 2001 (see in particular p. 8 on the hypothesized relationship of the Hungarians to Huns and Sumerians, controversial among scholars but endorsed by many Hungarians).

36 Endre Ady, *The Explosive Country: A Selection of Articles and Studies 1898–1916*, trans. G.F. Cushing, Budapest: Corvina Press, 1977, pp. 110–12. The origins of the Hungarians are one theme of the essays in this collection; see e.g. pp. 103–6 (on Mongols) and p. 110 (on Scythians).

37 Endre Ady, *Poems*, trans. Anton N. Nyerges, Buffalo NY: Hungarian Cultural Foundation, 1969, p. 76. Since the late nineteenth century, the Tisza had served as a symbol of Hungary's backwardness (see Lee Congdon, 'Endre Ady's Summons to National Regeneration in Hungary, 1900–1919', *Slavic Review* 33:2 (1974), p. 309, note 26).

38 Ady, *Poems*, p. 68.

39 Ibid., pp. 66–8.

40 Ady, *The Explosive Country*, pp. 82–93; for the ferry image, see pp. 83 and 85.

41 Ibid., pp. 90–1; see also Congdon, 'Endre Ady's Summons', pp. 315–16.

42 Ady, *The Explosive Country*, pp. 118–19.

43 René De Clercq, *Toortsen*. Amsterdam: Van Looy, 1909, p. 73.

44 Quotations from Hendrik De Man, *Persoon en ideeën. V. Een halve eeuw doctrine. Verspreide geschriften*, ed. H. Balthazar, Amsterdam/Antwerp: Standaard Wetenschappelijke Uitgeverij, 1976, pp. 67–9.

45 Cf. Sheehan, *Where Have All the Soldiers Gone?*, p. 52.

46 See the joint 2005 website of the Norwegian national library and the Swedish national archives at nb.no/baser/1905/english.html.

47 Based on Astrida B. Stahnke, 'Aspazija's Drama *The Silver Veil* and her Role in the 1905 Revolution', in Andrew Ezergailis and Gert von Pistohlkors, *Die Baltischen Provinzen Russlands zwischen den Revolutionen von 1905 und 1917*, Cologne: Bohlau, 1982, pp. 219–43, and Stahnke, *Aspazija, Her Life and Her Drama*, Lanham MD: University Press of America, 1984, and Arvids Ziedonis, *The Religious Philosophy of Janis Rainis, Latvian Poet*, Waverly IA: Latvju Gramata, 1969.

48 Stahnke, *Aspazija*, p. 36.

49 Stahnke, 'Aspazija's Drama', p. 230.

50 Ibid., p. 241.

51 Ibid. and Andrejs Plakans, *The Latvians: A Short History*, Stanford: Hoover Institution Press, Stanford University, 1995, pp. 104–7 (quotation from Rainis's play at p. 107). DM from the Dutch.

52 Friedrich Nietzsche, *Thus Spake Zarathustra*, trans. Thomas Common, ed. Oscar Levy, Edinburgh: Foulis, 1911, available at philosophy.eserver.org.

53 Henri Bergson, *L'évolution créatrice*, Paris: Quadrige Presses Universitaires de France, 1986 (1907), p. 193; English translation by Arthur Mitchell (1911), available at gutenberg.org (p. 195).

54 The biographical information about Marinetti is drawn from Giovanni Lista, *F.T Marinetti. L'anarchiste du Futurisme. Biographie*, Paris: Séguier, 1995, and forewords and annotations in Filippo Tommaso Marinetti, *Critical Writings*, trans. Doug Thompson, ed. Günter Berghaus, New York: Farrar, Straus and Giroux, 2006.

55 Filippo Tommaso Marinetti, *Selected Writings*, trans. R.W. Flint and Arthur A. Coppotelli, New York: Farrar, Straus and Giroux, 1972, p. 42.

56 Marinetti, *Critical Writings*, p. 19.

57 Estimates of the number of victims range from 70,000 to 300,000, but the most authoritative sources estimate the total to be around 160,000. On this subject, see e.g. Charles Morris, *Morris's Story of the Great Earthquake of 1908, and Other Historic Disasters*, Philadelphia, 1909, and Stephen J. Spignesi, *Catastrophe! The 100 Greatest Disasters of All Time*, New York: Citadel Press, 2004, pp. 62–4.

58 Cecil Kisch, *Alexander Blok, Prophet of the Revolution: A Study of his Life and Work Illustrated by Translations from his Poems and Other Writings*, London: Weidenfeld & Nicolson, 1960, p. 116. Cf. Vladimir Orlov, *Hamayun: The Life of Alexander Blok*, Moscow: Progress Publishers, 1980, pp. 237–8. For more about Blok and his response to the Messina catastrophe, which he described as having changed their lives, see Konstantin Mochulsky, *Aleksander Blok*, trans. Doris V. Johnson, Detroit: Wayne State University Press, 1983 (1948), pp. 245–6.

59 Alexander Blok, *Gedichten (gevolgd door enkele gedichten van Solovjov en Fet)*, trans. Frans-Joseph van Agt, Leiden: Plantage/G&S, 1991, p. 29.

60 Guy Tosi, *La vie et le rôle de D'Annunzio en France au début de la grande guerre (1914–1915). Exposé chronologique d'après des documents inédits*, Florence: G.C. Sansoni, 1961, p. 16, and Alfredo Bonadeo, *D'Annunzio and the Great War*, Madison, NJ: Fairleigh Dickinson University Press, 1995, p. 69.

61 On this subject, see Modris Eksteins, *Rites of Spring: The Great War and the Birth of the Modern Age*, Boston: Houghton Mifflin, 1989.

62 Charles Péguy, *Œuvres poétiques complètes*, Paris: Gallimard, 1975, p. 1028. DM from the French.

63 The list of cultural centres comes from 'Par ce demi-clair matin' in Charles Péguy, *Œuvres en prose complètes*, Paris: Gallimard, 1988, p. 95, as do the references to endangered cultures (pp. 104ff).

64 On this subject, see e.g. David Fromkin, *Europe's Last Summer: Who Started the Great War in 1914?*, New York: Alfred A. Knopf, 2004, p. 76, and Strachan, *The First World War. Volume I*, pp. 15–17. The latter judges Germany much less severely.

65 On Péguy's intellectual evolution, see Roland N. Stromberg, *Redemption by War: The Intellectuals and 1914*, Lawrence: Regents Press of Kansas, 1982, pp. 31–2 and 72–4.

66 Cf. Eksteins, *Rites of Spring*, pp. 64–73.

67 Wuthenow in Uwe Schneider and Andreas Schumann (eds.), *Krieg der Geister. Erster Weltkrieg und literarische Moderne*, Würzburg: Konigshausen & Neumann, 2000, p. 111.

68 The standard edition of George's works gives early February 1914 as the date. See Stefan Anton George, *Der Stern des Bundes*, Stuttgart: Klett-Cotta, 1993, p. 118. Verwey received his copy on 30 January. See P.N. van Eyck and Albert Verwey, *De briefwisseling tussen P.N. van Eyck en Albert Verwey*, ed. H.A. Wage, The Hague: Nederlands Letterkundig Museum en Documentatiecentrum, 1988–95, p. 265.

69 George, *Der Stern des Bundes*, p. 31. DM from the German.

70 Georg Heym and Nina Schneider, *Am Ufer des blauen Tags. Georg Heym, sein Leben und Werk in Bildern und Selbstzeugnissen*, Glinde: Bockel, 2000, p. 70.

71 Ibid., p. 136.

72 Ibid., p. 163.

73 See Strachan, *The First World War. Volume I*, pp. 24–6, Fromkin, *Europe's Last Summer*, pp. 77–8, and Heym and Schneider, *Am Ufer des blauen Tags*, pp. 163–4.

74 Georg Heym, 'War', in Jon Silkin (ed.), *The Penguin Book of First World War Poetry*, London: Penguin Books, 1996, pp. 237–8. Translated from the German by Patrick Bridgwater.

75 Heym and Schneider, *Am Ufer des blauen Tags*, p. 164.

76 Ibid., pp. 203, 194.

77 See Marinetti, *Critical Writings*, p. 74.

78 In Mike Jay and Michael Neve (eds.), *1900. A Fin-de-siècle Reader*, London: Penguin, 1999, p. 305. For a remarkably similar statement made by Theodore Roosevelt in 1897, see Fromkin, *Europe's Last Summer*, p. 41.

79 Sheehan, *Where Have All the Soldiers Gone?*, p. 12.

80 See the map in Gilbert, *Atlas of World War I*, p. 8, Strachan, *The First World War. Volume I*, pp. 49–52, and Fromkin, *Europe's Last Summer*, pp. 83–103.

81 On this episode, see Fromkin, *Europe's Last Summer*, pp. 70–5. The Russian foreign minister had not initially objected to the annexation, but he changed his mind when it became clear that Austria was reneging on an earlier agreement and refusing to provide Russia with territorial compensation in the east.

82 *Blast*, no. 1, 20 June 1914, pp. 22–8.

83 On Newbolt's patriotic poetry, see Cecil D. Eby, *The Road to Armageddon: The Martial Spirit in English Popular Literature, 1870–1914*, Durham, NC: Duke University Press, 1987, pp. 98–108.

84 *Blast*, no. 1, 20 June 1914, pp. 141, 133, 132.

85 For an English-language anthology of these ballads, see George Rapall Noyes and Leonard Bacon, *Heroic Ballads of Servia*, Boston: Sherman, French & Company, 1913, and Helen Rootham (ed.), *Kossovo, Heroic Songs of the Serbs*, Oxford: B.H. Blackwell, 1920.

86 The story has been told countless times; see, for example, Fromkin, *Europe's Last Summer*, pp. 113–49, and Strachan, *The First World War. Volume I*, pp. 64–7.

87 Poetic ambitions: Fromkin, *Europe's Last Summer*, p. 121, and Strachan *The First World War. Volume I*, p. 65; reading list: Fromkin, *Europe's Last Summer*, p. 120.

88 Fromkin, *Europe's Last Summer*, p. 138.

89 Based on Miloš Crnjanski, *Kommentare zu 'Ithaka'*, trans. from the Serbian by Peter Orban, Frankfurt am Main: Suhrkamp, 1967, pp. 40–3.

90 Based on Vanita Singh Mukerji, *Ivo Andrić: A Critical Biography*, Jefferson, NC: McFarland, 1990, pp. 1–13.

91 This detail comes from a note by Miroslav Krleža quoted in Reinhard Lauer, 'Ivo Andrić – der Lyriker', in Peter Thiergen (ed.), *Ivo Andrić, 1892–1992. Beiträge des Zentenarsymposions an der Otto Friedrich-Universität Bamberg im Oktober 1992*, Munich: O. Sagner, 1995, p. 58.

92 Diary entry, 8 June 1912, Singh Mukerji, *Ivo Andrić*, p. 10, and Njegos M. Petrović, *Ivo Andrić. L'homme et L'œuvre*, Montreal: Leméac, 1969, p. 34. In the Balkans, the term *hajduk* refers to an armed rebel or outlaw.

93 Reinhard Lauer, 'Ivo Andrić – der Lyriker', in Thiergen, *Ivo Andrić*, p. 54.

94 Singh Mukerji, *Ivo Andrić*, pp. 161–2.

95 Mario D. Fenyo, *Literature and Political Change: Budapest, 1908–1918*, Philadelphia: American Philosophical Society, 1987, p. 71.

96 Biographical information from Orlov, *Hamayun*, p. 341.

97 Quoted in Mochulsky, *Aleksander Blok*, p. 350. The author gives the date of 15 June but seems to use the old Russian calendar in his book. To make the chronological sequence of events as clear as possible, all dates in the present volume have been adapted from the pre-revolutionary Julian calendar to the Western, Gregorian system (for instance, 1 August 1914 was 19 July in Russia). Accordingly, 15 June on the old Russian calendar was 28 June.

98 Alfred Lichtenstein, *Gesammelte Gedichte*, ed. Klaus Kanzog, Zurich: Verlag der Arche, 1962, p. 94.

99 The second wife of the pacifist minister Joseph Caillaux had murdered the editor-in-chief of the right-wing newspaper *Le Figaro* to prevent it from publishing love letters between Calliaux and his second wife written before his first marriage had officially ended. The trial was set to begin on 20 July 1914. This was much more than a private affair, since *Le Figaro* claimed to have in its possession deciphered German telegrams about Caillaux. Many foreign embassies responded, in July, by changing their own secret codes, and for a while France was deprived of important information. On this subject, see e.g. Fromkin, *Europe's Last Summer*, pp. 141–3, and Strachan, *The First World War. Volume I*, p. 79. On the British and Home Rule, see Fromkin, *Europe's Last Summer*, p. 140, and Robert Kee, *The Green Flag: The Turbulent History of the Irish National Movement*, New York: Delacorte Press,

1972, pp. 512–17. On the Serbian field marshal, see Crnjanski, *Kommentare zu 'Ithaka'*, p. 44. On the German generals' summer furlough, see Fromkin, *Europe's Last Summer*, pp. 201–2.

100 Prose translation by Patrick Bridgwater, in Tim Cross (ed.), *The Lost Voices of World War I: An International Anthology of Writers, Poets and Playwrights*, Iowa City: University of Iowa Press, 1989, p. 164. On the inevitability of a major European war as a theme in Germany and elsewhere in Europe, see Wolfgang J. Mommsen, 'German Artists, Writers and Intellectuals and the Meaning of War, 1914–1918', in John Horne (ed.), *State, Society and Mobilization in Europe During the First World War*, Cambridge: Cambridge University Press, 1997, pp. 1–38.

2 *A Hot Summer*

1 Louis Couperus, *Brieven van den nutteloozen toeschouwer*, Amsterdam: L.J. Veen, 1918, p. 26.

2 Biographical information compiled from Jessie Davies, *Anna of all the Russias: The Life of Anna Akhmatova (1889–1966)*, Liverpool: Lincoln Davies & Co, 1988; Roberta Reeder, *Anna Akhmatova: Poet and Prophet*, New York: St Martin's Press, 1994; Michael Basker, 'Introduction' and 'Notes' in Nikolay Gumilyov, *The Pillar of Fire: Selected Poems*, trans. Richard McKane, London: Anvil Press Poetry/Survivor's Poetry, 1999, pp. 17–32, 219–42, 248–52; Nancy K. Anderson, *The Word That Causes Death's Defeat, Poems of Memory*, New Haven: Yale University Press, 2004; and from documents, introductions and annotations in Anna Akhmatova, *My Half Century: Selected Prose*, Ann Arbor: Ardis, 1992, and Akhmatova, *The Complete Poems: Updated and Expanded Edition*, trans. Judith Hemschemeyer, ed. and introduced by Roberta Reeder, Boston: Zephyr Press, 1997.

3 Davies, *Anna of all the Russias*, p. 13.

4 Akhmatova, *My Half Century*, p. 285.

5 Ibid.

6 For a day-by-day account of the escalation see Fromkin, *Europe's Last Summer*, pp. 206–50.

7 Unless otherwise indicated, the chronology of the war described in

this book is based on Edward Gleichen, *Chronology of the Great War, 1914–1918*, London: Greenhill Books, 2000; Christine Bent, *The New York Times Book of World War I*, New York: Arno Press, 1980; David F. Burg and L. Edward Purcell, *Almanac of World War I*, Lexington: University Press of Kentucky, 1998; Gerhard Hirschfeld et al. (eds.), *Enzyklopädie Erster Weltkrieg*, Paderborn: Verlag Ferdinand Schoningh, 2003, pp. 985–92; and Stephane Audoin-Rouzeau and Annette Becker, *14–18, retrouver la Guerre*, Paris: Gallimard, 2000, pp. 1283–96.

8 The quotes from the correspondence between the Czar and the Kaiser come from The World War I Document Archive at lib.byu.edu; see also Willem Melching and Marcel Stuivenga (eds.), *Ooggetuigen van de Eerste Wereldoorlog in meer dan honderd reportages*, Amsterdam: Bert Bakker, 2006, pp. 35–6, and Fromkin, *Europe's Last Summer*, pp. 220–35.

9 Flagrant diary entries and commentaries to this effect can be found, e.g., in Fromkin, *Europe's Last Summer*, pp. 239–42.

10 Original Russian version in Geert Buelens (ed.), *Het lijf in slijk geplant. Gedichten uit de Eerste Wereldoorlog*, Amsterdam: Ambo, 2008, p. 88; English translation from the Russian by Lydia Razran Stone (p.c.), 2012.

11 From the poem 'Iambic Pentameter', included in his 1916 collection *The Quiver*, in Nikolay Gumilyov, *De giraffe*, selected, translated and introduced by Hans Boland, Amsterdam: Meulenhoff, 1985, p. 39; English translation by Lydia Razran Stone (p.c.), 2012. Information from Basker in Gumilyov, *The Pillar of Fire*, pp. 225–6. Orlov, *Hamayun*, p. 431, also describes the weather as exceptionally dry and hot and the sun as dark red. This Soviet biographer also describes the smell of burning in this context and the sun as a red ball and the moon as purple. Whether this apocalyptic vision is extrapolated from Akhmatova and Gumilyov's classicist poems or based on historical sources is difficult to tell from Orlov's book. Gippius, in her diary, likewise describes a stinging haze that hung over the landscape that summer. See Ben Hellman, *Poets of Hope and Despair: The Russian Symbolists in War and Revolution (1914–1918)*, Helsinki: Institute for Russian and East European Studies, 1995, p. 27.

12 Akhmatova, *My Half Century*, pp. 11, 26, 48.

13 Orlando Figes, *Natasha's Dance: A Cultural History of Russia*, London:

Penguin, 2003, p. 251, and Melching and Stuivenga, *Ooggetuigen van de Eerste Wereldoorlog*, pp. 39–40.

14 Contemporary patriotic verse, quoted anonymously in Alexander Solzhenitsyn, *August 1914*, trans. Michael Glenny, Harmondsworth: Penguin, 1974, p. 60.

15 Leonid I. Strakhovsky, 'Three Sojourners in the Acmeist Camp: Sergei Gorodetsky, Vladimir Narbut, Mikhail Zenkevich', *Russian Review* 9:2 (1950), pp. 135–6; Orlov, *Hamayun*, pp. 343–4; Hellman, *Poets of Hope and Despair*, pp. 84–102; and Hubertus F. Jahn, *Patriotic Culture in Russia During World War I*, Ithaca: Cornell University Press, 1995, p. 106.

16 Hellman, *Poets of Hope and Despair*, pp. 88ff.

17 Cf. Ibid., 86–91; James H. Billington, *The Icon and the Axe: An Interpretative History of Russian Culture*, New York: Random House, 1966; pp. 19, 635; Figes, *Natasha's Dance*, p. 335, 615.

18 Hellman, *Poets of Hope and Despair*, p. 95.

19 Ibid., p. 33.

20 Ibid., pp. 40–1.

21 Sketch based on Vladimir Markov, *Russian Futurism: A History*, Berkeley: University of California Press, 1968; Wiktor Woroszylski, *The Life of Mayakovsky*, New York: Orion Press, 1970; Viktor Borisovich Shklovsky, *Mayakovsky and His Circle*, New York: Dodd, Mead, 1972; and Edward J. Brown, *Mayakovsky: A Poet in the Revolution*, New York: Paragon House Publishers, 1973.

22 V.V. Majakovski, *Werken*, trans. Marko Fondse, Amsterdam: G.A. van Oorschot, 1993, p. 702. See also Brown, *Mayakovsky*, p. 36 (Mayakovsky uses the word *revplaksivo*).

23 For English versions of the manifestos, see Anna Lawton and Herbert Eagle (eds.), *Russian Futurism through its Manifestoes, 1912–1928*, Washington DC: New Academia Publishing, 1988.

24 Cf. Perloff, *The Futurist Moment*, pp. 121–7. Illustrations of the Futurist volumes can be found in Margit Rowell (ed.), *The Russian Avant-Garde Book, 1910–1934*, New York: Museum of Modern Art, 2002, and Susan P. Compton, *The World Backwards: Russian Futurist Books, 1912–16*, London: British Museum Publications, 1978.

25 Markov, *Russian Futurism*, p. 151.

26 Khlebnikov, *Collected Works*, pp. 87–8.

27 Markov calls Khlebnikov 'Germanophobic' (*Russian Futurism*, p. 298). See also 'A Friend in the West', a highly critical 1913 essay about what he saw as the Slavophobic country of Germany (Khlebnikov, *Collected Works*, pp. 243–5).

28 Mayakovsky, *Werken*, p. 29.

29 John Horne and Alan Kramer, *German Atrocities, 1914: A History of Denial*, New Haven: Yale University Press, 2001, pp. 81–2.

30 For a similar description, see e.g. Virginie Loveling, *Oorlogsdagboeken 1914–1918*, ed. Sylvia van Peteghem and Ludo Stynen, Antwerp/Amsterdam: Meulenhoff/Manteau, 2005. p. 7.

31 Based on Sing Mukerji, *Ivo Andrić*, pp. 13ff., and the introduction to Ivo Andrić, *Ex Ponto/Unruhen*, trans. Leonore Sheffler, Frankfurt am Main: P. Lang, 1988.

32 Andrić, *Ex Ponto*, p. 5.

33 Ibid., pp. 7, 11, 14.

34 Based on Crnjanski, *Kommentare zu 'Ithaka'*, pp. 40, 44ff.

35 'Austrian Attacks on Servia. "A Nest of Plague Rats"', *The Times*, 9 July 1914, p. 7.

36 In 1914 the population of the Habsburg Empire was 23 per cent German, 19 per cent Hungarian/Magyar, 13 per cent Czech, 10 per cent Polish, 8 per cent Ruthenian, 6 per cent Romanian, 6 per cent Croat, 4 per cent Serb, 4 per cent Slovak and 3 per cent Slovene, with a sprinkling of Italians, Bosniaks and Roma/Sinti. The official language of the imperial army was German, but officers were required to learn the language of their troops. More than half of the regiments were bilingual, twenty-four were trilingual, and in a few cases four or five languages were spoken. See Spencer Tucker (ed.), *The European Powers in the First World War: An Encyclopedia*, New York: Garland, 1996, p. 86.

37 These Jewish poets were part of the literary scene in Lemberg, which was then a primarily Polish city (Lvov) and is now part of the Ukraine (Lviv). When the war broke out, most of them were in Vienna. Theodor Daubler, a German speaker from Trieste (and thus an 'Austrian') was exempted from military service and spent the war in Germany. See Solomon Liptzin, *A History of Yiddish Literature*, New York: J. David, Middle Village, 1972, pp. 237–42.

38 Biographical information from Joseph Leftwich (ed.), *The Golden Peacock. An Anthology of Yiddish Poetry Translated into English Verse*,

Cambridge, MA: Sci-art Publishers, 1939, p. 240, and Liptzin, *A History*, pp. 244–6.

39 Gabriele Kohlbauer-Fritz (ed.), *In a Schtodt Woss Schtarbt. In einer Stadt, die stirbt. Jiddische Lyrik aus Wien*, Vienna: Picus, 1995, p. 61.

40 On this subject, see e.g. Aviel Roshwald and Richard Stites (eds.), *European Culture in the Great War: The Arts, Entertainment and Propaganda, 1914–1918*, Cambridge: Cambridge University Press, 2002, passim, and on the killing of Jews by Jews, pp. 97–8.

41 S.J. Imber (ed.), *Modern Yiddish Poetry: An Anthology*, New York: The East and West Publishing Co., 1927, pp. 90–5.

42 On this subject, see Harold B. Segel, 'Culture in Poland During World War I', in Aviel and Stites, *European Culture in the Great War*, pp. 58–88; especially p. 63. On the divided country of Poland, see also Norman Davies, *Heart of Europe: A Short History of Poland*, Oxford: Clarendon Press, 1984, pp. 109–15.

43 See Czeslaw Milosz, *The History of Polish Literature*, Berkeley: University of California Press, 1983, pp. 230–1.

44 Based on a translation in Jerzy Peterkiewicz and Burns Singer (eds.), *Five Centuries of Polish Poetry: 1450–1950*, London: Secker & Warburg, 1960, pp. 107–8. Adapted by DM, partly on the basis of the Dutch translation by Karol Lesman in Buelens, *Het lijf in slijk geplant*, pp. 82–4.

45 List in Segel, 'Culture in Poland during World War I', pp. 65–6.

46 Information from Milosz, *The History of Polish Literature*, p. 342, and Cross, *The Lost Voices of World War I*, pp. 330–1.

47 Cross, *The Lost Voices of World War I*, p. 332.

48 Andrea Orzoff, 'The Empire Without Qualities: Austro-Hungarian Newspapers and the Outbreak of War in 1914', in Troy R.E. Paddock (ed.), *A Call to Arms: Propaganda, Public Opinion, and Newspapers in the Great War*, Westport, CT: Praeger Publishers, 2004, p. 175.

49 Ibid., pp. 190–1. DM from the German.

50 Eric Lohr, 'The Russian Press and the "Internal Peace" at the Beginning of World War I', in Paddock, *A Call to Arms*, p. 109.

51 Couperus, *Brieven van den nutteloozen toeschouwer*, p. 18.

52 Jeffrey Verhey, *The Spirit of 1914: Militarism, Myth and Mobilization in Germany*, Cambridge: Cambridge University Press, 2000, p. 2.

53 On the German attitude toward Enlightenment ideals and Anglo-Saxon pragmatism, see e.g. Mommsen, 'German Artists, Writers and Intellectuals and the Meaning of War', pp. 28–33.

54 The von Schlieffen plan has been a cause of great controversy in recent years. For a revisionist theory postulating that the plan never existed in this form, see Terence Zuber, *Inventing the Schlieffen Plan: German War Planning, 1871–1914*, Oxford: Oxford University Press, 2002. For a more concise account, see Fromkin, *Europe's Last Summer*, pp. 34–5, and Strachan, *The First World War. Volume I*, pp. 163–80.

55 For the whole story, see Sophie De Schaepdrijver, *De Groote Oorlog. Het koninkrijk België tijdens de Eerste Wereldoorlog*, Amsterdam: Atlas, 1997, pp. 55–65, and Larry Zuckerman, *The Rape of Belgium: The Untold Story of World War I*, New York: New York University Press, 2004, pp. 15–32. For the international context, see e.g. Fromkin, *Europe's Last Summer*, pp. 243–50.

56 Cf. Niall Ferguson, *The Pity of War*, New York: Basic Books, 1999, p. 163.

57 Fromkin, *Europe's Last Summer*, pp. 160–1, 260 and 299–302.

58 For an estimate of the number of First World War poems, see Buelens, *Het lijf in slijk geplant*, pp. 12–13.

59 Elizabeth A. Marsland, *The Nation's Cause: French, English and German Poetry of the First World War*, London: Routledge, 1991, p. 2. Albert Verwey gives the same figure (Albert Verwey, *Holland en de oorlog*. Maatschappij voor goede en goedkope lectuur, Amsterdam, 1916, p. 67). Klaus Vondung mentions some 1.5 million in August alone (Klaus Vondung [ed.], *Kriegserlebnis. Der Erste Weltkrieg in der literarischen Gestaltung und symbolischen Deutung der Nationen*, Göttingen: Vandenhoeck & Ruprecht, 1980, p. 13; Vondung's source: Carl Busse [ed.], *Deutsche Kriegslieder 1914/16*, Bielefeld/Leipzig, 1916. p. VI).

60 Quoted in Ernst Volkmann (ed.), *Deutsche Dichtung im Weltkrieg, 1914–1918*, Leipzig: P. Reclam jun., 1934, p. 51; English translation from Patrick Bridgwater, *The German Poets of the First World War*, London: Croom Helm, 1985, p. 191.

61 Lichtenstein, *Gesammelte Gedichte*, p. 96; English translation from Bridgwater, *The German Poets*, pp. 173–4.

62 Biographical information from Wolfgang Leppmann, *Rainer Maria Rilke. Zijn leven en werk*, trans. Theodor Duquesnoy, Amsterdam: Balans, 1990.

63 Ibid., p. 171.

64 Couperus, *Brieven van den nutteloozen toeschouwer*, pp. 7, 8, 9 (all the quotations in this passage are from a letter written on 1 August).

65 DM from the German and from the Dutch translation by Ton Naaijkens in Buelens, *Het lijf in slijk geplant*, p. 53.
66 Cross, *The Lost Voices of World War I*, p. 105.
67 Ernst Stadler, *Dichtungen, Schriften, Briefe*, ed. Klaus Hurlebusch & Karl Ludwig Schneider, Munich: C.H. Beck, 1983, p. 523.
68 Ibid., pp. 518–19.
69 Ibid., p. 529.
70 Ibid., pp. 530, 532.
71 Ibid., p. 532.
72 Ibid., p. 533.
73 Ibid., p. 534.
74 Ibid., p. 535.
75 Anecdote in Cross, *The Lost Voices*, p. 101.
76 Information and quotes from Marcel Jean's introduction to Hans Arp, *Collected French Writings: Poems, Essays, Memoirs*, trans. Joachim Neugroschel, London: Calder, 2001, p. xvii. Quotes translated by DM from the Dutch. The anecdote could be apocryphal, considering that war between France and Germany was not declared until 3 August. It may have been the general mobilization (on 1 August) rather than the declaration of war that was responsible for Arp's financial troubles.
77 Guillaume Apollinaire, *Œuvres Poétiques* pp. 207–8; English translation in *Calligrammes: Poems of Peace and War (1913–1916)*, trans. and annotated by Anne Hyde Greet, Berkeley: University of California Press, 1980, pp. 105–11.
78 The photographs have been converted into a short film, 'Apollinaire en film', which can be viewed at wiu.edu.
79 On the difference between popular image and reality, see Jean-Jacques Becker, *1914, comment les Francais sont entrés dans la guerre. Contribution à l'étude de l'opinion publique printemps-été 1914*, Paris: Presses de la Fondation nationale des sciences politiques, 1977 (on France) and Verhey, *The Spirit of 1914* (on Germany).
80 Quoted in Olivier Rony, *Jules Romains, Ou, L'appel au monde*, Paris: R. Laffont, 1993, p. 210.
81 Couperus, *Brieven van den nutteloozen toeschouwer*, pp. 27, 28, 29.
82 Marcel Martinet, *Les temps maudits. Suivi De la Nuit*, foreword by Leon Trotsky, Paris: Union générale d'éditions, 1975, pp. 55–60, at 57, 60.
83 Gabriele D'Annunzio, *Versi d'amore e di Gloria*, Milan: Mondadori, 1968, p. 993. DM from the French.

84 Ibid., p. 997.

85 Tosi, *La vie et le rôle de D'Annunzio*, p. 25.

86 Ibid., pp. 21–2. Luigi Albertini would later write a three-volume Italian standard work about the outbreak of the war, *Le origini della guerra del 1914* (1942–3).

87 Fromkin, *Europe's Last Summer*, p. 245.

88 Enzo Berrafato, Laurent Berrafato and Jean-Pierre Verney, *L'Italie en Guerre: 1915–1918*, Verdun: 14–18 Éditions, 2006, p. 28.

89 Cf. Christine Poggi, *In Defiance of Painting: Cubism, Futurism, and the Invention of Collage*, New Haven: Yale University Press, 1992, p. 224; colour reproductions, p. 24; black-and-white reproduction in *Lacerba*, 1913–1915, Archivi d'arte del XX secolo/G, Rome/Milan: Mazzotta, 1970 (reprint), p. 233. Some studies distinguish between the 'true' Futurists in Marinetti's circle and the *Lacerba* group led by Papini and Soffici. For convenience's sake, that distinction is disregarded here.

90 Paolo Buzzi, *Conflagrazione. Epopea Parolibera*, Florence: Il Fauno editore, 1963, p. 29.

91 Letter, 26 August 1914, in Van Eyck and Verwey, *De briefwisseling*, p. 24.

92 Fernando Pessoa, *Gedichten 1913–1922*, trans. and afterword by August Willemsen, Amsterdam: De Arbeiderspers, 2006, p. 193.

93 Ibid., pp. 195–7.

94 Ibid., p. 195.

95 Ibid., p. 197.

96 Ibid., p. 201.

97 Sorley, *Collected Letters*, p. 177.

98 Ibid., pp. 176, 214, 264, 265, 266. In a letter to his school-friend Hutchinson, Sorley later revealed that he himself had spread the rumour that the British had declared war on Russia (p. 181).

99 Ibid., p. 267.

100 Anonymous poem quoted in Stephen Martin (ed.), *Never Such Innocence: Poems of the First World War*, London: J.M. Dent, 2003, p. 35.

101 Quoted in David Roberts (ed.), *Minds at War: The Poetry and Experience of the First World War*, London: Saxon Books, 1996, p. 45.

102 Based on Luc de Vos, *De Eerste Wereldoorlog*, Leuven: Davidsfonds,

1996; Burg and Purcell, *Almanac of World War I*; and Horne and Kramer, *German Atrocities, 1914*.

103 The zeppelin attack of 6 August found its way into Buzzi's collage diary on the ninth, and the fate of the city was also central to his diary entries of 11 and 12 August (Buzzi, *Conflagrazione*, pp. 32, 34–5).

104 Emile Verhaeren, *Les ailes rouges de la guerre. Poèmes*, Paris: Mercure de France, 1916, p. 25.

105 Hellman, *Poets of Hope and Despair*, p. 64.

106 Henri Guilbeaux, *Du champ des horreurs*, Geneva: Édition de la revue 'Demain', 1917, p. 19.

107 Horne and Kramer, *German Atrocities, 1914*, pp. 436, 437.

108 Biographical information on Benemann from Maria Benemann, *Leih mir noch einmal die leichte Sandale. Erinnerungen und Begegnungen*, Hamburg: Christians, 1978, pp. 178, 183; Margaret R. Higonnet (ed.), *Lines of Fire: Women Writers of World War I*, New York: Plume, 1999, pp. 483–4; information on Visé from Horne and Kramer, *German Atrocities, 1914*, p. 24, 436; L. Mokveld, *De overweldiging van België beschreven*, Rotterdam: W.L. & J. Brusse, 1917, pp. 43–50; and Rob Kammelar, Jacques Sicking and Menno Wielinga (eds.), *De Eerste Wereldoorlog door Nederlandse ogen. Getuigenissen, verhalen, betogen*, Amsterdam: Nijgh & van Ditmar, 2007, pp. 47–52. See also Sophie De Schaepdrijver, 'Gemartelde steden en verwoeste gewesten. Twee legaten van 1914–1918', in Jo Tollebeek et al. (eds.), *België: Een parcours van herinnering*, Amsterdam: Bert Bakker, 2008, vol. II, pp. 194–207.

109 DM from the Dutch translation by Ton Naaijkens in Buelens, *Het lijf in slijk geplant*, p. 172.

110 Mokveld, *De overweldiging*, p. 47; Kammelar et al., *De Eerste Wereldoorlog*, p. 50. The events described here took place on 15 and 16 August. According to Horne and Kramer, the plundering continued until the 18th. The war diary of Gerhard Benemann, the poet's husband, states that on Wednesday, 19 August, his company arrived in Visé, 'which was utterly devastated and in flames'. He also repeats the story of the snipers: 'Die ersten Schüsse von unde auf Freischärler' ('The first shots by and at snipers'; Benemann, *Leih mir noch einmal*, p. 178, cf. 183). Reports of German drunkenness while committing these and other war crimes are legion; see e.g. Luc Vandeweyer, *De Eerste Wereldoorlog. Koning Albert en zijn soldaten*,

Antwerp: Standaard Uitgeverij, 2005, p. 92, and a letter from Karel Van den Oever to Maria Viola dating from 16 to 19 September, based on eyewitness reports by Van den Oever's brother, an itinerant priest in the Leuven region: 'The horrible "soudards" [German soldiers] were often as drunk as beasts; all around Werchter, the ground was littered with 90,000 empty bottles of Jacop [a local beer] and from Werchter to Boortmeerbeeck countless bottles of wine lay on either side of the cobbled road; they also drank from the huge brewery vats in which strong Flemish beer is stored and then staggered their way to Paris! [sic] ... The battle cry was "Sauffen, sauffen al was wir haben!" [Guzzle, guzzle everything we've got!].' The same letter also includes a story related by another priest about German soldiers nailing a baby to the wall – a tale that may primarily serve to illustrate the moral outrage of the downtrodden Belgian civilian population (Viola Archive, KDC Nijmegen).

111 Horne and Kramer, *German Atrocities, 1914*, p. 427.

112 Ibid., passim. Besides in this poem by Benemann, stories about snipers are found in a number of other literary accounts. In a letter to his sweetheart on 16 August, the young Expressionist Ernst Wilhelm Lotz complained of 'die Schande und Schmach, die elsässischen Französlinge, die Franktireurs, Spione und Leichenräuber' ('the shame and disgrace, the Francophile Alsatians, the snipers, spies and body snatchers', Lotz, *Gedichte, Prosa, Briefe*, Munich: Edition Text + Kritik, 1994, p. 195, cf. 202). In his war diary, Ernst Stadler wrote vaguely of the 'shameless conduct of the Belgians' (Stadler, *Dichtungen, Schriften, Briefe*, p. 547), perhaps an allusion to stories about civilians taking up arms. He later made a similar reference to 'stories about the Belgian civilian population' (p. 552). Stadler also reports stories of French 'atrocities' targeting injured Germans (p. 545). On 21 August, the poet and physician Wilhelm Klemm wrote in a letter from Belgium that the village where he was billeted had been attacked by snipers and that in reprisal 'a few houses were burned down, people shot dead, horses stolen etc.' (Wilhelm Klemm, *Gloria! Kriegsgedichte aus dem Feld*, Munich: Langen 1915, p. 109).

113 An example of a French poem on a postcard (the picture shows a young boy with a toy gun being executed by German soldiers, another legend) can be found in Horne and Kramer, *German Atrocities, 1914*, p. 208.

114 The poem is included in H.B. Elliott, *Lest We Forget: A War Anthology*, London: Jarrold & Sons, 1915, p. 24.

115 Valentine de Saint-Point, 'Futurist Manifesto of Lust', at unknown. nu. Véronique Richard de la Fuente's monograph about Valentine de Saint-Point includes the original French manifesto, but, strikingly, it does not include the passage quoted here (Véronique Richard de la Fuente, *Valentine de Saint Point (1875–1953). Une poétesse dans l'avant garde futuriste et méditerranéiste*, Céret: Editions des Albères, 2003, p. 38).

116 Jan Bernaerts and Hendrik Heyman (eds.), *Oorlogspoëzie. Verschenen in 1914 en 1915 en onuitgegeven gedichten*, Port-Villez: Drukkerij van het Militair Gesticht van Vakheropleiding voor Zwaar Gekwetsten uit den Oorlog, 1916, p. 7.

117 Letters from Van den Oever to Viola, 20 August 1914 and 16 to 17 September 1914 (Viola Archive, KDC, Nijmegen).

118 Based on Tom Kettle, *The Ways of War*, New York: C. Scribner's Sons, 1917; the foreword to that book by his wife Mary Sheehy; and Senia Paseta's chapter about Kettle in Adrian Gregory (ed.), *Ireland and the Great War: A War to Unite Us All?* Manchester: Manchester University Press, 2002.

119 Kettle, *The Ways of War*, p. 104.

120 Ibid., p. 106.

121 'Frontbeweging', *Nieuwe Encyclopedie van de Vlaamse Beweging*, Tielt: Lannoo, 1998, 3 vols. and CD-ROM.

122 Saunders, *Ford Madox Ford*, vol. 1, p. 461.

123 Ford Madox Ford, *War Prose*, New York: New York University Press, 2004, p. 207.

124 Ibid., p. 209.

125 'For All We Have and Are', in Rudyard Kipling, *Rudyard Kipling's Verse: Inclusive Edition, 1885–1932*, London: Hodder & Stoughton, 1933, p. 326.

126 See Roberts, *Minds at War*, pp. 54–60.

127 Ford, *War Prose*, p. 209.

128 August Stramm, *Gedichte. Dramen. Prosa. Briefe*, ed. Jorg Drews, Stuttgart: Philipp Reclam jun., 1997, p. 172.

129 Ibid.

130 Ibid., p. 173.

131 Quoted in Elaine Rusinko, 'The Theme of War in the Works

of Gumilev', *The Slavic and East European Journal* 21:2 (1977), p. 204.

132 Quoted in Reeder, *Anna Akhmatova*, p. 80, and Orlov, *Hamayun*, p. 347. DM from the Dutch.

133 Biographical information compiled from Kisch, *Alexander Blok*, pp. 116,130, Orlov, *Hamayun*, p. 341–7, and Mochulsky *Aleksander Blok*, pp. 348–51.

134 Orlov, *Hamayun*, p. 342.

135 Strachan, *The First World War. Volume I*, pp. 143–4.

136 Oleh S. Ilnytzkyj, *Ukrainian Futurism, 1914–1930: A Historical and Critical Study*, Cambridge, MA: Ukrainian Research Institute, Harvard University Press, 1997, p. 30.

137 John Keegan, *The First World War*, New York: Vintage Books, 1999, pp. 149–150. Hobsbawm believed that the 1905 revolution was the beginning of the end (Eric Hobsbawm, *Age of Extremes: The Short Twentieth Century 1914–1991*, London: Michael Joseph, 1995, p. 56).

138 Fromkin, *Europe's Last Summer*, p. 218.

139 Cf. Horne and Kramer, *German Atrocities, 1914*, p. 85.

140 Photographs of these atrocities can be found in A. van Tienhoven, *De gruwelen van den oorlog in Servië. Het dagboek van den oorlogs-chirurg Dr. W.L. & J. Brusse*, Rotterdam, 1915, pp. 14–21.

141 Ibid., p. 20.

142 De Vos, *De Eerste Wereldoorlog*, p. 41.

143 John Robert Woodhouse, *Gabriele D'Annunzio: Defiant Archangel*, Oxford: Clarendon Press, 1998, p. 275.

144 Tosi, *La vie et le rôle de D'Annunzio*, p. 41. DM from the French.

145 Quoted in Rony, *Jules Romains*, p. 213. DM from the French.

146 Charles Péguy, *Œuvres en prose, 1909–1914*, Paris: Gallimard, 1957, p. 1496.

147 Paul van Ostaijen, *Verzameld werk. Proza. Besprekingen en Beschouwingen*, Amsterdam: Bert Bakker, 1979, p. 413.

148 Leonard V. Smith, Stephane Audoin-Rouzeau and Annette Becker, *France and the Great War, 1914–1918*, Cambridge: Cambridge University Press, 2003, p. 39.

149 Figure based on firstworldwar.com/battles/marne1.htm. There were roughly equal numbers of French and German casualties, plus more than 10,000 among British forces. In the course of the entire campaign, there were 329,000 French fatalities in August–September

(Smith et al., *France and the Great War*, p. 40).

150 Bent, *The New York Times Book of World War I*, p. 38.

151 François Porché, *L'arret sur la Marne*, Paris: Éditions de la Nouvelle revue française, 1916, p. 63. DM from the French.

152 Anna de Noailles, *Les forces éternelles*, Paris: A. Fayard & cie., 1920, pp. 32–6.

153 Pessoa, *Gedichten 1913–1922*, p. 211.

154 Ibid., p. 213.

155 Buzzi, *Conflagrazione*, p. 58.

156 Filippo Tommaso Marinetti, *Selected Poems and Related Prose*, ed. Luce Marinetti, trans. Elizabeth R. Napier and Barbara R. Studholme, New Haven: Yale University Press, 2002, p. 118.

3 *The Voice of Steel*

1 Franz Marc, *Schriften*, Cologne: DuMont, 1978, p. 165. DM from the Dutch translation by Ton Naaijkens in the Dutch edition.

2 See e.g. H. Wildon Carr, 'Introduction', in Henri Bergson, *The Meaning of the War: Life & Matter in Conflict*, London: T. Fisher Unwin, Adelphi Terrace, 1915, p. 10.

3 Quoted in Leonid I. Strakhovsky, 'Georgi Ivanov – Paragon of Verse', *Russian Review* 8:1 (1949), p. 72.

4 Lichtenstein, *Gesammelte Gedichte*, pp. 97–8; English translation of 'Gebet vor der Slacht' in Cross, *The Lost Voices of World War I*, p. 165. English title and lines from 'After Combat' available at people.bu.edu. Translation of 'Die Schlacht bei Saarburg' from Bridgwater, *The German Poets*, pp. 174–5.

5 In Cross, *The Lost Voices of World War I*, p. 98.

6 Lotz, *Gedichte, Prosa, Briefe*, p. 193. DM from the Dutch, except for the lines from 'Aufbruch der Jugend', from Kirsten Painter, *Flint on a Bright Stone: A Revolution of Precision and Restraint in American, Russian, and German Modernism*, Stanford: Stanford University Press, 2005, p. 148.

7 Lotz, *Gedichte, Prosa, Briefe*, p. 193.

8 Ibid., pp. 198, 200, 201, 202, 205.

9 Stadler, *Dichtungen, Schriften, Briefe*, p. 559.

10 Ibid., p. 569.

11 Ibid., p. 522.

12 The same comment accompanied Klemm's first three war poems when they appeared in the 24 October issue of *Die Aktion* (p. 834), preceded by Pfemfert's proud declaration that these were the first worthwhile poems the war had produced.

13 *Die Aktion*, 21 November 1914, p. 872; also in Klemm, *Gloria!*, p. 38; English translation from Bridgwater, *The German Poets*, p. 178.

14 Date of Hinz's death from Franz Pfemfert (ed.), *Die Aktions-Lyrik. Nummern 1–7, 1916–1922*, Nendeln/Liechtenstein: Kraus Reprint, 1973, p. 41. Cross, *The Lost Voices of World War I*, p. 396, gives 7 July 1914, which is clearly a typographical error. Milton A. Cohen, *Movement, Manifesto, Melee: The Modernist Group, 1910–1914*, Lanham, MD: Lexington Books, 2004, p. 299, gives '1914'.

15 Cf. Eckhard Faul, 'Nachwort', in Hans Leybold, *Gegen Zuständliches. Glossen, Gedichte, Briefe*, ed. Eckhard Faul, Hanover: Postskriptum, 1989, pp. 111–12, and Cross, *The Lost Voices of World War I*, p. 149.

16 English translation (uncredited, probably by Philip Mann) from Cross, *The Lost Voices of World War I*, p. 153, edited by DM.

17 Wilhelm Klemm, *Ich lag in fremder Stube. Gesammelte Gedichte*, Munich: C. Hanser, 1981, pp. 110.

18 Ibid., pp. 115, 117–18.

19 These and other lists were compiled from the alphabetical list of writers, artists, composers and architects who died in the war in Cross, *The Lost Voices of World War I*, pp. 388–406. Several other people on that list died or went missing in action on 20 August, among them Étienne Collet, Robert Perréoux, Paul Rioux and Antoine Villermin.

20 This passage is based on Caroline Tisdall and Angelo Bozzolla, *Futurism*, London: Thames and Hudson, 1977, pp. 174–5; Richard Cork, *A Bitter Truth: Avant-Garde Art and the Great War*, New Haven: Yale University Press, 1994, pp. 61–3; Günter Berghaus, *Futurism and Politics: Between Anarchist Rebellion and Fascist Reaction, 1909–1944*, Providence, RI: Berghahn Books, 1996, pp. 73–8; Evelyn Benesch and Ingried Brugger (eds.), *Futurismus. Radikale Avantgarde*, Vienna/Milan: Ca-Ba Kunstforum/Mazzato, 2003, p. 243, and Marinetti, *Critical Writings*, pp. 226–37. For the geopolitical and military background, see Hew Strachan, *The First World War*, New York: Viking, 2004, pp. 151–4.

21 *Lacerba*, 1913–1915, pp. 241–4.

22 The original Italian version of the *Synthesis* can be found in Carlo Carrà, *Guerra pittura. Futurismo politico, dinamismo plastico, 12 disegni guerreschi, parole in libertà*, Milan: Edizioni Futuriste di 'Poesia', 1915, and an English translation in Marinetti, *Selected Writings*, pp. 62–3.

23 Reims Cathedral was shelled on a number of times in September, particularly between 17 and 19 September, just before the Futurist Synthesis was published. On Reims and the controversy following the German shellfire, see Horne and Kramer, *German Atrocities, 1914*: pp. 217–21.

24 Marinetti, *Selected Writings*, pp. 62–3.

25 Quoted in Peter Jelavich, 'German Culture and the Great War', in Roshwald and Stites, *European Culture in the Great War*, p. 44.

26 Verwey, *Holland en de oorlog*, pp. 11, 16; published in the October issue of *De Beweging*.

27 Gundolf wrote of a 'misguided essay with the narrow-mindedness of a small, neutral state', an essay that cried out for a response. (Mea Nijland-Verwey [ed.], *Albert Verwey en Stefan George*, Amsterdam: Polak & Van Gennep, 1965, p. 171.)

28 Paseta in Gregory, *Ireland and the Great War*, p. 18.

29 Poem in Tom Kettle, *Poems & Parodies*, Dublin: Talbot, 1916, pp. 84–6.

30 Jules Romains, *Europe*, Paris: Éditions de la Nouvelle revue française, 1919, p. 11.

31 Ibid., p. 10. Biographical information on Romains from Olivier Rony (ed.), *Correspondance Jacques Copeau-Jules Romains. Deux êtres en marche (1913–1946)*, Paris: Flammarion, 1978, p. 102, note 2.

32 Romains, *Europe*, p. 10.

33 Ibid., p. 12.

34 Ibid., p. 65.

35 Ibid., p. 31.

36 Ibid., pp. 23, 33, 43, 79, 80.

37 Ibid., p. 83.

38 This passage is based on Rupert Brooke, *The Letters of Rupert Brooke*, selected and ed. Geoffrey Keynes, New York: Harcourt, Brace & World, 1968, and Nigel H. Jones, *Rupert Brooke: Life, Death & Myth*, London: Richard Cohen Books, 1999.

39 Rupert Brooke, *The Complete Poems*, London: Sidgwick & Jackson, 1934, p. 144.

40 Van Ostaijen, *Verzameld werk. Proza. Besprekingen en Beschouwingen*, p. 416.

41 They had probably left Duffel on 28 September because the many large Red Cross flags on the military hospital set up across from the church there were making too much noise. Cf. 'The large and numerous flags of the Red Cross ... turned this asylum from suffering into a favourite target for our enemies.' (Jules Gernaert, *Souvenirs de la grande guerre. Les derniers jours de Duffel*, Brussels: A. Dewit, 1919, p. 19. DM from the French.)

42 Brooke, *The Letters*, p. 623.

43 Ibid., p. 625.

44 Van Ostaijen (n.p.)

45 Brooke, *The Letters*, p. 640.

46 Ibid., pp. 632–3.

47 Ibid., p. 629.

48 Hueffer on 12 September, in Ford, *War Prose*, p. 209 ('this present war is just a cloud – a hideous and unrelieved pall of doom').

49 Ford Madox Ford, *Selected Poems*, Manchester: Carcanet Press, 1997, p. 84.

50 Ford, *War Prose*, p. 210.

51 Ford, *Selected Poems*, pp. 83–4.

52 This passage is based on Vandeweyer, *De Eerste Wereldoorlog*, pp. 96–127 and Burg and Purcell, *Almanac of World War I*, pp. 29–39.

53 Brooke, *The Letters*, pp. 624–5.

54 Karel Van den Oever, *Verzen uit oorlogstijd (1914–1919)*, 's-Hertogenbosch: Teulings, 1919, p. 15.

55 This passage is based on Strachan, *The First World War. Volume I*, p. 281–373, Hans Weichselbaum, *Georg Trakl. Eine Biographie mit Bildern, Texten und Dokumenten*, Salzburg: O. Müller, 1994, pp. 165–180; and Evelyn de Roodt, *Onsterfelijke fronten. Duitse schrijvers in de loopgraven van de Eerste Wereldoorlog*, Soesterberg: Aspekt, 2005, pp. 75–113.

56 Fromkin, *Europe's Last Summer*, p. 302; Strachan, *The First World War. Volume I*, p. 356.

57 Weichselbaum, *Georg Trakl*, p. 169 (Dutch translation in De Roodt, *Onsterfelijke fronten*, p. 77).

58 Cross, *The Lost Voices of World War I*, p. 123.

59 Georg Trakl, *Werke, Entwürfe, Briefe*, ed. Hans-Georg Kemper

and Frank Rainer Max, afterword and bibliography by Hans-Georg Kemper, Stuttgart: P. Reclam, 1984, pp. 249–50; De Roodt, *Onsterfelijke fronten*, p. 104.

60 Biographical information from Cross, *The Lost Voices of World War I*, pp. 348–9 and John Neubauer, '1918: Overview', in Marcel Cornis-Pope and John Neubauer (eds.), *History of the Literary Cultures of East-Central Europe: Junctures and Disjunctures in the 19th and 20th Centuries*, Amsterdam: J. Benjamins, 2 vols., 2004, vol. 1, pp. 184–5. Opening lines from Géza Gyóni, 'Levél nyugatra' (*Lengyel mezőköon, tábortűz mellett*, 1914); English translation in Cross, *The Lost Voices of World War I*, pp. 121–2.

61 DM from the Dutch translation by Mari Alföldy in Buelens, *Het lijf in slijk geplant*, pp. 107–9.

62 Cf. the section 'Perfidy from the West' in Orzoff, 'The Empire Without Qualities', in Paddock, *A Call to Arms*, pp. 175–8.

63 Neubauer, '1918: Overview', p. 185, calls it arguable that this was Gyóni's intention, but does not offer any arguments for that view. Given the high profile of the magazine and the prominent role played in it by Ady, who had close ties to Paris culture, it strikes me as very improbable that Gyóni did not intend this as a critique of the *Nyugat* circle.

64 On *Nyugat*'s position, see Andras Mihályhegyi, 'Ambivalente Gefühle – eindeutige Stellungnahmen. Die ungarische Intelligenz im Ersten Weltkrieg', in Vondung, *Kriegserlebnis*, pp. 289–90, 301–4.

65 Zoltan Horváth, *Die Jahrhundertwende in Ungarn. Geschichte Der 2. Reformgeneration '1896–1914'*, Berlin-Spandau: Luchterhand, Neuwied a. Rh., 1966, p. 467; see also Ignotus, 'Háború', *Nyugat*, 1 August 1914.

66 Béla Balász, 'Párisz-e vagy Weimar?', *Nyugat*, 16 August–1 September 1914, p. 200.

67 Quoted in Hanno Loewy, 'Medium und Initiation. Béla Bálazs. Märchen, Ästhetik, Kino', PhD diss., Universität Konstanz, 1999, available at ub.uni-konstanz.deIkops, p. 170.

68 Stanza from Desző Kosztolányi, 'Öcsem', *Nyugat*, 16 August–1 September 1914. DM from the Dutch translation by Mari Alfoldy in Buelens, *Het lijf in slijk geplant*, p. 65.

69 Translated from Anton N. Nyerges, *Árpád Tóth: Song of Drywood*, Richmond, Kentucky, 1983 (unpublished typescript in the collection of the Library of Congress, Washington, DC), p. 51.

70 Quoted and paraphrased from Horváth, *Die Jahrhundertwende in Ungarn*, p. 490.

71 Ady, *Poems*, p. 427.

72 Ady, *The Explosive Country*, p. 281.

73 Ady, 'Az új militarizmus', *Nyugat*, 1 November 1914 (unpublished Dutch translation by Gyorgyi Dandoy).

74 Endre Ady, *Selected Poems*, trans. Eugene Bard, Munich: Hieronymus, 1987, pp. 112–13.

75 Based on the slightly abridged German translation of the article in Aranka Ogrin and Kalman Vargha (eds.), *'Nyugat' und sein Kreis: 1908–1941. Anhang, 'Magyar Csillag' 1942–1944*, Leipzig: P. Reclam, 1989, pp. 118–22 (p. 122). The complete article was published under the title of 'Egyszerű gondolatok' in the 16 December 1914 issue of *Nyugat*. The same title would be used for a postwar collection of his articles on the First World War, which were mostly pacifist in tenor (and some of which were also published in French and German newspapers).

76 Higonnet, *Lines of Fire*, p. 451.

77 Stanza from Géza Gyóni, 'Csak egy éjszakára …' (*Lengyel mezőköon, tábortűz mellett*, 1914); English translation in Cross, *The Lost Voices of World War I*, p. 349–50.

78 The lesser-known Acmeists Narbut and Zenkevich also fought in the war; see Strakhovsky, 'Three Sojourners in the Acmeist Camp', p. 42. Nikolai Tikhonov served in the war, and his Acmeism-tinged collection *The Horde* (1922) is based on his wartime experiences (Victor Terras, *Handbook of Russian Literature*, New Haven: Yale University Press, 1985, p. 475). The lesser-known Futurist Konstantin Bolshakov fought in the war from 1915 onwards. His collection *Solntse na izlete* (The Sun at the End of Its Flight, 1916) consists of war poems. His 'Poem on the Events', influenced by Mayakovsky's style, is a long requiem for a friend who had died in combat, in the form of a collage incorporating pieces of the friend's work (Markov, *Russian Futurism*, p. 266). For lists of mobilized Futurists, see ibid., p. 298 and Khlebnikov, *Collected Works*, pp. 92–3.

79 See Basker in Gumilyov, *The Pillar of Fire*, p. 228.

80 Vladimir Markov and Merrill Sparks (eds.), *Modern Russian Poetry: An Anthology with Verse Translations*, Alva: Macgibbon & Kee, 1966, p. 237.

81 Oljanov, quoted in Rusinko, 'The Theme of War in the Works of Gumilev', p. 207. Also compare Leonid I. Strakhovsky, 'Nicholas Gumilyov, the Poet-Warrior 1886–1921', *Slavonic and East European Review. American Series* 3:3 (1944), p. 22.

82 Based on Nikolai Gumilev, *Selected Works of Nikolai S. Gumilev*, Albany, NY: State University of New York Press, 1972, p. 70 and Gumilyov, *The Pillar of Fire*, p. 104.

83 Rusinko, 'The Theme of War in the Works of Gumilev', p. 210.

84 Cf. ibid., p. 207, and Basker in Gumilyov, *The Pillar of Fire*, p. 28–9.

85 English translation by Lydia Razran Stone (p.c.), 2012.

86 Brown, *Mayakovsky*, p. 109. This passage is also based on Woroszylski, *The Life of Mayakovsky*, pp. 129–35, Shklovsky, *Mayakovsky and His Circle*, pp. 71–3, Brown, *Mayakovsky*, pp. 109–12, and Nyota Thun, *Ich, so gross und so überflüssig. Wladimir Majakowski, Leben und Werk*, Düsseldorf: Grupello, 2000, pp. 82–4. The relevant Mayakovsky writings are in Mayakovsky, *Werke*, vol. 9, pp. 28–44, Lawton and Eagle, *Russian Futurism*, pp. 87–9, and Mayakovsky, *Werken*, pp. 633–7.

87 For descriptions and examples, see Brown, *Mayakovsky*, p. 110, and Cork, *A Bitter Truth*, pp. 51, 54.

88 Mayakovsky, *Werken*, p. 633.

89 Mayakovsky, *Werke*. vol. 5, pt. 1, p. 41.

90 Hellman, *Poets of Hope and Despair*, p. 111. The remainder of this passage is based on ibid., pp. 111–13.

91 Russian and Dutch versions in Buelens, *Het lijf in slijk geplant*; English translation from the Russian by Lydia Razran Stone (p.c.), 2012.

92 Hellman, *Poets of Hope and Despair*, p. 43.

93 Final stanzas, from Blok, *Selected Poems*, p. 112.

94 On Gippius and the war, see Temira Pachmuss, *Zinaida Hippius: An Intellectual Profile*, Carbondale: Southern Illinois University Press, 1971, pp. 179–88, and Hellman, *Poets of Hope and Despair*, pp. 139–55.

95 Quoted in Strakhovsky, 'Three Sojourners in the Acmeist Camp', p. 136.

96 Viktoria Schweitzer, *Tsvetaeva*, trans. Angela Livingstone, London: Harvill Press, 1992, pp. 39, 53–54; Marko Fondse, 'Afterword', in Marina Tsvetaeva, *Werken*, trans. Margriet Berg et al., Amsterdam: Van Oorschot, 1999, pp. 707–9.

97 Quoted in Schweitzer, *Tsvetaeva*, p. 54. DM from the Dutch.

98 Tsvetaeva, *Werken*, p. 61; English translation by Lydia Razran Stone (p.c.), 2012.

99 Sorley, *Collected Letters*, pp. 181, 187, 191, 193, 195, 196.

100 'Daddy's gone Hun-hunting', in the anonymous poem 'The War Baby', in Vivien Noakes (ed.), *Voices of Silence: The Alternative Book of First World War Poetry*, Stroud: Sutton, 2006, p. 45; Lissauer in Julius Bab, *1914. Der Deutsche Krieg im Deutschen Gedicht*, vol. 2, Berlin: Morawe & Scheffelt, 1914, pp. 36–7.

101 Brooke, *The Letters*, p. 632 (letter to Leonard Bacon).

102 Brooke, *The Complete Poems*, p. 148.

103 Thomas Anz and Joseph Vogl (eds.), *Die Dichter und der Krieg. Deutsche Lyrik 1914–1918*, Munich: C. Hanser, 1982, p. 44. DM from the German.

104 Karl Kraus, *In These Great Times: A Karl Kraus Reader*, trans. Harry Zohn, Manchester: Carcanet, 1984, p. 73.

4 The Smell of Mustard Gas in the Morning

1 Siegfried Sassoon, *Diaries 1915–1918*, ed. and introduced by Rupert Hart-Davis, London: Faber and Faber, 1983, p. 22.

2 John D. Gartner, *The Hypomanic Edge: The Link Between a Little Craziness and a Lot of Success in America*, New York: Simon & Schuster, 2005, p. 180. For the whole story of Ford's peace initiative, see Barbara Kraft, *The Peace Ship: Henry Ford's Pacifist Adventure in the First World War*, New York: Macmillan, 1978.

3 Gilbert, *Atlas of World War I*, p. 50.

4 On the names for the war and the striking fact that Germany spoke of the coming *Weltkrieg* even before 1914, while other countries tended to call the war 'great' or 'European', see Strachan, *The First World War. Volume I*, p. 694ff.

5 Daan F. Boens, *Van glorie en lijden. Sonnetten uit de loopgraven aan den Yser*, published and introduced by Dr. P.H. De Keyser, Drukkerij van de Werkschool, Kamp van Hardewijk, 1917, p. 90.

6 De Vos, *De Eerste Wereldoorlog*, p. 58, estimates that there were 14,000 casualties (due to death, injury, illness or disappearance) during the Battle of the Yser.

7 Boens, *Van glorie en lijden*, p. 91.

8 Ibid., p. 130; Cross, *The Lost Voices of World War I*, p. 394, and Association des écrivains combattants, *Anthologie des Écrivains Morts à la Guerre, 1914–1918*, vol. 3, Malfere, Amiens, 1925, pp. 766–7.

9 This passage draws on information from De Vos, *De Eerste Wereldoorlog*, p. 58, and Vandeweyer, *De Eerste Wereldoorlog*, pp. 130–5.

10 'Verzen', in Bernaerts and Heyman, *Oorlogspoëzie*, pp. 79–80.

11 Biographical information on Van Cauwelaert from J. Pauwels, 'De daad van August Van Cauwelaert', *Dietsche Warande en Belfort*, 1945, pp. 350–1, available at dbnl.org; and J. Rombouts, *August Van Cauwelaert en zijn tijd*, Antwerp: Standaard-Boekhandel, 1951, pp. 15–32.

12 On this subject, see Koen Hulpiau, *René De Clercq (1877–1932). Een monografie*, Ghent: Koninklijke Academie voor Nederlandse Taal-en Letterkunde, 1986, pp. 239–40.

13 Ibid.

14 René De Clercq, *De zware kroon. Verzen uit den oorlogstijd*, Bussum: Van Dishoeck, 1915, p. 29.

15 Ibid., p. 30.

16 Poems in Bernaerts and Heyman, *Oorlogspoëzie*, pp. 154, 155; on *De Vlaamsche Stem*, see Lode Wils, *Flamenpolitik en Aktivisme. Vlaanderen tegenover België in de Eerste Wereldoorlog*, Leuven: Davidsfonds, 1974, pp. 114ff.

17 On this subject, see Hulpiau, *René De Clercq*, pp. 244–5; Wils, *Flamenpolitik en Aktivisme*, pp. 114ff.; and the entries 'De Clercq', '*De Vlaamsche Stem*', 'Gerretson', 'Flamenpolitik' and 'activisme' in *Nieuwe Encyclopedie van de Vlaamse Beweging*. On the relationship between literature and activism, see e.g. Geert Buelens and Matthijs de Ridder, '"t Is allemaal een boeltje": over activisme, frontisme, zaktivisme, arrivisme, neo-activisme, Vlaamsch idealisme, jusqu'au-boutisme, Nieuw-Aktivisme, post-activisme en naoorlogs activisme', in Geert Buelens, Matthijs de Ridder and Jan Stuyck (eds.), *De Trust der Vaderlandsliefde. Over literatuur en Vlaamse Beweging 1890–1940*, Antwerp: AMVC-Letterenhuis, 2005, pp. 162–98.

18 De Clercq, *De zware kroon*, pp. 50–1.

19 Eric Hobsbawm, *Nations and Nationalism Since 1780: Programme, Myth, Reality*, Cambridge: Cambridge University Press, 1990, p. 32.

20 For a map and pie charts of the situation in the Habsburg Empire in 1910, see ibid., p. 198. For an overview of those same minorities and

the empire's ethnic composition in 1914, see Chapter 2, note 36 of the present volume.

21 Cf. Hobsbawm, *Nations and Nationalism*, p. 31.

22 Lyman Abbott (ed.), *King Albert's book. Een hulde aan den koning der Belgen en het Belgische volk vanwege voorname en gezaghebbende personaliteiten door de wereld heen*, London: Hodder & Stoughton, 1914, p. 5.

23 Ibid., p. 7.

24 Ibid., pp. 25, 181.

25 Ibid., p. 108.

26 Ibid., p. 59.

27 Verwey, *Holland en de oorlog*, p. 48.

28 Ibid., pp. 48–9.

29 Ismee Tames, *Oorlog voor onze gedachten. Oorlog, neutraliteit en identiteit in het Nederlandse publieke debat, 1914–1918*, Hilversum: Verloren, 2006, p. 44.

30 Verwey, *Holland en de oorlog*, p. 28.

31 Ibid., p. 25.

32 Ibid., pp. 10, 28.

33 Nijland-Verwey, *Albert Verwey en Stefan George*, p. 174 (poem of 28 January 1915).

34 Ibid., p. 176.

35 Cf. Tames, *Oorlog voor onze gedachten*, pp. 44–6.

36 Nijland-Verwey, *Albert Verwey en Stefan George*, p. 178.

37 Ford, *War Prose*, p. 210.

38 Ford Madox Ford, *When Blood Is Their Argument: An Analysis of Prussian Culture*, London: Hodder and Stoughton, 1915, p. xi.

39 Ibid., pp. 270, 305.

40 Ford, *War Prose*, p. 218.

41 Ford, *When Blood Is Their Argument*, p. 318.

42 Apollinaire, *Lettres à Madeleine*, p. 116.

43 Sorley, *Collected Letters*, pp. 217, 218, 219.

44 Sorley, *Collected Poems*, p. 70.

45 Sorley, *Collected Letters*, p. 236.

46 Ibid., pp. 243, 254, 261, 260.

47 Sorley, *Collected Poems*, p. 91.

48 Verhaeren, *Les ailes rouges de la guerre*, pp. 246, 243, 245. DM from the French.

49 'Tragic Death of Emile Verhaeren, Belgium's Most Famous Poet', *The Times*, 29 November 1916, p. 11.

50 Cf. the end of an article about Verhaeren that presented him as a beacon of hope, 'showing, what is perhaps the surest cause which our shattered Europe has for hope, that it is possible to have sympathies at once national and cosmopolitan' (Francis Bickley, 'Emile Verhaeren: The Poet of Belgium and of Europe', *The Living Age*, 5 December 1914).

51 Pierre-Jean Jouve, *Vous êtes des hommes*, Paris: Éditions de la Nouvelle revue française, 1915, pp. 22–3. DM from the French.

52 Ibid., p. 82.

53 Ibid., p. 83.

54 Ibid., pp. 84–5, 91.

55 Ibid., pp. 112–15.

56 Ludwig Rubiner, 'Ihr seid Menschen', *Die weissen Blätter* 3 (January-March 1916), pp. 389–91.

57 Van Ostaijen, *Verzameld werk. Proza. Besprekingen en Beschouwingen*, vol. 1, pp. 10, 12.

58 Ibid., p. 15.

59 For Van Ostaijen's fierce rejection of both 'pan-Gallicism' and 'pan-Germanism', see ibid., p. 420.

60 Darlene J. Sadlier, 'Nationalism, Modernity, and the Formation of Fernando Pessoa's Aesthetic', *Luso-Brazilian Review* 34:2 (1997), pp. 110–11.

61 See also Angel Crespo, *Het meervoudige leven van Fernando Pessoa*, trans. Barber van de Pol, Baarn: De Prom, 1992, pp. 285–94.

62 Fernando Pessoa, *Brieven 1905–1919*, trans., annotated and afterword by August Willemsen, Amsterdam: De Arbeiderspers, 2004, p. 110.

63 Ibid., p. 108.

64 Fernando Pessoa, *De anarchistische bankier & ander proza*, selected, translated and afterword by August Willemsen, Amsterdam: Meulenhoff, 1997, p. 64; a month later, in October 1914, he mentioned a 'Manifesto (Ultimatum, actually)' for the first time in a letter (Pessoa, *Brieven*, p. 114).

65 Pessoa, *Brieven*, p. 90.

66 Crespo, *Het meervoudige leven*, pp. 84–106, 164–8; Manuel Villaverde Cabral, 'The Aesthetics of Nationalism: Modernism and Authoritarianism in Early Twentieth-Century Portugal',

Luso-Brazilian Review 26:1 (1989), pp. 24–6; Sadlier, 'Nationalism, Modernity, and the Formation of Fernando Pessoa's Aesthetic'.

67 Crespo, *Het meervoudige leven*, p. 168.

68 Roberta L. Payne (ed.), *A Selection of Modern Italian Poetry in Translation*, Montreal: McGill-Queen's University Press, 2004, pp. 72ff.

69 Manifesto in Umbro Apollonio (ed.), *Futurist Manifestos*, New York: Viking Press, 1973, pp. 197–200.

70 See Gilbert, *Atlas of World War I*, pp. 36–7, for maps on which the areas in question are marked.

71 Bonadeo, *D'Annunzio and the Great War*, p. 73.

72 *Lacerba*, III, p. 161. DM from the Italian.

73 Soffici, 'Memento', *Lacerba*, III, p. 163. DM from the Italian.

74 *Lacerba*, III, p. 165. DM from the Italian.

75 Quoted in Strachan, *The First World War*, p. 155.

76 Information from Angelo Bazzanella, 'Die Stimme der Illiteraten. Volk und Krieg in Italien 1915–1918', in Vondung, *Kriegserlebnis*, pp. 340–1; Bonadeo, *D'Annunzio and the Great War*, pp. 69–124; and Woodhouse, *Gabriele D'Annunzio*, pp. 294–312.

77 Bonadeo, *D'Annunzio and the Great War*, p. 75.

78 Filippo Tommaso Marinetti, *Taccuini, 1915–1921*, Bologna: Il Mulino, 1987, pp. 5–42.

79 Original in Marinetti, *Selected Poems*, p. 116. DM from the French.

80 This section is based on Glenn E. Torrey, 'Rumania and the Belligerents, 1914–1916', *Journal of Contemporary History* 1:3 (1966), pp. 171–91, a very detailed reconstruction of Romania's diplomatic moves between 1914 and 1916.

81 Letter in Cornelia Bodea and Hugh Seton-Watson (eds.), *R.W. Seton-Watson Si Românii: 1906–1920*, Bucharest: Editura Stiintifica si Enciclopedică, 1988 (2 vols.), p. 403. DM from the German.

82 Ibid., p. 551.

83 Description of the newspaper from Torrey, 'Rumania and the Belligerents', p. 181; date and publication date from Octavian Goga, *Opere*, Bucharest: Univers Enciclopedic, 2001, p. 1307.

84 DM from the Dutch translation by Jan H. Mysjkin in Buelens, *Het lijf in slijk geplant*, p. 221.

85 Alain Bosquet (ed.), *Anthologie de la poésie roumaine*,Paris: Éditions du Seuil, pp. 100–1. See also John Neubauer, 'Transylvania's Literary

Cultures: Rivalry and Interaction', in Cornis-Pope and Neubauer, *History of the Literary Cultures of East-Central Europe*, p. 264.

86 Mario D. Fenyo, 'Writers in Politics: The Role of Nyugat in Hungary, 1908–19', *Journal of Contemporary History* 11:1 (1976), p. 189.

87 Ady, *The Explosive Country*, p. 285. On Goga's negotiations, see note in ibid., p. 310.

88 Ibid., p. 286.

89 Ibid., p. 287.

90 Based on letters to his wife in Jeremy D. Adler and John J. White (eds.), *August Stramm. Kritische Essays und unveröffentlichtes Quellenmaterial aus dem Nachlass des Dichters*, Berlin: E. Schmidt, 1979, pp. 143–52, and to Herwarth and Nell Walden in August Stramm, *Briefe an Nell und Herwarth Walden*, Berlin: Edition Sirene, 1988. The term 'Bundesbrüder' is used in Adler and White, *August Stramm*, p. 144 and again on p. 145.

91 Burg and Purcell, *Almanac of World War I*, p. 70.

92 Adler and White, *August Stramm*, p. 147.

93 Ibid., p. 147.

94 Anna Akhmatova, *The Complete Poems of Anna Akhmatova*, ed. Roberta Reeder, trans. Judith Hemschemeyer, Boston: Zephyr Press, 2000, p. 434–5.

95 See for this passage Davies, *Anna of all the Russias*, p. 27.

96 Stramm, *Briefe an Nell und Herwarth Walden*, p. 80.

97 colecizj.easyvserver.com/pgstrtri.htm. Trans. Anthony Vivis and Will Stone, 2002.

98 Adler and White, *August Stramm*, p. 152.

99 For the third battle (Loos), Strachan, *The First World War*, p. 181, reports a quarter-million Allied casualties and only 60,000 on the German side. According to German Werth, 170,000 Allied and 51,000 German soldiers died in Loos (Hirschfeld et al. *Enzyklopädie Erster Weltkrieg*, p. 684); for the same battle, Yelton gives 62,000 British, 48,000 French and 51,000 German casualties (in Tucker, *The European Powers in the First World War*, p. 80); Keegan, *The First World War*, p. 203, reports 143,567 French casualties in Artois and Champagne.

100 Keegan, *The First World War*, p. 202.

101 Miriam Cendrars, *Blaise Cendrars*, Paris: Balland, 1984, p. 424. DM from the French.

102 Blaise Cendrars, *Aujourd'hui: 1917–1929. Suivi de Essais et Réflexions 1910–1916*, Paris: Denoel, 1987, p. 22. DM from the French.
103 Strachan, *The First World War*, pp. 158–9.
104 Keegan, *The First World War*, pp. 255–6.
105 See Cross, *The Lost Voices of World War I*, p. 355, and Milne Holton and Vasa D. Mihailovich (eds.), *Serbian Poetry from the Beginnings to the Present*, New Haven: Yale Center for International and Area Studies, 1988, pp. 220–6.
106 DM from the Dutch translation by Reina Dokter in Buelens, *Het lijf in slijk geplant*, pp. 411–13.
107 See Gilbert, *Atlas of World War I*, pp. 32–41; Tucker, *The European Powers in the First World War*, pp. 525–7; Jones, *Rupert Brooke*, pp. 400–1; Strachan, *The First World War*, p. 99–123.
108 Cross, *The Lost Voices of World War I*, p. 54.
109 Based on Compère-Morel, *Apollinaire au feu*, and Pierre-Marcel Adema and Michel Decaudin, *Album Apollinaire. Iconographie*, Paris: Gallimard, 1971.
110 Apollinaire, *Calligrammes*, p.181.
111 Cf. Cross, *The Lost Voices of World War I*, p. 203.
112 Apollinaire, *Calligrammes*, p. 127.
113 Apollinaire, *Calligrammes*, p. 203.
114 See the chapter 'Les armes chimiques' by Olivier Lepick in Audoin-Rouzeau and Becker, *14–18, retrouver la Guerre*, pp. 269–79.
115 Bent, *The New York Times Book of World War I*, p. 65.
116 Karl Kraus, *Weltgericht*, Munich: A. Langen, G. Müller, 1965, p. 16.
117 On gas as a theme in British war poetry, see Hilda D. Spear and Sonya A. Summersgill, 'Poison Gas and the Poetry of War', *Essays in Criticism* XLI (1991), pp. 308–22.
118 See note 74 above.
119 Figures from Vincent Dulcert, 'La destruction des Arméniens', in Audoin-Rouzeau and Becker, *14–18, retrouver la Guerre*, pp. 381–92, and Alan Kramer, *Dynamic of Destruction: Culture and Mass Killing in the First World War*, Oxford: Oxford University Press, 2007, p. 150.

5 *A Europe of Words, a Europe of Action*

1 Evermar van Moere, *Soldatenleven. Eene bijdrage tot de oorlogsfolklore van den Vlaamschen soldaat*, Leuven: Vlaamsche Boekenhalle, Leuven, 1919, pp. 76–7.

2 The plan was for Belgian Congo to become part of *Mittelafrika*, Germany's colonial empire. On *Mitteleuropa*, see e.g. Alfred D. Low, *The Anschluss Movement, 1918-1919, and the Paris Peace Conference*, Philadelphia: American Philosophical Society, 1974, pp. 20–3; Gerard Delanty, *Inventing Europe: Idea, Identity, Reality*, New York: St. Martin's Press, 1995, pp. 101–9; Peter Bugge, '"Shatter Zones": The Creation and Re-creation of Europe's East', in Menno Spiering and Michael J. Wintle, *Ideas of Europe Since 1914: The Legacy of the First World War*, Basingstoke: Palgrave Macmillan, 2002, pp. 47–68; Antoine Prost and Jay Winter, *Penser la Grande Guerre. Un essai d'historiographie*, Paris: Seuil, 2004, p. 68.

3 Anon., 'The New Europe', *The New Europe* 1:1 (19 October 1916), p. 1.

4 Cf. Bugge, '"Shatter Zones"', p. 64, n. 1.

5 Guillaume Apollinaire, 'Mitteleuropa. La Mise en tutetelle de l'Autriche', *Paris-Midi*, 18 February 1917. Also in Apollinaire, *Œuvres en prose complètes*, Vol. 3, Paris: Gallimard, 1993, pp. 478–81.

6 On the deliberate German policy of destabilizing existing state structures and supporting nationalist and revolutionary groups, see Wils, *Flamenpolitik en Aktivisme*, and Sebastian Haffner, *De zeven hoofdzonden van Duitsland tijdens de Eerste Wereldoorlog*, trans. from the German by Ruud van der Helm, Afterword by Sophie De Schaepdrijver, Amsterdam: Mets & Schilt, 2002, pp. 82–5.

7 See Jozsef Galántai, *Hungary in the First World War*, Budapest: Akademiai Kiado, 1989, p. 158, and Gyorgy Litván, *A Twentieth-century Prophet: Oscár Jászi, 1875–1957*, Budapest: Central European University Press, 2006, p. 97.

8 Biographical sketch based on Lela Zeckovic, 'Miroslav Krleža 1893–1981', *Raster* 73 (1996), pp. 6–20.

9 Quoted in ibid., p. 8.

10 Miroslav Krleža, 'Achter de coulissen van het jaar 1918 / Dagboeken 1942–1943', *Raster* 75 (1996), pp. 124–5.

11 Ibid., p. 125.

12 Miroslav Krleža, 'Vervlogen dagen. Dagboek maart 1916 ', *Raster* 73 (1996), p. 31.

13 Ibid., p. 39.

14 Reconstructed from Anton N. Nyerges, 'Endre Ady: The World of Gog and God', in Ady, *Poems*, pp. 38–55; Congdon, 'Endre Ady's Summons to National Regeneration in Hungary', p. 321; Ady, *The Explosive Country*, pp. 288–90; and John Neubauer, '1918: Overview', in Cornis-Pope and Neubauer, *History of the Literary Cultures of East-Central Europe*, pp. 184–5. The entire affair is recounted in Hungarian in László Kardos, *Az Ady-Rákosivita. Egy irodalmi per aktái 1915–16-ból*, Debrecen, 1940.

15 Nyerges, 'Endre Ady: The World of Gog and God', p. 55. DM from the Dutch.

16 Excerpt from Mihály Babits, 'Hüsvét előtt', *Nyugat*, 1 April 1916, trans. Peter Zollman, available at c3.hu.

17 In *Nyugat*, 16 August 1915; English translation in Ady, *Poems*, p. 414. Babits's poem about the pinky of his beloved appeared in the same issue.

18 William English Walling (ed.), *The Socialists and the War. A Documentary Statement of the Position of the Socialists of all Countries; with Special Reference to their Peace Policy: Including a Summary of the Revolutionary State Socialist Measures Adopted by the Governments at War*, New York: H. Holt and Company, 1915, p. 343.

19 Karl Kautsky devoted his 1 May speech to this subject in 1911. Available at marxists.org. The term was also used in an appeal for peace made by the socialist parties in the Entente countries. See Randolph Silliman Bourne (ed.), *Towards an Enduring Peace: A Symposium of Peace Proposals and Programs, 1914–1916*, New York: American Association for International Conciliation, 1916, p. 260.

20 Herman Gorter, *Het imperialisme, de wereldoorlog en de sociaal-democratie*, Amsterdam: SDP, 1915, pp. 101–2.

21 Herman de Liagre Böhl, *Herman Gorter. Zijn politieke aktiviteiten van 1909 tot 1920 in de opkomende kommunistische beweging in Nederland*, Nijmegen: SON, 1973, pp. 133–4.

22 Herman Gorter, *Pan* (second, greatly expanded edition), Bussum: C.A.J. van Dishoeck, 1916, p. 276.

23 For all the related documents, see Horst Lademacher (ed.), *Die Zimmerwalder Bewegung. Protokolle und Korrespondenz*, The Hague:

Mouton, 1967, 2 vols.; for the story of the conference and an analysis of it, see R. Craig Nation, *War on War: Lenin, the Zimmerwald Left, and the Origins of Communist Internationalism*, Durham, NC: Duke University Press, 1989. On Roland Holst's role and experiences there, see Elsbeth Etty, *Liefde is heel het leven niet. Henriette Roland Holst, 1869–1952*, Amsterdam: Balans, 1996, pp. 311–21; on Gorter, see De Liagre Böhl, *Herman Gorter*, pp. 135–9.

24 Nation, *War on War*, pp. 35, 82, 86.

25 The manifesto states, 'The right of self-determination of nations must be the indestructible principle in the system of national relationships of peoples.' Available at marxists.org.

26 V.I. Lenin, 'The Socialist Revolution and the Right of Nations to Self-Determination' (1916). Available at marxists.org.

27 Claes Ahlund, *Diktare i krig. K.G. Ossiannilsson, Bertil Malmberg och Ture Nerman från debuten till 1920*, Hedemora: Gidlund, 2007, p. 375.

28 DM from the Dutch translation by Lisette Keustermans and Eric Metz in Buelens, *Het lijf in slijk geplant*, pp. 309–15.

29 Based on Lademacher, *Die Zimmerwalder Bewegung*, vol. 2, pp. 481, 544–50, and Ahlund, *Diktare i krig*.

30 Lademacher, *Die Zimmerwalder Bewegung*, vol. 2, p. 481, note 1.

31 'Nyorientering', in *Bläck och blod. Dikter av Z. Höglund, Wilhelmssons boktryckeri*, aktiebolag, 1917. DM from the Dutch translation by Lisette Keustermans in Geert Buelens, *Europa Europa! Over de dichters van de Grote Oorlog*, Amsterdam: Ambo, 2008.

32 Paraphrased from Pierre-Jean Jouve, 'Á la Belgique', *Demain*, pp. 318–21.

33 C.S. Adama van Scheltema, *Zingende stemmen*, Rotterdam: Brusse, 1918, p. 50.

34 Cf. the biography of Adama van Scheltema at socialhistory.org.

35 Verwey, *Holland en de oorlog*, p. 47.

36 Based on Kee, *The Green Flag*, pp. 548–89.

37 This term was used by the Irish poet Padraic Colum in Joyce Kilmer, 'Poets Marched in the Van of the Irish Revolt Pearse and MacDonagh, Executed Last Week, Well Known for Their Verse – Other Writers Prominent in Sinn Féin Ranks', *New York Times*, 7 May 1916.

38 Quoted in Cross, *The Lost Voices of World War I*, p. 41.

39 In Kilmer, 'Poets Marched in the Van'.

40 Kee, *The Green Flag*, p. 569.

41 Padraic Colum (ed.), *Poems of the Irish Revolutionary Brotherhood, Thomas MacDonagh, P. H. Pearse (Padraic MacPiarais), Joseph Mary Plunkett, Sir Roger Casement*, Boston: Small, Maynard & Company, 1916, p. viii.

42 William Butler Yeats, *The Collected Poems of W.B. Yeats: A New Edition*, ed. Richard J. Finneran, New York: Collier Books, 1989, p. 182.

43 Ibid.

44 Anon., 'Het oproer in Dublin', *Nieuwe Rotterdamsche Courant*, 30 April 1916, morning edition.

45 Gaston Burssens, *Alles is mogelijk in een gedicht. Verzamelde verzen 1914–1965*, ed. with an afterword by Matthijs de Ridder, Antwerp: Meulenhoff/Manteau, 2005, p. 36.

46 Ibid., p. 37.

47 This idea is worked out in detail by Erik Spinoy in his analysis of the early Van Ostaijen. See Spinoy, *Twee handen in het lege. Paul van Ostaijen en de esthetica van het verhevene (Kant, Lyotard)*, unpublished PhD diss., KU Leuven, 1994, available at dbnl.org.

48 Paul van Ostaijen, *Verzameld werk. Poëzie. Music-Hall, Het Sienjaal, De Feesten van Angst en Pijn*, Amsterdam: Bert Bakker, 1979, p. 115.

49 Stanza from 'Aan die van Havere toen zij vergaten dat ook Vlaanderen in België lag', in René De Clercq, *De Noodhoorn. Vaderlandsche Liederen*, Utrecht: Dietsche Stemmen, 1916, p. 14.

50 Burssens, *Alles is mogelijk*, p. 726.

51 Rudolf Medek, '1914', in Paul Selver (ed.), *Modern Czech Poetry*, London: K. Paul, Trench, Trubner & Co., Ltd., 1929, pp. 294–6.

52 See also 'The Story of Latvia', Chapter V, at latvians.com.

53 Ziedonis, *The Religious Philosophy of Janis Rainis*, p. 73.

54 'The Story of Latvia', Chapter V, at latvians.com.

55 Kārlis Skalbe, 'Latvju bataljonem', DM from the Dutch translation by Kurt Engelen in Buelens, *Het lijf in slijk geplant*, p. 353.

6 *Writing Poetry After Verdun and the Somme*

1 Sassoon, *Diaries 1915–1918*, p. 83.

2 Virginie Loveling, *Oorlogsdagboeken 1914–1918*, ed. Sylvia van

Peteghem and Ludo Stynen, Antwerp/Amsterdam: Meulenhoff/Manteau, 2005, p. 74.

3 Alexander McAdie, *War Weather Vignettes*, New York: The Macmillan Company, 1925. As early as December 1914, an article was published in America placing the impact of the war on the weather in historical perspective. This article confirms Loveling's recollections (reporting that the Franco-Prussian war took place amid 'torrential rains; floods; icy roads; muddy fields') and points out that similar weather had an impact on military engagements in Namur, along the Meuse, and in Flanders in wars in 1586, 1692 and 1708–9. See Robert DeCourcy Ward, 'The Weather Factor in the War', *The Journal of Geography* 13 (1914), pp. 169–71.

4 The dismal weather during the third Battle of Ypres prompted Blunden to write, 'It was one of the many [rainstorms] which caused the legend, not altogether dismissed even by junior officers, that the Germans could make it rain when they wanted to' (Edmund Blunden, *Undertones of War*, London: Cobden-Sanderson, 1928, p. 216).

5 Marc de Larreguy de Civrieux, *La Muse de Sang*, Foreword by Romain Rolland, Paris: Librairie du Travail, 1926, p. 47. DM from the French.

6 Jean-Jacques Becker, 'Mourir à Verdun', in *14–18: Mourir pour la patrie*, Paris: Seuil, 1992, p. 159.

7 Quoted in Melching and Stuivenga, *Ooggetuigen van de Eerste Wereldoorlog*, p. 153, italics added. See also Keegan, *The First World War*, pp. 277–8, and Strachan, *The First World War*, p. 188, who notes that in fact this sentence did not come into being until after the war, when von Falkenhayn wrote his memoirs. Krumeich and Audoin-Rouzeau emphasize that the memorandum in question has never been found (in Stephane Audoin-Rouzeau and Jean-Jacques Becker, *Encyclopédie de la Grande Guerre 1914–1918. Histoire et culture*, Paris: Bayard, 2004, p. 305).

8 Burg and Purcell, *Almanac of World War I*, p. 102. This passage also draws on Becker 'Mourir à Verdun'; Smith, Audoin-Rouzeau and Becker, *France and the Great War*, pp. 75–92; and Strachan, *The First World War*, pp. 184–97.

9 Becker, 'Mourir à Verdun', p. 155.

10 Granier in Ian Higgins (ed.), *Anthology of First World War French Poetry*, Glasgow: University of Glasgow, French & German Publications, 1996, pp. 58–60.

11 Anton Schnack, *Lyrik*, ed. Hartmut Vollmer, Berlin: Elfenbein, 2003, pp. 64 ('Eine Nacht'). English translation in Bridgwater, *The German Poets*, pp. 184–6.

12 Schnack, *Lyrik*, p. 68.

13 DM from the Dutch translation by Ton Naaijkens in Buelens, *Het lijf in slijk geplant*, p. 599.

14 Apollinaire, *Calligrammes*, pp. 256–9.

15 Stramm, *Gedichte. Dramen. Prosa. Briefe*, p. 174 ('Morden ist Pflicht ist Himmel ist Gott').

16 Peter Baum, *Gesammelte Werke*, ed. Hans Schlieper, Berlin: Ernst Rowohlt, 1920.

17 Cross, *The Lost Voices of World War I*, pp. 174–7.

18 Paul Samuleit, *Kriegsschundliteratur; Vortrag, Gehalten in der Offentlichen Versammlung der Zentralstelle zur Bekämpfung der Schundliteratur zu Berlin am 25. März 1916*, Berlin: C. Heymann, 1916, pp. 3–4.

19 Ibid., pp. 38–9.

20 On the workings of censorship in Germany and Austria, see John D. Halliday, *Karl Kraus, Franz Pfemfert, and the First World War: A Comparative Study of 'Die Fackel' and 'Die Aktion' Between 1911 and 1928*, Passau: Andreas-Haller-Verlag, 1986, pp. 168–90. On war poetry more generally and the relative lack of censorship in France, Germany and England, see Marsland, *The Nation's Cause*, pp. 186–9, as well as Nicolas Beaupré, *Écrire en guerre, écrire la guerre. France-Allemagne, 1914–1920*, Paris: CNRS, 2006, pp. 74–95.

21 Johannes R. Becher, 'An Deutschland', *Das Tribunal* 1:5 (May 1919), p. 1.

22 Bridgwater, *The German Poets*, p. 184.

23 Sassoon, *Diaries 1915–1918*, pp. 75, 76.

24 Information on the Somme from Martin Middlebrook, *The First Day on the Somme, 1 July 1916*, London: Allen Lane, 1971, pp. 87–106; Keegan, *The First World War*, pp. 286–99; Strachan, *The First World War*, pp. 190–7.

25 Middlebrook, *The First Day on the Somme*, p. 97.

26 E.A. Mackintosh, M.C., *A Highland Regiment*, Edinburgh: Turnbull & Spears, n.d., p. 37.

27 Siegfried Sassoon, *The War Poems*, London: Faber and Faber, 1999, p. 27.

28 Middlebrook, *The First Day on the Somme*, p. 107.
29 List and dates based on Cross, *The Lost Voices of World War I* and scuttlebuttsmallchow.com/killedsomme.html.
30 Ford, *War Prose*, p. 221.
31 See Saunders, *Ford Madox Ford*, vol. 2, p. 2.
32 See ibid., pp. 7–15.
33 Quoted in Samuel Lynn Hynes, *A War Imagined: The First World War and English Culture*, New York: Atheneum, 1991, p. 105.
34 Ibid., p. 106.
35 Ford, *Selected Poems*, pp. 87–8.
36 Both newspapers can be viewed at the Gallica Digital Library, available at gallica.bnf.fr.
37 François Broche, *Anna de Noailles. Un Mystère en pleine lumière*, Paris: R. Laffont, 1989, p. 331.
38 Noailles, *Les forces éternelles*, p. 15.
39 Elisabeth Higonnet-Dugua (ed.), *Anna de Noailles, cœur innombrable. Biographie, correspondance*, Paris: Michel de Maule, 1989, pp. 281, 283.
40 Noailles, *Les forces éternelles*, p. 37.
41 Higonnet-Dugua, *Anna de Noailles*, p. 286.
42 Noailles, *Les forces éternelles*, p. 13. English translation from Higonnet, *Lines of Fire*, p. 491.
43 Edmond Rostand et al., *Les livres de la guerre, août 1914-août 1916*, Paris: Agence générale de librairie et de publications, 1916, p. vi.
44 Ibid., p. vii.
45 Strachan reports that estimates of German losses vary from 465,000 to 650,000, depending on whether slight injuries are counted. There were 614,000 Allied casualties, including 420,000 British soldiers (*The First World War*, p. 195). Krumeich and Audoin-Rouzeau write of a half million British casualties, as many Germans, and 200,000 French troops (in Audoin-Rouzeau and Becker, *Encyclopédie de la Grande Guerre*, p. 307).
46 Blunden, *Undertones of War*, p. 139.
47 Anon., 'The Story Told by the Dead', *Guardian*, 22 November 1916 (reprinted on the newspaper's opinion pages without further comment on 22 November 2007).
48 Estimate made by Krumeich and Audoin-Rouzeau in Audoin-Rouzeau and Becker, *Encyclopédie de la Grande Guerre*, p. 305.
49 Rony, *Jules Romains*, pp. 239, 240.

7 *Café Dada*

1 Leppmann, *Rainer Maria Rilke*, p. 314; English translation in Rainer Maria Rilke, *Letters, Volume Two: 1910–1926*, trans. Jane Bannard Greene and M.D. Herter Norton, New York: W.W. Norton, 1948. Rilke received three weeks of military training in the Vienna region and then, after a great deal of lobbying by other poets and influential friends, was assigned to the historical division of the Dual Monarchy's war archives (Leppmann, *Rainer Maria Rilke*, p. 315).

2 George Bacovia, *Lead*, Romanian–English bilingual edition, trans. Peter Jay, introduced by Marian Popa, Bucharest: Minerva, 1980, pp. 60–1.

3 See American Jewish Committee, *The Jews in the Eastern War Zone*, New York, 1916, pp. 89–92; I.C. Butnaru, *The Silent Holocaust: Romania and Its Jews*, New York: Greenwood Press, 1992; Irina Livezeanu, *Cultural Politics in Greater Romania: Regionalism, Nation Building and Ethnic Struggle, 1918–1930*, Ithaca: Cornell University Press, 1995, p. 12; William Brustein and Ryan D. King, 'Anti-Semitism as a Response to Perceived Jewish Power: The Cases of Bulgaria and Romania before the Holocaust', *Social Forces* 83:2 (2004), p. 692.

4 Anon., 'Pogroms in Roumania on Outbreak Of War; Jews Flee for Their Lives', *Washington Post*, 8 October 1916; and Roshwald and Stites, *European Culture in the Great War*, p. 96.

5 Francois Buot, *Tristan Tzara. L'homme qui inventa la Révolution Dada*, Paris: Grasset, 2002.

6 Opening lines of Tristan Tzara, 'Furtuna i cîntecul dezertorului' (The Storm and the Deserter's Song). Part I was first published in *Chemarea*, 11 October 1915; English translation from Tristan Tzara, *Primele Poeme / First Poems*, trans. Michael Impey and Brian Swann, New York: New Rivers Press, 1976, p. 23.

7 See Jonathan Steinberg, *Why Switzerland?* Cambridge: Cambridge University Press, 1976, pp. 53–7, and Jean-Claude Favez, 'La Suisse pendant la guerre', in Audoin-Rouzeau and Becker, *Encyclopédie de la Grande Guerre*, pp. 867–75.

8 The terms *Dichtung* and *Volkstum* are used in this context; Hanns Bächtold-Stäubli, *Aus Leben und Sprache des Schweizer Soldaten*, Basel: Verlag der Schweizerischen Gesellschaft für Volkskunde, 1916, p. 5 and passim.

9 DM from the French ('Le monde peut de toi, Suisse, beaucoup attendre, / Et ton devoir est grand, si tu sais le comprendre'). Jules Carràra, *Solidarité: Poèmes*, Geneva: Atar, 1914, n.p.

10 'Unser Schweizer Standpunkt', Carl Spitteler, *Gesammelte Werke, Band 8, 'Land und Volk'*, ed. Gottfried Bohnenblust, Zurich: Artemis-Verlag, 1947, pp. 579–94; English translation available at currentconcerns.ch (edited by DM). Background, origins and rhetorical analysis of the lecture in Walter Müri, *Carl Spittelers Rede vom 14. Dezember 1914. Unser Schweizer Standpunkt rhetorish betrachtet*, Bern: Herbert Lang, 1972.

11 Spitteler, *Gesammelte Werke, Band 8, 'Land und Volk'*, p. 592.

12 Henri Guilbeaux, 'et demain?...' *Demain. Pages et Documents* 1:1 (January 1916), pp. 1–7.

13 On Dada and the First World War, see Geert Buelens, 'Reciting Shells: Dada *and*, Dada *in* & Dadaists *on* the First World War', *Arcadia* 41:2 (2006), pp. 275–95.

14 Hugo Ball, *Briefe 1911–1927*, Einsiedeln/Zurich/Cologne: Benziger, 1957, pp. 40, 34.

15 See Bridgwater, *The German Poets*, p. 71.

16 Ball, *Briefe 1911–1927*, p. 40.

17 Hugo Ball, 'Totentanz 1916', *Der Revoluzzer*, vol. 2, no. 1 (January 1916). These are the opening stanzas; DM from the German.

18 On the sources of inspiration for this poem, see Ludger Derenthal, 'Dada, die Toten und die Überlebenden des Ersten Weltkriegs', *zeitenblicke* 3 (2004), no. 1, available at zeitenblicke.historicum.net, and Rudolf E. Kuenzli, 'Dada gegen den Ersten Weltkrieg: Die Dadaisten in Zürich', in Wolfgang Paulsen and Helmut G. Hermann (eds.), *Sinn aus Unsinn. Dada International*, Bern/Munich: Francke, 1982, p. 91.

19 Jan H. Mysjkin (ed.), *Een avond in Cabaret Voltaire*, Nijmegen: Vantilt, 2003, p. 79.

20 'Totenklage' in Karl Riha and Waltraud Wend-Hohenberger (eds.), *Dada Zürich. Texte, Manifeste, Dokumente*, Stuttgart: Reclam, 1992, p. 69; 'Gadji beri bimba' in ibid., p. 68.

21 Hugo Ball in Mysjkin, *Een avond in Cabaret Voltaire*, p. 8.

22 Statement made by Huelsenbeck in spring 1916; in Riha and Wende-Hohenberger, *Dada Zürich*, p. 29; English translation in Herbert Grabes, *Making Strange: Beauty, Sublimity, and the (Post)Modern 'Third Aesthetic'*, Amsterdam/New York: Rodopi, 2008, p. 34.

23 Tristan Tzara, *Œuvres complètes. Tome 1, 1912–1924*, edited, introduced and annotated by Henri Behar, Paris: Flammarion, 1975, p. 82; English translation in Robert Motherwell (ed.), *The Dada Painters and Poets: An Anthology*, Cambridge, MA: Harvard University Press, 1981, pp. 75–6.

24 This accusation was corroborated with quotes in the Bryce Report distributed in thirty languages by the British government in 1915, available at gwpda.org. For a recent critical analysis of this report, see Zuckerman, *The Rape of Belgium*, pp. 153–9.

25 Tristan Tzara, 'Seven Dada Manifestoes', in *The Dada Painters and Poets: An Anthology*, ed. Robert Motherwell, Boston: Harvard University Press, 1981, p. 75.

26 In Riha and Wende-Hohenberger, *Dada Zürich*, p. 78. English translation of 'Flüsse' (Rivers) from Richard Huelsenbeck, *Memoirs of a Dada Drummer*, ed. Richard Kleinschmidt, Berkeley: University of California Press, 1991, p. xlv.

27 Ibid., p. 28.

28 See Mayakovsky, *Werken*, pp. 708–9, Mayakovsky, *Werke*, vol. 4, p. 444, Woroszylski, *The Life of Mayakovsky*, p. 141. Maxim Gorky is said to have used his connections to keep Mayakovsky away from the front (Shklovsky, *Mayakovsky and His Circle*, p. 88).

29 For a summary and analysis of the poem, see Brown, *Mayakovsky: A Poet in the Revolution*, pp. 146–52.

30 Mayakovsky, *Werken*, p. 219; English translation of the two complete verses from the Russian by Lydia Razran Stone (p.c.), 2012. Other quotes translated by DM from the Dutch. See also the translation of 'War and the World' in Vladimir Mayakovsky, *Electric Iron*, trans. Jack Hirschman and Victor Erlich, Berkeley: Maya, 1971, p. 37.

31 Mayakovsky, *Werken*, pp. 219–21.

32 Ibid., pp. 225, 231, 227, 241.

33 Ibid., pp. 247, 263, 273–5.

34 Rozanova's exact role in the creation of the second work remains unclear. On this subject, see Markov, *Russian Futurism*, p. 336; Alexei Kruchenykh, *Suicide Circus: Selected Poems*, trans. Jack Hirschman, Alexander Kohav and Venyamin Tseytlin, Los Angeles/Copenhagen: Green Integer, 2001, p. 78; and Juliette R. Stapanian, '*Universal War* and the Development of *Zaum*: Abstraction Toward a New Pictorial

and Literary Realism', *The Slavic and East European Journal* 29:1 (1985), pp. 18–38.

35 Kruchenykh, *Suicide Circus*, pp. 80–1.

36 Markov, *Russian Futurism*, p. 336; Kruchenykh, *Suicide Circus*, p. 68.

37 Velimir Khlebnikov, *Collected Works, Volume III: Selected Poems*, trans. Paul Schmidt, ed. Ronald Vroon, Cambridge, MA: Harvard University Press, 1998, pp. 50–61.

38 For an introduction to his thought, see Charlotte Douglas, 'Kindred Spirits', in Khlebnikov *Collected Works, Volume I*, pp. 165–94. For an introduction to his life, work, numerological theories and views on language, see Willem G. Weststeijn, 'Inleiding', in Velimir Khlebnikov, *Ik en Rusland*, selected, translated and introduced by Willem G. Weststeijn, Amsterdam: Meulenhof, 1986, pp. 7–27.

39 Khlebnikov, *Collected Works, Volume I*, p. 99.

40 Ibid., pp. 100, 103, 106–7, 108.

41 DM from the Dutch translation by Willem Weststeijn in Buelens, *Het lijf in slijk geplant*, p. 341.

42 Khlebnikov, *Collected Works, Volume 1*, p. 160. During the war and the revolution and civil war that followed, more than a thousand pogroms took place in Russia. See Steven Marks, *How Russia Shaped the Modern World: From Art to Antisemitism, Ballet to Bolshevism*, Princeton: Princeton University Press, 2003, p. 144.

43 See American Jewish Committee, *The Jews in the Eastern War Zone*; Roshwald and Stites, *European Culture in the Great War*, pp. 92–6; Strachan, *The First World War*, pp. 147–8; and Kramer, *Dynamic of Destruction*, p. 151.

44 Diana Burgin, *Sophia Parnok: The Life and Work of Russia's Sappho*, New York: New York University Press, 1994, p. 127.

45 Tsvetaeva, *Werken*, p. 137.

46 Quoted in Zinaida Gippius, *Journal sous la Terreur*, Foreword by Jacques Michaut-Paterno, trans. Marianne Gourg, Odile Melnik-Ardin and Irene Sokologorski, Monaco: Collection Anatolia, Éditions du Rocher, 2006, p. 263. Gippius herself used similar language in 1918, when she made the cynical observation that the Russian delegation 'at least includes *one* Russian now, along with the eight yids' (ibid., p. 362).

47 Hellman, *Poets of Hope and Despair*, pp. 81–4.

48 Leon Levison, *The Tragedy of the Jews in the European War Zone*, Edinburgh: Russian Jews Relief Fund, 1916, pp. 3–7.

49 Vilna, now called Vilnius, was then the centre of Jewish spiritual life in Lithuania. English translation quoted in David G. Roskies, *Against the Apocalypse: Responses to Catastrophe in Modern Jewish Culture*, Cambridge, MA: Harvard University Press, 1984, p. 93.

50 Moyshe-Leyb Halpern, *In New York: A Selection*, trans. Kathryn Hellerstein, Philadelphia: Jewish Publication Society of America, 1982, pp. 131–3. This excerpt is from the earliest version of the poem, which was published in New York in 1916 in the Yiddish collection *East Broadway*.

51 Cf. Roshwald and Stites, *European Culture in the Great War*, p. 94; Roskies, *Against the Apocalypse*, pp. 79 ff.

8 Total War

1 Gippius, *Journal sous la Terreur*, p. 128.

2 Verwey, *Holland en de oorlog*, p. 10.

3 For the specifically French interpretation of the term *culture de guerre*, see Audoin-Rouzeau and Becker, *14–18, retrouver la Guerre*, pp. 145–8, and Prost and Winter, *Penser la Grande Guerre*, pp. 217–24. For a critique of this interpretation as elitist, see Frederic Rousseau, *La guerre censurée. Une histoire des combattants européens de 14–18*, Paris: Seuil, 2003, pp. 9–23.

4 Audoin-Rouzeau and Becker, *14–18, retrouver la Guerre*, pp. 135–45.

5 Rousseau, *La guerre censurée*, pp. 337–40.

6 This passage is based on information in Ferguson, *The Pity of War*, pp. 176–279; Jay Winter, 'Nourrir les populations', in Audoin-Rouzeau and Becker, *Encyclopédie de la Grande Guerre*, pp. 581–9; and Kramer, *Dynamic of Destruction*, pp. 152–5.

7 Loveling, *Oorlogsdagboeken*, pp. 614–15.

8 Information in this section comes from the chapter 'War Aims and Peace Negotiations' in David Stevenson, *Cataclysm: The First World War as Political Tragedy*, New York: Basic Books, 2004.

9 For peace plans until 1916, see Bourne, *Towards an Enduring Peace*; for peace plans from December 1916 to November 1918, see James Scott (ed.), *Official Statements of War Aims and Peace Proposals, December 1916 to November 1918*, Washington: Carnegie Endowment for International Peace, 1921.

10 Arnold Toynbee, in Bourne, *Towards an Enduring Peace*, pp. 54–5.

11 Quote from Owen Seaman, 'More Peace-Talk in Berlin', in Noakes, *Voices of Silence*, p. 267. For five other British poems about the German peace proposals, see ibid., pp. 267–70.

12 For the peace proposals and all the responses, as well as the declaration of unrestricted submarine warfare, see Scott, *Official Statements of War Aims*, pp. 1–66; for an overview of the peace proposals, responses and hidden agendas, see Tucker, *The European Powers in the First World War*, pp. 549–51.

13 Information from Stevenson, *Cataclysm*, pp. 247–54; Orlando Figes, *A People's Tragedy: The Russian Revolution, 1891–1924*, London: Jonathan Cape, 1998 (1996), pp. 307–405; Hellman, *Poets of Hope and Despair*, pp. 249–80.

14 Stevenson, *Cataclysm*, p. 248. Figes, *A People's Tragedy*, p. 307, gives an average temperature of 30 degrees below zero in February. Considering that 33 degrees below zero is the absolute minimum in February in St Petersburg today (bbc.co.uk/weather), an average of 30 below seems highly improbable.

15 In other words, the February Revolution took place in March according to the Western/Gregorian calendar (and the October Revolution in November). The dates that follow are always in the Gregorian calendar and therefore do not correspond to the dates given in Russian sources (such as diaries and dated poems).

16 Keegan, *The First World War*, p. 334, and Figes, *A People's Tragedy*, p. 308.

17 Woroszylski, *The Life of Mayakovsky*, pp. 173–4.

18 Reeder, *Anna Akhmatova*, p. 107.

19 Gippius, *Journal sous la Terreur*, p. 135.

20 Richard Minne, *In duizenden varianten. Historisch-kritische uitgave van Richard Minnes gedichten*, 3 vols., ed. Yves T'Sjoen, Ghent: Koninklijke Academie voor Nederlandse Taal-en Letterkunde, 2003, vol. 1, p. 48.

21 Mihályhegyi, in Vondung, *Kriegserlebnis*, p. 309.

22 Cross, *The Lost Voices of World War I*, p. 349.

23 Date in Marcel Martinet, *Les temps maudits. À bas les pharisiens de l'art. Carnets des années de guerre* (1914–1918), Marseille: Agone, 2003, p. 192.

24 Henri Guilbeaux, *Du champ des horreurs*, Geneva: Édition de la revue 'Demain', 1917, p. 75 (poem, 72–5). DM from the French.

25 Figes, *A People's Tragedy*, p. 321, calls it a liberal myth that the February Revolution was bloodless. In Petrograd alone, it is reported that 1,500 died and 6,000 were injured.
26 Gippius, *Journal sous la Terreur*, p. 133.
27 Ibid., pp. 174, 182.
28 Schweitzer, *Tsvetaeva*, p. 139; Figes, *A People's Tragedy*, p. 351; and Mochulsky, *Aleksander Blok*, pp. 380–1.
29 Gippius, *Journal sous la Terreur*, p. 171.
30 Andrew Parrott, 'The Baltic States from 1914 to 1923: The First World War and the Wars of Independence', *Baltic Defence Review* 2:8 (2002), p. 144.
31 See the eight principles of government advanced by the revolutionary soviets as conditions for recognition of the Provisional Government, in Figes, *A People's Tragedy*, p. 335.
32 Ibid., p. 465.
33 On this subject, see Keegan, *The First World War*, pp. 303–6.
34 Figes, *A People's Tragedy*, pp. 406–21.
35 Leonid Kannegiser, quoted in ibid., p. 410.
36 Hellman, *Poets of Hope and Despair*, p. 249.
37 Ibid., p. 267.
38 In 1916 there were 1,203 deserters, and in 1917 no fewer than 5,603 (see the entry 'Frontbeweging' in *Nieuwe Encyclopedie van de Vlaamse Beweging*).
39 Vandeweyer, *De Eerste Wereldoorlog*, p. 266.
40 Joris Van Severen, *Die vervloekte oorlog. Dagboek 1914–1918*, ed. Daniel Vanacker, Kapellen: Pelckmans, Studiecentrum Joris Van Severen, Ypres, 2005, p. 166.
41 E.g. ibid., p. 169 ('orthodox revolutionary'), p. 170 ('seriously revolutionary'), p. 175 ('I am becoming what I must … to the devil with it all … revolutionary, tough').
42 In Filip De Pillecyn and Jozef Simons, *Onder den hiel*, Tielt: Lannoo-Maes, 1920, p. 43.
43 Cf. the entry 'Frontbeweging' in *Nieuwe Encyclopedie van de Vlaamse Beweging*.
44 See Rombouts, *August van Cauwelaert*, p. 18, and Van Severen, *Die vervloekte oorlog*, p. 368. The descriptive phrase comes from ibid., p. 120.
45 Opening stanza of Van Cauwelaert, 'Voor onze Regeering', quoted in full in Rombouts, *August van Cauwelaert*, pp. 19–21.

46 De Clercq, *De Noodhoorn*, p. 13.
47 Rombouts, *August van Cauwelaert*, p. 21.
48 Quoted in De Schaepdrijver, *De Groote Oorlog*, p. 188.
49 Keegan, *The First World War*, pp. 326–32.
50 The final stanza of the English translation by Mark K. Jensen, in the entry 'La Chanson de Craonne' at wikipedia.org.
51 Transcript of the speech available at stahlgewitter.com. DM from the German. English and German versions of the poem in question can be found in Bridgwater, *The German Poets*, pp. 194–5 and 134–5.
52 See the article about desertion by Christoph Jahr in Hirschfeld et al., *Enzyklopädie Erster Weltkrieg*, pp. 435–7.
53 See Tucker, *The European Powers in the First World War*, pp. 298–9.
54 Carl Zuckmayer, '1917', trans. David Colmer, in *mpT* (2014), no. 3, p. 75. Original German version online at files.melusine-literatur.org.
55 French original in Nancy Sloan Goldberg, *En l'honneur de la juste parole: la poésie française contre la Grande Guerre*, New York: P. Lang, 1993, p. 155 ('Hi! Hi! Hi! / L'Europe à la barbarie! / Elle s'y vautre, elle en jouit, / Elle s'amuse et se suicide'). DM from the French.
56 'Les tendances nouvelles. Interview avec Guillaume Apollinaire', *SIC*, August–October 1916 (reprint, pp. 58–9).
57 Francis Steegmuller, *Apollinaire: Poet Among the Painters*, New York: Penguin, 1986 (1963), pp. 257–60.
58 Quoted in Christophe Prochasson, *Les intellectuels, le socialisme et la guerre: 1900–1938*, Paris: Seuil, 1993, p. 151.
59 Steegmuller, *Apollinaire*, pp. 259–60.
60 Ibid., pp. 263–4.
61 Sassoon, *Diaries 1915–1918*, pp. 119.
62 'A Listening Post', in Roberts, *Minds at War*, p. 287.
63 Sassoon, *Diaries 1915–1918*, p. 133.
64 Ibid., pp. 151, 154.
65 Ibid., pp. 133, 173–4.
66 Ibid., p. 175.
67 Eddie Marsh, in ibid., p. 179.
68 Ibid., p. 181.
69 Information about military operations and developments is drawn from Keegan, *The First World War*, pp. 343–50; Berrafato, Berrafato and Verney, *L'Italie en Guerre*, pp. 77–106; Bazzanella, 'Die Stimme der Illiteraten'; and Strachan, *The First World War*, pp. 255–8.

70 Bazzanella, 'Die Stimme der Illiteraten', p. 341.
71 On this subject, see Bonadeo, *D'Annunzio and the Great War*, pp. 69–124, and Woodhouse, *Gabriele D'Annunzio*, pp. 294–312.
72 Bonadeo, *D'Annunzio and the Great War*, p. 89.
73 From 2,137 in April to 5,471 in August (Strachan, *The First World War*, p. 257). There were almost as many Italian deserters in the latter month alone as Belgian deserters in the entire year of 1917.
74 Woodhouse, *Gabriele D'Annunzio*, p. 306.
75 Bonadeo, *D'Annunzio and the Great War*, p. 79.
76 Ibid., p. 109.
77 Cf. Zygmunt G. Baranski, 'Italian Literature and the Great War: Soffici, Jahier and Rebora', *Journal of European Studies* 10:2, no. 39 (1980), pp. 161–5.
78 Piero Jahier, 'Prima marcia alpina', available at archive.org. DM from the Italian, with reference to the Dutch translation by Bart van den Bossche in Buelens, *Het lijf in slijk geplant*, pp. 331–3.
79 Keegan, *The First World War*, p. 346.
80 Excerpt from 'Ospedale da campo 026' (Field Hospital 026); English translation from Payne, *A Selection of Modern Italian Poetry*, p. 81.
81 Quoted in Tucker, *The European Powers in the First World War*, p. 373.
82 Gabriele D'Annunzio, *The Rally*, trans. Magda Sindici, Milan: Bestetti & Tumminelli, 1918, pp. 15, 30, 31, 35, 40.
83 Opening lines of untitled poem, Fernando Pessoa [Alberto Caeiro], *De hoeder van kudden en andere gedichten*, trans. and afterword by August Willemsen, Amsterdam/Antwerp: De Arbeiderspers, 2003, p. 227.
84 Pessoa, *De anarchistische bankier & ander proza*, p. 54.
85 Ibid., p. 79.
86 Ibid., pp. 78–9.

9 Last Man Standing

1 Georges Duhamel, *Civilisatie 1914–1917. Arts aan het front van WOI*, trans. Mechtild Claessens, afterword by Wouter van Raamsdonk, Amsterdam/Antwerp: Oorlogsdomein, De Arbeiderspers, 2007, p. 179.

2 Figures from Anne Dumenil, 'Les combattants', in Audoin-Rouzeau and Becker, *Encyclopédie de la Grande Guerre*, p. 323.
3 Guillaume Apollinaire, *Selected Writings*, trans. Roger Shattuck, New York: New Directions, 1971, p. 229.
4 Gilbert, *Atlas of World War I*, pp. 106–9.
5 Keegan, *The First World War*, pp. 338–43; Parrott, 'The Baltic States from 1914 to 1923', p. 139; Figes, *A People's Tragedy*, pp. 438–500.
6 Gippius, *Journal sous la Terreur*, p. 222.
7 Ibid., p. 266.
8 Information from Hellman, *Poets of Hope and Despair*, pp. 300–24.
9 Victor Terras, *Vladimir Mayakovsky*, Boston: Twayne, 1983, p. 10.
10 Khlebnikov, *Collected Works, Volume 1*, p. 25.
11 Quoted in Katherine Bliss Eaton (ed.), *Enemies of the People: The Destruction of Soviet Literary, Theater, and Film Arts in the 1930s*, Evanston, IL: Northwestern University Press, 2002, p. 76.
12 Victor Serge, *Memoirs of a Revolutionary*, Iowa City: University of Iowa Press, 2002, p. 59.
13 Reeder, *Anna Akhmatova*, p. 110.
14 Tsvetaeva, *Werken*, p. 155.
15 Ibid., p. 157.
16 Gippius, *Journal sous la Terreur*, p. 235.
17 Ibid., pp. 262–3; Hellman, *Poets of Hope and Despair*, p. 307. On the condemnations by other authors, see the Soviet critic Orlov, *Hamayun*, p. 371.
18 Hellman, *Poets of Hope and Despair*, pp. 279–80.
19 Mochulsky, *Aleksander Blok*, p. 388.
20 Hellman, *Poets of Hope and Despair*, pp. 308, 309.
21 Blok, *Selected Poems*, pp. 127–8.
22 See Figes, *A People's Tragedy*, pp. 540–50.
23 When the premiere of *Le Sacre du printemps* caused a scandal in Paris in 1913, it was above all the Asiatic/Scythian features of the costumes that shocked the critics. See Figes, *Natasha's Dance*, p. 409.
24 Blok, *Selected Poems*, p. 129.
25 Ibid., p. 131.
26 Hellman, *Poets of Hope and Despair*, p. 312.
27 Blok, *Selected Poems*, p. 131.
28 Calculation by Alan Moorehead in Hellman, *Poets of Hope and Despair*, pp. 311–12. Figes, *A People's Tragedy*, p. 548, gives slightly different

figures, based on Wheeler-Bennett's 1938 study *Brest-Litovsk: The Forgotten Peace, March 1918*: 34 per cent of the population (55 million people), 32 per cent of the agricultural land, 54 per cent of industry, and 89 of the coal mines.

29 Quoted in Figes, *A People's Tragedy*, p. 547.

30 Gippius, *Journal sous la Terreur*, p. 374. DM from the French.

31 Figes, *A People's Tragedy*, p. 548.

32 Edith Södergran, *Complete Poems*, trans. David McDuff, Newcastle upon Tyne: Bloodaxe Books, 1984, p. 102.

33 See Keegan, *The First World War*, pp. 378–80. Keegan reports 30,000 casualties. An official Finnish report from 2004 gives a figure of just fewer than 10,000 deaths during the actual civil war. In addition, both sides executed large numbers of opponents without trial. At the end of the war 500 prisoners were sentenced to death, but not all were executed. After the war, just under 13,000 civilians died in captivity of starvation and epidemics. See the entry for 'Finnischer Bürgerkrieg' at wikipedia.org.

34 Blunden, *Undertones of War*, pp. 152–3.

35 Ibid., p. 222.

36 On the third battle, see Keegan, *The First World War*, pp. 360–9; Strachan, *The First World War*, pp. 250–4; Koen Koch, *De derde slag bij Ieper 1917*, Amsterdam: Ambo, 2007; for a revisionist view, see Sheffield, *Forgotten Victory*, pp. 204–16.

37 Blunden, *Undertones of War*, 216.

38 Cross, *The Lost Voices of World War I*, pp. 393, 37.

39 Ibid., p. 38.

40 *The Wipers Times: The Complete Series of the Famous Wartime Trench Newspaper, 1916–1918*, Foreword by Ian Hislop, introduced by Malcolm Brown, annotated by Patrick Beaver, London: Little Books, 2006 (reprint), p. 205.

41 Ivor Gurney, *War Letters*, selected by R.K.R. Thornton, London: Hogarth Press, 1984, p. 186.

42 Ibid., p. 196. On the peace conference organized by Camille Huysmans and the attitudes of Europe's socialist movements, see David Kirby, 'International Socialism and the Question of Peace. The Stockholm Conference of 1917', *The Historical Journal* 25:3 (1982), pp. 709–16; Jan Hunin, *Het enfant terrible Camille Huysmans 1871–1968*, Amsterdam: Meulenhoff, 1999, pp. 165–92.

43 Gurney, *War Letters*, p. 201.

44 Koch, *De derde slag bij Ieper 1917*, p. 17.

45 Sir Herbert Edward Read, *The Contrary Experience*, New York: Horizon Press, 1973, p. 112.

46 As so often, almost every source consulted gives slightly different figures. For an overview, see Koch, *De derde slag bij Ieper 1917*, p. 243.

47 See the poem 'Sick Leave', also published under the title of 'Death's Brotherhood', in Sassoon, *The War Poems*, p. 83.

48 Sassoon, *Diaries 1915–1918*, p. 192.

49 Wilfred Owen, *The Poems*, ed. Jon Silkin, Harmondsworth: Penguin, 1985, p. 86.

50 Opening stanzas of Daan F. Boens, *Menschen in de grachten. Werk gedegen in de loopgraven*, Nieuwpoort: Juul Filliaert, 1918, p. 59.

51 'Moed in lijden' (Courage in Suffering), speech delivered by Corporal Daan F. Boens at the Volkshuis in Fulham, London, 16 December 1917. Collection of the AMVC Letterenhuis, Antwerp, Call number B 675 I H (2), Registration number 71603I1–4.

52 August Vermeylen, 'Vlaamsche en Europeesche Beweging', *Van Nu en Straks*, Nieuwe Reeks 4:5–6 (November 1900), p. 310.

53 Boens showed greater sympathy for the radical Front Movement on the Yser (which was in some ways related to and allied with the activist movement). On the punished, exiled Front members, see the poems 'De Boete-jongens I' and 'De boete-jongens II', in Boens, *Menschen in de grachten*, pp. 86–9.

54 On the political aspects of his life in this period, including the story of Van Ostaijen's job application to an organization intended to become a Flemish gendarmerie (*Rijkswacht*), see Marc Reynebeau, 'Geschapen als activistisch mannequin. Het politieke avontuur van Paul van Ostaijen in de Eerste Wereldoorlog', *Spiegel der Letteren* 39:2 (1997), pp. 161–81. On Van Ostaijen's poetic evolution and its relationship to everyday reality in occupied Belgium, see Geert Buelens, *Van Ostaijen tot heden. Zijn invloed op de Vlaamse poëzie*, Nijmegen: Vantilt, 2001, pp. 74–80.

55 The German offensives began on 21 March (see Keegan, *The First World War*, pp. 392–408), by which time large parts of Van Ostaijen's *Het Sienjaal* had already been written.

56 Van Ostaijen, *Verzameld werk. Poëzie. Music-Hall, Het Sienjaal, De Feesten van Angst en Pijn*, p. 105.

57 Ibid., p. 119.

58 Van Ostaijen, *Verzameld werk. Proza. Besprekingen en Beschouwingen*, p. 165.

59 Excerpt from 'Het Sienjaal', in Van Ostaijen, *Verzameld werk. Poëzie. Music-Hall, Het Sienjaal, De Feesten van Angst en Pijn*, p. 147.

60 Cf. Spinoy, 'Twee handen in het lege', pp. 455–68.

61 Van Ostaijen, *Verzameld werk. Poëzie. Music-Hall, Het Sienjaal, De Feesten van Angst en Pijn*, p. 119.

62 For the original passage, see Scott, *Official Statements of War Aims*, p. 236, and Van Severen, *Die vervloekte oorlog*, p. 360.

63 On the endgame, see Keegan, *The First World War*, pp. 392–414, and Strachan, *The First World War*, pp. 295–325.

64 Excerpt from 'Break of Day in the Trenches', Isaac Rosenberg, *Collected Poems*, London: Chatto & Windus, 1949, p. 73.

65 Isaac Rosenberg, *The Collected Works. Poetry, Prose, Letters, Paintings and Drawings*, Foreword by Siegfried Sassoon, ed. Ian Parsons, Oxford: Oxford University Press, 1979, p. 268.

66 Woodhouse, *Gabriele D'Annunzio*, p. 312.

67 Cross, *The Lost Voices of World War I*, p. 83.

68 Paraphrased from a long quoted passage from a letter, in Bridgwater, *The German Poets*, p. 144.

69 Ibid., p. 151.

70 Information for this passage from Dominic Hibberd, *Wilfred Owen: A New Biography*, Chicago: Ivan R. Dee, 2002, pp. 341–66.

71 Ibid., p. 352.

72 Apollinaire, *De mooiste*, p. 173.

10 11/11 and After

1 Paul van Ostaijen, *Verzameld werk. Proza. Grotesken en ander Proza*, Amsterdam: Bert Bakker, 1979, p. 242.

2 Arnulf Øverland, 'The Thousand-year Reich'. DM from the Dutch translation by Janke Klok in Buelens, *Het lijf in slijk geplant*, p. 585.

3 Quoted in Erik Goldstein, *The First World War Peace Settlements, 1919–1925*, London: Longman, 2002, p. 22.

4 Thomas G. Masaryk, *The Problem of Small Nations in the European*

Crisis, London: The Council for the Study of International Relations, 1916, p. 31.

5 John Mavrogordato, 'From Nationalism to Federation', *The New Europe*, 2 May 1918, pp. 69–71, 70.

6 Quoted in Herman de Liagre Böhl, *Met al mijn bloed heb ik voor U geleefd. Herman Gorter 1864–1927*, Amsterdam: Balans, 1996, p. 396.

7 Ibid., p. 408.

8 Quoted in Paul Moeyes, *Buiten schot. Nederland tijdens de Eerste Wereldoorlog 1914–1918*, Amsterdam: De Arbeiderspers, 2001, p. 335.

9 Ibid., p. 337.

10 On Eisner and the revolution in Bavaria, see Sebastian Haffner, *De Duitse revolutie. 1918–1919: de nasleep van de Eerste Wereldoorlog*, trans. Piet Jaarsma, Afterword by Ronald Havenaar, Amsterdam: Mets & Schilt, 2003, pp. 227–42.

11 Rainer Maria Rilke, *Wartime Letters, 1914–1921*, New York: W.W. Norton, 1940, pp. 100–3.

12 Ibid., p. 102. On Czechs and Slovaks, see W.V. Wallace, 'From Czechs and Slovaks to Czechoslovakia, and from Czechoslovakia to Czechs and Slovaks', in Seamus Dunn and T.G Fraser, *Europe and Ethnicity: The First World War and Contemporary Ethnic Conflict*, London: Routledge, 1996, pp. 47–66; Margaret MacMillan, *Peacemakers: The Paris Conference of 1919 and Its Attempt to End War*, London: John Murray, 2002, pp. 240–53; and Goldstein, *The First World War Peace Settlements*, pp. 22–31.

13 Some 100,000 of the 450,000 Hungarian prisoners of war ultimately fought with the Red Army (Mihályhegyi, in Vondung, *Kriegserlebnis*, pp. 300–1).

14 Excerpt from 'Victorious Retreat' by Miloš Jirko, in Selver, *Modern Czech Poetry*, p. 297.

15 Excerpt from Oskar Kanehl, *De schande. Gedichten van een dienstplichtig soldaat uit de moordjaren 1914–1918*, trans. Jac. Knap, Amsterdam: De Fakkel, 1925, pp. 30, 31.

16 Clarence Augustus Manning (ed.), *An Anthology of Czechoslovak Poetry*, New York: Columbia University Press, 1929, pp. 37–8.

17 Selver, *Modern Czech Poetry*, pp. 241–3.

18 Leppmann, *Rainer Maria Rilke*, p. 323.

19 MacMillan, *Peacemakers*, p. 257.

20 Ady, *Selected Poems*, p. 136.

21 Agnes Huszar Vardy, 'Trianon in Transylvanian Hungarian Literatur: Sandor Remenyik's "Vegvari Poems"', in Bela K. Kiraly et al., *Essays on World War I: Total War and Peacemaking, a Case Study on Trianon*, New York: Brooklyn College Press, Social Science Monographs, 1982, pp. 407–22.

22 Nyerges, Árpád Tóth, pp. 66–7.

23 Neubauer, '1918: Overview', p. 186.

24 Rilke, *Wartime Letters*, pp. 106–7.

25 See Woroszylski, *The Life of Mayakovsky*, pp. 242–60, and Brown, *Mayakovsky*, pp. 191–218.

26 Mayakovsky, *Werken*, p. 732. Translation of excerpt from 'It's too Early to Rejoice' partly based on excerpt in Woroszylski, *The Life of Mayakovsky*, p. 248.

27 Mayakovsky, *Werken*, p. 733.

28 Ibid., p. 357.

29 Ibid.

30 Woroszylski, *The Life of Mayakovsky*, p. 248.

31 Mayakovsky, *Werken*, p. 359

32 On this subject, see Matei Calinescu, *Five Faces of Modernity: Modernism, Avant-garde, Decadence, Kitsch, Post-modernism*, Durham, NC: Duke University Press, 1987, pp. 112–13.

33 Mayakovsky, *Werke*, vol. 3, p. 122.

34 Akhmatova, *The Complete Poems*, pp. 538–9.

35 Gippius, *Journal sous la Terreur*, pp. 502, 507.

36 Goldstein, *The First World War Peace Settlements*, pp. 11–21, and MacMillan, *Peacemakers*, pp. 167–214.

37 Verwey in *De Beweging*, March 1919, also quoted in Nijland-Verwey, *Albert Verwey en Stefan George*, pp. 282–3.

38 See the entries for 'Ward Hermans' and 'Houthakkers' in *Nieuwe Encyclopedie van de Vlaamse Beweging*.

39 Van Ostaijen, *Verzameld werk. Poëzie. Music-Hall, Het Sienjaal, De Feesten van Angst en Pijn*, p. 137.

40 Van Ostaijen, *Verzameld werk. Proza. Besprekingen en Beschouwingen*, p. 126.

41 Van Ostaijen, *Verzameld werk. Poëzie. Music-Hall, Het Sienjaal, De Feesten van Angst en Pijn*, p. 147.

42 Sassoon, *Diaries 1915–1918*, pp. 280, 282.

43 See Saunders, *Ford Madox Ford*, vol. 2, pp. 26, 77–9.

44 Information in this section is drawn from John Lucas, *The Radical Twenties: Writing, Politics, and Culture*, New Brunswick, NJ: Rutgers University Press, 1999.

45 Robert Graves, *Goodbye to All That*, Harmondsworth: Penguin, 1965 (1929), p. 235.

46 Information is drawn from MacMillan, *Peacemakers*, pp. 288–314; Woodhouse, *Gabriele D'Annunzio*, pp. 315–52; and Bonadeo, *D'Annunzio and the Great War*, pp. 125–43.

47 MacMillan, *Peacemakers*, p. 304.

48 Ibid., p. 309.

49 Woodhouse, *Gabriele D'Annunzio*, p. 347; Michael Ledeen, *The First Duce: D'Annunzio at Fiume*, Baltimore: Johns Hopkins University Press, 1977, pp. 177–81.

50 Berghaus, *Futurism and Politics*, pp. 134–43; Marinetti, *Critical Writings*, pp. 269–84.

51 Marinetti, *Critical Writings*, p. 45. D'Annunzio, the manifesto explained, had to be opposed because he stood for decadence, sentimentality, eroticism and the love of the past.

52 Bonadeo, *D'Annunzio and the Great War*, p. 134.

53 Ibid., p. 135.

54 MacMillan, *Peacemakers*, p. 124.

55 Ljubomir Micić, 'Manifest an die Barbaren des Geistes und Denkens auf allen Kontinenten', in Holger Siegel (ed.), *In unseren Seelen flattern schwarze Fahnen. Serbische Avantgarde 1918–1939*, Leipzig: Reclam, 1992, p. 130.

56 Ibid.

57 Hugo Ball, *Zur Kritik der deutschen Intelligenz*, Frankfurt am Main: Suhrkamp, 1991, available at gutenberg.spiegel.de. DM from the German.

58 Richard Huelsenbeck (ed.), *Dada Almanach. Im Auftrag des Zentralamts der deutschen Dada-Bewegung*, Berlin: E. Reiss, 1920, pp. 108–9.

59 Ibid., p. 109.

60 Ibid., p. 147.

61 See Buelens, *Van Ostaijen tot heden*, pp. 131–46.

62 See Kee, *The Green Flag*, and Seamus Dunn and Thomas W. Hennessey, 'Ireland', in Dunn and Fraser, *Europe and Ethnicity*, pp. 177–96.

63 MacMillan, *Peacemakers*, p. 19.

64 Terence Brown, *The Life of W.B. Yeats: A Critical Biography*, Malden, MA: Blackwell, 1999, p. 300.

65 Presentation speech by the Nobel Committee chairman Harald Hjärne, 10 December 1920, available at nobelprize.org.

66 Ziedonis, *The Religious Philosophy of Janis Rainis*, p. 78; other information in this passage drawn from Stahnke, *Aspazija, Her Life and Her Drama*, pp. 114–17, and Aleksis Rubulis, *Baltic Literature: A Survey of Finnish, Estonian, Latvian, and Lithuanian Literatures*, Notre Dame: University of Notre Dame Press, 1970, p. 117.

67 See Livezeanu, *Cultural Politics in Greater Romania*, pp. 277–9.

68 Anon., 'Charges Officials Aided in Pogroms. German Correspondent in Lemberg Says They Encouraged Killing of Jews. Ghetto was Laid in Ruins. Looting by the Polish Officers and Soldiers Widespread in Three Days of Slaughter', *New York Times*, 2 December 1918.

69 On this pogrom, see William H. Hagen, 'The Moral Economy of Popular Violence: The Pogrom in Lwow, November 1918', in Robert Blobaum (ed.), *Antisemitism and Its Opponents in Modern Poland*, Ithaca, NY: Cornell University Press, 2005, pp. 124–47.

70 Opening lines, Irving Howe et al. (eds.), *The Penguin Book of Modern Yiddish Verse*, New York: Viking, 1987, pp. 484–5.

71 On the new Poland, see MacMillan, *Peacemakers*, pp. 217–39.

72 Information about that evening and the literary group comes from Barry Keane, *Skamander: The Poets and Their Poetry 1918–1929*, Warsaw: Agade, 2004, pp. 15ff, and Marci Shore, *Caviar and Ashes: A Warsaw Generation's Life and Death in Marxism, 1918–1968*, New Haven: Yale University Press, 2006, pp. 1–26.

73 DM from the Dutch translation by Karol Lesman in *Het lijf in slijk geplant*, pp. 556–9. Original Polish included there, and also in Jan Lechón and Antoni Słonimski, *Faceje Republikańskie*, Warsaw, 1919, pp. 4–5.

74 Keane, *Skamander*, p. 16.

75 Ibid., p. 17.

76 Tuwim and his friends formed the group Skamander a short time afterwards; in 1921, Wat would describe the Polish Futurists' temporary collaboration with this group as one of their 'greatest tactical errors' (Bogdana Carpenter, *The Poetic Avant-garde in Poland, 1918–1939*, Seattle: University of Washington Press, 1983, p. xvii).

77 Keane, *Skamander*, p. 19, and Shore, *Caviar and Ashes*, pp. 24–5.
78 Based on the translation in Peter Grzybek, 'Ivo Andrić's "Put Alije Đerzeleza" – The Dethronement of Heroism?', *Essays in Poetics* 23 (1998), British Neo-Formalist Circle, University of Keele, 1998, p. 197. Edited by DM.
79 Anatol Stern, *Europa: A Poem*, illustrated and layout by Mieczyslaw Szczuka, trans. Stefan Themerson and Michael Horovitz. Foreword by Oswell Blakeston, London: Gaberbocchus, 1962, n.p.
80 Ibid.

Afterword

1 Originally published in English under the title of 'The Crisis of the Mind', in two parts, in *The Athenaeum* (London), 11 April and 2 May 1919. The French version, 'Le Crise de l'esprit', appeared in August 1919 in *La Nouvelle Revue Française*.
2 On this subject, see e.g. Thomas von Vegesack, *De intellectuelen. Een geschiedenis van het literaire engagement 1898–1968*, trans. Petra Broomans and Wiveca Jongeneel, Amsterdam: Meulenhoff, 1989.
3 See Peter Sloterdijk, *Theorie der Nachkriegszeiten. Bemerkungen zu den deutsch-französischen Beziehungen seit 1945*, Frankfurt am Main: Suhrkamp, 2008.
4 This passage was inspired by Sheehan, *Where Have All the Soldiers Gone?*
5 Some exceptions, specifically on the subject of poetry, are Julia García Games, *Contribución al estudio de la poesía de la Gran Guerra*, Buenos Aries: Talleres Gráficos 'La Internacional', 1921; C.M. Bowra, *Poetry and the First World War*, Oxford: Clarendon Press, 1961; Michael Hamburger, *The Truth of Poetry: Tensions in Modern Poetry from Baudelaire to the 1960s*, New York: Harcourt, Brace & World, 1970, pp. 148–74; Marsland, *The Nation's Cause*; and Perloff, *The Futurist Moment*. For a comparative look at the general intellectual and literary climate, see Robert Wohl, *The Generation of 1914*, Cambridge, MA: Harvard University Press, 1979, Stromberg, *Redemption by War*; Wohl, 'Introduction', in Cross, *The Lost Voices of World War I*, pp. 1–10, Eksteins, *Rites of Spring*; Jay Winter, *Sites of Memory, Sites of Mourning: The Great War in European Cultural History*, Cambridge:

Cambridge University Press, 1995; and Roshwald and Stites, *European Culture in the Great War*. For an overview of other studies and anthologies, most of which are limited to one language or nation, see Buelens, *Het lijf in slijk geplant*, pp. 675–8. For the present state of Anglo-American literary studies of the First World War, see Joanna Scutts, 'Contemporary Approaches to the Literature of the First World War. A Critical Survey', *Literature Compass* 3:4 (2006), pp. 914–23. Paula Kepos (ed.), 'World War I Literature', in *Twentieth-Century Literature Criticism, Topics Volume 34*, Farmington Hills, MI: Gale Research, 1990, pp. 320–414, is a survey article that covers the major language areas and includes a substantial bibliography. Two interesting comparative studies of the visual arts are Annegret Jürgens-Kirchhoff, *Schreckensbilder. Krieg und Kunst im 20. Jahrhundert*, Berlin: Reimer, 1993, and Cork, *A Bitter Truth: Avant-Garde Art and the Great War*.

6 On this subject, see e.g. Joseph Theodoor Leerssen, *National Thought in Europe: A Cultural History*, Amsterdam: Amsterdam University Press, 2007.

Index of People

Index of Places

Index of Places